ESL (ELL) LITERACY INSTRUCTION

This comprehensive research-based text provides both ESL and mainstream teachers with the background and expertise necessary to plan and implement reading programs that match the particular needs and abilities of their students. *ESL (ELL) Literacy Instruction: A Guidebook for Theory and Practice, Second Edition*:

- applies current ESL and reading research and theory to practice
- is designed for use by pre-service and in-service teachers at all levels from kindergarten to adult learners
- explains different models of literacy instruction from systematic phonics to whole language instruction and includes specific teaching methods within each model
- encourages teacher choice in instructional decisions and provides a systematic rationale and approach for teachers to design their own teaching programs within their own models of literacy
- addresses multicultural issues

Changes in the Second Edition include:

- more research based discussions and more practical teaching suggestions
- a brief history of reading instruction
- updated coverage of views on reading instruction for ESL/ELL students including the National Reading Panel and National Literacy Panel results
- new section on second-language theory and research
- new chapter on the importance of culture in second-language literacy contexts
- expanded, revised chapters on teaching reading to young ESL students, teaching reading to older students, and teaching academic reading, including include discussions of phonemic awareness training and developments related to new technologies
- information on how published resources can be accessed on the Internet

As the number of ESL students in public schools continues to grow, so grows the need for teachers to have the background and skills necessary to provide these students with the best possible programs. This book is dedicated to that task.

Lee Gunderson is Professor of Language and Literacy Education at the University of British Columbia where he teaches courses in second language reading, language acquisition, literacy acquisition, and teacher education. He received the David Russell Award for Research, the Killam Teaching Prize at the University of British Columbia and has been awarded the Kingston Prize for contributions to the National Reading Conference.

ESL (ELL) Literacy Instruction

A Guidebook to Theory and Practice

Second Edition

Lee Gunderson
University of British Columbia

Routledge
Taylor & Francis Group

NEW YORK AND LONDON

First published 2009
by Routledge
270 Madison Ave, New York, NY 10016

Simultaneously published in the UK
by Routledge
2 Park Square, Milton Park, Abingdon, Oxon OX14 4RN

Routledge is an imprint of the Taylor & Francis Group, an informa business

Typeset in Minion by
Keystroke, 28 High Street, Tettenhall, Wolverhampton
Printed and bound in the United States of America on acid-free paper by
Edwards Brothers, Inc.

This book was previously published by Pearson Education, Inc.

Library of Congress Cataloging in Publication Data
Gunderson, Lee —
  [ESL literacy instruction]
  ESL (ELL) literacy instruction : a guidebook to theory and practice / Lee
Gunderson. — [2nd ed.].
       p. cm.
    Includes bibliographical references and indexes.
    Rev. ed. of: ESL literacy instruction, New York : Routledge, c2005.
    1. English language—Study and teaching—Foreign speakers.   2. Literacy
programs.   I. Title.
    PE1128.A2G79 2008
    428.407—dc22   2008002955

ISBN 10: 0–415–98971–X (hbk)
ISBN 10: 0–415–98972–8 (pbk)
ISBN 10: 0–203–89421–9 (ebk)

ISBN 13: 978–0–415–98971–8 (hbk)
ISBN 13: 978–0–415–98972–5 (pbk)
ISBN 13: 978–0–203–89421–7 (ebk)

To Dianne Fouladi, the world's
greatest ESL teacher and mentor

Brief Contents

Contents

Preface

This book is a revision of *ESL Literacy Instruction: A Guidebook to Theory and Practice*, published in 1991. Many readers of that book have contributed suggestions for changes to be made in this revision. Many asked for more research-based discussions, while others asked for more practical teaching suggestions. As far as possible, both of these suggestions have been incorporated into this book. However, the book will not contain exhaustive lists of published materials, but will instead report how such resources can be accessed and located.

In 1991, this author noted that the number of ESL students was continuing to increase. Not much has changed since 1991, except that the increase appears to have accelerated. Indeed, the number of students who speak a language other than English in classrooms continues to increase in the United States and Canada. The National Center for Education Statistics (NCES, 2004) reported that "The number and percentage of language minority youth and young adults—that is, individuals who speak a language other than English at home—increased steadily in the United States between 1979 and 1999" (p. 1). They add:

> Of those individuals ages 5–24 in 1979, 6 million spoke a language other than English at home. By 1999, that number had more than doubled, to 14 million. Accordingly, of all 5- to 24-year-olds in the United States, the percentage who were language minorities increased from 9 percent in 1979 to 17 percent in 1999. (p. 1)

The number of ESL students in U.S. public schools has almost tripled over the past decade (Goldenberg, 2006). In 2004, Crawford observed that one-fourth of the school-age students in the United States were from homes where a language other than English was spoken. The school-age population (K–12) will reach about 40 percent ESL in about 20 years (Center for Research on Education, Diversity and Excellence, 2002). Between 1990 and 2000 the number of Spanish speakers increased from about 20 to 31 million (U.S. Census Bureau, 2001). The census report also showed a significant increase in the number of speakers from other linguistic groups, particularly Chinese and Russian. Learning to read English represents a major hurdle for many second language students. Many do not succeed, and their lives are significantly impacted. As ESL numbers increase, the number of individuals who are not successful in learning to read English also increases. Indeed, when they enter school with limited exposure to English, they are at risk for reading difficulties (Snow, Burns, & Griffin, 1998).

Reading Achievement and English Language Learners (ELLs)

The term "English as a Second Language" (ESL) is incorrect in many cases because students may actually be learning English as a third, fourth, or additional language. Recently the term "English Language Learner" (ELL) has been used in the United States to refer to students who speak a language other than English at home. The term "ESL," however, will be used in this text for historical reasons and because the term "English Language Learners" can be easily applied to most young students in North America because they are actively learning English. It could be argued that language learners are lifelong learners. It is not unusual, for instance, for a 60-year-old native English speaker to learn new vocabulary. For the sake of convenience, the term "ESL" will be used throughout this book.

Most elementary teachers seem convinced that one of their primary goals is to teach students to become critical readers able to read, comprehend, understand, and learn from their instructional materials. Most secondary teachers, on the other hand, appear convinced that their primary goal is to teach academic content, not to teach students reading skills (Gunderson, 1985, 1995, 2000, 2007). Teachers of adult students appear as convinced that their primary goal is to teach their students "survival English skills."

The sad truth, however, is that many students who speak English as a second language are failing to learn to read in English, are failing to read and learn from their textbooks, are failing to learn from lectures in their academic classes, and are failing to acquire the literacy skills they need to get work in anything but low-level labor-intensive work. It is also shocking to learn how few ESL students actually complete high school. Indeed, not only are they failing to learn, but they disappear from academic-stream courses and about 40 percent drop out of school (Gunderson, 2007). Many teachers do not understand the sheer size of the problem of reading failure in elementary, secondary, and adult classes that enroll students who speak a primary or home language other than English.

The Consequences of Failing to Learn to Read

It is an exaggeration to claim that those human beings who fail to learn to read are doomed to unfulfilling and desperate lives. It is likely true that the overwhelming majority of human beings in the world manage to live full, productive, and happy lives without ever having to read or to learn to read. There are consequences, however, for those who live in jurisdictions in which the government's goal of being part of the global economy is basic or in countries in which the goal is to become a global economic power or in which technology is viewed as vital. While many individuals with poor reading skills are able to function in such societies, their potential for both financial and academic success appears significantly limited.

There are those who have argued that learning to read and write is a basic requirement for success for all human beings. Gunderson (2004) concludes,

"Many in North America view learning to read and write as the prerequisite that allows both native-born and immigrant students' participation in schools, socialization into society, ability to learn, and academic and professional success" (p. 1). Others, including teachers, are convinced that English should be required for those who wish to immigrate to the United States, Canada, New Zealand, or Australia.

English, and learning to read English, are important in these countries. For instance, the authors of the 2005 *National Assessment of Adult Literacy* report in the United States conclude that those individuals who have higher literacy levels make on average about $50,000 a year, which is $28,000 more than those who have only minimal literacy skills (NCES, 2005). There is certainly a stigma associated with those who are unable to learn to read or who have very low reading ability. All too often, it seems, politicians and the popular press demonize teachers as those individuals responsible for students' poor reading achievement. These same critics, however, do not appear to understand the complexities of learning to read English.

Disappearing Students and Declining Reading Scores

Many students speak languages other than English at home in the United States and Canada. The problem is that students who speak a language other than English at home are less likely to succeed in schools (NCES, 2004; Statistics Canada, 2001). In the United States, Spanish-speaking students are less likely to complete high school than English speakers and are also less likely to go on to university (NCES, 2004; Alemán, 2006). The number of non-English speakers is increasing. As immigration increases their numbers, the problems they encounter in schools increase. Rumberger (1995) noted that immigrants in the United States have a higher dropout rate than native-born students. Hispanic students have alarmingly high dropout rates varying from 14 percent to 30 percent (Zehr, 2003). In Canada, Radwanksi's (1987) Ontario study revealed that 53 percent of the ESL high school population left early, while Watt and Roessingh's (2001) study showed a 73 percent dropout rate in Alberta. Pirbhai-Illich concluded that both American and Canadian studies have indicated that students likely to drop out

> come from families from low socio-economic backgrounds, are from various ethnic and linguistic groups, perform poorly academically, perform poorly on standardized tests, demonstrate signs of disengagement, have been retained at grade level, take on adult roles prematurely, work more than 15 hours out of school, have family structures that are not stereotypically middle-class, and have at least one parent who has not graduated from high school.
>
> (2005, pp. 38–40)

Gunderson (2007) found that socio-economic status was an important variable related to ESL students' academic success in secondary schools. He also found that there were unfortunate interactions between socio-economic status and ethno-linguistic groups that had significant social consequences for students from particular groups. Spanish-speaking students who entered Canada were, for the most part, from refugee families. They received the lowest grades in secondary school and had the highest dropout rates. This pattern was similar for speakers of languages such as Kurdish, Amharic, Vietnamese, Punjabi, and Tagalog. The terms "Vietnamese" and "Spanish" became negative signifiers in the local media in headlines reporting street crime and drug offenses. Students who do not finish high school are at risk. The authors of the NCES (2004) report note that

> In general, language minority youth and young adults lagged behind their counterparts who spoke only English at home on most education and economic indicators. However, among those who finished high school, no differences were found by English-speaking ability in the percentage that enrolled in postsecondary education. Among language minority groups, those speaking Spanish fared less well than those speaking other languages.
>
> (p. 6)

The percentage of the population who speaks Spanish in the Gunderson (2004, 2007) study was approximately 5.5 percent. This is a significant proportion of the school-age population. However, the NCES report notes, "In 1999, the majority (63 percent) of all language minorities (aged 5–24) were native-born—that is, they were born in the United States or its outlying areas" (p. 4). It also notes, "Language minorities were more likely to be Hispanic (65 percent) than to be members of any other racial/ethnic group." The largest group of individuals in the United States who have difficulty learning to read English is the Spanish-speaking group.

Special English classes at all levels enroll students in oral English development programs. Most often they are taught to read, however, in regular or mainstream classrooms. Gunderson, Eddy, and Carrigan (submitted for publication a) observed that reading instruction in the elementary schools they observed generally involved the use of literature, but no systematic direct reading instruction. In the past, and in many cases in the new millennium, the practice has been that ESL students are generally assigned to the "low" reading group with the poorest native English readers. They are often taught using an adopted basal series and are asked to read orally in an unrehearsed fashion. The new millennium has seen the adoption of approaches involving scripted reading instruction.

The majority of ESL students are enrolled in mainstream classrooms where they are taught to read using mainstream methods, practices, and materials (Gunderson, 1983a, 1985, 1986b, 2004, 2007). It is no coincidence that they are approximately two years behind their native English-speaking classmates by the time they are in the sixth grade (Cummins, 1981). It is also obvious that classes for secondary and adult students are not succeeding, either (http://nces.ed.gov/naal/, accessed on January 27, 2007). There is a crisis in the schools for ESL (ELL) students. Simply using standard materials, methods, and approaches designed to teach native English-speaking students has not been successful.

Teachers are faced with the difficult task of teaching their ESL students how to speak, read, and write a second, sometimes a third, fourth, or fifth language. In the past they have concentrated on teaching students oral communication skills. Recently, the skills of reading and writing, also, have been acknowledged as vitally important to survival in English-speaking societies. Digital literacy and use of the Internet have taken on an urgency as their development has changed the way human beings search for and use information. All too often, however, the adopted instructional approaches, practices, and programs are those designed for native English speakers (see Gunderson, 1985, 1986b, 2004). Ironically, these approaches are often vehemently condemned by researchers as being inappropriate even for native English speakers! And for many years they have failed to teach ESL students to read (see Carter, 1970; U.S. Commission on Civil Rights, 1975; NCES, 2004). The discussions in the following chapters are based on the application of research to instruction. They focus on literacy programs designed for ESL students at all age levels. The discussions also equip the reader to make critical decisions about placing ESL students into appropriate literacy programs and constructing teacher-made materials within different models of literacy instruction.

Chapter 1: A Brief History of Reading Instruction

Chapter 1 begins with a brief history of reading instruction. An analysis of the history of reading instruction reveals the roots of the standard reading practices used to teach ESL students in classrooms across North America. A description of the current trends and major theoretical contentions of various influential authors is presented. Finally, different programs are described and discussed in reference to the needs and abilities of ESL students.

Chapter 2: Language Proficiency, Literacy Background, Purpose for Reading, L2 Reading Ability

Selecting and/or designing literacy programs for ESL students is often more complicated than selecting programs for native English speakers. Procedures for selecting appropriate reading programs are delineated in Chapter 2 based on students' ages, literacy backgrounds, purpose for reading, and oral English ability. The reader is asked to make decisions about programs within his or her own personal theoretical viewpoint. Assessment procedures are described and demonstrated; instruments are presented that allow students' English proficiency, English reading ability, content reading knowledge, and background knowledge to be considered when literacy programs are designed and/or adopted and adapted for ESL students. L2 assessment at all levels is demonstrated.

Chapter 3: Language and Culture as Literacy Variables

Culture is an important learning and instructional variable. Students who have learned to read a first language in a system that focuses on the rote memorization of characters or printed words on flash cards will likely have some difficulty with a system that focuses on meaning and appreciation of literature. Teachers who focus on process rather than product may face difficulties in designing programs for students who have cultural expectations for product-based learning. Culture is described and methods for assessing culture in local small communities are presented.

Chapter 4: Teaching Young ESL (ELL) Students to Read

Thousands of new ESL students are enrolled in elementary schools every year in North America. Schools and school districts face yearly crises as they attempt to cope with the influx of ESL students. Thousands are simply enrolled in mainstream classrooms in which teachers valiantly attempt to teach basic literacy skills. Chapter 4 highlights the elementary-level ESL student. The chapter contains decision heuristics to help place students in programs that match their abilities and backgrounds, within both different theoretical positions and different pedagogical approaches. The chapter contains discussions of such topics as ESL phonics instruction, whole-language instruction and ESL students, L2 basal reading approach, and L2 comprehension instruction. The chapter is filled with practical ideas to teach beginning ESL students literacy skills. The basic notion developed in this chapter is that comprehensible input is the most important feature of reading instruction.

Chapter 5: Teaching Older ESL/ELL/EFL Students to Read

Older ESL students represent unique problems to teachers. Decision heuristics are presented to enable a teacher to design and/or select programs that match students' needs and abilities. Special emphasis is put on programs that do not offend older students by presenting them with obviously childish material. Survival and special reading programs are discussed and examples are given. The adult-level students' needs are delineated.

Chapter 6: Teaching Academic Reading

At some point, ESL students must be able to read, comprehend, and learn from text. This chapter discusses intermediate, secondary, university, and adult-level ESL students and their special content-area reading needs. General content skills are discussed. In addition, examples of methods for teaching students to read content texts are provided. Critical literacy and multiliteracies are discussed and suggestions for instruction are included. Examples from the Internet are provided. The notion of co-sheltering of instruction is described in situations where the academic content is outside of the ESL teacher's area of expertise.

Chapter 7: The Past, Present, and Future of ESL Reading Instruction

The last chapter in the book contains some final observations and conclusions about ESL/EFL reading instruction. It makes suggestions for further classroom research and speculates on the direction of curriculum development for ESL/EFL students. The chapter ends with the suggestion that the classroom teacher must become the agent of change in order to improve the ESL/EFL student's chances at becoming a functioning member of society.

Appendix: Informal Primary-Level Language and Literacy Test

There are very few primary-level language and literacy tests designed for ESL (ELL) learners. The Appendix contains instructions for constructing such a test that can help primary teachers to decide whether or not individual students should be included in instruction. Scores obtained by about 1,300 primary-level ESL students are presented to allow the teacher to assess their students' English levels.

Conclusion

In 1991 this author argued that the fastest-growing segment of the public school population across North America was the ESL group. Now, more than a decade and a half later, the ESL population has grown incredibly. However, the growth is actually accelerating. ESL students from age 4 to 80 are enrolled by the hundreds of thousands in public and private elementary and secondary schools, and private and public English institutions such as the YMCA, community colleges, and universities, where they are taught to speak, read, and write English. The purpose of this book is to provide both ESL and mainstream teachers with the background and expertise necessary to plan and implement reading programs that will match the special needs and abilities of their students at whatever their age levels.

Reading is a vital skill, one that allows individuals to become thinking, participating members of society. Teachers must have the knowledge and expertise to provide ESL students with the best possible programs. This book is dedicated to that task.

Acknowledgments

This book is dedicated to Dianne Fouladi, a good friend and colleague who has encouraged this author many times and in so many ways over the years. Thank you, Dianne, for your tireless efforts on behalf of ESL teachers and their students. The author also thanks Tony Carrigan, Catherine Eddy, and Sylvia Helmer for their strong and consistent support for research and for the various research efforts this author has undertaken over the years. Without their encouragement and assistance, none of the research this book is based on would have been undertaken or completed.

Thank you, Reginald D'Silva and David Ward, for your assistance and faith in this author's work. A special thank-you to Oliver and Lavina D'Souza, and all the other Mangaloreans who have included me in their special celebrations, in their lives, in their families, and helped this writer through difficult times when his mother died during the writing of this book.

And hearty thanks to the thousands of immigrant students who have contributed to this book in such significant ways.

Thank you, Peter Harrison, for your meticulous and thoughtful attention to the details of this book.

Finally, thank you, Naomi Silverman, the world's best editor, for your support and faith in this book.

Figures

Tables

Abbreviations

ABE	Adult Basic Education *or* Adult Basic English
BICS	Basic Interpersonal Communicative Skill
CALLA	Cognitive Academic Language Learning Approach
CALP	Cognitive Academic Language Proficiency
CTBS	Comprehensive Test of Basic Skills
DRA	Directed Reading Activity *or* Directed Reading Approach
DRTA	Directed Reading–Thinking Activity
EAL	English as an Additional Language
EAP	English for Academic Purposes
EBP	English for Business Purposes
EFL	English as a Foreign Language
ELL	English Language Learner
EOP	English for Occupational Purposes
ER	Expected Response
ESL	English as a Second Language
ESP	English for Special Purposes
EVP	English for Vocational Purposes
i.p.a.	International Phonetic Alphabet
IRI	Informal Reading Inventory
K-W-L	Know, Want to Know, Learned
LEA	Language Experience Approach
LEP	Limited English Proficient
NRP	National Reading Panel
OR	Obtained Response
PQRST	Preview, Question, Read, Summarize, Test
SCI	Sheltered Content Instruction
SDAIE	Specially Designed Academic Instruction in English
SEI	Structured English Immersion
SIN	Skill in Instructional Nonsense
SIOP	Sheltered Instruction Observation Protocol
SQ3R	Survey, Question, Read, Recite, and Review
SQRQCQ	Survey, Question, Read, Question, Compute, Question
SSR	Sustained Silent Reading
TBE	Transitional Bilingual Education
TESOL	Teaching English to Speakers of Other Languages

TOEFL	Test of English as a Foreign Language
USSR	Uninterrupted Sustained Silent Reading
WRAT	Wide Range Achievement Test
WRMT	Woodcock Reading Mastery Test

A Brief History of Reading Instruction

ESL or ELL?

It is important to clear up from the beginning a problem of vocabulary. The term "English as a Second Language" (ESL) has traditionally referred to students who come to school speaking languages other than English at home. The term in many cases is incorrect, because some who come to school have English as their third, fourth, fifth, and so on, language. Some individuals and groups have opted for the term "Teaching English to Speakers of Other Languages" (TESOL) to represent better the underlying language realities. In some jurisdictions the term "English as an Additional Language" (EAL) is used. The term "English Language Learner" (ELL) has gained acceptance, primarily in the United States. The difficulty with the term "ELL" is that in most classrooms, everyone, regardless of their linguistic backgrounds, is learning English. The native English speaker in first grade is an English Language Learner, as is her classmate who speaks a language other than English as his first language. For the purposes of this book the traditional term "ESL" will be used, but on occasion the reader will be reminded that "ESL" is a traditional term referring broadly to ELL/TESOL/EAL. In classrooms, mostly in non-English-speaking countries, English as a Foreign Language (EFL) is taught. The difference between ESL and EFL will be discussed later in this book. The distinction is an important one to make.

That a book on ESL reading instruction should contain a discussion of programs designed for native English speakers may be a surprise. Most ESL (ELL) students, however, are enrolled in mainstream classrooms in North America, where they are involved in reading and writing instruction along with their native-English-speaking peers. If they receive special English support, most often they do so in pull-out or sheltered content classes (Gunderson, 2007). The programs used to teach students to read English are most often those that have been developed for native English speakers. It is important to know about the different approaches designed to teach both native English speakers and those who speak a language other than English at home, but are included in English reading instruction in their classrooms. This chapter contains a discussion of the history of reading instruction over a period of about three thousand years. It presents the major theoretical notions that led to different reading programs and approaches.

Teaching Reading in the Greek Fashion

In ancient Greece, boys were taught to read in a simple fashion. First they learned the names of the letters of the alphabet in order, then backwards. Then they practiced putting consonant sounds together with vowels; that is, they practiced reading syllables. Finally, they read aloud with their teacher. Although there was some experimenting in different countries with different methods over the period of some three thousand years, the basic reading methodology remained the same (see Mathews, 1966) until well into the nineteenth century. The system worked well for the Greeks because their alphabet reliably represented the phonemes of their language. However, events conspired against the students and teachers of English.

English was written using the Roman alphabet as early as the twelfth century. Of course, there were both students and teachers of English during the twelfth to the fifteenth centuries, but little is known about how reading was taught. The reading program of the fifteenth century was very much the same as that of the ancient Greeks. English teachers taught with one additional aid, however: a hornbook, a paddle-shaped device that contained the letters of the alphabet, some selected syllables, and the Lord's Prayer. It was covered with a transparent piece of horn to protect it from little fingers (see Figure 1.1).

Students learned the names of the letters of the alphabet in order, then backwards. They practiced syllables and read the Lord's Prayer aloud. A student who was successful in this enterprise was given a book of religious material, a primer, to read. Learning to read English, however, was getting more and more difficult.

In the fifteenth century the art of printing was introduced to England. This tended to fix spelling (Mathews, 1966). Unfortunately for the students of reading, while the sounds of English changed, spelling was not altered to account for the changes. Mathews (1966) notes that "today we spell about as they did in the time of James I (1603–25)" (p. 23). And how were students of the time taught to read?

Hoole ([1660] 1912) reports that students learned "by oft reading over all the letters forwards and backwards until they can say them." Hoole reports that bright students learned quickly, but less bright ones "have been thus learning a whole year together (and though they have been much chid, and beaten too for want of heed) could scarce tell six of their letters at twelve monts' [sic] end" (p. 33).

The early schools of North America borrowed both the hornbook and the pedagogy, one essentially unchanged since the time of the ancient Greeks. The first North American schoolbook was the *New England Primer*, published toward the end of the seventeenth century (Harris, c. 1690). Students were taught to use the primer by having them learn to name the letters of the alphabet, practice syllables, and read aloud the primarily religious material in the primer. Material in the primer can be seen at http://www.sacred-texts.com/chr/nep/1777/index.htm (accessed on October 23, 2007).

In 1787, Webster's *Blue-Back Speller* was published. This reading program had students memorize the names of the letters of the alphabet, learn letter–sound correspondences, and read orally. Content was primarily religious, but it also contained material related to the history and the Constitution of the United States.

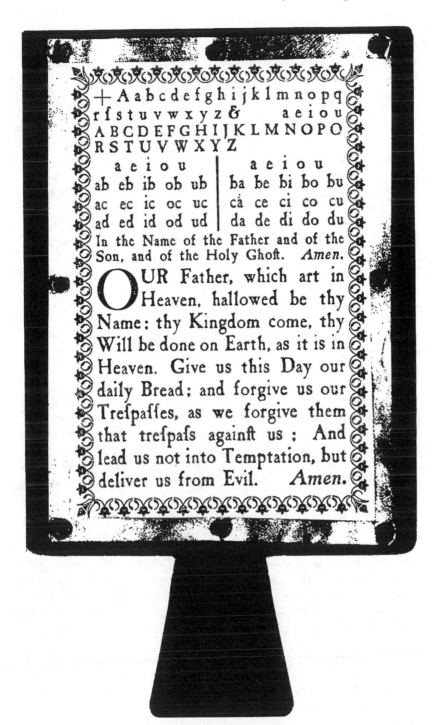

Figure 1.1 Replica of the Hornbook

There were many moralistic selections to help guide the development of the youth of America. The emphasis on letter–sound correspondences makes this reading program one of the first to focus students' attention on phonic relationships.

The beginning of the nineteenth century brought an amazing revolution to reading pedagogy. McGuffey's Eclectic Readers, first published in 1836, were a series of books aimed at different grade levels. Grade levels had not been considered important before McGuffey. His material also contained more illustrations than other reading programs. It stressed phonic relationships, syllables in isolation, and the repetition of words. The material contained moralistic and patriotic text and some literary selections at the upper levels. Producing good oral readers was a goal of the McGuffey program. In addition to providing multilevel texts, McGuffey also included a teacher's guide with each volume to improve instruction. The guide informs the teacher on how to teach good oral reading. For instance, in the revised edition of the *Fifth eclectic reader*, McGuffey's first comment is: "The great object to be accomplished in reading, as a rhetorical exercise, is to convey to the hearer, fully and clearly, the ideas and feelings of the writer" (*Fifth eclectic reader*. New York: American Book Company, 1879, p. 9). The teacher's guide contains advice on how to improve articulation and intonation. Such features of oral speech are presented as the "absolute emphasis," "emphatic pause," and "pitch and compass." The following, an excerpt from McGuffey's *Fifth eclectic reader*, is an example of the kind of material students read:

The Venomous Worm
Who has not heard of the rattlesnake or copperhead? An unexpected sight of either of these reptiles will make even the lords of creation recoil; but there is a species of worm, found in various parts of this country, which conveys a poison of a nature so deadly that, compared with it, even the venom of the rattlesnake is harmless. To guard our readers against this foe of human kind is the object of this lesson.

(p. 77)

The nineteenth century also brought a great deal of public criticism to schools and to the teaching of reading. Many individuals bitterly attacked the teaching of reading. Individuals such as Gallaudet (1888), Keagy (1824), Mann (1844a), Palmer (1837), Peirce (1844), and Rice (1893) denounced the Greek-developed pedagogy as out of date and, indeed, harmful. It may be that Mann's (1844a, b) criticisms were the most influential (Mathews, 1966). Mann, in evaluating the ABC method, stated:

If the child is bright, the time which passes during this lesson is the only part of the day when he does not think. Not a single faculty of the mind is occupied except that of imitating sounds; and even the number of these imitations amounts only to twenty-six. A parrot or an idiot could do the same thing.

(1844a, p. 5)

Each of the authors mentioned above suggested an alternative to the three-thousand-year-old ABC method used in the schools of North America. They suggested that "the word" should be the focus of instruction, rather than letters. However, even though the ABC method was greatly criticized, it continued to flourish in schools across North America, as measured by the sales of Webster's old *Blue-Back Speller* and the McGuffey readers.

The most famous educational innovator of the time was Colonel Parker, who became a leader in the battle to focus reading pedagogy on the word as a unit. Mathews (1966) notes, "Although Horace Mann is commonly regarded as having played a decisive role in the initiation of this movement, what he said was far less significant than what Parker and his teachers did" (p. 204). The basic pedagogy involved having students memorize whole words and ignore letters. Letter names were not taught until later. Thus, the traditional Greek ABC system of teaching reading had been significantly altered after some three thousand years.

Parker's career was filled with public criticism. He finally found himself with John Dewey at an elementary school attached to the University of Chicago. Students were taught to read at the university schools by focusing on the word as a unit. The word method or the "look–say" method was soon thoroughly entrenched in North American schools, as noted by Huey (1908). The notion of teaching whole words to students resulted in an intense interest in words, in vocabulary. The basic notion was that students should be introduced to reading that contained words that were in their speaking vocabulary. Their initial reading task was to learn to recognize them in print.

The increased interest in vocabulary was associated with another force beginning to exert influence on reading and reading instruction, textbook publishers. Large publishing firms began to become interested in reading texts. Ginn, for instance, published the Beacon Street Readers in 1912. Scott, Foresman & Co. published the Elson Readers during the same period. This was a significant reading series because it was the forerunner of one of the most famous series ever written, which will be discussed later in this chapter.

By the 1920s there were many different reading series. Their authors were interested in controlling the vocabulary they included in their books. Individual researchers began to look at vocabulary quite carefully. Gates (1926) produced a list of the top 500 words of the 1,000 words occurring in the primary school readers of the 1920s. The Wheeler–Howell list consisted of the 453 most frequent words in ten primers and ten grade 1 readers published between 1922 and 1929. The International Kindergarten List, produced by the International Kindergarten Union, contained 2,596 words obtained from a body of 893,256 running words spoken by a group of kindergarten children in Washington, D.C. Each of these studies became important to reading instruction because they contributed to Dolch's (1936) "A basic sight vocabulary of 220 words."

Dolch created a list that contained all words common to each of these lists, except for nouns. He added some words not common to all lists, however, because "which belongs with 'who,' 'what,' and 'that'; 'done' and 'goes' belong with 'did' and 'go'; and 'start' belongs with 'stop,' and 'write' with 'read.'" This list is still in use in classrooms across North America. Indeed, it is a powerful list that accounts for about 70 percent of all the vocabulary in beginning reading texts and about 50 percent of the vocabulary encountered in academic texts (Dolch, 1960). Teachers often teach students to read the words on sight because they believe knowing the words helps students learn to read more efficiently (Gunderson, 1983b). Publishers were interested in producing reading texts, and textbook authors were interested in controlling the vocabulary they wrote in their texts. Vocabulary control became an important textbook concern.

Vocabulary Control in Textbooks

The whole-word or sight-word approach meant that students were introduced to words, not to letters. It was thought by many that they should be high-frequency words so that students would know them. Such words as "the," "have," "of," and "come" are very high-frequency words. Most students have them in their speaking vocabularies when they enroll in first grade. Textbook authors selected them for use in their primary texts. (It will be shown later why this might not be such a good idea.) So, the first kind of vocabulary control involved selecting only high-frequency or common words. A second kind of vocabulary control was instituted. Dolch thought only a few words should be introduced at a time so students would have a better chance of learning them. Finally, vocabulary was controlled in one last fashion. If it is the students' task to learn new words, they should see the words often; that is, the words should be repeated. The three kinds of vocabulary control affecting primary texts, then, were: 1) include only high-frequency words, 2) introduce only a few at a time (Dolch recommended ten at a time), and 3) repeat them in text often enough so students successfully learn them. The pattern for our modern basal readers was set.

The 1920s and 1930s brought an emphasis on reading readiness. Publishing companies brought out pre-primers designed to give students a basic recognition vocabulary. Silent reading was in vogue. Indeed, there were entirely silent programs, including teachers' instructions (see Watkins, 1922). In general, students received whole-word training, practice on phonics within the context of whole words, and comprehension exercises. Publishers produced more complete teachers' guides to help support reading programs. Basal reading series were becoming an important part of elementary school. The well-respected Arthur Gates stated:

> The purpose of the basal program is to pave the way and provide the foundation and incentive for much wider, more enjoyable reading than would otherwise be possible. It is designed to free the teacher of much of the work that she would otherwise have to do, so that she can give more attention to the proper selection of other reading materials and the proper guidance of children in their total reading program.
>
> (1940, p. 2)

The Directed Reading Approach

The 1930s and 1940s saw the development of a basic reading lesson that quickly became part of most teachers' guides, the Directed Reading Activity or Approach (DRA). It is difficult to pinpoint when, where, and by whom the DRA was invented. Most likely it was the result of the combined genius of reading researchers and publishers wishing to produce a foolproof lesson plan for teachers. Betts (1946) notes that most of the teachers' guides of the day were organized around the basic DRA plan and that the basal authors "are in general agreement" about the contents of the plan. It has been estimated that about 80–90 percent of elementary teachers across North America used basal readers and the DRA to teach students to read into the 1980s (Aukerman, 1981). About 80–90 percent of the teachers in surveyed elementary schools in the 1980s reported that they taught their ESL students to read using basal readers and DRA (Gunderson, 1984a). The DRA has been in use for years, and most individuals can remember it from their own school experiences. Indeed, DRA is so pervasive that it can be found in use around the world in the new millennium in such diverse places as the People's Republic of China, India, Indonesia, and Zimbabwe. The use of basal readers also returned to the United States in the mid-1990s in the form of scripted readers (see p. 18).

There are basically five steps in a typical DRA:

1. Background development
2. Introduction of new vocabulary
3. Guided reading
4. Following up the reading—comprehension check
5. Skills-development exercise.

This basic lesson plan should sound familiar to most North Americans. The teacher asks a group to come to the reading circle; or sometimes he or she might work with the entire class. The teacher introduces the activity by saying that the group will be reading a story about, say, the zoo.

Teacher: Today we are going to read a story about a trip to the zoo. Has anyone been to the zoo? Can you tell us what you saw?

This portion of the DRA is to develop background for a particular story. It is one of the basic tenets of the DRA that comprehension demands some knowledge of background, and there is good evidence to support such a contention. Background is certainly an important element in ESL comprehension.

Teacher: Before you read the story I would like to show you some new words that you will find in this story. Look at this word [written on a flash card, the chalkboard, or a wall chart]. Can someone read this for me? Yes, you are right; this is the word *tiger*.

Students practice reading all of the new words. The teacher knows which words are new in the series because vocabulary is controlled and the publisher has identified them in a teacher's guide. After practicing the new words, the teacher progresses to step 3.

Teacher: If you turn to page 36, you will see a story entitled "Our trip to the San Diego Zoo." This is a story about a family that visits one of the most famous zoos in all the world. I want you to read carefully to find out how many different animals the family sees on their trip.

In this portion of the DRA the teacher has guided the silent reading; he or she has given them a reason to read, so that they read for a purpose. When the reading is complete, the teacher wishes to find out about comprehension; so there is a question period. All too often teachers have come to consider this the worksheet portion of DRA. The final step is to teach some skills. The basal series are very well organized, with scope and sequence charts delineating what skills should be taught and when. This is the time when students learn about such things as plural possessives.

As was mentioned earlier, Scott, Foresman & Co. produced one of the very first successful basal reading series. In the 1930s, William S. Gray of the University of Chicago, as an author for Scott, Foresman, introduced real people doing real activities in his basal series: Dick, Jane, Nan, Puff, and Spot. The readers were colorful, contained real children doing real things, and were written under the strictest of vocabulary control guidelines. That is, they used high-frequency words selected from a list collected from other basal texts; they introduced only a very few of the words at a time; and they repeated them. Does this sound familiar? The following is an excerpt from Gray's *Our Big Book*, published by Scott, Foresman in 1951:

Dick
Look, Jane.
Look, look.
See Dick.
See, see.
Oh, see.
See Dick.
Oh, see Dick.
Oh, oh, oh.
Funny, funny, Dick.

(pp. 11–15)

The vocabulary control is quite obvious. Gray had compelling reasons to produce the text the way he did, reasons based on the notion that vocabulary control as discussed above is vitally important. Many ESL texts written today have vocabulary control that is as strict as that found in Dick and Jane.

The *YES!* series was designed to teach reading in English in the Philippines by Mellgren and Walker (1977/78). It is a typical basal reading series containing different levels for students. It also has very strict vocabulary control. Rebane (1985) put all of the text from these readers into the computer and came up with a list of the 50 most frequent words. They were, in descending rank order: *the, is, a, he, you, to, in, and, what, she, I, are, it, did, was, they, my, can, of, this, his, on, do, at, how, your, where, no, does, there, for, her, when, but, that, it's, one, were, go, have, with, two, what's, we, yes, as, our, car, old, going, name.* These are standard very high-frequency words. There are only ten words repeated about three times each. There is one difference, however. Instead of using past-tense verbs, as basals designed for native English speakers do (e.g., *run, came, had*), these readers use words containing the lexical morpheme "ing." There is logic in choosing such words for use with ESL students. This is the first lexical morpheme learned by both ESL and native English speakers, as discussed in Chapter 2. Doesn't it make sense to use it in writing for beginning L2 learners?

Basal reading series became extremely important in elementary schools. They were well designed, they contained important high-frequency vocabulary, introduced a few words at a time, and repeated them often enough for students to learn them.

From Dick and Jane to Whole Language: The 1950s to the 1980s

By the early 1950s, reading instruction had become standardized and regularized. Basal readers were carefully written within the parameters of very strict vocabulary control. The basic lesson plan was the DRA. Basal readers had become big business. It was not very long before they also came under fire from both professional and lay critics.

In 1955, Rudolph Flesch published a book entitled *Why Johnny Can't Read* that maintained teachers should get back to the teaching of phonics and abandon the whole- or sight-word approach. Ironically, he recommended a program very similar to the one that was criticized by Mann in 1844. The real problem was that beginning readers were filled with words that did not have consistent one-to-one grapheme–phoneme correspondences. The great care taken to control basal vocabulary had resulted in a body of high-frequency words that contained items not pronounced the way they were spelled (e.g., *have, come,* and *of*). Some individuals thought beginning readers should be introduced to regularly spelled words so they learn that English orthography is, to an extent, regular, that words can be decoded. Two alternatives were explored: i.t.a. and "linguistic" readers.

The Initial Teaching Alphabet

Some proposed that since many important, high-frequency words are not spelled the way they are pronounced, the alphabet should be changed so that it adequately represents English phonemes. Sir Isaac Pitman well over a century ago developed a system of symbols to represent English. His grandson, Sir James Pitman, developed the Initial Teaching Alphabet (i.t.a.) at the beginning of the 1960s. The i.t.a. is shown in Figure 1.2. It contains 44 symbols to represent the approximately 44 phonemes of English. The Janet and John series contained the first English readers printed in i.t.a.

During the early 1960s, hundreds of schools and thousands of students across North America began their reading experiences with i.t.a. These programs were very successful. There have been studies conducted with ESL students learning to read using i.t.a. (e.g., Robertson & Trepper, 1974). These authors tested i.t.a. against standard orthography with 53 Mexican-American bilingual fourth graders in east Los Angeles, California. They conclude, "The results tend to confirm that i.t.a. can be an effective tool with which to teach beginning reading of English to Mexican-American bilingual children. To that end, it appears to be superior to the traditional orthography." Especially impressive is the fact that the children who were in the i.t.a. group were tested in traditional orthography, and yet had only been reading traditional orthography for about one year (p. 136). Downing (1962) was i.t.a.'s most ardent supporter.

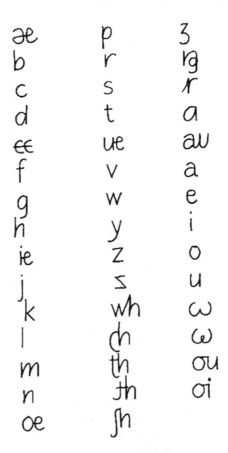

Figure 1.2 The Initial Teaching Alphabet

Over the past few decades, fewer and fewer teachers have used i.t.a. materials, however. Teachers make two basic complaints about i.t.a., namely that there is not enough material written in it and i.t.a.-trained students become poor spellers. The former is true. However, there are no reliable data to suggest the latter is true.

The Miami Linguistic Readers

An alternative to changing the orthography is to select regularly spelled high-frequency words. The most regular spelling patterns involve what reading teachers call short vowel words such as "pin." Minimal contrasts are used in "linguistic" readers to teach students regular spelling patterns. So, a story is written with such words as *man, Nan, Dan, fan,* and *can.* Students learn that English does have regular spelling patterns. Manning (1975) referred to these sorts of reading texts as the "Can Nan fan Dan" texts. The Miami Linguistic Readers were designed for ESL students and are based on the principle of selecting vocabulary that is regularly spelled. This can be seen in an example taken from the Level 1A text (R.F. Robinett, P.E. Bell, and P.M. Rojas, *Miami Linguistic Reading* (Boston: D.C. Heath & Co., 1971, pp. 3–13):

Biff and Tiff
Tiff Tiff. Tiff!
Sit, Tiff.
Sit, Tiff, sit!
Biff is sitting.

The classic features of "linguistic" vocabulary control are evident. The other vocabulary control features are also evident: the introduction of a limited number of words, and repetition. Bilingual programs will be discussed in some detail later in this chapter.

The 1960s were exciting years in the area of reading education. By the middle of the decade the basal business was huge. Indeed, this period represents the acme of the development of basal readers. A typical series of the day contained students' readers, and such pedagogical devices as comprehension workbooks, skills workbooks, audio and video material, criterion tests, pre- and post-unit assessments, and scope and sequence charts. They were often referred to as complete reading programs. They continued to be viewed as complete programs by individuals in many school districts into the late 1980s and early 1990s. This view has, as we will see, returned in the minds of many individuals in the twenty-first century.

Publishers were anxious to meet the needs of students in different areas of North America. At the time, the civil rights movement in the United States resulted in an interest in the content of basal readers. Gray brought real people to basal readers in the 1930s. Many complained, however, because the people portrayed in the basals of the 1960s were middle-class, white people in stereotypic sex roles. Publishers responded with material containing a broader representation of society. They also included material showing both men and women in various non-stereotypic roles. There were critics, however, who suggested the changes were only superficial, and that the underlying problem with basals is the unusual—yes, bizarre—language containing strange syntactic patterns in odd, repetitive ways. Other critics suggested basal readers did not account for the individual needs and abilities of students. Programs were needed that could account for an individual student's needs and abilities.

Grouping for Instruction

There is a kind of folklore about grouping for instruction in reading. Somehow, somewhere, someone decided the best method for accounting for different levels of students' needs and abilities was to divide classes into ability groups. Three seems to be a magic number. The typical elementary classroom had three reading groups variously named after colors, animals, or famous rock bands. However, many thought the wide range of abilities in a typical classroom could not be accounted for by instruction in three reading groups. Individualization was the answer. Each student was to have his or her own program, designed to meet individual needs. It did not take long for publishers to get in on the act. Individualized reading kits allowed teachers to provide students with individualized programs.

The typical reading kit had a series of short stories that varied in difficulty. Students were given an entry test. On the basis of their scores, they were assigned to different levels. As they read each story there were accompanying exercises to test for comprehension. The icon of reading kits is the "SRA Kit." This author is convinced that it is a rare school in North America that does not have at least one SRA Kit. The SRA Kit was developed in 1957 by Science Research Associates. The kit included graded material so that the difficulty level increased as the learners moved from one story to the next and one level to the next. It is also interesting that SRA also produced DISTAR (renamed *Reading Mastery*) and in the 1990s acquired the *Open Court* reading program. These developments will be discussed later in this chapter. This author used the SRA Kit and other individualized programs to teach reading to ESL students. His experiences convinced him that they were difficult for the teacher to manage adequately.

Managing an individualized program required the teacher to have "conferences" with students. The conference was a way of monitoring progress. During the conference, students were asked questions about stories they had read (some kits provided the questions for the teacher). The teacher took careful notes during the conference. In effect, rather than dividing a class of 30 into three groups of 10 each, they were divided into 30 groups. Management was the teacher's biggest headache. It was not always possible to meet with 30 to 35 students during a week. Other forces were also exerting themselves on reading instruction.

The Language Experience Approach (LEA)

Many people complained that basal readers were inappropriate for students because they contained language that was far from normal. It was thought that students should be taught to read by providing them with material that contained both content and language that was familiar to them—indeed, their own language and own stories. Sylvia Ashton-Warner (1963) was one of the Language Experience Approach's best-known advocates.

As a teacher of Maori students in New Zealand, Ashton-Warner believed the reading material given to her by her education ministry was inappropriate for her students. She used the Language Experience Approach (LEA) to teach them to read. LEA consists of students helping to create their own reading material. Students write or dictate their own stories, which are then used as reading material. If students have done something as a group, say taken a field trip, they help compose and dictate a group story to the teacher, who writes it on a large group story chart. In addition, students are asked individually what words they would like to know how to read. The teacher writes these words on cards and the student saves them as "key" words. LEA is an important development because many researchers believe it is the preferred way to teach ESL students. There is, however, little research to suggest that LEA is superior in teaching ESL students to read. Another significant development for ESL students was the development of the "psycholinguistic model."

The Psycholinguistic Reading Model

Instructional programs are generally based on a model of reading called the "skills model." The skills model is based on the notion that learning to read is the acquisition of a large set of skills. It is often called the "bottom-up" model because its adherents believe that text "drives" the comprehension process. Goodman (1965), however, proposed that reading is a psycholinguistic process in which readers act in a "top-down" fashion. They come to a text with expectations based on their knowledge of English syntax and semantics and their experience with the world. In Goodman's view, a reader selects "the fewest, most productive cues necessary to produce guesses which are right the first time" (Goodman, 1976, p. 498). In his view, miscues (instances in which what is read differs from what is on the page) are not always indications of poor reading. When a miscue does not alter the meaning of a sentence, it shows that the reader is comprehending what is read. Indeed, miscues show that readers are actively predicting from what they understand from print. Predictions are based on a reader's knowledge of syntax (the systematic ordering of words in English), semantics (the meaning of words), and world knowledge. The following sentence is an illustration of the predictability of English: "I think s/he is a blithering ———." Gunderson (1995) suggested there would probably be 100 percent agreement concerning the missing word if native English speakers were asked to supply it. How would they know? They know from their knowledge of syntax that the word cannot be a verb or an adjective. A noun is appropriate, but not just any noun. Since there is the pronoun "she" (or "he"), an animate noun is predicted. A knowledge of semantics suggests that the missing word is associated with a particular noun learned through experience. One would not normally supply such nouns as *bird, boy, rider,* or *policeman.*

Goodman developed the notion of "miscue analysis." In a miscue analysis, the oral reading behavior of students is examined critically to discover as much information about their reading abilities as possible. Miscue analysis will be discussed in Chapter 2. Goodman had considerable impact on reading instruction. He suggested, for instance, that "much of reading required of children in schools deters rather than promotes critical reading" (Goodman, 1976). Many teachers began to abandon basal readers for material that was more meaningful to students, material that better represented students' own language. Indeed, it had become "fashionable to bash basals" (McCallum, 1988), to ascribe all of reading education's ills to their use.

The psycholinguistic model of reading has been adopted by ESL experts as being a good model for L2 instruction. Unfortunately, there is very little evidence to suggest that psycholinguistic programs are superior to other programs. Bernhardt (1991, 2000) argues that it is unfortunate that first-language reading models are simply borrowed to represent second-language reading processes.

Clay developed a program to teach primary-level students who were having difficulty learning to read. Her approach is called Reading Recovery. Reading Recovery involves one-on-one sessions with students. Clay also developed the notion of "running records," a miscue-like approach to track students' progress in reading (Clay, 1979, 1985, 1988, 1991, 2001).

Another development of note in initial literacy training is referred to as "whole-language" instruction.

Whole Language

During the 1970s and early 1980s there was great interest in students who learned to read before they entered school. Many researchers observed the development of individual students growing up in environments where literacy and literacy activities were highly valued. The children they observed began to make letters and letter-like forms spontaneously. Indeed, there appears to be a developmental sequence in which students begin to understand that print represents language. The writing of preschool children appears to progress through developmental stages: scribbling (with meaning), perceiving print and drawing as synonymous, representing things with individual letters, writing initial consonants to represent words beginning with particular sounds, spacing between words, representing sounds with letters, invented spelling, and producing the mature conventions of spelling and writing (DeFord, 1980; Dyson, 1981; Ferreiro, 1986; Hipple, 1985; Sulzby, 1986). Preschool children also learn to "read" environmental print. That is, they recognize and understand the significance of such visual stimuli as the "Golden Arches." They can produce and read their own material even though it may bear little resemblance to the mature writing model produced by literate adults.

These findings suggest to advocates of whole language that the traditional developmental sequence upon which language programs are built—listening, speaking, reading, writing—is incorrect. For years, one of the basic tenets of ESL teachers has been that speaking and listening should precede reading, and that reading should precede writing. Students, advocates maintain, should be involved in an integrated program. Indeed, they should start writing immediately. First-grade whole-language teachers involve their students in writing activities from the very first day. Secondary ESL teachers who are whole-language teachers, this author has observed, involve their students in writing activities from the very first day. How does whole-language instruction work?

Gunderson and Shapiro (1987) observed two grade 1 classrooms in which whole-language instruction was the goal of the teachers. From the very first day of grade 1 the students were asked to write in logbooks. The logbooks were to contain material that was important to the students. Four categories of early-September writers were observed: 1) those who could not or would not write on their own, 2) those who wrote strings of letters, 3) those who wrote strings of letters containing some invented spelling, and 4) those who could write text, usually with much invented spelling.

In fact, it was found that about 52 percent of the students could not or would not write that September (Shapiro & Gunderson, 1988). Their teachers then asked them what they would like to write and transcribed their text for them. Students carefully copied the text. Teachers also responded in writing to their students' writing. Both were read aloud by teachers and students. Some students began writing groups of letters representing their text. The teachers asked them to read their stories aloud and wrote a paraphrase so that the students would see a related form. Teachers never "corrected" students' texts. They always made interested, positive comments. About 10 percent began their writing experiences with groups of letters. About 38 percent began writing recognizable text. Again, the teachers always responded positively. About the end of November, students were given draft books and were asked to write special stories. In addition, students were involved in reading big books aloud with their teachers. Students were allowed to read material they wanted to read, what interested them. An important element in some, but not all, whole language is LEA, both individual- and group-dictated activities.

Thousands of teachers across North America introduced their students to language in this fashion. Indeed, it seems that many features of whole-language instruction, especially in the higher grades, are still abundant in classroom instruction in the new millennium. There is no empirical evidence to suggest that whole-language instruction is superior to any other program in teaching ESL students to read, although Pressley (2006) argues strongly that whole-language instruction works better for very young students than phonics instruction, but that older students benefit more from systematic phonics instruction. In 1991 this author suggested that it would be interesting to see what the outcomes would be of the use of whole language over a period of years with ESL students. Unfortunately, a raging, bitter debate erupted between whole-language advocates and those who viewed direct systematic phonics instruction as superior. The "Reading Wars" pitted researchers against researchers, teachers against teachers, and eventually got the U.S. government into the search for scientific evidence to support the best reading instructional programs. In the minds of some individuals, whole language acquired a negative connotation and was viewed by many as loosey-goosey and warm and fuzzy, but not appropriate to teach students the skills they need to read independently.

For about a decade, from about the mid-1980s to the mid-1990s, whole-language approaches appeared to be the predominant teaching program used particularly by primary teachers. The approach resulted in the use of children's literature, called trade books, in hundreds of thousands of classrooms. Teachers, often using their own money, set up classroom library centers where students could select the books they wanted to read. It is interesting that this feature of whole language continues to have an influence in elementary classrooms (Gunderson, Eddy, & Carrigan, submitted for publication b). Goodman (1992) noted that "Sales of children's books have quintupled since 1982, and the use of children's rooms in public libraries is skyrocketing" (p. 355). One serious difficulty was that the definition of whole language varied from teacher to teacher (Gunderson, 1989, 1997). Some referred to whole language as a philosophy.

WHAT IS WHOLE LANGUAGE?

This author reviewed hundreds of studies of whole language and concluded that it was not a philosophy; rather, different versions existed in classrooms depending on individual teachers' views (Gunderson, 1997). Specifically, he argued that "each construal is a framed composite propositional intertext" (p. 225). So, the definition of whole language varies from teacher to teacher. Each teacher believes in a set of propositions about teaching and learning. However, Gunderson notes:

> For purposes of discussion and debate, it is proposed here that the minimal set of propositions includes:
>
> · that meaningful language is intact language;
> · that active learning is meaningful learning;
> · that speaking, listening, reading, writing, and watching are integrated, mutually reinforcing language activities;
> · that the aesthetics of language are fundamental;
> · that language is functional;
> · that the learning of content and the learning of language are inseparable; and
> · that literacy learning should involve the learning of process.
>
> (1997, p. 226)

Unfortunately, the notion that there is not a single, unified definition of whole language is bothersome to some individuals, especially to those who wish to compare it with other instructional approaches. Instruction that varies from classroom to classroom is best studied at the classroom level, and probably by teachers. The research employed to study whole language is typically qualitative research that does not seek to develop universal generalizations about teaching and learning. Goodman (1992) concluded that "We are in a period when many teachers are producing useful, applicable knowledge while many researchers have locked themselves into a paradigm *de rigueur* that produces little that is useful to teachers" (p. 356). McKenna, Robinson, & Miller (1993) lament that "Mainstream researchers are often frustrated by the lack of a coherent, universally applicable definition" (p. 141). They add, "If whole language varies from teacher to teacher, general definitions and generalizeable conclusions are difficult to make precise" (p. 142).

Stahl & Miller (1989) reviewed studies related to whole language and concluded, "From the data reviewed, it appears whole-language has not, in fact, been rigorously tested by empirical research." They also concluded that "From the data reviewed, it appears that whole-language approaches may have an important function early in the process of learning to read, but that as a child's needs shift, they become less effective" (p. 111). The difficulty with the Stahl & Miller review, however, was that they included studies that involved language experience approaches. Debate concerning best method became intense. These debates were referred to as the Reading Wars or the Paradigm Wars. They were referred to as the Paradigm Wars because whole-language researchers focused on the use of qualitative research methodologies to explore classroom differences while phonics or skills-based advocates argued strongly for the need to use what they referred to as scientific studies to compare in objective ways which approach resulted in the highest reading achievement scores.

WHOLE-LANGUAGE- AND LITERATURE-BASED BASAL READING PROGRAMS

Publishers of basal reading programs in the 1980s attempted to get into the whole-language field by producing literature-based basals. These basal reading series contained children's literature that was considered to be of high quality. However, there were individuals in a number of different jurisdictions who were offended by these materials because part of their content involved witches, devils, and monsters, which they considered to be the work of the devil. Such responses were loud and strident in such places as California, Texas, and British Columbia, Canada. The issues were brought to critical attention by a trial in a federal court in Tennessee (1987, *Mozert v. Hawkins County Public Schools*). DelFattore wrote about the trial:

> The protesters, who described themselves as born-again fundamentalist Christians, based their entire understanding of reality on their particular interpretation of the Bible. In their way of looking at life, all decisions should be based solely on the Word of God; using reason or imagination to solve problems is an act of rebellion. Everyone should live in traditional nuclear families stuctured on stereotyped gender roles. Wives should obey husbands, and children their parents, without argument or question.
>
> (1992, p. 36)

The literature-based programs contained many stories involving imaginary creatures, fantasy, and fairy tales. Parents were upset about the material, but they were as upset about the notion of asking learners to become critical readers. DelFattore (1992, p. 44) notes:

> Imagination, like independent thinking and tolerance for diversity, has no place in the Hawkins County protesters' world view. They alleged that the *process* of imagination, regardless of the content, distracts people from the Word of God. Once the mind is open to imagination, all kinds of of alien

thoughts may enter, and the soul may be lost. Moreover, using imagination to solve problems substitutes a human faculty for the absolute reliance on God that is necessary for salvation. [emphasis in the original]

So, whole-language- and literature-based instruction faced opposition from others. Some complained that literature-based programs did not contain vocabulary that was decodable. Hoffman *et al.* (1998) concluded that "in the mid-1990s many readers struggled with the challenge level of the materials." They noted that the problem was especially bad for "at-risk" students. Hoffman *et al.* also observed that "In their 1996 adoption, the California legislature demanded that publishers attend to more explicit teaching of skills, but offered no specific requirements for the decodability of the text." They also concluded that

> Basal publishers responded. At the same time, there was an influx of "little books" specifically designed to support the development of decoding. Early on, these little books were imported directly from New Zealand, where they were used in association with the Reading Recovery program. Basal publishers in the United States began to produce similar materials to support decoding.
>
> (1998, p. 170)

There was opposition to the use of basal readers from individuals from many different points of view. Some argued that basal readers took control away from teachers, while others argued that there should be more control. Baumann & Heubach (1996) surveyed teachers and concluded that a large majority of them argued that the basal reading programs in their classes did not take away from their pedagogical decision making. There was an effort to make certain that teaching programs were regularized and controlled, and scripted programs received renewed attention.

The two best-known scripted reading programs are *Open Court* and *Reading Mastery*. *Reading Mastery* was developed by Siegfried Engelmann of the University of Oregon, and was originally called Direct Instruction and subsequently DISTAR. These programs provide written scripts and step-by-step instructions for teachers to follow. In 2000, *Open Court* was used in one in every eight elementary schools in California (Helfand, 2000). The Los Angeles Unified School District, with over 300,000 K–5 students, adopted *Open Court* in 2000. MacGillivray *et al.* (2004) note that the program is still in use in Los Angeles. Moustafa and Land (2002) "suggest that *Open Court* limits what children are able to achieve in literacy relative to what they are able to achieve via many other programs." The amount of angst and turmoil generated by different arguments for and against different points of view concerning reading instruction has no boundaries. But other arguments have also focused on literacy and how it represents a political or Eurocentric point of view that should be challenged.

Critical Literacies—Multiliteracies

Olson (1992) notes that proponents have proposed the "somewhat overblown" notion that "learning to read and write is not only necessary to permit one to participate in literate society, but also necessary for the full development of one's intellectual resources" (pp. 18–19) and that "literacy has come to be seen as an interesting problem in its own right rather than being seen as the solution to every other problem" (p. 19). Olson concludes that

> Literacy is a resource that is particularly appropriate to some forms of discourse, to solving a certain range of problems and to functioning in contemporary social institutions. But literacy does not exhaust the range of valued forms of discourse and valued forms of rationality.
>
> (1989, p. 13)

Reading and writing and political and personal power and choice are related in interesting and complex ways. Literacy has been equated to "cultural capital." Those who have it, some contend, can participate in society and learn from the words written in wise texts. In essence, they believe literacy is liberating. However, knowing how to read and write does not mean, necessarily, participation in society. Literacy is not necessarily liberating (Harman & Edelsky, 1989). Harman & Edelsky add that "*merely knowing how to read and write guarantees neither membership in the dominant culture nor the concomitant political, economic, cognitive, or social awards of that membership*" (p. 393; emphasis in original). Gee noted:

> To read is to respond appropriately to a specific hegemonic or displaced consensus centered on the values of the dominant Discourses, a consensus achieved among persons (in dominant groups or not) whose paths through life have [for a time and place] fallen together with the members of the dominant Discourses.
>
> (1992, pp. 74–75)

Critical literacy theorists argue that students must read texts to analyze how and when their own discourse differs from the Discourses of the dominant society.

Freire (1975) believed that one should learn to read the word and to read the world. His early efforts trained fishers to identify objects in their environments and to write them on cards, which helped to lead them to become literate. His views influenced educators to help to teach workers the literacy skills needed to advance themselves in their work; to become shop stewards and share in power. He developed the view that the metaphor for teaching was the banking model where teachers poured bits of knowledge into their students' empty heads. Luke (2004) notes, "Freire's work has become a canonical example of what we might term *point of decolonization* educational theorizing about emancipation, consciousness raising, and education" (pp. 21–22; emphasis in original). Cummins ([1985] 1991) argued that "students from 'dominated' societal groups are 'empowered' or 'disabled' as a direct result of their interactions with educators in the schools" (p. 375). Teachers consciously or unconsciously reproduce the political system of domination. Eurocentric views and beliefs form the core of the educational thought that guides curriculum development and instructional practice. Critical literacy seeks to deconstruct the underlying hegemonies that define power relationships that may not be apparent from the surface-level discourses of texts—in other words, what does a particular text actually say from a feminist viewpoint about male–female relations or what does it say about right and wrong from a Eurocentric viewpoint? Students are taught to deconstruct texts to understand the underlying messages. The basal readers mentioned previously, for instance, presented views of families that were white and middle-class and excluded other family structures. They also marginalized human beings of color and portrayed men and women in stereotypic roles. The purpose of critical literacy is to produce readers who read and deconstruct the underlying, possibly hegemonic, messages in text. Power and privilege are issues that critical literacy seeks to explore.

The concept of multiliteracies was developed in some detail by a group of ten individuals referred to as the New London Group (New London Group, 1996). These individuals met in New London, New Hampshire, to discuss the teaching of literacy. They argued that literacy education was focused on print, but that literacy should be broadened to include non-print material, art, architecture, the Internet, and the world. They proposed that

> A pedagogy of multiliteracies, by contrast, focuses on modes of representation much broader than language alone. These differ according to culture and context, and have specific cognitive, cultural, and social effects. In some cultural contexts—in an Aboriginal community or in a multimedia environment, for instance—the visual mode of representation may be much more powerful and closely related to language than "mere literacy" would ever be able to allow. Multiliteracies also creates a different kind of pedagogy, one in which language and other modes of meaning are dynamic representational resources, constantly being remade by their users as they work to achieve their various cultural purposes.
>
> (New London Group, 1996, p. 10)

The concepts of critical literacy and multiliteracies have been powerful forces in guiding educators in developing programs to equip students to be critical readers and to question texts in political and philosophical ways. The local literacy curriculum is developed by those who view reading and writing through a particular lens. It is disconcerting for government curriculum developers to see their work read and evaluated critically. They often respond negatively to this view and try to seek out what they view as the best way to teach students to read, but always within their own point of view. The argument is focused on what kind of instruction would help students develop their reading skills—always in terms of such issues as phonics instruction, word recognition, and traditional comprehension measures, not the development of critical literacies or multiliteracies.

Which Instructional Approach Works Best?

American politicians determined that they wanted to find the best approach to teach reading. The U.S. Congress in 1997 provided impetus for the creation of a National Reading Panel (NRP) that would "assess the status of research-based knowledge, including the effectiveness of various approaches to teaching children to read" (NICHD, 2000). Panel members conducted an extensive search and evaluation of the available studies of reading. Their conclusions were:

a) Teaching phonemic awareness to children improves their reading more than instruction that does not have a focus on phonemic awareness.
b) Systematic phonics instruction works best for students in kindergarten to grade 6 and for children who have reading difficulties.
c) "Older students receiving phonics instruction were better able to decode words and spell words and to read text orally, but their comprehension of text was not significantly improved" (p. 9).
d) "Guided repeated oral reading procedures that included guidance from teachers, peers, or parents had a significant and positive impact on word recognition" (p. 12). However, the panel concluded there was no evidence concerning oral reading and fluency over more than one year.
e) The panel found no evidence to suggest that independent silent reading resulted in the improvement of reading.
f) The panel found that instruction in vocabulary resulted in increases in comprehension.
g) The panel concluded that teaching a combination of techniques is the most effective way to improve comprehension.
h) It was concluded that to be most effective, teachers needed to be taught explicitly strategies.

Garan (2001) evaluated the panel's findings and concluded that there were significant problems. For instance, she pointed out that the conclusion (item b above) concerning systematic phonics instruction was not supported by the panel's study. Indeed, the subgroup studying the issue reported that "There was insufficient data to draw any conclusions about the effects of phonics instruction with normally developing readers above first grade." Overall, Garan concludes that "the panel's own words have established that the research base in its report on phonics is so flawed that the results do not even matter" (p. 502). Yet regardless of the problems with the panel's report—and there were many—the generalizations derived from the study were supported by influential researchers and politicians. They were viewed as scientific and as such were influential.

In 2002 the No Child Left Behind Act was signed into law. This piece of legislation was based on the findings of the NRP. The law established The Reading First Initiative, which was "a new, high-quality evidence-based program for the students of America" (NICHD, 2000). The law was designed to ensure that the students received the best instruction possible. Based on the findings of the panel, the development of literacy coaches was established. Literacy coaches were individuals who were reading specialists who were designated to help teachers become more effective reading teachers. Again, the notion of literacy coaches came out of the findings of the panel (see, for instance, items g and h in the list above). The Reading First initiative mandates the use of coaches in K–3 classrooms. No Child Left Behind has itself created a great deal of controversy concerning such issues as funding and the adoption of programs that are approved because they conform to the findings of the NRP. Programs featuring systematic phonics instruction and instruction in which teachers follow scripts often containing the precise word-by-word lessons they are to use were approved for adoption, while other programs were not.

The U.S. Inspector General released a report in September 2006 that concluded that procedures had been used that were inappropriate because policy "prohibits Department officials from exercising any direction, supervision, or control over the curriculum or program of instruction of any educational institution, school, or school system" (p. 2). The report further notes:

> "Specifically we found that the Department:
> - Developed an application package that obscured the requirements of the statute;
> - Took action with respect to the expert review panel process that was contrary to the balanced panel composition envisioned by Congress;
> - Intervened to release an assessment review document without the permission of the entity that contracted for its development;
> - Intervened to influence a State's selection of reading programs; and
> - Intervened to influence reading programs being used by local educational agencies (LEAs) after the application process was completed.
> (Accessed on January 17, 2007 from
> http://www.ed.gov/about/offices/list/oig/aireports/i13f0017.pdf)

Many teachers have felt coerced to make pedagogical choices *not* based on their own views of teaching and learning by No Child Left Behind, and the Inspector General's report appeared to confirm their fears that they had no choice. Systematic phonics instruction and scripted instruction involving preferred published programs have become features in many jurisdictions across the United States. It is ironic that the members of the NRP wished to consider the best scientific evidence, yet their own report appears to be flawed scientifically.

Many individuals in the mid-1990s thought the Reading Wars could be ended by including features of both points of view into a unified instructional program: some aspects of whole language and some aspects of phonics instruction. The notion of balanced instruction was introduced, and one of the champions of the approach was Pressley (2006). There were critics of this approach, however. This author, for instance, responded strongly to Pressley's call for balanced instruction, noting that it was a dangerous concept because teachers needed to have an unbalanced approach. They need to respond to the needs of individual students, rather than providing all students with a one-size-fits-all program (accessed on January 17, 2007 from http://literacyconference.oise.utoronto.ca/papers/gunderson.pdf). Others have strongly supported the notion (see www.balancedreading.com, accessed on January 21, 2007), while others have criticized it (see http://www.edexcellence.net/foundation/publication/publication.cfm?id=45, accessed on January 21, 2007). Quite a number of influential reading researchers have lent their support to the notion of balanced instruction (see, for instance, Morrow, Gambrell, & Pressley's 2003 edited volume). The difficulty is that defining the term "balanced instruction" turns out to be difficult and there is little apparent consensus on what balanced instruction looks like in the classroom. Connor *et al.* (2007) disagree with the notion of balanced instruction because it represents a single approach to teach all students. They conclude that various approaches must be used relative to individual students' needs, abilities, and backgrounds. They argue that "the impact of any particular instructional strategy appears to depend on children's language and literacy skills" (Connor *et al.* 2007, accessed at www.sciencemag.org/cgi/content/full/315/5811/464/DC1 on February 2, 2007). This is also the view described and argued in this book. The overall goal of this book is to provide teachers with the tools to allow them to account for the incredible diversity of backgrounds, needs, abilities, and motivations in their classes. To accomplish this task, opposing viewpoints will be presented.

The language of instruction also became a focus of debate and contention beginning about the mid-1980s. The essential question for educators, the public, and, of course, politicians is "What language is best for a student's initial reading instruction?"

English-Only or Bilingual Instruction?

The history of the United States is one that contains many instances in which the language of instruction was not English (Kloss, 1978). Bilingual instruction was widely distributed across the United States. The first large-scale bilingual programs were started in Florida in the 1960s, as has already been noted in this chapter. There is contention, however, concerning what language should be used to teach students to read (Gunderson, 2008).

The commonsense answer would seem to be that students should speak English before being involved in reading instruction. Some researchers many years ago maintained that they should not be taught to read until they have become orally proficient in English (Sharp, 1973; Ching, 1976), while others argued they should be involved regardless (Saville & Troike, 1971). One major approach used to teach students oral language is referred to as the "audiolingual" method, which involves mimicry, memorization, and pattern drills. Indeed, proponents believe students "need to overlearn the target language, to learn to use it automatically without stopping to think" (Larsen-Freeman, 1986). One of the major tenets of the audiolingual approach that continues to receive support, even though the audiolingual method itself has received considerable criticism, is that students should be fluent in oral English before they begin reading instruction. Sharp (1973), for instance, in writing about teaching in the United Kingdom, suggested that language learning should be entirely oral until students are about 10 or 12 years old, or until they are in secondary school if they are slow learners. Ching (1976) noted that "before bilingual children can learn to read English, they must be able to understand it effectively."

A study conducted in Montreal casts some doubt on the native-language-first approach. Lambert and Tucker (1972) placed native English speakers in a total French immersion program. Their students became fluent in French and their English skills were not significantly different at the end of the project from those of native English speakers enrolled in regular English-speaking classrooms. Critics have pointed out that the subjects in this project were from upper-middle-class families who were actively involved in English-language activities at home. Studies of other populations, however, have generally supported these findings, suggesting that students do not necessarily learn to read best in their native language (Tucker, Lambert, & d'Anglejan, 1973; Barik & Swain, 1975).

First-Language, Bilingual, and English-Only Instruction

A number of researchers 30 years or more ago argued that a student's beginning reading instruction should be in their "mother tongue" (Gamez, 1979; Gutierrez, 1975; Hillerich, 1970; Kaufman, 1968; Lewis, 1965; Modiano, 1968; Mackey, 1972; Rosen, 1970; Yoes, 1967). Natalicio (1979) referred to this notion as the "native-language literacy axiom." Some early researchers, particularly those who looked at French-immersion students who were native English speakers enrolled in French immersion classes, concluded that students do not necessarily learn to read best in their first language (L1) (Barik & Swain, 1975; Tucker, Lambert & d'Anglejan, 1973). Andrew, Lapkin, & Swain noted:

> While it is not clear that the superior performance of the immersion centre students in these academic areas is due to the language environment of the immersion centres, it is clear that a French language environment in these schools has no detrimental effects in the achievement of the immersion students in any of the academic areas tested.
>
> (1978, p. 27)

This early research into French immersion was viewed as supporting the notion that students do not necessarily learn to read best in their L1. Generally, the English-speaking immersion students in these early studies were from families in which both English and French were highly valued and the dominant language was English. Auerbach concluded that

> Whereas research indicates that immersion programs can be effective in the development of language and literacy for learners from dominant language groups, whose L1 is valued and supported both at home and in the broader society, bilingual instruction seems to be more effective for language minority students, whose language has less social status.
>
> (1993, pp. 15–16)

Bilingual Programs

The decision of the United States Supreme Court in 1974 was that all students had the right to access to educational programs in schools and that L1 was a key to such access (*Lau v. Nichols*, 1974). Proponents of bilingual programs in the United States argue that the only effective way for students to be able to learn academic content is through use of their L1s, especially students who have little or no proficiency in English (see, for instance, Moll, 1992; Ramirez, 1992; Ramirez, Yuen, & Ramey, 1991; Willig, 1985). They suggest that since it takes a long time to learn English language skills, students immersed in English will not acquire the academic skills their English-speaking peers are learning. And it is likely they will fall further behind their peers in academic development as they concentrate on English (Lucas & Katz, 1994). There is good evidence to suggest that students enrolled in English-only high schools do not do particularly well and disappear from academic classes as at about a 60 percent rate (Gunderson, 2007).

The U.S. Supreme Court decision in *Lau v. Nichols* included a number of comments. A significant one was:

> Basic English skills are at the very core of what public schools teach. Imposition of a requirement that, before a child can effectively participate in the educational program, he must already have acquired those basic skills is to make a mockery of public education.

The use of languages other than English in schools in the United States is contentious and politically charged. Many states have passed English-only laws, and a group called U.S. English has organized to lobby for an amendment to the United States Constitution that would establish English as the official language (Crawford, 1989). In 1998, 63 percent of the voters in California supported an anti-bilingual proposition called Proposition 227 (Crawford, 1997), and Arizona has passed a similar law (Zehr, 2001). The passage of the law in California did not eliminate the debate concerning bilingual education, however, nor did it eliminate bilingual education. Moore, a visiting fellow at Stanford University's Hoover Institute, noted:

> The bilingual lobby is now simply defying the law. A front-page story in the San Francisco Chronicle headline "Educators Working Around Prop. 227" reports that "in many Bay Area school districts, bilingual education lives." When kids got back to school "they found bilingual education waiting for them." The bilingual-education director in Contra Costa County defiantly said, "If a child is very limited in English proficiency, we will offer [native] language instruction. It's essentially the same as what we offered last year."
> (1998, p. 23)

In the mid-term federal election of 2006 in the United States a majority of voters in Arizona voted 849,772 (66 percent) to 295,632 (26 percent) in favor of

Proposition 103 to make English the official language and businesses to enforce the measure (accessed on November 10, 2006 from http://www.foxnews.com/politics/youdecide2006/races.html?AZ). Gunderson notes:

> The scandalous situation is that ESL students are not learning the academic skills to allow them to enter into our technological society and they are dropping out at high rates; some groups more than others. In the meantime, educators, researchers, politicians, and others seem intent on proving that their views of English-only or bilingual instruction are right rather than on searching for the best programs to assure that all students, including ESL students, learn the vital skills they need to participate in this technologically based society.
>
> (2006, p. 6)

Students in jurisdictions outside of the United States are often enrolled in schools in which the language of instruction is different from their home languages. The language of instruction in the People's Republic of China, for instance, often differs from the languages spoken by students in different areas and provinces. The language of instruction has also been the focus of contention in places like Malaysia, where university programs were conducted in L1 until recently. It is not clear from or well supported by research that English-only programs are necessarily detrimental to second-language students' language development in either L1 or L2. There is a great deal of contention and argument, however. Indeed, proponents from both sides cite research that they argue supports their particular points of view.

Large-scale, systematic bilingual programs in the United States first appeared in Florida in the 1960s. Early bilingual programs were designed to be transitional in that the use of first language was employed to support students until their English skills developed and they could learn academic content from books written in English. The majority of students' early education in this model is conducted in first language with a daily "period" reserved for English instruction. Students begin to transition to English after they have attained a degree of English proficiency. At this point they are taught to read and learn academic content in English. These programs have come to be known as transitional bilingual education (TBE).

Rossell & Baker (1996) reviewed 300 studies of bilingual education and concluded that only 72 were "methodologically acceptable studies" and that they revealed "no consistent research support for transitional bilingual education as a superior practice for improving language achievement of limited English proficient children" (p. 21). Rossell & Baker also concluded, "Seven percent of the studies show transitional bilingual education to be superior, 64 percent show it to be inferior, and 29 percent show it to be no different from submersion or doing nothing." They add, "Altogether, 93 percent of the studies show TBE to be no different from or worse than doing nothing at all" (p. 22). Among their most damning comments were "One cannot trust an author's conclusion to be an accurate representation of the data on which it is supposedly based" and "Moreover, this is as true of studies done by supporters of bilingual education as it is of those done by its critics" (p. 25).

However, other researchers have strongly criticized Rossell and Baker. Greene (1998) noted, "It is clear that Rossell and Baker's review of studies is useful as a pool for a meta-analysis, but the lack of rigor and consistency in how they classify studies and summarize results prevent their conclusions from being reliable" (p. 8). In addition, he argued that "unfortunately, only 11 of the 75 studies identified as acceptable by Rossell and Baker actually meet their own criteria for an acceptable study" (p. 4). Greene concluded that "despite the relatively small number of studies, the strength and consistency of these results, especially from the highest quality randomized experiments, increases confidence in the conclusion that bilingual programs are effective at increasing standardized test scores measured in English" (p. 9). Greene asserted that scores on standardized tests were higher when children with limited English proficiency were taught using at least some of their native language than when only English was used to teach similar children. He also concluded that

> The limited number of useful studies, however, makes it difficult to address other important issues, such as the ideal length of time students should be in bilingual programs, the ideal amount of native language that should be used in instruction, and the age groups in which these techniques are most appropriate.
>
> (1998, p. 6)

Finally, he noted that "the results from the 5 randomized experiments examined here clearly *suggest* that native language instruction is useful" (p. 6; emphasis added). These five randomized experiments were among the 11 methodologically acceptable studies from the Rossell and Baker review. Greene's response to Rossell and Baker's review identified many problems, a critique that was echoed by other authors (e.g., Crawford, 1999; Cummins, 1998; Krashen, 1999). There are alternatives to TBE.

Bilingual Immersion Programs

Bilingual immersion programs were designed "to rapidly introduce minority students to English in a meaningful fashion during the early years of school by sensitively integrating second language instruction into content area instruction" (Gersten, Woodward, & Schneider, 1992, p. 5). Gersten, Woodward & Schneider compared the achievement of students enrolled in transitional bilingual classrooms to that of students in bilingual immersion programs and found that the immersion students showed an early significant advantage in achievement at grade 4 that disappeared by grade 7. There were a number of methodological problems with the Gersten, Woodward & Schneider study, however, some of which the authors themselves acknowledge. They noted that they did not adequately describe the degree to which the two programs were implemented in the study. They also noted the difficulty of the use of standardized tests with second language students. They concluded, however, that the results of the study were suspect because the design did not involve random selection; it included only those students who remained in the programs over four years. They note that

> Neither the bilingual immersion program nor transitional bilingual education brought its students up to the national norms, especially in the areas of reading (23rd–24th percentile for the bilingual immersion program and 21st percentile for the transitional bilingual education program) and vocabulary (16th and 15th percentiles respectively by the seventh grade).
>
> (1992, p. 29)

A different approach to bilingual instruction gained significant interest in the 1990s.

Two-Way or Dual Immersion Programs

Howard & Sugarman define two-way immersion programs as the integration of language-majority and language-minority students in the same classrooms where:

> 1) language-minority and language-majority students are integrated for at least 50% of the day at all grade levels; 2) content and literacy instruction in both languages are provided to all students; and 3) language minority and language-majority students are balanced, with each group making up one third to two thirds of the total student populations.
>
> (2001, p. 1)

There are a number of programs that involve two-way or dual immersion. The research base is fairly extensive, although it does contain a large number of studies that have not been subjected to blind review, including many Ph.D. dissertation studies. This author is aware of one difficult situation where Spanish- and Cantonese-speaking students were enrolled in a two-way kindergarten program. The difficulty was that the program was Spanish–English and half of the students spoke Cantonese at home, not English. The available research is not compelling in the case of two-way or dual immersion programs.

One major difficulty in evaluating bilingual studies is that there are so many variations in programs across studies. A second major difficulty is that many studies are neither well designed nor well evaluated. A third difficulty is that authors often take for granted that what other authors claim is true of their findings is, in fact, true. Cazabon et al., for instance, state, "research on the most effective forms of bilingual education (usually in terms of English achievement) suggests two way programs may be the best" (1998, p. 2). The research they cite to support this conclusion is that of Thomas & Collier (1997). It is not clear, however, that this conclusion is a valid interpretation of the results of their study.

Thomas & Collier (1997) reported on findings of their study of "700,000 language minority students, collected by five participating school districts between 1982 and 1996, including 42,317 students who have attended our participating schools for four years or more" (p. 30). Unfortunately, they did not identify or describe any of the demographics related to the school districts, nor did they provide enough information to allow the reader to evaluate whether or not their results are valid, reliable, or accurate. The study does not appear to have been published in a refereed publication, so it has not received critical independent blind review. In addition, its dissemination by the National Clearinghouse for Bilingual Education adds the possibility that it is more a political document than an independent research effort. Thomas and Collier indicated that they only recorded data from "well-implemented programs in school systems with experienced, well-trained staff" (p. 28), but no data were presented to substantiate such claims. Although they themselves criticized other reports of studies of language minority education as frequently more "pseudo-scientific" than scientific, they did not provide enough information needed for the reader to judge whether or not they themselves had been rigorous in the application of what they called scientific methods. On the basis of their cryptic report, one that focused more on the methodology than on the details of their research results, it is difficult to conclude whether they have provided strong evidence to support their claims.

Rossell (1998) is less kind. In a review of the Thomas & Collier (1997) study, she noted that "the methodology of the study is unscientific, as is the case with all of Virginia Collier's research" (p. 1). Crawford (1999), a proponent of bilingual education, remarked that "unfortunately, for reasons that remain unclear, Thomas and Collier have thus far declined to release sufficient data to support these findings" (p. 11). He added, "so, when asked about the Thomas–Collier study, bilingual education researchers usually respond that, while the early reports are intriguing, this remains *unpublished research*" (p. 12; emphasis in original). Thomas & Collier (2002) published a subsequent study through the Center for Research on Education, Diversity, and Excellence at the University of California in Santa Cruz. This more recent effort focused on data collected between 1985 and 2001 in five sites, but again the data are not easy to interpret, and the report appears not to have been subjected to the rigors of a blind review. The data are not convincing. The U.S. government again decided to intervene and seek the truth about which approach worked best: English-only or bilingual instruction.

Which Is Better, English-Only or Bilingual Instruction?

The National Literacy Panel was established to review the research literature of studies comparing bilingual and English-only programs (National Literacy Panel, 2003). Members of the panel reviewed hundreds of research articles and identified those that met their stringent requirements. When they completed their study, however, in August 2005, the United States Department of Education declined to publish the report of the National Literacy Panel reportedly "because of concerns about its technical adequacy and the degree to which it could help inform policy and practice" (staff writer, 2005, p. 1). In a related study, Slavin and Cheung (2005) conducted a meta-analysis of studies comparing bilingual and English-only instruction. They note, "The most important conclusion from research comparing the relative effects of bilingual and immersion programs for English learners is that there are too few high-quality studies of this question" (p. 273). Their study showed that of the 17 studies that fit their qualifications, 12 revealed that bilingual education resulted in higher scores, while English immersion resulted in no superior performances. The majority of their qualifying studies involved Spanish-speaking students in primary-level classes. One study involving secondary students found bilingual education superior to immersion in a ninth-grade program involving Spanish-speaking students. The research base related to secondary students is extremely limited, indeed, almost non-existent.

August & Shanahan (2006) conclude, "by and large, for language-minority children, word-level components of literacy (e.g., decoding, spelling) either are or can be (with appropriate instruction) at levels equal to those of their monolingual peers" (p. 13). However, they also note, that "this is not the case for test-level skills, like reading comprehension, which rarely approach the levels achieved by their monolingual peers" (p. 13). They also conclude that second-language oral proficiency is significant in second-language literacy development. The authors also conclude that "Language-minority students who are literate in their first languages are likely to be advantaged in the acquisition of English literacy" (p. 17). By the way, this was one of the foundational premises of the Gunderson (1991) instructional heuristics that are also used in the present book. The authors also note that "language-minority students instructed in their native language (primarily Spanish in this report) as well as English, perform on average, better on English reading measures than language-minority students instructed only in their second language (English in this case)" (p. 17). The panel's findings support the approach taken by this author in producing the 1991 text. The basic approach is to identify variables that have been shown to be important in research to assist teachers in designing their own or selecting literacy programs for their ESL students.

Unfortunately, it seems clear that the claims that one instructional approach is superior to any other appear to be founded on limited or questionable evidence. At best, inferences about best approaches appear to have limited empirical support. As Ovando (2003) concluded, one reason it has been difficult to derive a clear view of the effectiveness of bilingual education programs is that, often, program evaluation research and basic research have been confused, and "much of the adverse publicity for bilingual education stems from a set of poor program evaluation results" (p. 15). The research on bilingual education, especially in terms of its effects on secondary-age immigrant students, is inconclusive.

During the 1990s an astounding parallel development in literacy occurred: the Internet and other, related technologies.

The Internet

Developments in technology allow texts and other materials to be easily recorded, stored, and accessed in digital forms. A related revolution occurred during the 1990s: the average human being in North America gained fairly easy access to the

Internet and to the digital information it contains. The Internet provided access to materials from around the world and its usefulness to reading instruction was recognized. However, the problem of classroom access (Gunderson & Anderson, 1999) has changed dramatically over the past decade as hundreds of thousands of teachers around the world have become involved in its use in their teaching and learning programs (Leu & Zawilinski, 2007). The use of the Internet and other digital information technologies has become a significant feature of instruction in many classrooms. Reading instruction has taken on a global context as teachers integrate technology into their classrooms (see, for instance, Leu & Leu, 2000). Digital technologies have had significant impact on reading instruction. Gunderson (2000b) predicted that a new kind of disability will become apparent in classrooms—difficulty reading digital texts—and that teachers will be blamed. A number of recognized experts in digital technologies and literacy produced models of the process (see, for instance, McEneaney, 2006; Leu *et al.*, 2004).

The background information discussed so far has focused on school-age (K–12) students, except for the issues related to digital technologies. Reading research has, for the most part, been designed to explore the teaching of reading to young human beings. However, immigrants come in all ages, and, surprisingly, the majority of immigrants are adults over the age of 19.

Reading Instruction for Adults

Teaching adult ESL students to read is an important undertaking, particularly for those who need English to enter the job market at levels higher than manual labor. In addition, many immigrants are highly trained professionals who lack the English skills needed to be hired for or to become professionally certified for positions such as lawyers, accountants, teachers, and doctors. Programs designed to teach adults English reading skills are simply borrowed from programs designed to teach native English speakers, often school-age students. This is also the lamentable case related to research: models and theories are simply borrowed from the first language (English) research base (Bernhardt, 1991, 2000; Gunderson, 2007).

So, it should not be surprising to find a program utilizing a modified orthography designed for ESL students (Bourne, 1972). Bourne's orthography contains 33 symbols standing for phonemes and is designed for adult illiterates. It contains a series of basic rules such as the three basic vowel rules. Bourne suggests that the program works very well with adult students. Unfortunately, the program has not been tested with ESL adults. It should also not be a surprise that Dauzat *et al.* (1978) created the Steck-Vaughn Adult Reading program. The Steck-Vaughn program contains reading material designed for two levels: 1) prereading, word recognition, and word-attack skills presented in seven student books; and 2) comprehension skills taught throughout eight student texts. The students' texts contain self-correcting material so that the students receive feedback on their progress. Receiving such feedback is referred to as programmed instruction. The basic approach, however, is a sight-word approach, with individual items being taught within the context of sentences. This author has seen many groups of adult ESL students working together with a teacher practicing the recognition of sight-words presented to them.

Adults are often asked to read using programs designed for younger students. Very often this results in negative attitudes toward reading and reduced motivation to learn. Several publishing companies have produced reading series that have high motivation (i.e., they are interesting) and low vocabulary (i.e., they have easy words). *Series Canada*, for instance, contains stories that are interesting and have simplified vocabulary (published by Collier Macmillan in 1984). Another approach is to take a familiar classic and make it easier to read. The Longmans readers contain such material as *Ivanhoe* and *The Time Machine* (London: Longmans, Green, 1969).

Many teachers have adopted a basic approach recommended by Paulo Freire (1985) that is based on his work in Brazil with adult workers who could not read. He compiled lists of vocabulary that were essential for them to learn. In addition, he also compiled lists of "generative words" to help students learn basic reading skills. His ideas and approaches have been adopted and adapted by NGOs, schools districts and other organizations to teach second-language adults how to read. His approach has also been referred to as liberatory education since its goal is to allow students to become part of a society through literacy. Indeed, the literacy program focuses on issues from the learners' life experiences so that what students learn helps to liberate them from the social conditions that oppress them.

Educators of adults have also adopted Language Experience Approach and whole-language programs to teach adults. Both are interesting approaches that utilize students' language and focus on their needs and experiences. Those interested in adult reading have followed their colleagues who have interests in younger learners by organizing a survey project to discover the best practices. The Partnership for Reading produced a report titled *Research-based principles for adult basic education reading instruction* in 2002 in cooperation with the National Institute for Literacy, the Department of Education, the National Institute of Child Health and Human Development, and the Department of Health and Human Services (accessed on January 17, 2007 from http://www.nifl.gov/partnershipfor reading/publications/html/adult_ed/adult_ed_1.html). The purpose of this project was "to identify and evaluate existing research related to adult literacy reading instruction in order to provide the field with research-based products including principles and practices for practitioners" (p. 5 of 14). The reviewers used the same guidelines for selecting research that the National Reading Panel used. However, they also included studies related to reading assessment and some non-experimental studies. Unfortunately, their strongest finding was that "In general, the review of ABE reading instruction research found that much more research is needed in almost all of the topic areas addressed" (p. 8 of 14). They did suggest that their findings showed that direct or explicit instruction of the various reading components is effective and that "computer-assisted instruction can improve achievement in some aspects of reading." Findings were basically that more research needs to be conducted. This author contends that the need for further research is particularly vital for adults who speak a language other than English at home. This author has also concluded, related to efforts such as the National Reading Panel and the National Literacy Panel, that

> As social institutions containing microsocieties comprised of students, teachers, administrators, counselors, paraprofessionals, librarians, custodians, secretaries, parent volunteers, occasionally police officers, and others, schools are not the best places to conduct scientific research. The normal state of affairs in a school is one of great flux and change. It is likely impossible to conduct scientific research in a typical school because there are too many confounding variables to control.
>
> (Gunderson, 2007, p. 248)

This is particularly true when the definition of scientific research includes only experimental studies, as the two panels did.

Teaching reading is an important undertaking, but it is not the only instructional task teachers must undertake in the area of reading. It does get slightly more complex. There are a number of different kinds of reading skills students should learn. Teaching these skills is essential since they help students to learn from written texts.

Learning to Read versus Reading to Learn

Someone who cannot read must be taught; he or she must learn to read. The student who studies an academic course such as physics must learn a great deal from a text written about physics. Reading authorities generally call instruction in the skills of learning from reading "content reading" instruction. Remedial instruction normally refers to the instruction of students who for some reason are behind. Many educators have suggested that adult ESL students are remedial, most often enrolled in programs designed to teach remedial reading to native English speakers. Unfortunately, as we have seen, reading programs for adult native English speakers are not particularly well developed.

Reading to Learn from Text

Students are often asked to read text and to learn content from the texts. This is actually a more difficult task than it sounds because content (academic) teachers do not change their approaches to teaching content or content reading when they have ESL students in their class. Reading, comprehending, and learning from text is the secondary, university, and adult students' most difficult task. They must deal with the real demands of learning a second or third language and of learning from text. In many cases, they have to learn new technical vocabulary, the uses of known items in new contexts (e.g., the word *conductor* in a physics class), and the features of particular discourse styles (e.g., narrative versus argumentation).

Students must learn to change their reading style to match their purposes for reading (i.e., scanning for specific content is different from skimming for general content). Most skilled adult readers have learned to change their reading style to match their reading purpose. These are specific content skills and there are literally hundreds of suggested pedagogical methods to teach them. There is, however, no single approach or program that carefully teaches students such content skills. The computer and access to the Internet and its different search engines have made the learning of academic content considerably more interesting but also considerably more complex for students and for their teachers. These issues will be addressed in Chapter 6.

Conclusion

There are hundreds of programs designed to teach native English students to read. In most cases, ESL students are taught to read using such programs. Unfortunately, there is considerable controversy about the programs designed for native English speakers. The popular press on a continuing basis enters into the debate with demands for a "return to the basics," a return to the teaching of "phonics." The research concerning "best methods" for teaching reading has been conducted at various times over the past fifty or sixty years. The "First-Grade Studies" involved 27 separate research endeavors designed to discover the best methods for teaching reading (Stauffer, 1967). Results were mixed, however, with no clear-cut method that was superior. The First-Grade Studies research coordinators concluded that a combination of instruction approaches was superior to consistent reliance on one approach and that a far more significant relationship affecting the learning of reading involved the personal characteristics of both students and teachers (Bond & Dykstra, 1967).

Chall (1967) reviewed 50 years of reading research and concluded that despite their shortcomings, which were many, findings indicated that programs stressing early phonics instruction helped below-average and average students more than programs stressing early emphasis on meaning. She also concluded that there was no superior phonics teaching method and that early phonics instruction did not necessarily guarantee that students would be successful in learning to read. The Reading (or Paradigm) Wars of the 1990s involved researchers and others arguing, sometimes vehemently, about which approach, whole language or phonics, was associated with the highest gains in reading scores. The U.S. federal government sought to settle the argument in the late 1990s by empowering first the National Reading Panel and then the National Literacy Panel. The first was authorized to seek out the scientific evidence that showed which approach was superior for English speakers, while the second was organized to survey research involving comparisons of bilingual and English-only programs. Results were not compelling, however, although the NRP results directly affected in dramatic ways the instruction going on in classrooms across the United States. The research implications of both panels have been questioned. The review that involved adult reading studies was also unimpressive in its findings.

No clear-cut "best methods" for teaching reading have been isolated. How can it be that ESL students are generally placed into programs designed for native English speakers when there is controversy within the reading community concerning those very programs? It is no wonder that ESL students are not successfully learning to read.

Some have argued that critical literacy is important for learners because it equips them to understand the underlying political messages they read and write. Some have also suggested that literacy should be broadened to include the notion of multiliteracies that include non-print materials and the Internet. These individuals also believe that the notion of critical literacy should be broadened to include the context of multiliteracies. The presence of the computer and digital technologies has complicated the definition of literacy. Literacy educators can no longer avoid a discussion of computer technologies and the Internet and their role in teaching and learning to read and write.

The remainder of this book contains discussions relating to ESL students and reading instruction. These discussions will delineate reading programs for primary, elementary, secondary, university, and adult ESL students. A rationale will be developed for matching students with programs within different models of reading.

Explorations

Work with a partner if possible.

1. Try to reconstruct the way you were taught to read in your early primary years. How are your memories the same or different from those of your partner? Can you identify a clear-cut model or approach in either case? How has the way you remember being taught to read affected your notion of what reading instruction should be?
2. There is a fairly common belief that all students should be taught to read through direct instruction of phonics. This view is often referred to as getting back to the basics. Explore with your partner the notion of teaching phonics to ESL students. What would this kind of instruction look like, do you think?
3. The history of reading instruction reveals that oral reading has been a standard classroom feature for thousands of years. What do you think of oral reading? What do you and your partner remember about the oral reading you did in your elementary and high school classrooms? Was it something positive or was it something negative?
4. Has the Internet changed your view of reading in any way? Do you and your partner read from electronic texts or from the Internet? How is it different from the reading of standard print?

Language Proficiency, Literacy Background, Purpose for Reading, L2 Reading Ability

Introduction

The teacher's initial pedagogical decision is to match students' abilities with the difficulty levels of materials. This is as true for literacy as it is for every kind of instructional program. As discussed in the first chapter, there are hundreds of reading programs; selecting the right one or designing a unique program for a student depends on many factors. While findings of research are not unequivocal in supporting certain kinds of instruction, they do suggest that there is reason to teach certain kinds of skills. Results of research surveys of the National Reading Panel, the National Literacy Panel, the Partnership for Reading, and other research will be considered in the design of the instructional strategies described and discussed in this book. The first consideration concerns teachers' models of reading and instruction.

Reading Models: Bottom-Up versus Top-Down versus Interactive

There is considerable controversy concerning the appropriate model of reading. It is important to be aware of models because they determine what a reading teacher believes about instruction and subsequently does in the classroom. The predominant paradigm or model involves the teaching of skills. Advocates of the skills approach believe that students learn to read and comprehend by acquiring a large set of skills in a particular sequence. Basal readers are designed on this principle. Skills advocates believe meaning is in the print. This view is also referred to as the bottom-up model. Most teachers believe that skills should be taught (see Gunderson, 1991). Indeed, most ESL teachers appear to believe students should be taught skills such as phonics and letter–sound relationships.

The top-down theorists believe that meaning resides in the heads of readers, not in print. They believe students should be asked to read meaningful material. Through the act of reading they acquire such basic skills as phonics. These theorists have not actually produced top-down reading programs. Meaningful reading material may be good books or students' own dictated LEA stories. Teachers would never directly teach the "ch" spelling correspondence, for example, as they do in the skills-based program.

A third view of reading is that it is "interactive." This model suggests that readers use both bottom-up and top-down information as they read. No one has suggested what an interactive reading program would be. Finally, the "holistic" school of thought has proponents who believe students should write and read as soon as they enter school. Most of these teachers are offended by the idea that students should be directly taught a skill. They are convinced, rather, that students will come to learn such skills through meaningful manipulation of language. Some subtle differences in teaching approaches exist between whole-language teachers who believe in the completely independent model and those who believe in implicit modeling (see Chapter 4).

A teacher's model has definite effects on what that teacher does in the classroom. It is vital for all teachers, and indeed for all potential teachers, to determine what their view of reading is. This is best done in a small group or individually and includes brainstorming answers to the following: "How should students be taught to read?" or "To learn to read, students must ————." An item analysis of brainstormed ideas reveals an individual's viewpoint. If, on the one hand, the list is overwhelmingly made up of items such as "Students must learn phonics, word recognition, names of the letters of the alphabet, prefixes, affixes, punctuation, spelling, and antonyms," then that individual has a skills-based viewpoint and, most likely, believes students should be directly taught skills. If the list contains such items as "meaningful reading, student-created reading material, word recognition in context, active prediction during reading," then the individual has a top-down notion of reading and will involve students in activities that are meaningful. If, on the other hand, the list contains a mixture of the two, then the individual may have an interactive viewpoint. Further, those who believe that all language activities should be taught together, and that students will learn to read by writing, are members of the holistic school of thought about language learning. A teacher's model determines the kinds of activities that teacher designs for his or her students. Indeed, the reader of this text will select those activities that fall within the parameters of a particular model. On the other hand, it is also true that teachers sometimes abandon their own instructional models as a result of strong pressure from other teachers, administrators, and/or politicians. It is this author's experience, however, that such programs are seldom successful.

As was noted in the previous chapter, teaching students to read in their mother tongue may be preferable to teaching them in English; few mainstream teachers are prepared to teach them these skills, especially in classrooms where four or more first languages (L1s) are represented. The prevailing methodology appears to include them in reading instruction in elementary school and to let them "sink or swim" in secondary school. Teaching approach is also affected by the overall percentage of ESL students in a class (Gunderson, Eddy, & Carrigan, submitted for publication b). Indeed, upwards of 60 percent of classrooms were more like EFL than ESL classrooms. In essence, these researchers found that there can, in fact, be too many ESL (ELL) students in a class to continue standard ESL instructional practices. Teachers in these high ESL classrooms must change their instruction to account for the lack of English models available to their students. Adults, on the other hand, appear to be taught English using teacher-developed programs. A number are also involved in online, cyberspace-based programs.

ESL reading instruction is, in many respects, a more complicated concern than reading instruction for native English speakers. Generally, teachers of native English speakers can assess students' reading abilities and assign them to an appropriate program—one that is either skills based, whole language, LEA, or some other integrated reading/language arts program, depending on the teachers' beliefs and the school system they are in. The ESL teacher's task, however, is not so simple. There are several factors to consider: 1) the students' first language (L1) literacy background, 2) their second language (L2) proficiency, 3) their L2 reading ability, 4) the cultural and age appropriateness of the L2 materials, 5) students' reasons for learning to read English relative to their age, 6) their purposes for reading, 7) the difficulty level of the material to be read, and 8) the overall percentage of ESL students in the class. A 55-year-old illiterate Burmese student needing to learn enough survival reading skills to get a job has different needs and purposes than 12-year-old Burmese students who have had six or seven years of schooling in reading their own language and who are enrolled in an elementary school where they need to be able to read and comprehend English-language textbooks.

The difficulty is to establish a systematic, research-based approach to designing appropriate literacy programs for a wide variety of human beings who differ dramatically in age, intellectual development, motivation, literacy background, experience, and language aptitude. This is no easy task. The purpose of the following discussion is to map out just such an approach. First, it is necessary to talk about the acquisition of English.

Language Acquisition

First-Language Acquisition—English

Human beings are not born with a language. However, it is well established that they are normally born with the ability to learn a language. Indeed, babies are born ready to learn any language. Chomsky (1975) referred to what he calls the Language Acquisition Device (LAD) to explain how human beings are equipped to learn language. The language they learn is usually the one spoken by their parents. There also appear to be developmental differences that are roughly related to age. Children do not learn, for instance, to use past-tense verbs accurately before they learn to use present-tense verbs in English (Clark & Clark, 1977). A number of researchers have investigated the acquisition of English in very young children. The one truly interesting finding related to the purpose of this book is that parents turn out to be outstandingly good language teachers.

North American children begin to produce their first words in English somewhere between 12 and 20 months on average (Bates *et al.*, 1977; Clark & Clark, 1977). The present progressive "ing" form is the first lexical form that native English speakers seem to develop (Brown, 1973). By the time they are about 6 or 7 years old they are fairly competent in understanding and producing complex sentences and are able to communicate well with their peers and the important adults in their worlds. By the time they are about 6 years old, most English-speaking children have well-established and fairly extensive vocabularies. That these young human beings have acquired their language abilities is due, to a large extent, to their parents' outstanding teaching approaches.

Brown (1973) carefully observed early mother–child communicative interactions and found a number of interesting features. Children began producing one-word utterances at about 18 months. These early one-word utterances were observed to be holophrastic in that they meant more than was evident from their surface structures. The child who said "more" actually meant something like "I want some more milk." Mothers did not simply repeat what the child said, but responded with something like "Does baby want more milk?" The relationships between mothers and children were supportive. The child produced an utterance and the mother responded with an expansion that provided the correct models without overt and critical correction. Magnificent teaching interactions continue as the child begins to produce simple sentences and different grammatical forms. So, for instance, if the child says, "I goed to the park yesterday," mothers usually respond by saying something like "Yes, you went to the park yesterday." The mothers' expanded and elaborated forms provide examples of the "correct" sentences (Bates, 1976; Bates et al., 1977; Brown, 1973; Clark & Clark, 1977). The product of this masterful parent–child synergy is a child who can understand and produce fairly complex language, including relatively appropriate vocabulary, syntax, and pragmatics, by about age 6 to 7. It is often at about 6 or 7 years of age that children begin to go to school, where they encounter the task of learning to read and write, and teachers who are nowhere near as good at teaching language as their parents. Gunderson (2007) found that immigrant students from very different first languages and first cultures were reported to have begun to say single words and simple sentences in their first languages at about the same ages as native English speakers. This finding in itself is quite extraordinary. However, they had begun to read at significantly different ages that related to when they actually began school. He concluded that reading instruction begins at a culturally relative age and that parents appear to largely get out of the language teaching business, which, he concludes, is an unfortunate state of affairs since they are such good language teachers.

As was noted in the previous chapter, vocabulary control is important for authors designing reading instructional texts because they assume that the words they should introduce are already known to native English speakers. The same cannot be said of second language learners. Indeed, the student who is learning English may differ from her English-speaking classmates in her knowledge of vocabulary, syntax (grammar), semantics (word meaning), pragmatics, literacy and cultural background knowledge, and sociolinguistic or socially embedded meaning making. A second language learner may not comprehend connected discourse because she does not have the experiential background knowledge to allow her to do so.

Learning or Acquiring English as a Second or Additional Language

It has been argued that there is a difference between acquiring and learning a language. This view is referred to as the "acquisition/learning hypothesis" (Krashen & Terrell, 1983). Language acquisition occurs naturally, usually at home within the context of a family. Learning language often is more formal and usually occurs in school. Reading instruction is a difficult undertaking because learners vary in so many ways from the native English speaker. However, there is evidence that second-language learners learn English in much the same way as native speakers. For instance, present-tense verbs are learned before past-tense verbs. This has been referred to as the "natural order hypothesis" (Krashen, 1982). Gunderson (2007) found solid evidence supporting this view. Krashen also developed the notion of comprehensible input.

The notion of comprehensible input is that learners must be able to understand information before they can learn. Piaget (1973) referred to the notion of moderate novelty, which is essentially the same idea. Krashen (1982) argues that the success of a language program depends on the provision of comprehensible input. Comprehensible input is a relative term, however. It varies among different human beings depending upon their background. The difficulty with packaged instructional programs is that they are designed to match the needs of human beings who do not always exist: "average" learners. And additionally, language learning is more complex for the second-language learner because in addition to sequence, there appear to be two basic kinds of language.

Cummins (1981) proposed that there were two kinds of language proficiencies to be learned: "basic interpersonal communicative skill" (BICS), the language of ordinary conversation or "the manifestation of language proficiency in everyday communicative contexts" (Cummins, 1984, p. 137); and "cognitive academic language proficiency" (CALP), the language of instruction and academic texts. It has been suggested these labels might lead to a misinterpretation of the complexities they seek to describe (Edelsky et al., 1983; Rivera, 1984) and imply a deficit model of language. Edelsky (1990) likens CALP to "test-wiseness" and developed an additional acronym, SIN, "skill in instructional nonsense" (p. 65). Cummins (2000) provides strong support for continued use of the terms and concepts, and the two labels have generally come to represent two categories of proficiency: that associated with face-to-face conversation (BICS) and that associated with learning in the context-reduced cognitively demanding oral and written environment of the classroom (CALP) (Cummins, 1981; Swain, 1981; Cummins and Swain, 1983). Older students use knowledge of academic material and concepts gained studying L1 to help them in L2 and the acquisition of L2 occurs faster. So, the child who has learned to read in a first language has skills that can be transferred to the task of learning to read English. Aukerman (2007) argues, on the basis of the results of her study of one primary-level child, that CALP is not really context-free in primary classrooms. The difficulty, however, is that primary-level curricula are extremely contextual in that teachers normally try to provide as much scaffolding as possible. This author has also argued that the Cummins model is static and that the underlying relationships are really relative to individual students' backgrounds, motivations, skills, and interests. This will be explained in some detail in what follows.

Second-Language Literacy: Some Principles

The potential number of variables a teacher should or could consider in planning an instructional program for a single human being is immense. Planning gets more complex when those human beings come to a classroom speaking a language other than the language of instruction. Indeed, students who speak a first language that is different from the language of instruction who have learned to read their L1s are different from those who have not learned to read L1. Young L1 non-readers are different from older non-readers for various important reasons. Immigrant ESL students are different in many important ways from native-born ESL students. Gunderson (2007) found that some immigrant students do enter their new countries with some English literacy skills. However, those who arrive with some English skills are significantly behind their grade levels in English reading ability. Indeed, the older immigrants who had some English skills were as much as seven or eight years behind their grade levels in reading comprehension. The National Reading Panel also reported that comprehension was usually significantly lower in ESL students than in native English speakers. The purpose here is to reduce the number of issues a teacher must consider to be able to design appropriate reading instructional programs to match the needs and abilities of human beings who differ so greatly in so many ways.

BICS, CALP, COMPREHENSIBLE INPUT, AND INSTRUCTIONAL HEURISTICS

Cummins (various dates) argued that language learning occurs in different contexts. Some contexts provide substantial cues to the learner. Usually these contexts are informal and involve face-to-face interactions. Learners are able to comprehend in context-embedded situations because the input is more comprehensible. The context is filled with multiple cues that help the learner. Body language, intonation, and simple direct communications contribute to a learner's understanding. Figure 2.1 shows these relationships. In it the context axis varies from embedded to reduced (disembedded). The second axis represents cognitive demand, sometimes referred to as difficulty. The informational material in a lecture or a chapter on phenomenological epistemologies is usually cognitively more demanding than a narrative of a trip to the zoo. Cummins hypothesized that BICS occurred in context-embedded, cognitively undemanding situations (quadrant A), while CALP occurred in context-reduced cognitively demanding situations (quadrant D). The difficulty with this model is that it is static. The informativeness of context and cognitive demand vary from individual to individual and also within an individual depending upon a particular task and a whole lot of other individual variables. Aukerman (2007) suggested that CALP was more embedded in context than Cummins proposed. The difficulty with this view, however, is that primary-level classes are highly social environments in which teachers provide scaffolding in significant ways. Instruction is a significant variable that affects CALP in direct ways.

Comprehensible input is also a relative term. There are many different variables that affect the degree to which a particular task is cognitively demanding or comprehensible for some individuals and not for others. Teenage learners who want

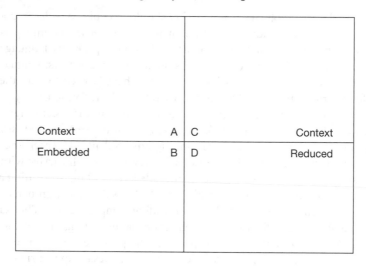

Figure 2.1 Context and Cognitive Demand

to get a driver's license are highly motivated to read the driver's license guide and will often be more successful reading it than they will be at trying to read social studies material at a comparable reading level. Learners interested in particular subjects such as dinosaurs or jet planes will find such material less cognitively demanding than comparable reading material on community resources. Comprehensibility and cognitive demand are relative, not static. The difficulty is to make relative judgments about individual learners—an especially difficult task for teachers with 30 or 40 students in their classrooms at one time.

Instructional Matrices

This author has worked with second-language learners since the 1960s and has developed the following Two-Factor ELL Instructional Matrices based on theory and research to help guide the design and implementation of literacy programs. The instructional heuristics presented in the following pages are based on extensive teaching practice and work with teachers. The number of potential background variables is huge. The instructional matrices represent a systematic reduction of variables into two that are very powerful. They also have support from the research of the National Literacy Panel (August & Shanahan, 2006; Gunderson, 2007).

Literacy Background and English Level

The following matrices were developed in 1989 on the basis of intuition and experience in classrooms in Chinese-majority schools, as a Title I reading teacher in a Spanish–English bilingual school in California, and as a teacher-educator working with teachers in schools with many ESL students. Over the years they have served teachers well as instructional guides. However, originally they were not, strictly speaking, supported by research. Since 1991, however, this author has conducted long-term research involving thousands of immigrant students (see Gunderson, 2000a, 2004, 2007). This research explored the relationships existing among about 150 variables, including developmental, language, family, and literacy variables. There is research to support the foundations of the heuristics.

The research involved approximately 25,000 immigrant students whose families were interviewed following a protocol that included items concerning such issues as individual development, literacy learning background, first and second language interactions, school history, English study, and health history. Both children and parents were encouraged to respond, and interviews were conducted in English when possible. However, for families unable to be interviewed in English, interpreters were hired who were native speakers of the family's first language and generally knew the customs and cultural background of the families. Following the interviews, students' English skills were assessed using various standardized and holistic instruments, beginning with an individual oral language assessment.

The oral assessment begins with the assessor asking simple questions in an effort to begin to understand the student's English ability. Items include:

1. What's your name?
2. How old are you?
3. Where are you from?
4. What did your mother do in ———?
5. What did your father do in ———?
6. Do you have any brothers or sisters? Tell me about them.
7. What is your favorite food?

Students' responses begin to inform the assessor about the students' English ability. The following items were designed to discover specific information about different kinds of English knowledge.

1. Tell me the days of the week.
2. What day was yesterday?
3. What day will tomorrow be?

The student is asked to count from one to as high as possible, and then to name numbers shown in random order. Eleven basic colors are shown and students are asked to name them. Reciting the alphabet is followed by the recognition and naming of letters at random. Nineteen different body parts are shown in pictures, and students are asked to name them, followed by the naming of six different school items such as a pencil and crayons. These items generally require students to have a basic English vocabulary. The second portion of the oral assessment focused on English structure.

The student was asked:

1. "Tell me two things you did yesterday."
2. "Tell me two things you are going to do tomorrow."
3. "Tell me one thing you would like to do when you grow up."

The student was shown a series of pictures containing objects that are in different positions relative to each other. The teacher demonstrates the process by showing a picture and saying, "The ball is on the table." The subsequent pictures are each prompted by the assessor saying, "The ball is ———. The student is asked to fill in the correct preposition.

The student's ability to formulate questions is assessed by the teacher saying, "Now it's your turn to ask me some questions:

1. Ask me my name.
2. Ask me where I live.
3. Ask me what I did yesterday.
4. Ask me what I am going to do tomorrow."

Performance on these items is informative and helped to guide the assessors in selecting further appropriate reading assessment instruments. Elementary students who have some English ability were administered the word recognition and comprehension sections of the Woodcock Reading Mastery test. Older students were administered the "NewGap" test (McLeod & McLeod, Novato, CA: Academic Therapy Publications, 1990), the "GAP" (McLeod & McLeod, Sydney: Heinemann, 1977), or the Comprehensive English Language Test (Harris & Palmer, New York: McGraw-Hill, 1986). All students were administered a math skills test developed by local curriculum consultants.

There were a number of interesting findings. The longitudinal portion of the study observed which of the variables mentioned earlier predicted students' achievement in secondary schools. A number of findings supported the matrices. There were strong relationships between the number of years students had studied in their home countries and the various oral and literacy measures in English, even for students who were reported not to have studied English formally. There were very strong relationships existing among the oral and literacy measures for students who had studied English in their home countries. However, there was an interesting plateau effect for students who had studied English. After five years of reported study, students' literacy scores did not increase. On the basis of mean scores, students on average did not acquire CALP in five to seven years of English study in their home countries. The strong relationships between the oral measures and reading provide support for the use of oral English as one of the axes in the heuristic. Likewise, the relationship between length of literacy study in home country and the English measures provides strong support for the use of this as a variable. There is support in both the NRP and NLP for the use of these two variables.

Two-Factor Instructional Matrices

The purpose of the matrices is to provide comprehensible input for learners who vary in many different ways. A general outline is shown in Figure 2.2.

First-language educational history is divided into none (zero level), one to two years, and three or more years. These are rough or fuzzy indicators, but experience has shown they are broadly predictive of a student's literacy background. One to two years of schooling is usually associated with knowledge of literacy behaviors and processes. These students understand that print represents language, that scanning of text, regardless of the orthography, is basic to reading, and that reading involves a relationship between them and the text. Relationships vary from the basic decoding and oral reproduction of the language of the text to understanding, interpreting, and making inference about the text. These one- to two-year students have been introduced to the act of reading in ways related to their cultural backgrounds. Those who have no schooling most often lack this knowledge. Students with three and more years of school have deeper knowledge of reading that they can apply to the task of learning to read English. In many cases they have been involved in reading to learn content of some kind; they have begun to learn CALP in their first languages. In essence, the heuristic predicts broadly the potential for the transfer of underlying proficiencies. As was noted earlier, there is good research evidence that the number of years of schooling in home countries is a predictor of English achievement, even for students who have not specifically studied English. The findings of the National Literacy Panel were that those who are literate in their first languages are likely to be advantaged when faced with the task of learning to read English. The heuristic uses a measure of L1 literacy background to determine what learning tasks will be comprehensible.

The other broad predictor of comprehensible input is English oral language skills. The Literacy Panel also found strong evidence to suggest that English proficiency is related to English reading achievement for minority-language learners. Four broad categories are used here: zero-level; very limited; limited; and limited fluency. In essence, there are three English proficiency levels. Note that English, like other languages, does not actually have levels. Speaking about levels is a way

	Non-English	Very limited	Limited	Limited fluency
L1 literacy				
None				
1–2 years				
3+ years				

Figure 2.2 Two-Factor Elementary Instructional Matrix

educators—and sometimes linguists—categorize learners so they can group them for instruction, or for study in the case of linguists. There are a number of different schemes involving five, seven, or sometimes nine levels. The basic difficulty is that the more levels one creates, the more difficult it becomes for different human beings to agree on them. So, the scheme in this book is to limit them to three. The assessing of oral English into these categories will be described later in this chapter.

Students who have never been to school and have zero-level English skills will most often find the task of learning to read English difficult, usually impossible at first. These students will find little comprehensible input in the English-medium classroom. They should not be involved in English reading instruction because the task will have no comprehensible input and generally these students will have no underlying literacy proficiencies that they can transfer to the task of learning English literacy skills. The student who arrives with zero-level English but has gone to school for one to two years does have some L1 knowledge that can be transferred to English. The student who arrives with no literacy background but has limited fluency skills can be introduced to some limited English literacy activities. Planned literacy activities vary for each of the squares noted above. They also vary somewhat relative to the age of the student.

The Primary-Level Student

The primary-level student is most often not included in literacy instruction because she has neither a L1 literacy background nor any English ability. However, there are some who do have some English skills. These students will be discussed later in this chapter in the section titled "English Assessment for Very Young Learners" (p. 56).

The Elementary Student

The matrix shown as Figure 2.2 is fairly straightforward. First, L1 literacy history reveals whether students are likely to understand that print represents language— one of the first, and often most difficult, skills to acquire. Second, it roughly matches students' language patterns with the material they are to read. Discovering the L1 literacy history is usually quite easy. One simply asks a parent, an aunt or an uncle, an older sibling, or the student him- or herself—through an interpreter, if necessary. In those cases in which no L1 literacy history can be discovered, zero-level is assumed. One to two years of L1 literacy instruction is associated with the basic understanding that print and language are related. Teachers who have used this heuristic have not found any differences between students of languages written in the Roman alphabet and students who had learned some literacy skills in non-Roman writing. That is, students who were Spanish or Portuguese did not differ from those who were Arabic or Chinese in the Gunderson (2007) study. Indeed, first-language instructional practices seemed to be the most powerful variable. That is, the way a child was taught to read in their first language established a strong cultural expectation concerning the way they thought they should learn to read English.

The next consideration involves assessing English oral-language proficiency. The following is a "shotgun" approach. To obtain a more accurate picture of an ESL student's English ability, one can contact a school or school district ESL consultant or teacher for more detailed and extensive testing. In addition, an assessment of beginning language skills for very young students will be described in some detail later in this chapter.

Oral Language Assessment

Oral English ability is divided into three general proficiency categories; the fourth is actually no English at all: 1) 0-Level (or non-English); 2) very limited; 3) limited; and 4) limited fluency. The first level is usually the easiest to identify. In a typical multi-L1 school, new students are continually enrolled during the school year. 0-Level speakers are immediately apparent. They usually seem dazed, afraid, and anxious. One can locate these students readily on the playground; they are the ones literally on the periphery, usually standing next to a fence surveying the activities before them (see, for instance, Gunderson, 1983a). This author's more recent observations confirm these observations, particularly in schools where there are a significant number of different L1s present.

0-LEVEL STUDENTS

0-level students cannot answer questions in English or identify objects. It is vital for them to be placed in an appropriate program of language learning. All too often they are simply placed in the lowest reading group, where they regularly hear the worst oral reading models possible (Gunderson, 1983a, 1985; Bartoli, 1995). For example, Fitzgerald (1995) concluded that English language learners tended to receive instruction heavily oriented toward lower-level skills, such as phonics and pronunciation. Instruction in these situations focuses on lower-level skills of decoding with little attention to the comprehension and higher-level thinking observed in reading instruction for other students. The 0-level students with limited or no L1 literacy instruction must *not* be placed in a reading program, because it will only confuse them. These students must be placed in an oral language program. They should be placed in a reading program, either formal or informal, only after their language ability has progressed to the "limited" level or higher, depending on their L1 history.

Zero-level students can be introduced to some reading activities that actually help oral language development if they have had three or more years of L1 literacy instruction. Immersing those who have not been in a reading program is a disservice. If one is uncertain about what an oral language development program should be, a local ESL consultant or teacher should be able to help in designing a program. The most difficult task is to avoid feeling compelled to place 0-level ESL students in a formal reading program. Often teachers are convinced they must include everyone.

VERY-LIMITED-ENGLISH STUDENTS

Very limited students can speak some words, usually responses to simple questions. Their utterances are short, most often two or three words. These students seldom initiate conversations. They respond best in yes/no situations and produce such utterances as "no go," "no have," and "run now." If one observes their verbal behavior in both formal (during lessons) and informal (on the playground) situations, it is extremely easy to recognize them. It is often possible to identify students from these first two levels by simply observing their behavior on the playground (see Gunderson, 1983a). Indeed, very limited students are confused by reading activities *unless* they have a minimum of one to two years of L1 literacy instruction.

LIMITED-ENGLISH STUDENTS

Limited-English students are able to produce a fair quantity of English, often initiate conversations, and are able to answer most questions. Their language is often filled with overgeneralized grammatical forms such as "we goed." Most often their speech lacks proper pronoun references, especially he/she and article use. Most of their utterances are simple, declarative sentences. Limited-English speakers are ready for some reading instruction, regardless of their L1 literacy background.

LIMITED-FLUENCY STUDENTS

Limited-fluency speakers are quite adept at English. They are able to produce fairly substantial sentences without overgeneralized forms. They understand and use the language well. They usually speak with an accent, but can actively question and respond in many different settings. These students often organize games in multi-lingual school settings (see Gunderson, 1983a). One fascinating feature of limited-fluency students is that they can switch codes very well. That is, they learn very quickly that there is an approved classroom language and one that is more appropriate for the schoolyard. Limited-fluency students sound like speakers of the dominant English group. Indeed, in the Gunderson (1983a) study, ESL students produced "black" speech while in the schoolyard, because it was the dominant English dialect. These students are ready for reading instruction regardless of their L1 literacy history. The following is a list of features to be used to identify students' L2 (second-language) proficiency.

At this point the teacher's task is to place a student in a program that matches both the student's background and the teacher's theoretical notions of language learning. The particular program selected must take into account both the cultural setting of the material in the program and the teacher's theoretical bias. Both of these concerns will be discussed in later chapters that specify programs and materials for each of the 12 potential reading groups identified in the decision heuristic above.

TABLE 2.1 English Oral Language Proficiency Features

L2 Oral Proficiency

0-Level English
    a. Cannot answer even yes/no questions
    b. Is unable to identify and name any objects
    c. Understands no English
    d. Often appears withdrawn and afraid

Very Limited English
    a. Responds to simple questions with mostly yes/no or one-word responses
    b. Speaks in one- to two-word phrases
    c. Attempts no extended conversations
    d. Seldom, if ever, initiates conversations

Limited English
    a. Responds easily to simple questions
    b. Produces simple sentences
    c. Has difficulty elaborating when asked
    d. Uses syntax/vocabulary adequate for personal, simple situations
    e. Occasionally initiates conversations

Limited Fluency
    a. Speaks with ease
    b. Initiates conversations
    c. May make phonological or grammatical errors, which can then become fossilized
    d. Makes errors in more syntactically complex utterances
    e. Freely and easily switches codes

The Secondary ESL Student

Secondary ESL students can be classified into two groups: 1) those who need to learn to read, and 2) those who need to learn how to learn from reading. Secondary teachers must also find out about students' L1 background and English ability. Generally, secondary ESL students do not benefit from academic instruction unless they can manage to read and understand their textbooks. Generally, secondary students with a good literacy background (i.e., a minimum of six years of L1 or L2 training) who are limited or limited-fluency students are able, with assistance from a teacher, to read and comprehend from text, *if the level of the text is not more than two years higher than their ability*. Students of lower English ability and with less L1 background *are not ready to learn from text*. No amount of help from the teacher will make these students successful content comprehenders. They must be immersed in a reading program. They must be brought to a level of English proficiency that is limited or limited-fluency before they can begin to face the challenges of content reading. A decision heuristic for the secondary student is shown in Figure 2.3 and will be discussed in detail in Chapter 5.

	0-level very limited	Limited	Limited fluency
L1 literacy			
None			
2–6 years			
6+ years			

Figure 2.3 Two-Factor Secondary Instructional Matrix

Learning to Learn from Text

Beginning at about the fourth grade, students regularly begin to read to learn new material. The material they read varies from social studies to science. In each case the textbook authors have identified material that they consider it important for the students to learn. They present the material in different formats, such as illustrations, maps, graphs, charts, number lines, and diagrams. Indeed, the material is written in different styles: exposition, description, argumentation, narration. Content material differs from basal material in significant ways. In many cases, vocabulary items have meanings that depend upon the subject—for example, a *product* in math is different from a *product* in economics. In addition, students need to identify their purpose for reading in order to select the correct reading style. Since 1991, use of Internet-based activities has increased significantly. Such use will be addressed in the following chapters, as will content programs.

The University Academic ESL Student

Two different categories of ESL students are enrolled in most English universities. First are those who want to increase their general abilities in English and who are anxious to learn to read and understand material such as books, newspapers, magazines, and novels. Their interests are general. Many of these general interest students are attempting to increase their English ability in order to pass a test to be admitted to a university. Second, however, are the academic majors, wanting to increase their ability to read and comprehend in a particular area, students who are interested in learning how to read newspapers and other general interest periodicals but who also want to learn to read and comprehend material in a particular academic area, such as economics. Often they are very frustrated. General courses in reading instruction do not provide them with the skills they need to read their special texts or, for that matter, the complex material they encounter on the Internet. In addition, many university-level adult students want to learn from "technical" texts in subjects such as electronics, medicine, and logic. Technical reading is difficult to teach because the material is often difficult for the reading teacher to comprehend. In Chapter 6, programs to teach content and technical reading to these students will be described and discussed.

Both categories of students have long histories of L1 instruction. Often they have had a minimum of four years of ESL or EFL instruction, including English reading instruction. The teacher's first task is to discover their L2 reading ability and to discover whether their current reading material matches their ability level. The gravest error that universities make is to assume that a certain TOEFL (Test of English as a Foreign Language) score, say 550, is equated with the ability to comprehend text in a particular academic area, even though the TOEFL is used by almost all English-speaking college and university faculties to judge students' preparation for studies. This is a deadly assumption since many very talented L2 speakers are not equipped to deal with typical academic texts, because they have not been taught the skills necessary to comprehend them. There is a more recently developed online version of TOEFL. It is not yet clear whether it predicts success at university better than the older version. The difficulty at this point is that is costs U.S.$140.00 to take and this price may be prohibitive for potential students in many countries. Special programs to teach these students will be discussed in Chapter 6.

The Adult ESL Student

Adults have many reasons for studying English. Often the instruction is part of a governmental program. Or students may want to improve their English skills in order to advance at work or to get a job. This author once met a 65-year-old Chinese-speaking student in a San Francisco night school who wanted to read well enough to help her 6-year-old granddaughter with her first-grade studies. She was interested in learning to read basal readers and children's stories. Lao farmers recently enrolled in an English program in an inner-city school in California, for instance, could not have known what they were doing there, since they had never learned to read or write their own language. They had no idea what the vocabulary exercises they were given were about.

Teachers of adults must discover students' L1 literacy history, their English proficiency, and, most important, their reasons for wanting to learn to read. Often there are very pragmatic reasons for adults to learn to read. A student who wants to be able to pass a driver's license test will not want to be taught to read using narrative material. English proficiency can be measured holistically, as noted above. In the best of all worlds, it would be preferable to design a program that accounted for students' oral proficiency and L1 literacy background. However, the reality of the situation is that this is seldom possible or desirable. Figure 2.4 represents a decision heuristic for adult ESL students.

Reading Approaches for the Adult ESL Student

SURVIVAL READING

The world is filled with print essential to survival—for example, words such as *STOP, DANGER, MEN,* and *WOMEN*. These are the first words students need to

	0-level very limited	Limited	Limited fluency
L1 literacy			
None			
2–6 years			
7+ years			

Figure 2.4 Two-Factor Adult Instructional Matrix

recognize. Others may be just as important to particular students. Teachers can develop their own lists of survival words, depending on a knowledge of their students. Yet there is another class of survival words: the words that represent the English core vocabulary, which are important because they form the bulk of the vocabulary used in speech and writing. As was mentioned before, Dolch was interested in this core vocabulary. He identified 220 essential sight words. Unfortunately, they are the most difficult words to teach to ESL students. Survival reading programs will be described in Chapter 5.

SPECIAL READING PROGRAMS

Adult students have difficulty with general reading programs—those designed to increase their overall reading abilities—because the material is usually unrelated to their needs, interests, and backgrounds. Special reading programs teach students reading skills in a restricted interest area, one related to their needs and backgrounds. Special reading programs are normally teacher designed. However, there are a few published programs. Special reading programs are more successful with adults because they are more motivated to learn than are younger students.

GENERAL READING PROGRAMS

There are general reading programs designed for adults that contain narrative material, comprehension and vocabulary exercises, and skills-development activities. One must be cautious about using general programs because the material they contain is often unrelated to the needs and interests of adults. The teacher must adapt the material. More about this later.

CONTENT READING PROGRAMS

Academic courses require students to read and comprehend text, text that is often difficult even for native English speakers. Content reading instruction helps students to learn to read and learn from academic texts.

TECHNICAL READING

Many students wish to retrain or to learn postgraduate university material. A graduate student in chemistry comes to a reading class not to learn general reading skills, but to learn how to comprehend material in incredibly complex and difficult texts. Some students wish to become recertified as doctors or lawyers. In these cases, they must read and learn from texts written in English. Technical reading programs are often called English for Special (or Specific) Purposes programs. Technical reading is differentiated from content reading, even though they are very similar, because technical reading is more difficult for both the reading teacher and the ESL student.

L1 literacy background is important. It seems, however, that the judgment to be made with adults is broader: no literacy background, elementary literacy background, and extensive university-level literacy background. The number of years in L1 literacy training is divided into three broad categories. L1 university graduates are often highly motivated to learn to read English. Indeed, they may have studied some English. There are three distinct levels of L1 background: 1) students with no L1 literacy training, who may not know that print represents languages; 2) students who are literate in L1 and do understand that print represents languages; and 3) those who have had a great deal of education and are usually highly motivated to learn, the "highly literate."

Categories of Adult Learners

0-LEVEL AND VERY LIMITED ENGLISH

These two categories can be combined when dealing with adults. Consider the individual with no L1 literacy training. After their English proficiency has been determined, a literacy program can be designed. There is little time to waste. Pragmatically, the student must begin immediately to learn survival reading skills. Chapter 4 contains the extraordinary comment that vocabulary should be taught in isolation to these students! But more about that later. The 0-level or very limited student must be taught initial survival reading skills right away. Those with no L1 backgrounds often become frozen at the survival level even with instruction.

LIMITED ENGLISH

Designing a reading program for a limited-English student is considerably easier than designing one for the less proficient student. The feature distinguishing the L1 illiterate from the L1 literate is the speed with which they learn initial English reading skills. The L1 literate students, especially the university-trained students, learn more quickly and remember better than the L1 illiterates. All must learn survival reading skills. The L1 literate students can begin a specific reading program designed with their needs in mind almost immediately.

Limited-fluency students are ready to begin learning to read. If they have no L1 history, it is best to teach survival skills first. Limited-fluency students usually learn quickly, especially if the program is a specific one designed to meet their needs. They are the best equipped of the adult students to cope with and master general reading programs, especially if they are university trained. These students' oral language development is aided by a reading program.

Reading Assessment and Readability

There are two final concerns to consider for all ESL/EFL students: 1) assessing L2 reading ability; and 2) assessing the difficulty level (including background content) or readability of L2 materials, in order to match students with materials.

Assessing L2 reading ability is not quite as simple as it seems. As a "reading specialist" in an elementary school with a large number of ESL students, Gunderson (1984a) noted that nearly all of the ESL students were enrolled in mainstream classrooms where they were required to take mandated group achievement tests— that is, the Comprehensive Test of Basic Skills (CTBS). Teachers were amazed at how well the ESL students performed, often posing the question, "How can Juan score at the 25th percentile when he can't read anything?" They were convinced that, for some unknown reason, the group test overestimated the reading ability of students. A study was designed to ascertain whether there was any validity in the suspicion that the group test overestimated ESL students' reading ability.

The reading achievement scores of students in four large urban elementary schools in a large California school district were analyzed. Their overall ESL population was approximately 54 percent. School records were consulted and a list of 457 students who had taken the CTBS in the fall of the school year was compiled. The CTBS is a group-administered instrument containing subtests ranging from vocabulary to computation. The CTBS uses a multiple-choice approach to assess vocabulary and comprehension. Total reading is measured by a composite score of vocabulary and comprehension, with comprehension given more weight. The test for vocabulary is fairly standard. Words are presented in context, as a phrase or sentence, and students circle the choice of four words that is most similar. Comprehension is tested by presenting a series of paragraphs followed by multiple-choice questions.

A random sample of 160 subjects was selected (51 grade 3, 54 grade 4, and 55 grade 5). Fifty-eight percent of the sample were ESL students (51 Spanish, 21 Tagalog, 3 Punjabi, 3 Vietnamese, 2 Cambodian, 2 Cantonese, 2 Samoan, 1 Fijian, 1 Hindi, 1 Ilocano). Surprisingly, the mean CTBS scores were as follows: vocabulary 39.50 L1, 38.70 L2; comprehension 39.40 L1, 39.71 L2; and total reading 38.80 L1 and 38.70 L2. When scores were broken down by number of years in English classrooms, the reasons for the finding of no differences became apparent. Students who had been in an English-speaking classroom for less than three years were significantly lower than native English speakers in reading ability; whereas those who had been in English classrooms for more than three years scored significantly higher than the L1 students. The L2s were good students from families that were interested in schools and learning (Gunderson, 1984a). There were no significant differences in the reading scores of L1 and L2 students. The native English-speaking students, on the mean, did not appear to read better than the ESL students!

Thirty grade 5 subjects were randomly selected for further study (9 Spanish, 6 Tagalog, 15 native English) and were individually tested using a standard individual reading assessment—the Woodcock Reading Mastery Test (WRMT), which has five subtests: letter knowledge, word recognition, word attack, word comprehension, passage comprehension, and total reading (a composite score). Mean WRMT scores were as follows: L1 letter recognition 45.70, word recognition 40.90, word attack 32.50, word comprehension 35.90, passage comprehension 34.20, and total reading 35.70; L2 35.50, 4.60, 17.00, 1.70, 3.70, and 3.20. The native English students' CTBS scores were not significantly different from their WRMT scores; however, the L2 scores were all significantly different. The group L2 scores were all significantly higher than the scores from the individually administered test. Either the CTBS overestimated L2 reading ability or the WRMT underestimated it. Two expert reading teachers assessed students' abilities using their own tried and trusted methods. Both stated that they had judged levels by listening to students' oral reading and asking four or five comprehension questions per passage. They had used reading texts at different levels as their assessment materials. Their estimations were lower than CTBS scores and higher than WRMT scores.

It would seem that L2 scores vary considerably according to the instrument used to measure reading ability. This is as true in the new millennium as it was in the 1980s and 1990s. This is a major problem for teachers wanting to correctly place L2 students in reading programs. The following procedures have been recommended by ESL experts. They are usually rather time-consuming to construct and/ or administer. The final procedures are designed to measure students' content/text reading needs and abilities.

Assessing L2 Reading Ability

In the first half of the twentieth century, many psychologists, teachers, and reading researchers maintained that an individual student had to be "ready" before reading instruction could be successful. The terms "readiness" and "readiness skills" were developed and teachers in kindergarten classrooms became dedicated to teaching the required skills so that their students would be able to begin to learn to read in first grade. The notion of readiness is based on the thesis that there is something called mental age. Morphett and Washburne (1931) conducted a study that, they argued, showed that a mental age of 6.5 was a prerequisite for beginning reading. It was thought that children before this age were not ready to begin to learn to read, regardless of the instruction they received. Publishers developed readiness tests and readiness activities. However, it has been shown that many human beings can learn to read when they are very young. Many children in Hong Kong, for instance, first begin to learn to read when they are 3 years old, well before they reach the mental age of 6.5 (Gunderson, 2007). The concept has generally received a great deal of criticism. However, the notion of readiness still has a great deal of influence in the primary grades (kindergarten to grade 3). There are a number of background skills that typical young students appear to have related to reading in English. For new students who are at the elementary level who appear to have zero-level or very limited English skills, a number of assessment measures are very informative.

English Assessment for Very Young Learners

The essential problem of assessment with second-language students is that it is generally assumed that the use of most test instruments is inappropriate because they were designed to measure the skills of native speakers and, in the case of standardized measures, are normed on the performance of native English speakers. The Gunderson (2007) study involved a number of measures designed to be used with very young second-language learners. The first battery of measures were designed by teachers in the school district; they represent background variables that the teachers believed would be important in these students' initial learning experiences. Some would likely call them readiness skills, but they will be referred to here as background variables.

The primary assessment is easy to administer and the instrument itself can be easily constructed with common classroom objects. Construction of the assessment package will be described in the Appendix. In addition, the assessment has been pilot-tested on about 1,300 primary-age immigrant students, so scores can be roughly interpreted and compared to this group of students. The 1,319 primary-aged students in the Gunderson (2007) study came from 82 countries and spoke 63 different languages such as Arabic, Bengali, Bulgarian, Cantonese, Cebuano, Dari, Danish, Gujarati, Hindi, Icelandic, Ilocano, Japanese, Kurdish, Korean, Mandarin, Pampango, Serbo-Croatian, Tagalog, Turkish, Urdu, and Vietnamese. However, the largest groups were from Asian countries, including Hong Kong, Taiwan, and China. See Chapter 4 for the interpretation of scores on this assessment.

There are a number of approaches available to measure the English reading ability of older students.

Methods of English Reading Assessment

Lado (1964) states that there is a simple method to test L2 reading ability, consisting of "presenting to the student passages containing reading problems and testing his comprehension of the passage precisely at those points at which the problems are crucial" (p. 232). According to Valette (1967), success in L2 reading is based on skills in two areas, vocabulary and structure—the most important being a knowledge of structure. Valette suggests that two types of tests can be constructed, one containing vocabulary items and one containing syntactic and morphological items. Obviously, these guidelines are very general. The following is a procedure that is effective in matching L2 students and reading material, a procedure that works well for students from grades 4 to adult level.

Generally, use of the term "readability" means that a book or passage is at a particular grade level. So, a third-grade readability level indicates that an average third-grade student would be able to read it. There is another meaning for the term that is related to an individual's potential for understanding a particular passage or book. In this case, readability is a qualitative measure that tells how well a student comprehends—whether they will comprehend the material independently or will need help. In this case, readability of a passage is determined for a particular student. It tells how readable a passage is for an individual—whether that student will find it easy or difficult. In this case it is also a comprehension measure.

If one wants to know whether or not a particular book is at a particular grade level, then a group of students who are known to be at that grade level are selected and tested. This reveals information about the material, since information is already known about the group of students. If one wants to know about how well a student comprehends a particular text, the readability of the text for the individual is determined. When one is speaking of individuals, the terms "readability" and comprehension are often synonymous.

THE CLOZE PROCEDURE

Taylor (1953) suggested that the "cloze procedure" is a good measure of readability. It has proved to be a useful device for matching both L1 and L2 students with text. The cloze procedure is a test in which words are systematically deleted and students supply the deletions (Bormuth, 1967; Klare, Sinaiko, & Stolurow, 1971; Potter, 1968). The cloze test has been used in numerous studies of ESL students (e.g., Carroll, Carton, & Wilds, 1959; Oller & Conrad, 1971; Bowen, 1969; Darnell, 1968). Knowledge of the syntactic and semantic systems of English allows them to supply correct words for the deletions. If one uses the cloze procedure as a test, the procedures are very clear. Since many older ESL students perform at very low reading levels, it is necessary to use material written for, say, grade 2. It is often difficult to find long enough passages. More about this later.

The cloze procedure puts students in direct contact with the material they are to read. One can easily manufacture a series of cloze passages to discover students' reading levels. Reading material should be surveyed, and if a reading series is being used, passages from the series should be selected. If newspapers are used, passages from several sections should be selected so that writing from different kinds of articles is included. The sports section usually is the most difficult!

The following steps are fairly well agreed upon for preparing a series of cloze passages:

1. A passage of about 250 running words that students have not read before is randomly selected, normally a passage from about the middle of the text. Students may not use their books as they fill in the deletions.
2. The title and the first and last sentences are left intact.
3. Beginning in the second sentence, every fifth word—including contractions, hyphenations, and numerals, such as 1999—is deleted.
4. The passage is typed and for each deletion a line of about 15 spaces in length is substituted. The passage should be double- or triple-spaced.

5. Students are asked to fill in the deletions. If one wishes to match students with text, it may be necessary to administer passages from different levels until the best student–text match is discovered.
6. The cloze is scored by accepting as correct only those items that are exactly the same as in the original.
7. The student–text match is determined according to one of the following criteria sets, to be discussed. Most educators appear to use the Bormuth (1967) criteria.

In order to establish individual students' appropriate text, it may be necessary to have students try four or five cloze passages. One should be sensitive to the demands of cloze since many ESL students struggle with the exercise. They especially have difficulty with idiomatic language (see Gunderson, Slade, & Rosenke, 1988).

TABLE 2.2 Different Reading Authorities' Scoring Criteria for Cloze Tests

Author	Independent Level	Instructional Level	Frustration Level
Bormuth (1967)	50% +	38–49%	37% and less
Rankin and Culhane (1969)	61% +	41–60%	40% and less
Ransom (1968)	50% +	30–49%	29% and less
Jones and Pikulski (1974)	46% +	30–45%	29% and less
Zintz (1975)	51% +	41–50%	40% and less

The three terms used in Table 2.2 are quite specific in meaning. A student operating at the "independent level" needs no help from the teacher; he or she will comprehend the text. "Instructional level" means the teacher will have to provide help. This is the ideal level. "Frustration level" means that no amount of help from the teacher will enable the student to comprehend the text; it is simply too difficult. These terms refer to how readable the text is for the student.

The different criteria may be a bit bewildering, but there is good evidence to support each set. Before considering which set to use with ESL students, however, the reader should consider the following passage, taken from Mary Ashworth's *The forces which shaped them* (1979, p. 3).

The Early Missionaries

Through the mercy of God, I have begun school today. It has been a ——— day to me, but ——— Lord helped me through. ——— the morning, I plainly ——— that a superstitious fear ——— spreading powerfully among the ———. Crowds wanted to come ——— school, but who were ——— be the first to ———? Here I reaped the ——— of my few weeks' ——— in the chief's house ——— last summer. The little ——— I had there eagerly ——— rushed to the school ——— they saw me coming, ——— even gladly mounted the ——— and struck the steel ——— me, to call their ——— ——— timid companions to the ——— . I had arranged to ——— the children in the ———, and the adults in ——— afternoon; but now I see ——— to change that plan, ——— have all together, at ——— for a while. My start ——— was with only ——— children; but, before we ——— finished, we had mustered ——— seventy. In the afternoon ——— about fifty adults, and ——— children. I felt it ——— difficult to proceed with ——— a company, and should ——— found it much more ——— , but for a few ——— whom I had already ——— training. Both morning and ——— I finished with an ——— previously prepared, in their ——— tongue; in which I ——— to show them my ——— , their need and condition, ——— also the glorious message ——— I had come to ——— known, namely, salvation through ——— Christ, the Son of ———. They were very attentive, and I hope and pray the Lord will now begin His work amongst them, to the glory of His great name.*

* *Deletions*: strange, the, in, saw, was, Indian, to, to, venture, fruit, labour, during, flock, enough, when, one, platform, for, more, place, have, morning, the, reason, and, least, first, fifteen, had, about, came, fifty, very, such, have, so, children, under, afternoon, address, own, endeavored, intention, and, which, make, Jesus, God.

The Ashworth selection is an intact unit from a textbook written in 1858, so the English is a bit different from today's standard English. The passage is 276 words long and contains 48 deletions. There are about 20 structure deletions such as *the* and "helper verbs" such as *have*. If the items that are easily inferred are counted, e.g., "Both morning and ———" (afternoon), a reader, through knowledge of English structure alone, could accurately predict about 41 percent of the deletions. Through knowledge of English structure alone, one would score at "instructional level" regardless of the criteria set used. If students are asked questions about the cloze passage, they have difficulty supplying some words that represent content, words representing the subject matter. A passage about telephones, for instance, will contain the same structure words, such as *the, and, have*, and *of*, as a passage like the Ashworth one, but it will also contain content vocabulary such as *receiver, busy signal*, and *dial tone*. It may also contain cultural content concerning such items as "telephone etiquette" and "conversational gambits" not found in a student's first culture. By possessing a basic knowledge of English syntax, an ESL reader scores at an instructional level.

The following criteria more accurately measure ESL students' comprehension levels. The criteria require them to know more of the content vocabulary and reveal a more realistic evaluation of their comprehension.

ESL Cloze Scoring		
Independent Level	*Instructional Level*	*Frustration Level*
70% +	50–69%	49% or less

Gunderson, Slade, & Rosenke (1988) studied the cloze performance of ESL adults compared with native English-speaking adults. They selected two passages of comparable difficulty: one a standard newspaper article and the other a parody on clichés. Each passage was made into a cloze test and given randomly to students in education classes or English classes for adults at an English language center. There were significant differences in the performances of the two groups. The native English speakers were superior on both tests; no surprise. They scored significantly higher on the idiomatic text, however, than they did on the standard text. Their knowledge of idioms improved their comprehension. The ESL adults scored significantly higher on the standard text than they did on the one filled with idioms. On both tests the content words were most difficult. Knowledge of the English syntactic system allowed the ESL adults to correctly fill in many structure words, somewhat inflating their comprehension levels, as in the case of the Ashworth selection. Overall, the ESL students scored a mean of 41 percent correct. This would suggest that the two passages were appropriate for them if the standard cloze criteria are used. However, if the ESL cloze scoring criteria are used, it can be seen that the passage was too difficult for most of the ESL students.

Some researchers have found that cloze is not sensitive to the overall context of a passage (Shanahan, Kamil, & Tobin, 1982), while others suggest that their findings are not conclusive (Cziko, 1983; Henk, 1982). Shanahan (1983) argued against their criticism, however. Use of the cloze procedure with ESL students should be cautious and, as noted above, it tends to overestimate their comprehension levels. It was also noted that the procedure is not useful for students below grade 4.

THE MAZE PROCEDURE

The "maze procedure" has been developed as an alternative to cloze (Guthrie *et al.*, 1974).

1. Select a passage of about one hundred words. Students should not have previously seen the passage.
2. As in the cloze procedure, the first and last sentences are left intact.
3. Instead of deleting every fifth word, provide three alternatives: a) the correct word, b) an incorrect word that is the same part of speech as the correct one, and c) an incorrect word that is a different part of speech than the correct one.
4. Students read the passage and circle the word they believe is correct.

Guthrie *et al.* define the instructional level for the maze procedure as between 60 percent and 75 percent accuracy. Independent level is 85 percent or better, while frustration level is below 50 percent. The maze is generally believed to be more reliable than the cloze in measuring ESL students' comprehension levels. The following is a portion of "The Early Missionaries" that has been turned into a maze activity.

The Early Missionaries

Through the mercy of God, I have begun school today. It has been

yellow	the	At

a <u>strange</u> day to me, but <u>an</u> Lord helped me through. <u>In</u> the morning,

run	two	Our

was	ran

I plainly <u>saw</u> that a superstitious fear <u>was</u> spreading

the	cats

Indians

powerfully among the <u>Eagles</u>.

Running.

The usual class contains students at many different reading levels. It is necessary, then, to construct a series of cloze or maze passages in order to find the appropriate reading material that will best suit individual students. One should be cautious because ESL/EFL students often become frustrated with both cloze and maze. The two procedures measure how readable particular texts are for individual students.

So far, cloze and maze have been discussed. They are methods for measuring a student's comprehension level. With caution, they can be used to help identify appropriate levels. However, they do not give much information about a student's reading performance. That is, a student's strengths and weaknesses are not identified. The procedures result in an overall estimation of comprehension level. Administering an informal reading inventory (IRI) to a student will provide diagnostic information regarding reading recognition and comprehension. It will also more accurately match students and reading materials.

THE INFORMAL READING INVENTORY

One of the first discussions of an informal reading inventory was made in Emmett Betts' text *Foundations of reading instruction* (1946). The best IRI is one containing the actual material students will be expected to read. That is, if they will be taught using a particular reading series, the inventory should be constructed from material from the series. By using the actual reading material, one assures a better match between students and reading level. Some teachers believe it takes too much time and effort to construct such inventories and opt to use a published one; however, the published tests are not as accurate at matching students and materials. Many basal reading series contain their own IRI. Scoring an IRI is an interesting experience.

Betts (1946) described four different reading levels to be measured by an IRI. In fact, these levels are still in use. While their names may vary from test to test, generally the levels are *independent, instructional, frustration,* and *capacity*. Different authors report different definitions of each of these reading levels. Generally, however, the following criteria are used. Independent reading level represents 99 percent or higher accuracy in word recognition and 90 percent or higher in comprehension. Ninety-five percent accuracy in word recognition and 75 percent comprehension indicate the instructional level. If a student scores 90 percent or less in word recognition and 50 percent in comprehension, that student is functioning at the frustration level. Capacity level indicates that the student can comprehend 75 percent of the material read aloud by the teacher. It is generally thought that this level represents a student's potential. An IRI consists of graded word lists and graded passages.

San Diego Quick Assessment

The words in each of the following lists should be typed on individual five-by-seven cards for use with students. Laminated cards last longer.

Pre-primer	Primer	1
see	you	road
play	come	live
me	not	thank
at	with	when
run	jump	bigger
go	help	how
and	is	always
look	work	night
can	are	spring
here	this	today

2	3	4
our	city	decided
please	middle	served
myself	moment	amazed
town	frightened	silent
early	exclaimed	wrecked
send	several	improved
wide	lonely	certainly
believe	drew	entered
quietly	since	realized
carefully	straight	interrupted

5	6	7
scanty	bridge	amber
certainly	commercial	dominion

develop	abolish	sundry
considered	trucker	capillary
discussed	apparatus	impetuous
behaved	elementary	blight
splendid	comment	wrest
acquainted	necessity	enumerate
escaped	gallery	daunted
grim	relativity	condescend

8	**9**	**10**
capacious	conscientious	zany
limitation	isolation	jerkin
pretext	molecule	nausea
intrigue	ritual	gratuitous
delusion	momentous	linear
immaculate	vulnerable	inept
ascent	kinship	legality
acrid	conservatism	aspen
binocular	jaunty	amnesty
embankment	inventive	barometer

11
galore
rotunda
capitalism
prevaricate
risible
exonerate
superannuate
luxuriate
piebald
crunch

Analysis:

Independent Level: 0–1 words missed

Instructional Level: 2 words missed

Frustration Level: 3 or more words missed

Source: M.H. LaPray & R.R. Ross (1969). The graded word list: Quick gauge of reading ability. *Journal of Reading, 12*, pp. 305–307. Reprinted with permission of the International Reading Association.

THE GRADED WORD LIST

Graded word lists comprise lists of words thought to be associated with particular grade levels. If one compares a student's performance on word lists with that student's performance on a comprehension test, there is always a positive correlation. One can roughly measure students' reading levels from their performance on graded word lists. The Wide Range Achievement Test (WRAT) (Jastak, Jastak & Wilkinson, 1984) is an often-used instrument that measures reading, using one word list (see also WRAT-Revised, Jastak, Wilkinson, & Jastak, 1984; Stone, Jastak, & Wilkinson, 1995). There are various graded word lists, but the San Diego Quick Assessment is a standard list. Word lists are useful for "shotgun" (i.e., rough) estimations of students' reading levels.

The San Diego gives a quick estimation of a student's general reading level. It is, as already stated, a shotgun approach and should not be used to place students in reading programs or to determine what reading materials they should use. The information gained from the San Diego forms the basis on which to decide what further assessments should be made. It also gives vital information about students' English phonological acquisition. As a student reads each card, the test administrator should take notes about which words the student has difficulty with. An error analysis reveals which English phonemes students have trouble articulating. A child whose first language is Javanese, for instance, may have trouble producing the final sounds in *fish* and *with*, producing *fis* and *wif* instead. This is important information that can be used to plan the student's overall language arts program.

IRIs use a series of word lists to measure word recognition in isolation and to estimate where testing should commence in the graded passages. The teacher makes careful notes during the reading of the word lists, indicating each time an Obtained Response (OR = what the student says) differs from the Expected Response (ER = what is actually in the text). The procedure is halted when the frustration level is attained, using the criteria noted previously (i.e., Independent = 99%+, Instructional = 95%+, Frustration = 90% and lower). The administration of the graded passages is, however, somewhat more complicated.

IRI PASSAGES

An IRI does require time. After some experience, many teachers develop their own miscue shorthand. Figure 2.5 shows a passage in which a fairly standard shorthand indicates miscues.

The ESL student who read this passage produced many miscues. That is, there are many cases in which the OR and the ER are different. She said "tree" instead of "three," but spontaneously self-corrected, so this miscue is not counted as an error. As she read, she ignored the period at the end of the first sentence, simply continuing as if the two sentences were one. The circle around the period signifies the omission. When she encountered "were," she substituted "went." The teacher gave her the word "trail" because she either could not or would not read it herself. "Track" was mispronounced as "turk," and she omitted the lexical morpheme "ed" in the words "shouted," "stopped," and "looked." The word "let's" was repeated

Lost in the Woods

The three young boys went home early in the afternoon. As they were walking down the trail one of the boys saw a deer running in the forest next to the old railroad track.

"Look," he shouted, "let's catch her." Immediately they began to chase the doe through the trees. The deer was very fast. Very soon the boys found themselves deep in the dark forest. They stopped, out of breath.

"Are we lost?" asked the youngest.

"I don't know," replied John, the oldest. They looked around. They ran to the top of a hill. There they saw John's house.

The following are miscues:

Substitution The student produces a real word, but not the one in the text.

Mispronunciation A nonword is produced.

Teacher-Assisted The student was unable or unwilling to produce the word so the teacher provided it: T

Insertion A word that does not occur in the text is inserted: ∧

Repetition A word or group of words is repeated: ∿

Omission A word is left out of the text: ◯

Reversal The order of words or letters in a word is reversed: ∿

Hesitation Pauses between words or phrases are too long so that the context of the passage is lost: /

Self-Correction A miscue is spontaneously changed to the ER in the text and should not be considered in the error count: SC

Figure 2.5 Portion of an IRI Passage

twice, whereas "dark" was omitted and "go" was inserted. Instead of producing "Are we lost?" the student read "We are lost." An extremely long pause was noted in the word "themselves." Finally, she said "home" instead of "house." Such a miscue, by the way, shows that she understood the content. Some would suggest that such a miscue should not be scored as an error.

The passage contains 100 words. One assesses the student's word recognition performance and decides whether she is functioning at the independent, instructional, or frustration level. The next procedure is to determine the student's comprehension level, so comprehension questions are asked:

1. How many boys were in the story? (Literal Question)
2. Where did they see the deer? (Literal Question)
3. Were the boys as fast as the deer? How do you know? (Inferential Question)
4. What is a dark forest? (Vocabulary Question)
5. Did the boys get lost? (Inferential Question)
6. What would you have done if you were one of the boys? (Critical/Evaluative Question)

The problem of constructing questions is a difficult one. When the passage is this short, it is difficult to ask a variety of questions. However, it is essential to ask different kinds of questions. Reading authorities disagree, but generally there are three kinds: 1) literal or detail, 2) inferential, and 3) applicative/critical questions. Each is related to a different level of comprehension. The easiest kind of question does not involve a reader operating on the meaning of a text, but rather on the surface structure.

COMPREHENSION LEVELS

Literal Comprehension: The reader is asked to supply items that are stated in the text. Literal comprehension requires a reader to operate on the surface level of text. He does not have to make inferences, other than low-level ones involving a knowledge of the syntactic and semantic constraints of English. So, for instance, if a text reads, "John was very hungry. He ate three plates of spaghetti", and the question is "Who ate three plates of spaghetti?", the question involves literal comprehension. However, to answer the question with "John" one has to make the inference that the pronoun "he" represents John. If it did not, then the author would be breaking the "given–new" contract inherent in text–reader relationships, and comprehension would not be possible. In this case, it is given that "he" refers to John. If "he" did not, the author would identify this new information with a name.

Inferential Comprehension: Literal comprehension deals mainly with the surface structure of the text. Generally, it does not involve inferred meaning. Inferential comprehension means that a reader deals with and understands the writer's ideas. He can make generalizations about the text, is able to understand the writer's purpose, and can anticipate and predict outcomes. In effect, the reader is able to go deeper than the surface structure of the text and operate on meaning.

Critical/Evaluative Comprehension: Many authors separate critical and evaluative (sometimes called applicative) comprehension. The term refers to a reader's ability to evaluate and make critical judgments about what is read. The reader is able to evaluate whether or not a text is valid, whether it expresses opinion rather than fact, and how she would apply the knowledge she gained from the text in other situations.

The following are the responses of an ESL student to the comprehension questions based on the story "Lost in the Woods."

1. "There were three boys."
2. "The deer was in the forest."
3. "I don't know."
4. "A dark forest is like one with no lights so it's dark, not even a moon or sun."
5. "Yes, because they didn't know where they were."
6. "I would have scream real loud so my mom could hear me."

The task is to analyze the student's responses and estimate her word recognition level in context and her reading comprehension. Again, the word recognition criteria are: Independent = 99% +, Instructional = 95% + , and Frustration = 90% and lower. There is a bit of a judgment call here regarding word recognition miscues: *were, trail, track, let's, go, dark, are we,* and *house.* There is some debate about counting repetitions. Some suggest they should be counted. Notice that in this case the omitted lexical morpheme "ed" was recorded three times but not counted as an error, because it was assumed that the omission was simply part of the student's English production at the time of the test. Some authorities would disagree. Word recognition in this case is 92 percent, a figure that falls between instructional and frustration. So, one makes another judgment call.

There is also room for making judgment calls when assessing comprehension. "I don't know" is obviously scored as an error. What about the other questions? Criteria are 90% + (Independent), 75% + (Instructional), and 50% and lower (Frustration). One must assess whether or not the student's answers show she comprehended the passage. Many teachers assign half-points. The final point is given if it is decided that the student did indeed understand the passage. Most individuals who have scored these questions agree that the student in this case understood the passage, since she answered five of the six questions. Even though that is only 80 percent comprehension, had there been more questions it is likely she would have scored higher.

To find the match between students' abilities and the requirements of a particular set of reading materials, one can construct an IRI with passages from the materials themselves. For teachers who do not feel they have the time or expertise to construct an IRI, published versions are available (see, for instance, Burns & Roe, 2002).

As was noted in Chapter 1, Marie Clay developed "running records" to allow teachers to see students' skills and needs in reading through an analysis of their miscues. The administration of a running record is fairly easy. The teacher records what the student reads. That is, the teacher records everything during the oral reading. This can be best accomplished on a photocopy of the reading material. It is suggested that the selections be of about 100 to 200 words and represent the three levels noted above: independent, instructional, and frustration. An analysis of the students' miscues reveals a great deal about their skills, weaknesses, and strategies (both appropriate and non-appropriate). The scoring of a running record is similar to that noted for IRIs above: 95–100% correct, independent; 90–94%, instructional; and less than 90%, frustration.

Three assessment procedures have been described and discussed that are effective in matching students with text. However, they do require a great deal of time and effort on the part of the teacher. The use of a graded word list such as the San Diego Quick Assessment will provide a gross estimation of students' reading abilities. One final consideration must be made: judging the appropriateness of the material.

Readability

As was discussed in the previous chapter, it was not until the early nineteenth century that people thought about "levels." Since McGuffey, educators have attempted to measure grade level. Textbook publishers "grade" their texts, usually from pre-primer to university level. There is very little agreement on what the word "level" actually means or how to accurately measure it. Generally, the term "readability" refers to measuring the difficulty level of a text. There are hundreds of readability formulas.

Interest in readability can be seen in Sherman's (1893) discussion of the effects of change in sentence length and degree of predication in English prose of the sixteenth century. Readability now, however, refers to the body of research surrounding the development or evaluation of readability formulas (Chall, 1958; Klare, 1963). The first readability formulas appeared in the late 1920s. Gray & Leary (1935) conducted a comprehensive investigation of text features to identify elements affecting readability in order to develop guidelines for writing easy materials. They surveyed librarians, publishers, and others, asking them to identify features that made texts "readable" for adults of low reading ability. One hundred respondents reported 289 features, which Gray & Leary categorized into four areas:

Format or Mechanical Features
1. Size of book
2. Number of pages
3. Quality of paper
4. Kind of type or printing
5. Length of lines (inches)
6. Binding
7. Illustrations

General Features of Organization
1. Title of book
2. Chapter divisions
3. Paragraph divisions
4. Reference guides

Style of Expression
1. Vocabulary
2. Sentences
3. Attitude of author
4. Method of presentation (literary genre)
5. Style of presentation (language style)

Content
1. Theme
2. Nature of subject matter (e.g., popular)

Their analysis revealed that content features were believed to be the most important factors in comprehension, followed by style, format, and organization. Factors within categories were also ranked. So, for instance, the most important features of content were timely subject matter and theme. The authors chose certain features to investigate further in order to develop a test that would involve the fewest possible elements that would still provide a reliable readability measure.

Selecting criteria to meet the demands of objective measurement imposed important constraints on the measurement instrument. First, quantifiable data were required. Of the four categories, stylistic features were most easily quantified. The need for quantification caused the content features, selected as most important, to be eliminated. Even though 82 elements of style were isolated, 18 defied objective measurement. The authors computed correlation coefficients for the remaining elements and a "criterion of difficulty" (i.e., a comprehension measure). The study, which began by investigating 82 readability elements, identified only 21 that were significantly correlated with the criterion. Of these, average sentence length in words, percentage of easy words, and numbers of first-, second-, and third-person pronouns were of interest to researchers (see Chall, 1958; Klare, 1963). "Easy words" were defined as items occurring in Thorndike's *The teacher's word book* (1921) and the word list of the International Kindergarten Union (1928).

Several features have become particularly important in readability formulas: number of syllables, number of sentences in selected samples, and number of uncommon words in selected samples. In summary, the selection of formula criteria has been greatly constrained. Many elements felt to be good indicators of difficulty were omitted, such as figures of speech, abstract vocabulary, and all factors related to a reader's interest in the content. Only features of style, items reliably quantified, have found their way into readability formulas. This is particularly unfortunate for ESL teachers and students because the formulas ignore the more important variables of interest and content.

The Fry Readability Graph

The standard readability instrument that is simplest to use and receives the most critical attention is the Fry readability assessment. The Fry continues in the new millennium to be the most widely used measure of readability. Its wide use is most likely a result of its simplicity. Fry uses a standard approach, one based on an operational definition of readability focusing on syllables and sentences. In fact, readability may be an artifact of the features of the formulas (Gunderson, 1986b). That is, readability formulas have been applied to reading texts for so many years that reading texts now reflect the features of the formulas. Readability measures should be thought of as extremely rough indications of level of difficulty, and no more. The Fry graph and instructions are shown in Figure 2.6.

The following discussion uses the passage entitled "Lost in the Woods" shown in Figure 2.5. The passage consists of 100 words; normally, three 100-word passages are randomly selected. It has been this author's experience that even university students have trouble determining what is a syllable and what is not. They are confused, for instance, by how many syllables are in the word "walked" as in "he walked through the forest." In a typical classroom of 30 students, at least five believe there are two syllables. There is one syllable. That is, there is one syllable in normal speech. If the word is pronounced "walk ed," then there are two. So what is the readability level of the passage? It has 122 syllables and 12 sentences, placing it at about the grade 2 level.

The Raygor Readability Graph

An alternative to Fry is the Raygor readability estimate. It is both easy and quick to apply. Raygor (1977) devised the graph to be used in elementary and secondary schools. Readability is determined by sentence and word length. Words of six or more letters are considered to be difficult. Individuals are more accurate in counting letters than in counting syllables! Baldwin & Kaufman (1979) found that Fry and Raygor produced equivalent readability levels but that Raygor was easier to use. (See Figure 2.7.)

In the Raygor system, the "Lost in the Woods" passage results in 12 sentences and 18 words of six or more letters. The Raygor estimation would seem to be about grade 3.

Fry and Raygor produce a rough grade-level estimate for material. They are helpful for most levels of materials. Fry is not as accurate at measuring primary material as it is higher-level material (Gunderson, 1986b). Raygor does not measure first- and second-grade material. In addition, neither measures the special reading skills required to be successful in a content area. Nor do they provide the information needed to determine whether elementary, secondary, university, or adult-level students will be able to cope with the special content-area reading skills necessary to read and learn from academic texts. Many computer-based programs contain readability measures that are easy to access and use. Microsoft Word, for instance, computes readability levels based on the Flesch–Kincaid procedures.

Average number of syllables per 100words

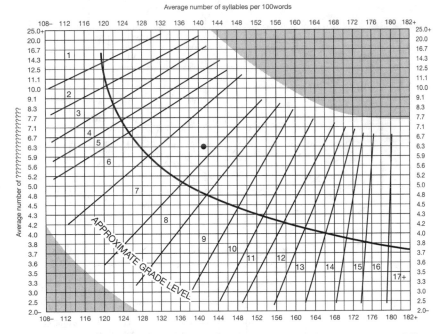

Figure 2.6 The Fry Readability Graph. The instructions for its use are as follows:

1. Randomly select three sample passages and count out exactly 100 words each, beginning at the beginning of a sentence. Do count proper nouns, initializations, and numerals.
2. Count the number of sentences in the hundred words, estimating the length of the fraction of the last sentence to the nearest one-tenth.
3. Count the total number of syllables in the 100-word passage. If you don't have a hand counter available, an easy way is simply to put a mark above every syllable over one in each word, then when you get to the end of the passage, count the number of marks and add 100. Small calculators can also be used as counters by pushing numeral 1, then pushing the + sign for each word or syllable when counting.
4. Enter graph with average sentence length and average number of syllables; then plot the dot where the two lines intersect. The area where the dot is plotted will give you the approximate grade level.
5. If a great deal of variability is found in syllable count or sentence count, putting more samples into the average is desirable.
6. A word is defined as a group of symbols with a space on either side; thus, *Joe*, *IRA*, *1945*, and *&* are each one word.
7. A syllable is defined as a phonetic syllable. Generally, there are as many syllables as vowel sounds. For example, *stopped* is one syllable and *wanted* is two syllables. When counting syllables for numerals and initializations, count one syllable for each symbol. For example, *1945* is four syllables, *IRA* is three syllables, and *&* is one syllable.

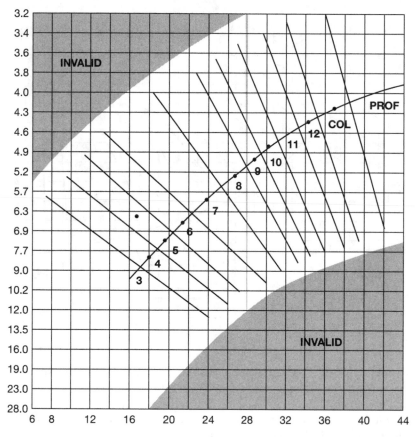

Figure 2.7 The Raygor Readability Graph. The directions for its use are as follows: Count out three 100-word passages at the beginning, middle, and end of a selection or book. Count proper nouns, but not numbers.

1. Count sentences in each passage, estimating to the nearest tenth.
2. Count words with six or more letters.
3. Average the sentence length and word length over the three samples and plot the average on the graph. Example:

	Sentences	6+ Words
A	6.0	15
B	6.8	19
C	6.4	17
Total	19.2	51
Average	6.4	17

Note the mark on the graph. Grade level is about 5.
Reprinted with permission of the National Reading Conference and A.L Raygor.

Content Reading Assessment

ESL teachers have a special responsibility to their students. They must discover whether or not students are able to cope with the special content reading skills required by their academic texts. Content teachers do not regularly make such an assessment (Gunderson, 1995).

Content textbooks vary in format according to the academic discipline involved. Social studies texts, for instance, contain many such items as illustrations, maps, and timelines. These texts differ from, say, science texts, which contain graphs, bar charts, and tables. Students must be able to "read" these special content features. If not, they will be unsuccessful even if they understand the written text. The following list delineates the content reading skills students normally need in order to read and learn from content texts:

1. Recognize the significance of the content
2. Recognize important details
3. Recognize unrelated details
4. Find the main idea of a paragraph
5. Find the main idea of large sections of discourse
6. Differentiate between fact and opinion
7. Locate topic sentences
8. Locate answers to specific questions
9. Make inferences about content
10. Critically evaluate content
11. Realize an author's purpose
12. Determine the accuracy of information
13. Use a table of contents
14. Use an index
15. Use a library card catalog
16. Use appendices
17. Read and interpret tables
18. Read and interpret graphs
19. Read and interpret charts
20. Read and interpret maps
21. Read and interpret cartoons
22. Read and interpret diagrams
23. Read and interpret pictures
24. Read and interpret formulae
25. Read and understand written problems
26. Read and understand expository material
27. Read and understand argument
28. Read and understand descriptive material
29. Read and understand categories
30. Adjust reading rate relative to purpose of reading
31. Adjust reading rate relative to difficulty of material

32. Scan for specific information
33. Skim for important ideas
34. Learn new material from text (Gunderson, 1995).

Adult readers often take for granted their ability to read and learn from text. Somehow, through experience with academic texts or through direct teacher instruction, they have learned many, if not all, of these content skills. Chapter 6 will contain discussions of programs to teach students these skills. The following is a content reading assessment that helps to judge whether students can cope with academic texts.

The first step is to assess carefully the text students are required to read. Such a process involves a review of the content skills listed above; each of these is a skill a student must learn. The question is, which skills are required by a particular text? Are students required to read and learn from graphs? Are they asked to remember details? Does the author expect them to extract the "main idea"? Are they expected to be able to use a glossary?

The best procedure for judging what the important content features are is to leaf through the text, tallying features on a chart like the Content Reading Skills List. It reveals the skills required by the text. Once the text has been reviewed, the next task is to produce an assessment. The purpose of the assessment is to determine students' needs and abilities in reference to a particular text. Chapter 6 will contain a brief discussion of some differences in style that occur between subject areas and that need to be considered when producing an inventory for a particular subject area.

As many questions as possible should be generated without making the assessment exhaustive; about 20 are usually adequate. If the text focuses on main ideas, the assessment should have many questions on main ideas (e.g., "Look at page six, read the paragraph about the Westward Expansion. What is the main idea of the passage?"). Content material is often filled with visual aids that make the text nearly incomprehensible for many ESL students. Indeed, many native English speakers struggle with content material.

Administration

It is explained to the class that the assessment is designed to find out what skills they know and don't know that are important in reading the text. It should be stressed that this is not a test in the usual sense of the word, since students will not receive a grade. The text should be available as they read. If absolute recall is expected, students should answer questions without the text after they have read the selections. Otherwise, they should use their texts during the assessment.

Scoring

This is an informal test and should not be used to establish grade levels. The following are rough guidelines requiring a judgment about the appropriateness of the text for individual students:

1. 90% +: the student is able to function independently with the content features
2. 65–90%: the student needs instruction in dealing with content features
3. 65% and less: if the student's cloze score is instructional or frustration, this text may be beyond his or her capacity to read and comprehend.

This scoring scheme is one suggested by Ruddell (1980). Such a content reading assessment helps to judge whether students will be able to read and learn from a particular text and is relatively easy to construct. One can produce a "class assessment table" that aids in grouping students for skills instruction. In this case, the identified content skills are coded at the top of a grid, with students' names down the side. The chart that follows identifies students with similar abilities and needs. The class record can be used to form instructional groups (see Chapter 6). Another factor to consider, if possible, is L2 cultural content, and it will be discussed in the next chapter.

Class Record

	1[a]	2	3	4	5	6	7	8
Jose								
Mohammed								
Suki								
Jakob								
Sylvana								
Duk Sue								

Note. [a] The meaning of the numbers is as follows: 1) table of contents, 2) glossary, 3) find main idea, 4) read maps, 5) follow directions, 6) follow a sequence of cause and effect statements, 7) read and interpret pie charts and bar graphs, 8) read and understand "flow" maps

Interest and Motivation

As was mentioned previously, interest and motivation are significant features in a student's potential for being able to read and comprehend texts. Unfortunately, interest is not an area that teachers often explore or utilize with their students (Gunderson, 1995). There are a number of ways to explore interest in elementary classrooms. The first is to use an informal small-group approach.

The group of six students listed above could be assembled, and the teacher would then take notes as the interview session progressed. The teacher would talk about his or her own reading interests to the group and then ask individuals in the group to name their interests. While the students responded, the teacher would take notes and record their different responses. An overall response record sheet like the following can be used to select reading materials and to form interest groups for instruction:

	Ghosts	Adventure	Science Fic.	Yng. Womens'
Jose		×		
Fernando			×	
Wai Chi			×	
Andrea	×			
Maria				×
Mohammed		×		

The group oral interest session is quite open and flexible, and the teacher can take opportunities to explore different areas of interest and students' reading backgrounds. The approach may be difficult in a large class, however, and so the teacher may opt for a written interest survey. The written survey is as good as the teacher's knowledge of what interests students. *The Reading Teacher*, published by the International Reading Association, has published a list of Students' Choices every year since 1974 (accessed on January 22, 2007 from http://www.reading.org/resources/tools/choices_childrens.html). This list can be used to help develop categories.

The written interest inventory can contain items such as:

1. When reading about airplanes I feel:
   Very Happy   Happy   Neither   Unhappy   Very Unhappy

For very young students, these five responses can be difficult, and so "faces" can be used, as shown in Figure 2.8.

The teacher can also survey what his or her students feel about reading generally by including items like the following:

1. When I read aloud to the class, I feel . . .
2. When I'm at home reading for fun, I feel . . .
3. When I hear my teacher reading aloud, I feel . . .
4. When I hear my friends read aloud, I feel . . .
5. When I am doing my math work, I feel . . .
6. When I am doing my reading worksheets, I feel . . .
7. When my teacher asks me to read aloud, I feel . . .
8. On my way to school, I feel . . .
9. When my friends hear me read aloud, they feel . . .
10. When my mother hears me read aloud, she feels . . .
11. When my teacher hears me read aloud, she feels . . .
12. When I read about science, I feel . . .
13. When I read social studies, I feel . . .
14. When I read math, I feel . . .
15. When someone gives me a book, I feel . . .

Figure 2.8 Primary Faces for Interest Inventory

16. When I get my homework back from my teacher, I feel . . .
17. When I get my report card, I feel . . .
18. When my mother gets my report card, she feels . . .
19. When I am reading silently to myself, I feel . . .
20. When I come to a word I don't know, I feel . . .

(Gunderson, 1995)

This author has constructed and used different kinds of interest inventories and has found the results to be very useful in planning instructional programs. Very often, the results are surprising. One group of third-grade students in a classroom with a large number of students from Hong Kong showed extremely positive attitudes about doing workbooks. The area of cultural differences will be explored in the next chapter.

The assessment measures discussed in this chapter produce information that is essential in designing reading programs that focus on the abilities and interests of students. They are measures that classroom teachers can adopt and adapt for their own purposes and needs.

Conclusion

ESL/EFL reading instruction is a complex undertaking. ESL students have complex language and literacy backgrounds that make it more difficult to plan teaching programs for them. The reader's view of teaching and learning also has an effect on instructional choices. The notion of comprehensible input was noted as an essential element in instruction. However, it was concluded that comprehensible input is relative to particular learners, not general to all. Students who have learned to read a first language have an advantage in learning an additional language over learners who have not learned to read another language because they can transfer some first-language reading skills to the learning of English reading.

A heuristic involving measure of first-language literacy and English ability was developed in 1991 to guide the process of assuring that instructional materials and approaches were comprehensible for learners with very different backgrounds. Results of more current studies confirm that English ability and first-language literacy background are good predictors of success in learning to read English (August & Shanahan, 2006; Gunderson, 2007). A detailed measure to assess English literacy background for very young students was described and discussed. In addition, a holistic oral proficiency measure was described, and secondary, university, and adult-level ESL students were each discussed. Those who needed to "learn to read" were differentiated from those who needed to "read to learn." Three reading programs were outlined: 1) survival reading, 2) specific reading, and 3) general reading. An adult decision heuristic was developed to aid teachers in placing students in reading programs.

Second-language (L2) reading assessment was also discussed. It was noted that standardized reading tests appear to overestimate students' reading abilities. The use of the "cloze procedure" was discussed and an alternative set of ESL scoring criteria was presented. In addition, "the maze" was suggested as an alternative to the cloze procedure. Informal reading inventories (IRIs) assess students' word recognition and comprehension abilities. An example of an IRI was given with suggestions for ESL students.

The chapter concluded with a discussion of readability, including the Fry and the Raygor graphs. The closing discussion also involved content reading skills and measures of interest. It was suggested that the ESL teacher must assess academic texts and students' ability to process and understand the varied skills they require, such as being able to read graphs and charts. It was also suggested that students' interests should be explored and approaches were described to do so.

The following chapters will delineate specific methods, procedures, activities, and programs within the context of different theoretical beliefs about language and language learning. However, the next chapter will contain a discussion in detail about the notion of culture and its importance in literacy instruction.

Explorations

Work with a partner if possible.

1. What model of reading best represents your view of reading and reading instruction? How does it vary from your partner's views, if it does? How do you think a teacher's model of reading affects her/his choice of teaching materials?
2. How much independent reading do you do? What kinds of material, if any, do you especially like to read for pleasure? How does this differ from your partner's interests? How do you think your personal interests will impact your teaching?
3. The concept of grade level is one developed by human beings to help them organize instruction. What do you think of the concept? Does it help you the teacher in designing instruction? If so, how; if not, why not?
4. Why should you know about your students' reading interests? Explore with your partner your reading histories relative to what you both find fascinating or highly interesting.
5. Many believe that readability is a real feature of books. Which is more important—readability or student motivation? Are they related in any way? What can you do to affect either of these in your classroom?

3
Language and Culture as Literacy Variables

Introduction

Classrooms across North America are becoming increasingly more culturally and linguistically diverse as new immigrants enter the United States and Canada (NCES, 2004; Statistics Canada, 2001). It is a sobering conclusion, however, that teachers must know about their students' cultures and languages or their students will fail in school (Gunderson, 2000a). This chapter contains information about cultures and how they are related to the teaching and learning of literacy. It is vital to remember that these discussions should not in any way lead to conclusions that can be generalized to large, broad populations or groups of human beings. The chapter includes discussions of some cultural differences that appear to characterize small groups in a particular geographic region. The conclusions can be used, however, as a guide to identify features that *may* also be important in other areas for teachers to explore.

Culture

Perception and Culture

This author once worked with an adult student from Indonesia who was attending the university as a graduate student. One rainy afternoon he brought with him a small umbrella with a floral pattern. When asked where he had borrowed it, he responded that he had purchased it himself. Why did he buy a woman's umbrella, he was asked. He was aghast! He had no idea that there were women's and men's umbrellas.

Cultural backgrounds *are* different. The same Indonesian student was asked to read an article about bedtime stories in a graduate class. He had absolutely no concept of what the term meant. After some explanation, he was able to read and comprehend the passage. He was amused at the concept of parents reading books to children at bedtime. When this author first read a newspaper item about curling, he had no idea what the article was about. The reporter, writing for an experienced audience, never once used the word *curling*. The text was filled with words like "short brooms" and "rocks," and they were all totally outside this author's understanding. Indeed, the text was not understandable for anyone without knowledge of curling in their background. Cultural background is significant in the way human beings understand and make sense of the world. A major difficulty, however, is that there is little agreement on what the word "culture" represents.

What Is Culture?

There has been considerable debate and controversy related to defining the term "culture." Fifty years ago, Kroeber and Kluckhohn (1954) identified 160 different definitions of the term. Larson and Smalley argued that culture was somewhat like a map or a blueprint that

> guides the behavior of people in a community and is incubated in family life. It governs our behavior in groups, makes us sensitive to matters of status, and helps us know what others expect of us and what will happen if we do not live up to their expectations. Culture helps us to know how far we can go as individuals and what our responsibility is to the group. Different cultures are the underlying structures which make Round community round and Square community square.
>
> (1972, p. 39)

Condon (1973) proposed that culture "is a system of integrated patterns, most of which remain below the threshold of consciousness, yet all of which govern human behavior just as surely as the manipulated strings of a puppet control its motions" (p. 4). Vontress (1988) concluded that each of us lives in five cultures that intermingle: the universal, the ecological, the national, the regional, and the racio-ethnic. Culture is more than a sum of its constituent parts, and each of us is more culturally complex than we know or can describe. Culture allows human beings to survive by providing the mental constructs through which to categorize the world. Murdock (1945) describes seven characteristics of cultural patterns: 1) they originate in the human mind; 2) they facilitate human and environmental interactions; 3) they satisfy basic human needs; 4) they are cumulative and adjust to changes in external and internal conditions; 5) they tend to form a consistent structure; 6) they are learned and shared by all the members of a society; and 7) they are transmitted to new generations. Culture can be viewed at a "macro level," a broad generalization consisting of shared features across a group, and at a "micro level," particular features related to an individual or a very small group of individuals.

A discussion of culture often includes descriptions, discussions and arguments for and against including such issues as race, ethnicity, socio-economic status, economy, gender, religion, and political philosophy. Often, culture is defined relative to the discipline of the individual doing the defining. In essence, culture is defined within the parameters of a particular academic culture. Sociolinguistic definitions differ from anthropological definitions, which differ in turn from ethnolinguistic definitions, and so on. Sociolinguists, for instance, focus on the language use that distinguishes communities. An individual, in this view, is a member of multiple cultural groups that can be identified by language and language use. Individuals are able to "code-switch" as they move from one community to another. Subgroups or subcultures can be identified by their use of jargon or "restricted codes." Individuals are "marked" by their membership in groups, so that an individual's language signals social status, gender, age, and so on. Culture affects the way an individual perceives the world, both on a macro and on a micro level. In particular, culture has a direct relationship with one's beliefs about, attitudes toward, expectations for, and views of teaching and learning and the importance of learning to read and write.

The notion of culture developed in this book is specific to the author's purpose; it is proposed that culture is the ideas, customs, language, arts, skills, and tools that generally characterize a given group of individuals in a given period of time, particularly as they relate to its members' learning in North American schools. The discussions that follow will include information about religious background, which often relates to what an individual believes about the value and place of learning to read; parental reasons for coming to North America, since they often reflect attitudes toward the importance of school and schooling; family dynamics, which reveal such features as gender roles; language (including phonological, syntactic, semantic, and pragmatic features that are informative about students' learning of English); and social patterns such as the role of eye contact in communication, particularly across generations. The complexity is that students do not simply adapt to a new culture or become bicultural. Rather, they acquire and reject some features of the new culture, retain and reject some features of their first cultures, adapt some features of the first culture to the second culture, and become socialized into a system that is uniquely individual, imbued with first- and second-cultural features in a way that is often predictable (Gunderson, 2000a).

Culture is a social phenomenon. When individuals move from one culture to another there are both micro- and macro-level consequences. There are a number of views concerning the consequences of entering a new culture. Ishiyama (1995), a counselling psychologist, notes that "Migrants inevitably face cultural, sociopolitical, and linguistic differences and various emotional and interpersonal consequences when they move to an unfamiliar culture" (p. 262). He goes on to define "cultural dislocation" as "a subjective experience of feeling displaced or not at home in a given sociocultural environment" (p. 263). He cautions that counsellors must know about cultural dislocation in order to provide appropriate services to individuals who have difficulties in a new culture. Micro-level features, according to Schumann (1978a, b), may include such phenomena as culture shock, motivation, and ego permeability. In 1986, Schumann categorized acculturation relative to the group of individuals involved; those who wish to assimilate fully into a culture and those who do not wish to assimilate.

Schumann (1978a, b) proposed that two factors affect the degree to which an individual learner acculturates: social distance and psychological distance. Social distance represents how well learners become members of the target-language community; that is, how well they are able to achieve contact with them. Psychological distance represents the degree to which a particular learner is comfortable learning the second language. Variables related to social distance include social dominance, integration pattern, enclosure, cohesiveness, size, cultural congruence, attitude, and a learner's intended length of residence. Psychological distance is related to language shock, culture shock, motivation, and ego permeability.

In Schumann's view, culture shock is often one of the most difficult experiences immigrants encounter. According to Schumann and others, an individual new to a culture begins to go through a process called acculturation, during which there are "stages" that represent the degree to which that individual becomes part of or adapted to the new culture. This is a view that suggests that immigrants or non-mainstream individuals must adapt to a new culture.

Culture Shock

Thus, "acculturation" is a term that refers to the notion that an individual from one culture must adapt to a new culture. The term "assimilation" refers to the case in which an individual's first culture is submerged in the new culture and there is often a loss of first-cultural values, beliefs, and behavior patterns. Acculturation is often associated with an individual's success in learning a new language. Indeed, many authors have suggested that failing to acculturate is often associated with failure to learn a second language (Ellis, 1986; Schumann, 1978a, b).

It has been observed by some that "normal" acculturation occurs in four stages: euphoria, culture shock, recovery, and acculturation. It is important to emphasize that these so-called stages are not particularly precise or accurate. "Under normal circumstances, people who become acculturated pass through all the stages at varying rates, though they do not progress smoothly from one stage to the next and may regress to previous stages" (Richard-Amato, 1988, p. 6). There is variation in acculturation both between and within cultural groups.

Overall, a number of factors appear to affect the degree to which individuals become acculturated: nation of origin, reasons for immigrating, age on entry, amount of prior schooling, economic status, difficulties related to travel, extent of disruption and trauma related to war, and a family's immigration status. Schumann's (1978a, b) model "seeks to explain differences in learners' rate of development and also in their ultimate level of achievement in terms of the extent to which they adapt to the target-language culture" (Ellis, 1994, p. 230). Schumann observes:

> We are concerned with variables which involve the relationship between two social groups who are in a contact situation, but who speak different languages. One group is considered the second-language learning (2LL) group and the other the target language (TL) group.
>
> (1986, p. 380)

Acculturation, according to Schumann, means "the social and psychological integration of the learner with the target language (TL) group" (1986, p. 379). However, a number of researchers view the notion of acculturation as a negative one.

Recently, second-language researchers have suggested that this view is a negative one (see, for instance, Duff & Uchida, 1997) because it characterizes the second-language learner as one who must give up a first culture. Socialization theorists have a more positive view. A central notion of language socialization theory is that children and other novices learn to function communicatively with members of a community by organizing and reorganizing sociocultural information that is conveyed through the form and content of the actions of others (Schieffelin & Ochs, 1986a, b). This theoretical framework views the acquisition of linguistic and of sociocultural competence as interdependent. Schieffelin & Ochs (1986b) conclude that as children learn to become competent members of their society, they also learn to become competent speakers of their language. Acquiring pragmatic competence—that is, the ability to use and interpret language appropriately in contexts—is an essential part of the language socialization process, because without pragmatic competence it is extremely difficult to participate in ordinary social life. In many respects, what is appropriate in a particular context is related to pragmatic cultural features. The language competence for giving advice, for instance, varies culturally (Matsumura, 2003).

Teaching and Learning

Teaching and learning—that is, schooling—is not culture-free. The Primary Program in British Columbia, for instance, begins its section on children's intellectual development with the following quotation:

> If intelligence develops as a whole by the child's own construction then what makes this construction possible is the child's curiosity, interest, alertness, desire to communicate and exchange points of view, and a desire to make sense of it all.
>
> (YEAR 2000, 1988)

Such a statement is based on the assumption that the development of "questioning" children who have a plurality of views and openness to them is meritorious. This is a value that is by no means universally shared, either by all Western teachers or by a number of students. Gunderson (2000a) concludes that "North American educators continue to view education within a 'mainstream' viewpoint, one that focuses on European values and beliefs, even though their school populations grow increasingly multi-cultural."

Teaching and learning differ considerably around the world. In the People's Republic of China, for instance, students begin school when they are 6½ years old. Free public education is available in every part of China, in government-supported public schools, company schools, or recently established private schools built mostly for the affluent. School hours are normally from 7:30 a.m. to 5:00 p.m. for five and a half days a week (Gunderson, 2007). There are several hundred languages and dialects spoken in China. Initial instruction involves the use of Pinyin, which is a form of the International Phonetic Alphabet (i.p.a.) used to transcribe speech sounds. Students are taught reading and writing in Putonghua (Mandarin), regardless of their L1s. The written language is the same in all of the schools, which makes it comprehensible across languages and dialects. On the other hand, students in Hong Kong often begin school at 3 years of age and they learn to read Chinese through rote memorization of traditional Chinese characters, although since the return of Hong Kong to China this approach has begun to change in many schools. Children from Hong Kong have often studied English from age 3.

To teach beginning reading skills in China, teachers use Pinyin, which is made up of 26 Roman letters, 59 International Phonetic Symbols, and four accents that mark tone. In addition, Chinese characters have been simplified, beginning in 1958. The use of Pinyin as a bridge to the learning of simplified Chinese characters is a feature of China but not Taiwan or Hong Kong. These differences have political significance. During Chinese New Year celebrations in Richmond, British Columbia, for instance, a parent from the People's Republic of China volunteered to produce large posters for display in and around one of the secondary schools. There were strong objections from parents from Taiwan, who complained that the signs were "communist" (Carrigan, 1998) because they used simplified Chinese characters.

There are a number of views of teaching and learning developed in schools in China that influence students' learning in North American schools. Many students expect to be involved in activities that focus on rote memorization, attention to facts and details, teacher-centered instruction, and a focus on grades. Unfortunately, when such students enroll in North American classrooms these differences can cause serious difficulties. Li (2006), for instance, found that the Chinese parents she studied rejected the teaching and learning going on in their children's school and opted instead to rely on outside school activities to give their children the skills they believed to be valuable. Interestingly, the visible minority in the school consisted of the white teachers, who were in a lower socio-economic group than were the Chinese families who were the visible majority. In essence, these families viewed Freire's banking metaphor of teaching as the preferred one.

Significant Cultural Variables

Learners from different cultures enter schools in North America with backgrounds that are complex. In many cases their expectations and their success are affected negatively because of differences between their cultures and the cultures of school and of their teachers. What an individual thinks about reading and writing is often determined by his or her first cultural views. It becomes even more complex because a student must also come to know about the culture related to school and schooling. For purposes of this book the following variables will be considered:

Significant cultural variables
- Privacy
- Cooperation/competition
- View of time
- Body movements
- Personal space
- Eye contact
- Physical contact
- Gender roles

- Individual vs. group family orientation
- Non-verbal communication norms
- Conversation rules (turn taking)
- Spirituality
- Fate vs individual responsibility
- Perceptual style (field dependence/independence).

Cognitive style
- Analytic
- Methodical
- Reflective
- Global.

Relational, Intuitive, Interpersonal
- Expression of emotion
- Family structures
- Roles of family members
- Educational expectations
- Perception and acceptance of individual differences
- Childrearing practices
- Modes of cultural transmission.

Diversity of ESL Students

Schools across North America enroll millions of students from all of the cultures in the world. In each cultural group, traditional beliefs, values, and customs may be retained to varying degrees by different individuals. Factors such as social class, religion, level of education, and region of origin in the home country (e.g., rural or urban) contribute to differences within immigrant groups. These factors influence the beliefs of the student and the student's family about teaching and learning, their help-seeking behavior, and their expectations of teachers. While there are usually shared beliefs, values, and experiences among people from a given group, there is also a widespread intra-group diversity. The degree of acculturation does not necessarily correlate with length of residence, and integration in one or more aspects of life does not imply a rejection of traditional ways. It is important to remember that every culture is dynamic. The existence of intra-group diversity precludes generalized assumptions about individual beliefs and responses to specific circumstances, and necessitates assessment on an individual basis. However, knowing about some of the key characteristics in the traditional cultures of specific groups may provide the beginning of a framework for mutual understanding and an improved ability to work effectively with students categorized as having limited proficiency in English. The key characteristics will help the teacher design systematic ways to explore cultural features that may affect his or her English literacy instruction.

The Role of Ethnicity and Race

Ethnicity, or race, is often related to culture in direct ways; but often it is not. Immigrants from Japan are almost always ethnically Japanese because there are few individuals from Japan who are not. Juan Hashimoto, on the other hand, is a Spanish-speaking immigrant from Peru whose grandparents were Japanese speakers from Osaka. Ethnically he was Japanese, but by most other behaviors he was Peruvian; he spoke only Spanish and knew little of the customs and practices of his grandparents, who had been farmers in Japan. As an 18-year-old, Juan was interested in finding a job. His aspirations for school and schooling were focused on this goal. He had no intention of enrolling in a post-secondary institution (Gunderson, 2007).

Three hundred and thirty-five students in the Gunderson (2007) study indicated that Hindi was their first language. There were considerable differences among this group, however. Hindi speakers from Fiji, for example, speak a kind of Hindi that is more similar to that spoken three hundred years ago than it is to the Hindi of India today. Many are farm workers and a large number are Christian. The culture they identify with is Indian-Fijian, and while it contains artifacts of Indian culture such as the celebration of Diwali (the festival of lights), it also contains Fijian beliefs and traditions such as the sharing of "grog" by Fijian males, a kind of male bonding ritual involving a drink made from the kava root. School and schooling are generally not viewed as central to the success of Indian-Fijians, particularly for women. But this view has changed dramatically in the past ten years.

Students from the subcontinent of India who indicated they were Hindi speaking differed from each other in many ways. Students from Mangalore, for instance, part of the region of Goa, are most often Catholic and have family names Westerners often associate with Portugal, such as D'Souza, D'Silva, and Peirera. They often speak Konkani as a home language, but they have learned both English and Hindi in school; however, they usually report Hindi to be their L1 for various reasons, but mostly because it is the "national language." On the other hand, Punjabi speakers, typically from northern India, report that they speak Punjabi, while they too have learned Hindi in government schools. Many Indian immigrants bring to Canada beliefs and traditions related to gender. It is not traditional in some Indian groups to view education as particularly important for females. Many immigrants from India continue to believe in arranged marriages. The local Indian-Canadian and Indian-American newspapers are often filled, even in the new millennium, with advertisements seeking marriage partners.

Caste Effects

In various parts of the world the social status of human beings within a particular society is marked by caste. In North America, social status markers are somewhat less obvious; however, generally socio-economic status, level of education, and profession mark one's status as, for instance, "middle class" or "upper middle class." Some societies mark status differences in their languages. In Bali the notion of caste was borrowed from the Indians who explored the region and is built into the language. The title "I" /i/, for instance, is the marker for the lowest caste, so that someone named "I Ketut" is from a family of the lowest caste. Almost as interesting in this case is that Ketut signifies that this individual was the third- or eighth-born child in the family, regardless of gender. There are only five names used in Bali. There are no family names, and each human being selects a name that she or he prefers to act as a second or family name. The notion of caste in Bali is no longer as strong a factor as it once was. In India, however, the notion of caste is still strong in some, but not all, areas. In 2005 a single 18-year-old refugee from Kenya arrived in Canada and was brought to Vancouver. She was from Somalia and was a Midgan-Madiban; that is, she belonged to the lowest caste of human being in Somali society (Samad, 2002), whose members are scorned and reviled. Samad notes, "To be a Midgan-Madiban, or an outcaste person, in Somali society is to suffer life-long indignities, to be deemed impure, unlucky, sinful, polluting, and thus meriting the disdain, avoidance, and abuse of others" (2002, p. 2). Samad continues, "Many Midgans have been denied food, medical treatment and protection just because of their outcaste status by many other Somalis" (2002, p. 2). This refugee arrived in Canada after a life in a refugee camp in Kenya. She had never been to school and could neither read nor write in any language. She lacked all of the basic readiness skills measured by every test known. Her life in English-only schools could only be described as extremely difficult and her potential for success is still doubtful. The categorization of human beings in a society into castes limits their social mobility, their access to educational and economic opportunities, and the overall potential for success within a society.

The students described so far also immigrated either having gone to school where they learned (or did not learn) to read and write their first languages or not having gone to school. Those who had attended school brought important aspects of their cultures that related to teaching and learning practices and beliefs, their teachers' beliefs about literacy, and the nature of the orthography of their L1s. These are all critical features of their backgrounds to consider in designing literacy programs for them.

Individuals come to school with rich, complex cultural and linguistic backgrounds, which they use to understand the world as they attempt to learn both language and academic content. Many of their views of teaching and learning, just as their teachers' views do, differ from each other and from those held by parents, teachers, administrators, and psychologists. Differences in their views and those held by teachers and other school personnel often contribute to the discrepancies that exist between their apparent capacities for learning and their actual levels of achievement.

Focus Group Issues

There are good publications that review cultural differences. Flaitz (2006), for instance, has published an in-depth analysis of features associated with individuals from 18 different countries. The reader will find this book to be informative because its discussions are organized around specific countries. The discussions that follow do not focus on individual countries. However, they involve a standard set of categories that can be used to develop local inferences about groups. The

Flaitz text also contains detailed information about educational and linguistic backgrounds that the reader may find useful. The basic approach used to discover the following information was to organize focus groups and to guide conversation through a set of focus questions:

1. Where do students come from?
2. What is the main religious orientation? (What might this mean for teaching–learning relationships? What might this mean for teacher–student, student–student, adult–student, male–female relationships in school?)
3. What are reasons for families to leave their home countries?
4. What is the naming system? (How should people be addressed?)
5. What are the family dynamics? (What is the family decision-making structure? Who should be contacted if needed at home?)
6. Are there strong overall cultural values that might make a difference in Western schools?
7. What are general attitudes toward school and schooling?
8. What are some specific language features that might make a difference?
9. Are there communication patterns associated with different roles such as parent, child, elder?
10. Are there ways in which the teacher can be sensitive to cultural differences?

Chinese Speakers

The following comments describe cultural features related to those who identify themselves as Chinese. Flaitz (2006) does not address issues related to speakers of Chinese. The comments have been derived from observations made by individuals from the cultures. The process began with a focus group of graduate Chinese and North American-born Chinese students developing a list of categories and contents. In addition, the following information was also derived from additional members of the school community who identify themselves as Chinese. Features have been changed or parts eliminated on the basis of their observations and reflections. All of the 18 individuals who reviewed and provided input on the following agreed that it was "generally" and "broadly" representative of the local Chinese immigrant community. Eight of the reviewers were graduate students from Hong Kong, the People's Republic of China, and Taiwan. Two were adults who were born in North America but who were self-identified as Chinese who knew about immigrants.

Individuals of Chinese background are found in every part of the world. The People's Republic of China has about one billion three hundred million inhabitants. It is particularly important, therefore, to keep in mind that the following comments are generalizations that are not necessarily accurate for many of those who are Chinese. Indeed, some Chinese-Canadians and Chinese-Americans interviewed argued that they were "100 percent Canadian or American." One Canadian-born Chinese-Canadian informant argued that the difficulty with immigration was that new Chinese immigrants were giving Chinese-Canadians a bad name by their behavior. This author has heard similar comments from fourth- and fifth-generation Chinese-Americans in California and Washington. Table 3.1 summarizes observations made by members of the focus group.

TABLE 3.1 Focus Group Observations: Chinese Students

Geographic origin	China, Hong Kong, Taiwan, Singapore, Thailand, Malaysia, Vietnam, Laos, Cambodia, Fiji, Africa, and the West Indies.
Religious background	Although some people from China may be Roman Catholic or Protestant, most Chinese are traditionally Buddhists. Central notions include a strong belief that one's past lives influence one's present and future lives (for example, evil deeds from a past life cause serious illness in the present and threaten the future), and the belief that man is inseparable from his universe, which is viewed as a vast, indivisible entity. Confucianism also exerts a strong influence in China. Confucius defined the rules that dictate relationships (i.e., between father and son, teacher and student, husband and wife, etc.).
Reasons for immigrating	To live in a modern and agreeable society; to obtain better job opportunities and better educational facilities for children; to join relatives who have already settled in North America; to escape from communist rule and live in a democratic society.
Naming system	The Chinese name usually consists of a one-word surname followed by a two-word given name. A woman may keep her own surname or use her own and her husband's surnames in hyphenated form. The more traditional Chinese may give a child a second name when schooling commences and a third name when marriage occurs. In Canada the child may have an additional name.
Family dynamics	*Structure*—A patrilineal extended family system that emphasizes family relationships, duties, discipline, filial piety, obedience, parental authority, and respect for the elderly. The family is often large, extended, living together, headed by the eldest working male, and is a source of pride. It is so important that the Chinese have specific terms for each member. For example, an "uncle" may be called "the second eldest brother of one's mother." The elderly are highly respected and the young are obliged to take care of them. The birth of a male child is considered more desirable than that of a female, since the male carries the family name and is entitled to a larger family inheritance.
	Roles—Traditionally, the husband interacted with the outside world, and to some extent this still obtains. He works, takes care of finances, usually disciplines the children, and makes the primary family decisions. Women have primary responsibility for the family.
	Discipline—May appear harsh to the Westerner, and open gestures of affection are seldom displayed.
	Problem solving—When dealing with conflicts, the Chinese may traditionally be persuaded by others without asserting their own rights. They prefer to listen to what others have to say instead of confronting them directly. And they may nod and smile when they neither understand nor agree with what is being said. They may then reply in an indirect way and try to handle the situation diplomatically.

TABLE 3.1 *continued*

Cultural values	The Chinese are generally pragmatic people. Hospitality is very important. Work and education are highly valued and are seen as the only means of climbing the social ladder. Harmony is highly valued in all things, a harmonious balance of yin, the negative female energy that produces darkness, coldness and emptiness, and yang, the positive, male energy that produces light, warmth, and fullness. To maintain this balance one must wholly adjust oneself to the environment.
Common attitudes toward education and society	High priority placed on work and education for children of both sexes. Expending time on jobs and schooling is considered much more important than leisure activities. Difficulties may arise when children do not meet their parents' high expectations of them in school. Parents may feel the rights and privileges accorded children in North America threaten their traditional authority and control. In traditional Chinese families, teachers are highly respected.
Language features	The Chinese people speak more than 80 different languages, not counting the hundreds of dialects and variations of those languages. Chinese language is tonal, non-inflectional, and essentially monosyllabic.
Significant social patterns	*Time*—Time is embedded in a lifestyle marked by formality and politeness.
	Physical contact—Touching the head or shoulder of another person in casual contact, particularly if he or she is older, is viewed as extremely disrespectful.
	Eye contact—The avoidance of eye contact is an expression of respect.
Culturally sensitive approaches	Chinese people place great emphasis on work and education, values that influence their education and their use of educational services. Chinese people come from various geographic locations and socio-economic classes, and vary in culture, religion, beliefs, and experience. It is important to respect each person as a unique individual with a distinct background and values.

It is important to identify country of origin because teaching and learning approaches vary rather dramatically from country to country. It is important to reemphasize the caution that these are not broad generalizations that apply to every human being who identifies him- or herself as Chinese. Indeed, as noted above, individuals from Hong Kong, the People's Republic of China, and Taiwan differ in many ways and there are interesting attitudinal differences. Individuals in the focus group argued that individuals from Hong Kong often look down on those from China as being primitive country folks. There are also negative views related to political differences between the People's Republic of China and Taiwan. During the 1990s, thousands of families left Hong Kong because of their fears related to the takeover by China. Nearly 90 percent of the families in the Gunderson (2007) study indicated that they came for a better education for their children.

In the past, after a child entered a school in North America it was traditional for someone like a school principal to give a child an "English" name. This author knew a principal who gave names such as Gordon and Winston because they were favorite items in her life. Many students continue to select their own English names (Gunderson, 2007). Students from Hong Kong often self-selected the names of favorite actors and singers.

Parents may feel the rights and privileges accorded children in North America threaten their traditional authority and control. In traditional Chinese families, teachers are highly respected. However, this view changes when they believe their children's education is not meeting their expectations (see, for instance, Li, 2006). It is not unusual for Chinese immigrants to keep information from school personnel about their children's schooling background, particularly if it includes learning difficulties. One interesting activity is to organize groups of parents to consider the features noted above and talk about their reasons for agreeing or disagreeing to their validity. This helps to establish some interesting discussions and local views about local cultures. It is important to remember that fourth- or fifth-generation Chinese have become Americanized or Canadianized and often have negative views of new immigrants. Gunderson (2000a) referred to the "shadow diaspora" as individuals who have only a few tokens of their parents' first cultures.

Central American Spanish Speakers

Many immigrants in this author's area of Canada come from Central America and arrive as refugees, largely from El Salvador, Guatemala, Honduras, Nicaragua, and Mexico, who have experienced considerable hardships, family losses, persecution, and lengthy journeys via several intermediary countries (Gunderson, 2007). The observations set out in Table 3.2 are consensus views of a group of five members of the community: two graduate students and three parents who had children enrolled in elementary and secondary schools.

For many, their immigration vectors are complex, often with stays in Mexico, Honduras and, more commonly, the United States. Many of the refugees come from California and have, in essence, worked themselves up the coast in various work situations. There are various agricultural communities located in California, Oregon, and Washington in which there are large Spanish-speaking communities of workers. These are interesting communities, by the way, because they have also attracted immigrant workers who speak other languages, such as Russian.

To many Central American parents the life of the urban teenager appears to be filled with reckless abandon. This is a view that is shared by other groups (see Gunderson, 2007). It was the conclusion of members of the focus group that every individual has a unique history and story of immigration and that generalizations or stereotyped images are likely to be inaccurate and can cause difficulty for both family members and school personnel. Life is difficult for many Spanish-speaking refugees, as it is also for other refugees. Gunderson notes:

TABLE 3.2 Focus Group Observations: Central American Students

Geographic origin	Largely El Salvador, Guatemala, Honduras, Nicaragua, and Mexico.
Religious background	While official statistics indicate that everyone is Roman Catholic, there is considerable diversity among the immigrants. Many are active Catholics, who accept the Church both as provider of social support and as a major participant in community life. Others are non-practicing members of the Church, with varying degrees of commitment to Catholic belief and ritual. Many are Protestants, either by birth or conversion. Some are Mennonite, Jehovah's Witnesses, Mormons, or Baha'i.
Reasons for immigrating	Poverty, violence, and a history of military dictatorship have forced many to flee, nearly all as refugees. For many, the road is an indirect one, with lengthy stops in Mexico and Honduras.
Naming system	When a woman marries, she both retains her father's name and takes her husband's name (Maria Sanchez, when she marries Juan Lopez, becomes Maria Sanchez Lopez). Thus, all elements in an immigrant family may have different last names. For a professional to call someone by his or her first name is seen as negative and patronizing.
Family dynamics	*Structure*—Elderly people are few. Families are intimately, though not physically, tied to the extended family, which is made up of both blood relatives and so-called fictive kin, such as godparents, creating a widespread net of social, business, professional, and bureaucratic connections. *Roles*—While the parents, especially the mother, are the primary sources of care, the extended family shares in these responsibilities. *Discipline*—Child discipline is variable. *Problem solving*—The husband is considered the head of the family, but important decisions will generally be made in consultation with the wider family. The belief in the helpfulness of talking about problems with close family or friends is not always recognized.
Cultural values	Children are universally welcomed and a large family is often a measure of status, especially in rural areas. Tremendous deference and respect is often shown to those in positions of authority.
Common attitudes toward education and society	While boys in Central America are allowed considerable freedom and have few domestic responsibilities, girls are not permitted to stay out late, to date, or to associate with whom they please. To Central American parents, the life of the urban Western teenager appears to be filled with reckless abandon.
Significant social patterns	*Time*—Respect for appointment times and deadlines varies among individuals. Many are punctual, others less so.

TABLE 3.2 *continued*

	Physical contact—Most Central American people relish physical warmth and closeness.
	Eye contact—Making immediate eye contact with strangers is uncomfortable.
Culturally sensitive approaches	Since every individual has a unique history and story of migration, stereotyped images serve no useful purpose and can cause difficulty for everyone involved. Uncovering the details of a student's story will help build an understanding of the situation left behind by the family.

One artifact of the state of affairs in the world that came to light was that linguistic groups and immigration status were related in unfortunate ways. Immigrants who arrived in the school district who spoke Mandarin differed from those who arrived as Spanish speakers in more than just first language. A significant number of Mandarin and Cantonese speakers were from entrepreneurial families who arrived with substantial amounts of financial resources, while a significant number of Spanish and Vietnamese speakers were from refugee families who arrived with limited or no financial resources. The social consequences of this artifact continue to be serious for students and for the social system in which they live. One consequence is that the linguistic markers take on features that are negative. "Vietnamese" has to a great extent become the "signifier" for "gang member." This is scandalous. It condemns a whole group, including the hard working law-abiding, participating members, in a grossly unfair manner.

(2007, p. 374)

Again, it is important to reemphasize that the views presented here must not in any way be considered to be reliable as generalizations across groups. One of the informants was an individual from El Salvador who is a single father of three. He entered British Columbia from the United States and has since become a successful Ph.D. student at a local university.

Indian Immigrants

It is predicted that India will become the world's most populous country sometime during this century. The subcontinent of India is the location of a number of independent countries. There is a long history of disagreement between India and Pakistan since they became separate countries in 1947. Individuals who identify themselves as Indian have spread around the world. The subcontinent has an extraordinary linguistic, cultural, and religious diversity that defies any attempt to make reliable generalizations. Table 3.3 shows the views of a focus group of six individuals who identified themselves as Indian, Indo-Canadian or from a variety of backgrounds. They agreed that the term "South Asian" is preferable to other names.

TABLE 3.3 Focus Group Observation: South Asian Students

Geographic origin	The Indian subcontinent, including Pakistan, India, Sri Lanka, Bangladesh, and Nepal, the South Pacific, and East Africa (Uganda, Kenya, and Tanzania). A linguistically, socially, and culturally diverse group sharing a common British colonial heritage.
Religious background	About 83% of the Indian population is Hindu and 11% is Muslim. Other small religious groups are Christians, Sikhs, Buddhists, and Jains. Pakistan is a Muslim nation; about 97% of the population practices Islam and 1.5% is Christian. The majority of South Asian immigrants from East Africa are Ismailis, although some are Hindus and Sunni Muslims. The majority of South Asians from Fiji are Hindu; about 15% are Muslim.
	Hinduism holds that all life is interdependent and is a continuous cycle without beginning or end, so that death and birth are merely transformations of form. After death the soul is reborn in another life form. All actions have consequences, and return to the perpetrator. The fortunes of the soul in each rebirth are determined by the behavior in former lives. This is the law of *karma*, whereby the present is affected by past action, and the future by present action. Society is organized into a hierarchy of social classes called castes, into one of which each person is born. Each caste has its own rules of behavior, which include social contacts with members of other castes. Sikhism believes in a single God and the equality of all people, rejecting the caste system.
	Sikhism includes Hindu concepts of reincarnation as well as *karma*. Unlike in Hinduism, the representation of God in pictures and the worship of idols are forbidden. Baptized Sikh men are enjoined to wear turbans and do not cut their hair or beards. In addition, baptized men and women do not smoke or drink alcohol. Most men and women, whether baptized or not, wear a steel bracelet on the right wrist.
	Islam literally means "submission". A Muslim is one who submits to the will of God, rejects all other gods, and follows the teachings of the Koran, the holy book that records the will of God as revealed to the prophet Muhammad. Islam imposes a code of ethical conduct encouraging generosity, fairness, honesty and respect. Muslims are required to pray five times daily, facing the direction of Mecca, after a ritual washing, and should additionally attend a mosque to pray together on Friday. They are to abstain from food, drink, and sexual activity from dawn to dusk during the month of Ramadan, the ninth month of the lunar Muslim calendar. Shortly after the death of Muhammad, Muslims divided into two major sects over the issue of who should succeed the prophet as religious leader. These sects are know as Sunni and Shia. Ismailis are one of the Shia subsects.

TABLE 3.3 *continued*

Reasons for immigrating	To pursue economic and educational opportunities that are perceived to be better than those of their home countries, and to escape from the traditional authoritarian patrilineal system. A relatively small number, mostly from Sri Lanka and Uganda, have come as political refugees. Some, like the Fijians, came as a result of racial conflict and increasing political and economic tension.
Naming system	South Asian names vary with religion and region. Women take their husband's surname at the time of marriage. Hindus generally have three names: a personal name followed by a complimentary name, and then a family name. However, many women have dropped the middle name after coming to Canada. Sikhs typically have three names: a personal name, then a title (*Singh* for men, e.g., Mohinder *Singh* Sandhu; *Kaur* for women, e.g., Raminder *Kaur* Gill), followed by the family name.
Cultural values	Interdependence is valued highly and the lifestyle is collective rather than individualistic. South Asian children may face a conflict between the values of their parents and U.S. or Canadian society.
Family dynamics	*Structure*—The extended family provides the identity of the individual as well as economic and emotional security. *Roles*—Traditional South Asian culture is male dominated and sex roles are well defined. Most decisions are made by the head of the household, who is usually the most established, financially secure male. The woman may be perceived as her husband's possession and taught to be submissive and obey him. Women and girls nevertheless have high social and religious status, and are considered to bear the honor of the family. The woman is in charge of nurturing and performing household duties. Her most important responsibility is to look after her family, and her childhood training may all be geared toward her role in the home. The eldest male is the most favored and the most privileged. In some cases, parents take on two jobs and work long hours, leaving children relatively unsupervised. Older children may be given the responsibility of babysitting younger ones. *Discipline*—In general there are no fixed schedules for young children; a child goes to bed when tired, eats when hungry. Parents may also expect teachers to take responsibility for disciplining children, as is the case in home countries. A less active, quiet child is often viewed as a good child. Children are not encouraged to take risks but rather to be cautious and observant. *Problem solving*—Some disabilities may be hidden because they reflect on the whole family, and some parents account for the situation in terms of karma. On all important matters close relatives are consulted and their opinions are given considerable weight.

TABLE 3.3 *continued*

Common attitudes toward education and society	Parents want children to be well educated and a high priority is placed on schooling. However, in home countries it is the role of the teacher to teach, and thus there is little or no parental involvement in schools. Consequently, South Asian parents new to the United States or Canada may not be used to participating in school activities or consulting with teachers. For some parents, extracurricular activities and social development may be considered unimportant and a waste of their children's time. New immigrants, both students and parents, are likely to find the Canadian school system more relaxed and liberal, very different from what they experienced at home. Some parents may be upset by the fact that sex education is provided to their children in schools, believing that sexual matters should not be discussed in front of children or adolescents, especially girls. Because education is felt to be important to upward mobility, failing a school examination may be devastating for a young person.
Language features	Hundreds of distinct languages and their dialects are spoken in East Asia, Southeast Asia, and the Pacific Islands, but the main languages spoken in Canada are Mandarin, Cantonese, Taiwanese, Hakka, Vietnamese, Khmer, Lao, Hmong, Mien, Chamorro, Samoan, and Hindi. Those who emigrate have various bilingual and biliterate backgrounds. Some are bilingual or trilingual, some are only monolingual; some come with prior education while others do not; some come with little experience of a written language.
Significant social patterns	*Physical contact*—The traditional greeting is with the palms of the hands pressed together in front of the chest. Shaking hands is not common. *Eye contact*—Customarily, eye contact is considered rude and disrespectful, especially with elders.
Culturally sensitive approaches	Help that is provided in an informal and egalitarian way is generally more effective. Work with and through a culturally acceptable agency or school when advising and helping a South Asian family, particularly when the student is an adolescent.

One major immigration vector involves Indians who have lived and worked in the Middle East in places such as the United Arab Emirates and Kuwait and opted to immigrate from there.

Gunderson & Anderson (2003) observed classrooms in which South Asian boys and white teachers did not have positive interactions because the boys appeared to view the teachers through their South Asian lenses. On all important matters, close relatives are consulted and their opinions are given considerable weight. Gunderson (2007) found that secondary-level female students were not allowed to participate in after-school activities because of their parents' views of appropriate gender roles and activities. Some teachers reported that South Asian students seldom completed their homework on time, and investigation showed it was because of their extended families. When someone came to visit, which was a common happening, it would have been rude for children not to attend to the company, and as a result they often did not have time to finish their homework (Gunderson & Anderson, 2003). New immigrants, both students and parents, are likely to find the American school system more relaxed and liberal, very different from what they experienced at home.

Vietnamese

The plight of the Vietnamese boat people is well known; many Vietnamese have entered as refugees. Vietnamese immigrant school-age students appear to have significant school-related difficulties at a rate that is higher than other immigrant groups (Gunderson, 2004, 2007).

TABLE 3.4 Focus Group Observations: Vietnamese Students

Geographic origin	Vietnam; several minority ethnic groups, including the Thai, Muong, Tho, Cham and Kha (Malay-Indonesians), East Indians and Chinese. About 95% of Vietnamese and Chinese-Vietnamese refugees are from urban backgrounds.
Religious background	Confucianism and Taoism exert a strong influence in Vietnam. People in Vietnam can also have a rather pluralistic view of religion. Confucius defined the rules that dictate relationships (i.e., between father and son, teacher and student, husband and wife, etc.). Central to the practice of Taoism is the belief that one must not interfere with nature, but must rather follow its course. This passivity can result in resignation and inaction. Most Vietnamese who have come to Canada are Buddhists; some are Christians (Roman Catholic). Supernatural forces are often used to explain illness.
Reasons for immigrating	Large numbers of people from Vietnam immigrated in two separate waves. The first immediately followed the end of the war in 1975–76. The second larger wave began in 1978, and is still not fully completed. The first wave included fairly well educated professional people and those who were high-ranking members of the Vietnamese armed forces, all of whom left the country for political reasons. Those in the second wave have left for political and economic reasons. Many are ethnic Chinese.
Naming system	Family names and given names are traditionally put in the opposite order from Western names so that the family name comes first and the given name last, with one or sometimes two names in between. For example, the Vietnamese name Nguyen Trong Thiet in terms of order is comparable to Smith Jim George. Women in Vietnamese communities usually do not change their names after marriage. Thus, married couples do not have family names in common.

TABLE 3.4 *continued*

Family dynamics	*Structure*—A hierarchical family structure; even older siblings have authority over younger and must be shown respect. For a person from Vietnam, the family is the main source of identity, and loyalty to family is primary. Many families were separated when attempting to leave Vietnam, so in Canada and the United States refugees have joined together to create substitute "families," while some intact families have taken in those who arrived as "extended" families.
	Roles—In the family, while elder men must be approached for major decisions, the wife or mother enjoys considerable although subtle power and independence. Even though large family networks may not actually live in the same home, the authority of elders, especially male elders, is still recognized, as is their right to be consulted when major family decisions are made.
	Discipline—Most child discipline and training is by example and thus is not usually a planned strategy. Vietnamese parents do expect their children to follow their guidance without discussion or question. One result of this is that children may not express anger openly but instead are more likely to appear stubborn or passively uncooperative.
	Problem solving—Many people in Vietnam are preoccupied with maintaining face and avoiding open disagreement and confrontation. It is important to smile and agree even when neither action really means consent or agreement. To a person from Vietnam, these actions are honorable and are meant to prevent mutual embarrassment.
Cultural values	In some instances, confusion about a child's age may arise since, traditionally, a baby is one year old at birth, rather than at the end of the first year of life. Sons are important because they perpetuate the family name and allow the family to fulfill its responsibilities to ancestors.
Common attitudes toward education and society	Families may be reluctant to agree that problems, such as adolescent problems at school, should be dealt with by a professional. Consulting a psychologist may be seen as an extreme measure. For many, a nostalgia for the old country still exists, as well as guilt over leaving friends and family members behind.
Language features	The Vietnamese language is tonal, non-inflectional, and essentially monosyllabic.
Significant social patterns	*Time*—Difficulty in adapting to the appointment system, often tend to arrive late, at least initially.
	Eye contact—Steady and direct eye contact may be uncomfortable for some, fleeting glances being preferred.
Culturally sensitive approaches	At least at first, be formal and unhurried, while attempting to establish a supportive mood and sense of trust. Be aware that open-ended questions may be an unfamiliar approach and perceived as threatening. Detailed questions about a student's life, past, or their family should be limited and should be connected to the needs of the student.

The focus group consisted of four parents and one Ph.D. student, all immigrants, who identified themselves as Vietnamese. Different groups of Vietnamese immigrants have arrived at different times over the past 30 or 40 years. Many professional people arrived during and after the war. These particular immigrants were often fluent in French. The "boat people" left Vietnam and many landed in Malaysia, Indonesia, the Philippines, and Hong Kong. Many of these individuals were ethnically Chinese and had actually been expelled from Vietnam. There are a number of different ethnic groups, including the Thai, Muong, Tho, Cham and Kha (Malay-Indonesians), Indians (South Asians), and Chinese. About 95 percent of Vietnamese and Chinese-Vietnamese refugees are from large urban backgrounds. A number of refugee children were born in Hong Kong but had grown up in isolation there because they were "boat people" who had arrived from Vietnam as refugees.

Those in the second group have generally been referred to as the boat people, although not all escaped Vietnam by boat. The experience of "the boat people" has been described as devastating: having to part with what little they had in order to pay bribes before embarking, dealing with victimizing sea pirates, and then living in refugee camps for months and years while waiting for reception by their new country. It is uncomfortable for many of these individuals to talk about being expelled from Vietnam because they were, in fact, ethnically Chinese.

Koreans

Members of the focus group included five graduate students, a teacher of Korean, and a retired school principal. The seven members of the group all maintained they were of Korean ancestry and by chance all were women.

There are a number of potential difficulties a teacher can experience with Korean students. In Korea, if an individual's name is written in red ink, that is taken as an omen that the individual's mother will die. Teachers who happen to "correct" written assignments using red ink will offend their Korean students.

West Indians

The focus group included four parents and a teacher-education adviser (Brown, 2001) in the local university, all of whom identified themselves as West Indians. The following individuals are broadly referred to as West Indians. They are speakers of Spanish, English, French or Creole. The West Indies today represent the aftermath of four "interrelated and sometimes overlapping orientations, the European, the African, the Indian, and the Chinese" (Braithwaite, 1974). Individuals from the West Indies have endured a history of anti-black racism. The unemployment rate for men is extremely high. Women in the West Indies may be a part of a variety of marriage, family, and household types: 1) nuclear and extended family structures; 2) monogamous, polygamous, and serial marriages; and 3) single and multiple generational households of various combinations of kin, friends, and sometimes strangers. Because of the importance of the income from migrant labor, partners in a marriage may not be co-residential. Partly as a consequence of

TABLE 3.5 Focus Group Observation: Korean Students

Geographic origin	Primarily South Korea, occasionally North Korea. Some immigrants who maintain they are Korean come from various other countries such as Brazil.
Religious background	Predominantly Buddhism and Confucianism until the middle of the nineteenth century, when Christianity was introduced. One of the best-known Christian groups was led by the Reverend Sun Myung Moon.
Reasons for immigrating	Access to better education. Older individuals often immigrate to access English training programs. Many teachers have immigrated to take formal English programs because of Korea's focus on English education in Korea. Many 20- to 25-year-olds visit to improve their English skills (and to enjoy their temporary independence) before they begin their working careers.
Naming system	Personal names include first a family name followed by a given name. Age and respect are related. An older brother or sister is not referred to by his or her given name but by a term like "big brother." There are about 350 family names in Korea; however, Kim, Lee, and Park are the most common, with Kim being the most frequent of all. Family names are associated with historical geographic roots. Older human beings are addressed by using their "positions."
Family dynamics	Individuals refer to parents by their children's names, particularly in the case of referring to a mother by her eldest son's name, e.g., "this is Jay's mother." The father is the absolute ruler of the family. Members of families feel a deep-seated responsibility for each other.
Cultural values	There is a deep respect for age and for a position in life. Teachers are highly respected individuals. It is considered very rude to address an individual by his or her given name.
Common attitudes toward education and society	There is a deep-seated respect for education and for teachers. The teacher is seen as the central figure in giving students the knowledge they need to succeed. Rote memorization is the most valued of classroom activities. Parents are convinced that success in school guarantees success in life.
Significant social patterns	Students have great respect for teachers, and even if they do not understand what a teacher says or is teaching, they nod their heads in apparent agreement. Looking another human being in the eyes is generally considered rude, especially with older people.
Culturally sensitive approaches	Korean students try very hard not to offend their teachers and often they remain silent in class. This may occur even though they do not understand. Students understand that there are cultural differences that cause difficulties in communication, and a polite explanation of the difference is often the best approach. This appears to work best with individual students rather than groups.

TABLE 3.6 Focus Group Observations: West Indian Students

Geographic origin	Mainly Trinidad, Tobago, Jamaica, Barbados, Haiti, Puerto Rico, and Cuba.
Religious background	The most common religions are Roman Catholic, Protestant, Sikh, Muslim, Rastafarian, and Voodun.
Reasons for immigrating	Unemployment has served as a major motive for immigration to Canada, where jobs, education, and training options are more numerous and accessible, particularly for middle-class West Indians. Employment as domestics is the pattern for individuals of lower economic status. The usual pattern of migration is that the wife, and possibly the husband, come to Canada first, leaving the children with their grandparents or aunts.
Naming system	In the West Indies it is common for the same person to be called by several different names. For example, most people may know Prescott Brown as simply "Brown"; those close to him may use a "pet name" like "Junior." In addition, he may have a nickname derived from some abbreviation of his other names, his initials, or a personal characteristic that is not always positive.
Family dynamics	*Structure*—Varies with social class and ethno-cultural background, but in many instances the family consists of more than the nuclear family unit living together. The extended family, although not necessarily sharing housing, may include close friends and hometown people with whom regular close contact is maintained over many years.
	Roles—Traditionally, women have played a strong and decisive role within the household.
	Discipline—A child may be physically punished for misbehavior or poor performance in school or at home. The method of discipline varies across social status.
	Problem solving—Revelation of problems to professionals such as counselors may be viewed as a weakness. The reciprocity of kin and community often breaks down after immigration.
Cultural values	Within the family, children are taught to respect and be obedient to authorities and elders; "to be seen and not heard," to listen rather than challenge or argue with adults.
Common attitudes toward education and society	Middle-class individuals from the West Indies tend to have little difficulty adapting to life after immigrating, perhaps because of the common British-influenced heritage and the previous multicultural experience in the home country. Lower-class individuals, those who have had to face anti-black racism, often have difficulty adjusting. However, given the usual pattern of migration, their children may struggle with the transition, particularly in adjusting to life away from their extended family custodians and with parents whom they may

TABLE 3.6 *continued*

	no longer know. Education is important to West Indian parents, most of whom want their children to advance as far as possible in school. In the West Indies, school is regarded as an extension of the home, and the child is entrusted entirely into the teacher's hands. Teachers are expected to know what is best for the child's education, and are more likely to keep in contact with parents over a child's progress, partly because of the individual initiative of teachers, and partly because of the quick flow of information within the close community network. West Indian parents may hesitate to attend conferences with the teacher because of their respect for the teacher's authority. They may assume that the teacher will notify them of problems, as would be the case in the West Indies.
Significant social patterns	*Time*—In the West Indies, the pace is slow, which can lead to difficulties in punctuality.
	Physical contact—Hand movements are frequently lively. Touching the arm, back or shoulder is frequent in friendly social conversation.
	Eye contact—Eye contact is used in some cases to avoid seeming rude or intrusive. Not making eye contact, depending upon the context, can be a sign of distrust for authority.
Culturally sensitive approaches	The approach should be sensitive. One should be aware of the effects of anti-black racism and how it is manifested in the curriculum and in social interactions. One should be aware of the unique gender roles within the family and the authority of the mother.

the social dislocation of the father from the family during slavery and partly because of high unemployment after slavery, there is a high frequency of female-dominated households. There is an authority status attributed to women that is highly significant.

Iranians

Table 3.7 lists generalizations concerning those who identify themselves as Iranian. There were six individuals in the focus group and there was some argument about the words "Persian" and "Iranian." Two members thought that the terms represented entirely different groups, whereas the others thought they were simply different words for the same group. It was also mentioned several times that Iranians are not Arabs and should not be called or referred to as Arabs. One member noted that he was half-Jewish and half-Iranian because his mother was Jewish and his father was Iranian.

Japanese

Six graduate students formed the focus group in discussion related to individuals who were Japanese. Two were born in North America.

TABLE 3.7 Focus Group Observations: Iranian Students

Geographic origin	Indo-Europe; ethnic Turks, Kurds, and Arabs from northern, western, and southern border areas of Iran; nomadic tribes, including the Bakhtiaris, Ghashghais, and the Turkomans, each with their own distinctive customs, dialects, and styles of dress.
Religious background	Ninety-eight percent of the Iranian population is Muslim, of which 93% belong to the Shi'ite sect. Two percent of the population is Baha'i, Zoroastrian, Jewish, or Christian. Submission to God's will is an important aspect of an Iranian's life. The deeply rooted cultural belief in fate or "Taghdir" remains strong in all classes. Iranians are expected to accept life's events and consequences with grace, based on the belief that "all is in the hands of God."
Reasons for immigrating	A trend toward a more traditional and religious lifestyle, making living conditions generally unbearable; never-ending persecution; the consequences and dangers of recent wars.
Family dynamics	*Structure*—Traditionally, the Iranian family is a strong patriarchal unit whose undisputed head is the oldest male of the extended family, all of whose members live together in the same household. In the family, the children are the least respected, enjoy limited freedom, but are expected at all times to safeguard the good name of the family. *Roles*—The father has authority over the entire family. Major decisions, such as the children's education, are usually made jointly by husband and wife. The actual implementation of plans and decisions is the husband's prerogative. The wife's role is to submit to her husband. However, should conflicts arise between father and the children, the wife usually intervenes because she is very close to the children. *Discipline*—Discipline (e.g., spanking) is usually administered by the father (and may be harsher than the Canadian or U.S. norm), since the mother is considered the more loving, caring, and protective figure in the family. *Problem solving*—Iranians are a people who dislike admitting mistakes for fear of losing face. Value is placed on extended family advice and support. Problem solving and conflict resolution usually occur in stages and according to a certain pattern. Every effort is made to keep a problem private. Should the parties involved fail to resolve the conflict, a third party from within the community who is trusted and respected by both sides is asked to intervene impartially. Reconciliation happens on the basis of "forgive and forget" and the problem is never mentioned again, whether it is truly resolved or not. Professional help is only reluctantly sought as a last resort.
Cultural values	Class and class consciousness are central factors in Iranian society. For many decades the traditional middle class, consisting of affluent, very religious Muslims, has controlled Iran's economy, as well as its

TABLE 3.7 *continued*

	political, religious, and ideological life. People tend to confine themselves to their own social class (which is defined mainly by levels of affluence and education), their own religious groups, and to those who share the same political views. For an Iranian, loss of Persian identity is shameful. An Iranian is usually judged by the name of his family, including grandparents, aunts, uncles, and cousins. The family is the most important element in Iranian culture and life is usually dominated by family values and relationships.
Common attitudes toward education and society	Fearful of Western influences, especially on their children. Iranian children, both male and female, are expected to do extraordinarily well at school. Iranian parents expect their children to achieve high marks but to avoid integration into the larger society.
Significant social patterns	*Time*—Punctuality is not a preoccupation; rather, time is taken to socialize and establish personal relationships before getting down to business.
	Physical contact—Touching, embracing, and kissing are very common among persons of the same sex, and conversational distance for Iranians is usually less than for North Americans.
	Eye contact—Eye contact may be far less than is typical for North Americans.
Culturally sensitive approaches	Spend time to establish a trust relationship before getting down to work. Emphasize the confidentiality of the assessment process and its results, and the need to work collaboratively with the family to determine how the information can best be used to support the student while preserving the family's sense of privacy.

Generally, Japanese parents appear to be very permissive with young children up to the age of about 6 or 7. Indeed, this author has observed a number of Japanese families interacting with their very young children, and it appeared to him that there was little or no control of behavior, except where a child's physical safety was in question. Once they start school, discipline is increased, and involves the mother using consistency and teaching consideration for others.

Filipinos

The focus group consisted of six professionals (nurses, teachers), who were all immigrants. Filipinos speak many different first languages. However, most speak Tagalog, the national language, and most have studied English in school. The history of the Philippines has been somewhat complex; the islands have come under the influence of Spain, the United States, and Japan. Both the language and the culture have been influenced by the presence of individuals from these countries.

TABLE 3.8 Focus Group Observations: Japanese Students

Religious background	In Japan, the principal religions are Shintoism, Buddhism, and Christianity. The majority of Japanese immigrants are from the Buddhist–Shinto traditions. Buddhism has exerted a tremendous influence on every aspect of traditional Japanese culture. Shinto is a polytheistic, indigenous religion which holds that all natural objects and phenomena have *kami* (Shinto gods), so that the gods of Shinto become innumerable. Shintoism is largely concerned with obtaining the blessing of the gods for future events. Most people in Japan are tolerant of religious beliefs and do not regard simultaneous involvement as incongruous.
Naming system	Customarily, the family name comes first, the given name second. Adults generally call each other by their surname and add the suffix *san*, meaning "Mr.," "Mrs.," or "Miss" (Tanada san). Adults call children by their first names, adding *kun* for boys and *chan* mainly for girls. Children do not call older siblings by their first names, but use special terms meaning older brother and older sister.
Family dynamics	*Structure*—The family structure is typically the nuclear family. Parents are devoted to meeting the physical and emotional needs of the children, and the children are obliged to respect, honor and obey their parents. The Japanese family has the duty and obligation to care for all its members, young and old, to take an active part in finding suitable partners for the children, and to teach the children proper conduct.

Roles—Within the family hierarchy, the father has the most authority, then the grandfather, eldest son, mother and daughter. The wife is responsible for raising the children and managing the household. All responsibility for child rearing is hers, including education. The mother is responsible for arranging tutoring, attending parent–teacher conferences, etc. Fathers may be reluctant to become involved in school activities, which they still believe to be the woman's role.

Discipline—Generally, parents are very permissive with young children up to the age of about 6 or 7. Once the children start school, discipline is increased, and involves the mother using consistency and teaching consideration for others.

Problem Solving—Family members are expected to stand together when dealing with outsiders. Within the family, the moods and feelings of others are highly respected, so that much interaction is indirect and non-verbal. Family problems (e.g., dropping out of school) tend to be hidden from outsiders, and are felt to bring shame on the whole family. Problem solving is dealt with by the family first. If it is unsuccessful, the family may seek an arbitrator, someone discreet whom the family respects, to assist without causing the family loss of face. It is very unlikely that the person chosen will be a |

TABLE 3.8 *continued*

	professional or a stranger. Head nodding indicates attentiveness and understanding but not necessarily agreement. Smiles may reflect a variety of emotions from joy to confusion, embarrassment, or politeness.
Cultural values	Family wishes and appropriate conduct take precedence over individual desires. Conformity to rules of conduct and etiquette is an important aspect of Japanese culture. Children are taught to respect elders and those in authority, to distinguish between relatives and close friends (insiders) and others (outsiders); to develop *giri* or social sensitivity to the needs of others and to be modest and considerate; to be stoical, and to endure adversity patiently and without complaint. Certain numbers are considered unlucky. The word "four" in Japanese is *shi*, which also means "death"; nine is associated with a word meaning "suffering."
Significant social patterns	*Physical contact*—Handshakes are acceptable with Westerners. Bowing indicates respect and is used for greeting and taking leave of others. *Eye contact*—Avoidance of eye contact traditionally denotes respect.
Culturally sensitive approaches	Avoid confrontation as it causes embarrassment and fear of losing face. Be aware that the educational problems of a student are difficult areas for the family to deal with because they may be considered extremely private.

Immigrants from the Philippines come to pursue economic and educational opportunities that are perceived to be better than those of their home country. Many who joined the U.S. armed forces have immigrated and have become U.S. citizens. A number have immigrated as nannies and housekeepers. This is also a major pattern of Filipinos who travel to the Middle East and to places such as Singapore and Brunei to work. Members of the focus group indicated that they no longer felt comfortable visiting the Philippines because of what they indicated was a fairly dramatic rise in public violence.

Filipinos generally believe in education as a path to success, and they respect scholars. Parents encourage their children to do well in school and to perfect their English skills. However, Gunderson (2007) found that many school-age Filipino students have difficulty in school and disappear from academic courses in high school at a very high rate. This finding was disturbing to many secondary teachers who believed that these students were ideal in many respects because they were thoughtful, attentive, and cooperative.

Arab Students

The reader is cautioned to consider the following as being an extremely limited view developed by five informants who themselves also made it clear that these

TABLE 3.9 Focus Group Observations: Filipino Students

Geographic origin	The Philippines is an archipelago of more than 7,200 islands situated south of China, southeast of Indochina.
Religious background	The Filipino populations have a variety of religious/philosophical beliefs; among the major ones are Buddhism, Confucianism, Taoism, Shintoism, animism, Roman Catholicism, and Islam.
Reasons for immigrating	To pursue economic and educational opportunities that are perceived to be better than those of their home country.
Family dynamics	*Structure*—The family is seen as a bilateral family system in which the individuals are obligated to both maternal and paternal sides of the family. Although the extended family is common, family patterns, practices, and values differ according to the area in which the families live, religious affiliation, ethnic group membership, and socio-economic status.
Cultural values	The repeated colonization of the Philippines (Spain, the United States, Japan) has made their culture a mixture of East and West.
Common attitudes toward education and society	The Filipino people believe in education as a path to success, and they respect scholars. Parents encourage their children to do well in school and to perfect their English skills.
Language features	The exact number of Philippines languages is uncertain, but there are three major languages: Tagalog, Ilocano, and Visaya. Since the study of English has been part of the Filipino educational system since the turn of the last century, the vast majority of immigrant Filipino students can speak English.
Culturally sensitive approaches	Help that is provided in an informal and egalitarian way is generally more effective. Work with and through a culturally acceptable agency or school when advising and helping a Filipino family, particularly when the student is an adolescent.

views were very limited and non-representative. They also concluded and argued strongly that there is no single view that could adequately represent the broad category "Arab." It was noted by one member of the group that there is a great deal of contention and often bitter vituperation related to the inclusion of Egyptians as Arabs. Many Egyptians have deep respect for their rich cultural and historical roots and view Arabs as being nomadic wanderers without established cultural and historical roots. They often resent being included in the category. This author wishes to note that he was encouraged to conduct a focus group in this area because the number of Arab students immigrating to North America continues to increase dramatically. The reader is cautioned to remember that the results are dependent on the experience and backgrounds of a local group and they are related directly to where the individuals came from (Saudi Arabia and the United Arab Emirates).

TABLE 3.10 Focus Group Observations: Arabic Students

Geographic origin	Originally individuals from the Arabian Peninsula, but presently this includes individuals from Sudan, Morocco, Algeria, Saudi Arabia, Iraq, Yemen, Syria, Libya, the United Arab Emirates and Oman. Although many insist that Egyptians are not Arabs, others maintain that they are. Arab immigrants have also come from Mexico, Argentina, Ecuador, Colombia, and Central America. The biggest group of Arabs living outside of the Middle East is in Brazil.
Religious background	Primarily Muslim; however, there are Arabic speakers who indicate that they are Christians or Jews.
Reasons for immigrating	Reasons for immigrating vary considerably from group to group. Individuals from regions outside of the Middle East usually immigrate for better educational and economic opportunities. Recently many have arrived in North America as refugees.
Naming system	The system seems complex, but it isn't. A man is given a name and it is followed by "bin Ali" (son of Ali) followed by "bin Saleh" (son of Ali's father, Aleh), which is followed by the family name. The pattern is the same for women, except that "bint" means daughter of. This is followed by the name of the father's father and the family name. This is the basic approach used in places such as Saudi Arabia. The system differs in other areas.
Family dynamics	Generally, families are led and dominated by the father or oldest male. Often there is an obvious separation of men and women even in the home. There are differences between individuals who have grown up in rural as against urban settings.
Cultural values	Generally, interactions between males and females are highly regulated by deeply held religious beliefs.
Common attitudes toward education and society	Generally, there is a strong belief in the value of education and a deep respect for those individuals who have successfully completed degrees. In some countries the possibility of completing degrees in prestigious English-speaking universities such as Oxford or Harvard is a highly coveted opportunity. Parental interactions with teachers in the West are often difficult because of gender-related issues. Students in many countries are separated by gender, and boys and men are almost never taught by women, and girls and women are almost never taught by men.
Significant social patterns	Members of the group concluded that good friendships were very deeply appreciated and were considered to be lifelong. Good friends are expected to be loyal and to be generous with their friends. One difficulty noted was that men appeared to be brutally blunt in their conversations, but that this was a communications style.
Culturally sensitive approaches	Interactions between parents and teachers can be difficult as a result of gender differences in communications. Initial communications are probably best arranged by men initially. Adult students are the most difficult since they have deeply ingrained male–female beliefs.

The author's university has a well-established English Language Institute that has a good home-stay program. Over the years, the institute has found that arranging home-stay programs for adult male students from countries such as Saudi Arabia and the United Arab Emirates needs to include considerable knowledge and finesse. Placing a male adult Jordanian student in a home with a Jewish family, for instance, may create difficulties for both the student and the family. Such placements must be made with care and a great deal of preparation and background development for both the student and the family. With good preparation these placements can be extremely successful. However, without it they can turn out to be disastrous.

Culture and Informants: A Cautionary Note

The information noted above was developed by small groups of informants who identified themselves as part of the different groups. Their statements should not and cannot be considered to be valid or generalizeable to everyone who identifies him- or herself as a member of a particular group. Indeed, no single human being or small group of human beings is able to represent the vast diversity of any large group of human beings who are grouped according to a category developed by other human beings. It is not possible, for instance, for this author to generalize about or characterize the culture of Norwegian-Americans outside of his own family, acquaintances, and community. Knowing the views of different members of the local school community, however, can be extremely helpful to the teacher in planning curriculum, which as noted previously is never culture free.

The category labels used above can be used to form focus groups of parents and others who identify themselves as members of the groups to explore local views of cultural features. It is essential for teachers and administrators to explore these issues locally and not to rely on the views of others such as the informants in the focus groups described above. In essence, the following points should be included in a locally developed cultural focus group:

- geographic origin
- religious background
- reasons for immigrating
- family dynamics
- cultural values
- attitudes toward education.

It is also important that the teacher involve an individual who is part of the culture to help lead the focus groups since, in many respects, the results may be dependent upon many of the cultural issues themselves.

First Languages and Cultures

It is beyond the scope of this book to present information about first languages and the ways in which they can affect the learning and assessment of English reading.

An outstanding resource in this respect is the book edited by Swan & Smith (2001) titled *Learner English: A teacher's guide to interference and other problems.* What follows is a brief discussion of Chinese because it represents an immigrant group that continues to increase in size.

Chinese consists of seven dialects or language groups referred to respectively as Mandarin, Wu, Hsiang, Hakka, Northern Min, Southern Min, and Yueh or Cantonese (Chang, 2001). According to Chang, Chinese dialects share not only a written language but also important basic features at all structural levels. Chang concludes that Chinese speakers find English hard to pronounce, and have trouble learning to understand the spoken language. It is interesting to note that Mandarin is the largest language group in the world, with an estimated 750 million speakers. There are a number of phonemes—separate language sounds in a language—that occur in English but not in Chinese and cause learners difficulty when they attempt to learn English.

Generally, English consonant clusters cause Chinese learners difficulty, particularly final consonant clusters, which tend to be either lost or glottalized. For example, back /bæk/ becomes /bæʔ/. In some dialects, / l/ and /r/ are confused so that "lice" and "rice" are produced the same. In general, English reduced vowels are difficult for Chinese speakers to perceive and to produce. Chinese languages have four to six tones that distinguish word meanings. English sentence intonation causes Chinese learners difficulty, since intonation in Chinese languages is used to affect the meaning not of a whole sentence, but of individual words. A question in English is signaled by a rising intonation. Chinese learners often use a word-by-word intonation and are often, as beginners, unable to produce or understand sentence-level intonation. In addition, Chinese is a monosyllabic language, and speakers therefore tend to emphasize every syllable. This makes their English sound "staccato." Words with complex consonant clusters are often "syllable-ized," such as "sipoon" for spoon.

Syntactic differences between Chinese and English often cause great difficulties for learners. Chinese does not use inflected forms. In essence, there are no tenses. Transitive and intransitive verbs are treated as the same in English, and adjectives and verbs are confused. Chinese does not use auxiliary verbs to form questions and produce negatives, particularly involving "to do." There are no articles in Chinese, no genders, and few expressions dealing with plurality. Word order is difficult in English because, unlike in English, it is the same in both questions and statements in Chinese. Prepositions, too, cause difficulty for the Chinese learner. The Chinese learner often has difficulty with personal pronouns, either omitting them or using incorrect ones, e.g., "John is friend, she is good friend." The ability to use prepositions in English correctly is a strong predictor of English reading comprehension (Gunderson, 2004, 2007).

Many of these features can become fossilized in speakers' English. A second-language learner attempts to learn the phonology, syntax, semantics, and pragmatics related to English. At any given time, the speaker's English contains features that are somewhere between their first language and English, called interlanguage. As the second-language speaker's abilities develop, he or she becomes more native-like. Her interlanguage approaches the target language in its repertoire of features. However, the primary goal of most second-language speakers is to develop the skills to enable her to communicate with individuals in the target culture. One does not need to be a native-like speaker to communicate. When a learner's language becomes comprehensible enough to be understood within the important second-language environment, say at work, fossilization can take place. The learner's English becomes frozen and stops changing. It is true that the features that get fossilized are often the ones that represent the kinds of features of first language we are talking about. In the case of Chinese, this includes such items as the deletion of final consonants and consonant clusters; the confusion of the two difficult English phonemes, the lateral and the American r; and the difficulty with personal pronouns.

Similar differences occur in every group described above. It is important to know about these differences. The cultural differences often affect interactions among students, teachers, and parents. They can also affect the learning going on in a classroom when a student–parent shared view of teaching and learning is contrary to the teacher's view. Language differences are especially important to know about during assessment sessions. It is also important to keep in mind that oftentimes there are differences related to views of subgroups of a culture. This is a reason this author selected Chinese for this discussion.

There are differences among groups of individuals who identify themselves as Chinese. Mandarin speakers from Taiwan, for instance, and Mandarin speakers from the People's Republic of China have views of each other that are not always positive. In addition, there are cultural differences between teachers' beliefs about teaching and learning and parents' beliefs. Teachers are human beings who differ from each other in many significant ways. In elementary school there has been the belief that learner-centered teaching and learning is the most appropriate approach. Pressley (2006) and others have argued strongly that teaching should be balanced. However, student-centered teaching is still quite powerful in elementary grades. Many immigrants, on the other hand, come from backgrounds that hold the teacher to be the center of the learning cycle, the person who has the knowledge that must be transferred to students. The following table contains a number of issues that teachers and immigrant parents often disagree on. In many respects, these polar binaries are reflected in a number of political debates going on in the United States. It would seem that the basic No Child Left Behind view is more similar to the general view of many immigrant students than it is of teachers and educators.

The Chinese secondary students and their parents in the study by Gunderson (2007) viewed teaching and learning differently from many of their teachers. The curriculum was focused on the creation of thinking, critical learners. As Gunderson (2000a) notes, this is a view that is, in effect, a cultural view. Parents of elementary students were also critical of this view. Indeed, Li (2006) described the difficulties occurring between immigrant parents and their children's teachers because of differences in views of teaching and learning. Students often complained: "We waste too much time in school. Too much time not working. Teachers are too lazy they don't tell you what to do (male, Cantonese, 15 years)."

TABLE 3.11 Comparison of Teacher and Parental Beliefs about Teaching and Learning

Teachers	Parents
Teaching should be learner-centered.	The teacher is the source of knowledge and should not be questioned.
Process is more important than product.	Correctness of form is important.
Meaningful language is intact language.	Learning should focus on skills.
Active learning is essential, so students should contribute to discussions and activities.	Students should be told what to learn. It's the teacher who should talk.
Learning should be meaningful.	Learning should involve memorizing.
Speaking, listening, reading, writing, and watching are integrated, mutually reinforcing language activities.	Learning the pieces of language is important.
The aesthetics of language are fundamental.	A focus on grammar is especially important.
Language is functional.	Language is a series of skills to be learned in order.
The learning of content and the learning of language are inseparable.	Content represents a set of facts that should be memorized.
Learning to read and learning to write involve the learning of process.	Learning to read and write means learning phonics, spelling, and how to write. The student should learn to produce a good product.
Error correction does not encourage language acquisition.	Errors should be corrected and students should be aware of their mistakes.
Invented spelling should be encouraged since it fosters language acquisition.	Poor spelling represents poor learning.
Independence in learning is critical. Critical reading and writing are basic.	Students should work on material given to them by the teacher.
Students should ask questions.	The teacher is the source of knowledge and should not be questioned.
Students should explore and attempt to solve problems.	The teacher should show students how to solve problems.
Workbooks are mindless make-work activities.	Practice is viewed as positive evidence that students are learning. The number of items correct is used to judge students' learning.

TABLE 3.11 *continued*

Skills are learned through interaction with good literature, not through explicit teaching.	Important skills are learned through explicit teaching and rote memorization.
Assessment and evaluation should be holistic.	Assessment should focus on how many skills a student has learned.
Problem solving should be deductive, learning should be exploratory.	Problem solving should be taught and students should learn it through induction.

Source: L. Gunderson (2001). Different cultural views of whole language. In S. Boran & B. Comber (Eds.) *Critiquing whole language and classroom inquiry* (p. 252). Urbana-Champaign, IL: National Council of Teachers of English. Copyright © 2001 by the National Council of Teachers of English. Reprinted with permission.

About 90 percent of the students from Hong Kong and Taiwan felt that the schools were not living up to their expectations and that teachers were not "giving" them the knowledge they needed to succeed in getting into university. Entrepreneurs were convinced that teachers had the "product" (knowledge) and that their task, one they were paid to do, was to make certain the students were given the knowledge. This is a product-oriented view of learning. Indeed, students from Hong Kong and Taiwan, but especially those from entrepreneurial families, were convinced that knowledge was a commodity, one composed of a corpus of facts and operations that should be transmitted to students. Doing homework was considered evidence that students were actively attempting to master the knowledge given to them by teachers. Finally, a grade was viewed as evidence of the degree to which students had mastered a set of skills.

Students from the People's Republic of China seemed much more accepting of the teaching and learning going on in the schools. One informant reported to this author that they were more accepting because they were generally from country areas and were somewhat naïve about the world. So what does this all mean for your reading instruction when it comes to students who identify themselves as Chinese, and, for that matter, for your students from other cultural and linguistic backgrounds?

It is important to remember that these observations were derived from local focus groups and they cannot be broadly generalized to other groups. It is also important to remember that there are significant and systematic differences between immigrant groups related to time. First-generation immigrant families often have very different views from fourth- and fifth-generation families. Fifth-generation individuals often have views that are very mainstream in character. Indeed, they often have negative views of new immigrants that are shared across cultural groups.

Culture, Language, and Reading Instruction

The classroom is a complex place where human beings attempt to learn and others attempt to teach. It is not an easy place to work, even though millions of people who should know better think it is. This author has argued that

> There is nothing more frustrating for teachers than to read the constant barrage of negative views promulgated by those who have little or no understanding of the realities of the classroom. The difficulty is that life in the classroom is considerably more demanding and complex than imagined by the armchair critics who believe their simplistic remedies will make it right. Teachers' actions, their personal beliefs, their strategies, their beliefs or theories about teaching and learning, and their ways of viewing the world have subtle but profound effects on their students.
>
> (Gunderson, 2007, pp. 328–329)

The teacher can often change students' lives in significant ways. Students who speak languages other than English and who come from backgrounds that differ culturally in significant ways from their teachers contribute a wonderfully complex diversity that is somewhat like a mosaic, although this author has referred to it as a "cultural slurry" (Gunderson, 2000a). Diversity also represents a significant challenge for teachers when they begin to plan and organize their instructional programs to meet the needs and abilities of their students.

Elementary Classrooms

This author has visited and observed in hundreds, probably thousands, of elementary classrooms, and has done so for about the past 40 years. What is clear is that ESL (ELL) student numbers have increased dramatically. In the 1960s, diversity was often a feature of classrooms in large urban districts, but primarily restricted to the coasts. This is no longer the case. Classrooms across North America are much more diverse than they were in the 1960s. This author has visited classrooms in Idaho, rural California, Louisiana, Connecticut, Saskatchewan, and Washington and has observed large numbers of ESL students. There are interesting pockets of Hmong speakers in Idaho, Arabic speakers in Michigan, Vietnamese speakers in Alberta, and Spanish and Russian speakers in rural Oregon and Washington.

The typical classroom appears to enroll about 30 to 35 students. One of the teacher's first tasks is to assess students' needs and abilities. The measures presented in Chapter 2 are recommended. In addition, as much information as possible should be collected about students' first-language literacy backgrounds. The following scenario is hypothetical and is based on the issues raised by the focus group mentioned earlier. It is not uncommon to find classrooms that have substantial numbers of students from families that have self-identified as Chinese. The assessment mentioned in Chapter 2 should be made for each student in such a class, and the teacher should be aware that many of the students will share some of the cultural views of teaching and learning mentioned above. Those students who have some English skills as measured by either the assessment for very young learners noted in the previous chapter, or have a history of being taught to read in their first languages, should be introduced to print in a way that is culturally appropriate. In the case of Chinese students who have learned to read previously using a sight-word and a rote memorization approach, this author has found that initial instruction should feature a sight-word approach and should focus on important basic vocabulary such as that discussed in Chapter 4. This is antithetical to the major notion developed in this book that teachers should design instruction within their own theoretical notions of what literacy and literacy education are or should be. This suggestion, however, is meant to be a bridge to connect cultures in a meaningful way: the teacher's culture and the student's culture.

Schools are social institutions funded by various governments. Their mandate is to teach what is approved and in ways that are also approved. In essence, they socialize human beings into various communities. Their purpose is to teach skills that will be useful to the society that funds them. Members of the focus group strongly maintained that human beings who identify themselves as Chinese have an educational history that trains them to rely on memory and quotation. They also argued that a focus on originality and analysis is difficult for such immigrants to understand and adopt. Many immigrants from Hong Kong have been socialized in an educational system—and many since they were 3 years old.

Li (2006) argues that teachers "can accommodate minority students' instructional needs in a variety of ways, such as including more systematic phonics instruction, explicit instruction in literacy skills, and homework" (p. 221). She also argues that the teacher can accomplish this task without "abandoning or dismantling" the teacher's model of instruction that may, in fact, be process oriented and meaning centered. She argues, "I suggest that teachers and schools give thoughtful consideration to the implementation of a progressive pedagogy in light of the social, cultural, and linguistic needs of English language learners who come from very different belief systems" (p. 221). The concept of parental input and participation should also be assessed in reference to the cultural features noted above, however, not to the specific conclusions reached by the focus groups, but by groups that represent local viewpoints. The school or school district is probably the agency that should organize such focus groups. Local background information can sometimes lead to astounding conclusions that can inform instruction in significant ways.

Lopez & Gunderson (2006), for instance, investigated the literacy practices and views of parents from Oaxaca, Mexico. Early childhood educators in the United States and Canada argue strongly that parental input and guidance are important in the literacy development of young children. They argue, for instance, that parents should set up home collections of good children's literature. However, Lopez & Gunderson found that poor families in Mexico could not afford to set up home libraries. They also found that Mexican families that could afford to do so opted to purchase workbooks instead. This was clearly related to parents' views of literacy and literacy learning. The suggestion that children be encouraged to go to the local library and borrow good children's literature was also found to be impossible since the library at the time did not have a collection of children's books. These authors also concluded that the notion of going to a library to borrow books was not part of the mindset of the families they studied. They concluded that teachers who have students from Mexico and other Latin American countries should explicitly teach about libraries and the concept of borrowing from libraries.

Early & Gunderson (1993) described how elementary school students could be trained to explore the literacy activities going on in the local school community. They argue that this is a valuable way to find out what literacy activities occur in the community and in students' homes. Their study showed a surprising repertoire of literacy uses in both L1 and L2. It is vital for teachers to be as informed as possible about their students' first cultures to be able to understand what instruction strategies work and don't work.

Many researchers have also argued that effective teachers and school programs are ones that encourage communications between home and school. Often, however, the culture represented by the teacher is different from that of students. Further complicating home–school connection is that teachers often believe they are culture-free. Schmidt & Izzo (2003) quote the teacher who said, "I'm an American; I don't have a culture." Schmidt developed a model she calls the "ABCs of Cultural Understanding," which is based on the notion that getting to know and understand human beings of other cultures is based on coming to know oneself (Schmidt, 1998, 2000, 2001). The process is begun with teachers writing auto-biographies including key details of their lives. These teachers then develop a biography of an individual who is culturally different from them. A comparison is made of similarities and differences between autobiographies and biographies. Schmidt explains that the comparison helps teachers develop a sense of cultural differences and helps them to develop their own self-perceptions of themselves as ethnocentric human beings. These activities help teachers develop plans to make connections with parents. The ABCs of Cultural Understanding and Communication focuses on teachers and homes, while the Early & Gunderson study mentioned above involves students in seeking out literacy connections in their communities. Xu (2000a, b) has also explored this model and found it to be useful in establishing cross-cultural understandings for individuals training to be teachers. Schmidt & Ma (2006) developed a series of strategies desgined to teach students about multicultural differences.

Secondary Classrooms

Life in a Western secondary school reflects in many respects the multiple cultures that are represented there. This author concluded that school cultures "consist, to some degree, of the expected behaviors prescribed by the curriculum guides, and to the multiple cultures within which students have membership" (Gunderson, 2007, p. 262). All students make accommodations to the culture of the school. Immigrant students do not simply become bicultural. Instead, they acquire and reject some features of the new culture, retain and reject some features of their first culture, adapt some features of first culture to second culture, and become socialized into a system that is uniquely individual, imbued with first- and second-cultural features, that is often, but not always, predictable. In many respects this could be referred to as an individual "inter-culture." "For immigrant students who are teenagers learning a new school culture is made more difficult because they do so as human beings whose bodies are filled with the raging hormones of their metamorphosis from children to adults" (Gunderson, 2007, p. 262). They are challenged further by the crisis of their developing and changeable multiple identities.

This author concluded, "School culture constructs the parameters within which students behave, learn, perceive, value, seek friendships, and construct identities" (Gunderson, 2007, p. 263). The irony is that this author found that secondary students wanted to learn English and thought that the best way to do so was to interact with native English speakers. However, for various cultural reasons they could not interact with such students. They concluded that the best way they had found to learn English was to watch television. Chinese students revealed their cultural preferences for learning strategies in a number of ways. One reported, "In Hong Kong all we do, memorize, memorize, memorize, day and night, 5 hours homework every day. In Vancouver all we do is think, think, think, nothing more. It's hard to think when the teacher doesn't tell you what to do" (female, Cantonese, 18 years) (Gunderson, 2000a, p. 695). In many respects this view was predictable for the Chinese students from Hong Kong because attitudes about teaching and learning were revealed by members of the focus group. Local focus groups can reveal vital information for secondary teachers. Indeed, teachers who do not take into account students' cultures will often fail to be successful in teaching them the academic skills they need.

Adult Students

Adults, in many respects, are more difficult as students than younger individuals because they have become more thoroughly inculcated into their first cultures by living in their first societies. Adults are more complex because there are those who need to learn basic English to survive in an English-speaking environment, those who wish to become licensed to practice a profession and must pass a qualifying examination, those who need to learn technical English in order to work in a particular profession such as aeronautical mechanics, those who wish to gain admission to a training institution, a college, or a university to pursue a degree, those who wish to gain admission to a graduate program in an English-speaking institution, or those who wish to pursue a career in a government body in an English-speaking environment.

There are cultural differences that interact negatively with students' learning and teachers' teaching at many different levels. A major problem for individuals from many different first cultures and languages has to do with pause time. North Americans take turns talking when they are communicating in small groups. Most North Americans unconsciously apply rules that govern interactions, although many do not, and often they are considered rude. Pause time is extremely short in such groups. Often if someone is speaking and wishes to pause but not lose a turn speaking, she inserts an "uh" or some other place holder. University-level classes often ask students to work in small groups. Life in a small group can be hell for an adult ESL student because they do not know the rules. In some cultures, pause time is considerably longer than in North America. Students from these cultures, at least until they learn the rules, if they ever do, are not able to engage in typical small-group conversations.

Adult students also face the problem that the English they may have learned in the EFL programs in their home countries was probably quite formal and proper. English speakers use different kinds of language depending upon the communicative context. Students in graduate classes asked to explore an issue in informal communicative contexts use reduced English that the student from, say, Indonesia will find incredibly difficult to understand. The following is an example.

Student A: Jawanna eat?
Student B: Yeah, ja have coin?
Student A: Nah, credit card.
Student B: Let's do it. The Pit?
Student A: Cool.

This author designed a study to test different teaching strategies on the reading comprehension of adult exchange students who spoke various first languages. One of the strategies being tested was DRTA (see the next chapter), which requires learners to predict aloud what happens next in stories. Students from one of the groups mentioned above found it impossible to answer such a question without actually going to the end of the story to find out what happened. They did not want to be wrong. Some told this author in follow-up interviews that individuals from their culture did not want to make a prediction and then turn out to be wrong for a number of interesting reasons. The reader should be able to predict which group this represents from reviewing the cultural features noted by the different focus groups. The group is identified in Chapter 5.

Culture is also important in the choice of materials a teacher selects to use with students as noted previously. In essence, a good English reading teacher must know about and consider culture in designing lessons for students. Not to do so is a significant error in planning.

Culture, Politics, and Reading Instruction

There is the view that teaching and learning are free from politics. Another fairly common assumption is that knowledge is culture-free and teachers are free to teach their students to seek the truth. However, teachers consciously or unconsciously reproduce the political system of domination. Eurocentric views and beliefs form the core of the educational thought that guides curriculum development and instructional practice. While the demographic data indicate that "five out of six people in the world are non-White" and that the "vast majority of the world's population is non-Christian" (Banks, 1991), North American educators appear to view education within a "mainstream" viewpoint, one that focuses on European values and beliefs, even though their school populations are growing increasingly multicultural. Teachers generally hold a view of teaching, learning, and the role of text that is imbued with features of their cultures. This is a problem (see "Critical Literacy" in Chapter 6 (p. 236)).

In countries around the world, teachers are required to teach the approved curricula. It turns out that this is also true in the United States. Many teachers have felt coerced to make pedagogical choices *not* based on their own views of teaching and learning by the outcomes of the No Child Left Behind initiative. In essence, it seems that the ruling party in the United States determined that certain teaching approaches would be rewarded and others would not. The consequences for teachers, schools, school districts, and states that do not teach using the approved materials and approaches is that they do not receive funding. They also face other consequences. So, it is essential that the discussions in the following chapters be contextualized so that they account for the needs and abilities of readers, taking into account their special linguistic and cultural backgrounds, their literacy backgrounds, their English skills, if any, their motivations, and the political climate within which the reader must make such decisions. This is no easy task.

Conclusion and Summary

Culture and cultural differences were discussed in this chapter. An approach to exploring culture was described. It involves organizing focus groups of individuals who self-identify themselves as belonging to a particular group. The focus groups described in this book were asked to brainstorm and come up with descriptions related to geographic origin, religious background, reasons for immigrating, naming system, cultural values, family dynamics, attitudes toward education, significant social patterns, and culturally sensitive teaching approaches.

The reader is again cautioned that the cultural conclusions reached by the focus groups here are not generalizations that can be applied to larger groups since they are in reference to human beings in a specific area of North America. They can be used, however, in other focus groups as points of discussion in other parts of North America. Some might question the relevance to reading and writing of certain of the focus-group categories such as religious background. It is related, however. Gunderson & Anderson (2003), for instance, found that members of a particular first cultural group doubted that the questioning of a text in a reading lesson was a good approach for their children because in their religion the text was not to be questioned, just reproduced orally in a perfect way. Culture is a significant reading variable that will be considered in the chapters that follow. The reader will also be reminded of the choices they have within what is best described as a charged political environment: the classroom.

The reader is also cautioned to consider local cultural differences in the United States and Canada as they relate to literacy, both content and process. There are some activities that may be abhorrent to some groups of parents who are native English speakers and who are not recent immigrants (see the discussion of *Mozert v. Hawkins County Public Schools* in Chapter 1). It is a significant error to assume that culture and cultural views are not factors in the way *all* parents and others perceive and evaluate the instructional programs and practices in which their children are involved. Every human being belongs to multiple cultures which form the lenses through which she or he perceives, evaluates, and judges the teaching and learning going on in classrooms.

The next chapter will contain discussions of the instruction of reading of very young ESL (ELL) students.

Explorations

Work with a partner, if possible.

1. Select a special day such as New Year's Day and compare and contrast the kinds of activities the two of you typically get involved in to celebrate the occasion. If the two of you share a common celebration such as Channukah, Christmas, Diwali, Eid ul-Fitr, Oban, or Vesak, compare the way you and your families celebrate the occasion. How is the way you celebrate the day different from the way your partner celebrates? If you do not share a common special day, choose one and explore how your views differ from your partner's views.
2. Cultural views and practices do differ, sometimes dramatically. Some cultures, for instance, value male children more than they value female children. Female fetuses are aborted in some cases because of this view. When should a cultural view be considered to be negative? In essence, the question is, where do you draw the line between actions that are generally abhorrent and those that are different but acceptable?
3. Students and their families often have different views of teaching and learning than do their teachers. As has been noted in this chapter, such differences often cause difficulties for both teachers and students. Should teachers accommodate students' different cultural views of teaching and learning or should students change their views to fit those of the teacher and the school?
4. Religious beliefs differ even within small communities concerning how students should be taught to read. Some human beings believe that written texts should not be questioned, while questioning is a central focus of many teachers' instructional approaches. In your view, can these two different views be accommodated in classrooms? If so, how?

4

Teaching Young ESL (ELL) Students to Read

Introduction

This chapter presents reading methods, procedures, and programs for young students. The activities are designed for elementary students, but they can be adapted and used with older students who need to learn to read. They can also be adapted for use in the English as a Foreign Language (EFL) classroom. The selection of methods and procedures depends upon what one believes about reading, whether one believes reading is bottom-up, top-down, or interactive. It also, unfortunately, depends upon what may be politically acceptable within particular jurisdictions. Different views are represented in the following discussions and the reader is encouraged to make decisions based on his or her own informed view and philosophy. The reader should keep in mind that Connor *et al.* (2007) conclude that "Many children fail to reach proficient levels in reading only because they do not receive the amount and type of instruction they need" (p. 464). In addition, they note, "Instructional strategies that help one student may be ineffective when applied to another student with different skills" (p. 464). Indeed, they argue that "the impact of any particular instructional strategy appears to depend on children's language and literacy skills" (Connor *et al.*, 2007, accessed at www.sciencemag.org/cgi/content/full/315/5811/464/DC1 on February 2, 2007). This same view guided the development of the 1991 educational heuristics and continues to guide the instructional recommendations that follow.

ESL versus EFL Instruction

As was noted previously, ESL and EFL instructional approaches differ in significant ways. ESL is based on the premise that English is the language of the community and the school and that students have access to English models. EFL is usually learned in environments where the language of the community and the school is not English. EFL teachers have the difficult task of finding access to and providing English models for their students. They do so by including activities involving such instructional aids as movies, magazines, literature, recordings, and other sources of English models. As the number of ESL students has increased in schools across North America, more classrooms and schools have become more like EFL than ESL environments. Indeed, Gunderson, Eddy, & Carrigan (submitted for publication b) studied the learning of English reading skills in schools and classrooms that varied in the number of ESL students. They found evidence that classrooms that had 60 percent or more ESL students achieved lower levels of English reading gains. They concluded that 60 percent was the ESL/EFL boundary. So, if your classroom is more than 60 percent ESL, you have to adjust your teaching strategies to include as many English models as possible. The computer and the Internet may be sources of such models, as will be discussed later in this chapter.

The National Reading and the National Literacy Panels

As was reported in Chapter 1, the findings of the National Reading Panel have been challenged. Overall, however, the following generalizations are cited by many authors, usually with the notion that they *may* also be valid for ESL (ELL) students. They are repeated here to remind the reader what they are, and caution is given to make a judgment about how strongly the reader believes in them.

a) Teaching phonemic awareness to children improves their reading more than instruction that does not have a focus on phonemic awareness.
b) Systematic phonics instruction works best for students in kindergarten to grade 6 and for children who have reading difficulties.
c) Older students receiving phonics instruction were better able to decode words and spell words and to read text orally, but their comprehension of text was not significantly improved.
d) Guided repeated oral reading procedures that included guidance from teachers, peers, or parents had a significant and positive impact on word recognition.
e) The panel found no evidence to suggest that independent silent reading resulted in the improvement of reading.
f) The panel found that instruction in vocabulary resulted in increases in comprehension.
g) The panel concluded that teaching a combination of techniques is the most effective way to improve comprehension.
h) It was concluded that to be most effective, teachers needed to be taught teaching strategies explicitly.

On the other hand, the National Literacy Panel, reviewing studies of ESL instruction, concluded:

a) By and large, for language-minority children, word-level components of literacy (e.g., decoding, spelling) either are or can be (with appropriate instruction) at levels equal to those of their monolingual peers.
b) [However,] this is not the case for text-level skills, like reading comprehension, which rarely approach the levels achieved by their monolingual peers.
c) Language-minority students who are literate in their first languages are likely to be advantaged in the acquisition of English literacy.
d) Language-minority students instructed in their native language (primarily Spanish in this report) as well as English, perform, on average, better on English reading measures than language-minority students instructed only in their second language (English in this case).

And, further, in a related study Slavin and Cheung (2005) concluded that:

a) "The most important conclusion from research comparing the relative effects of bilingual and immersion programs for English learners is that there are too few high-quality studies of this question."
b) [Of the 17 studies that fitted their qualifications] 12 revealed that bilingual education resulted in higher scores, while English immersion resulted in no superior performances.

August & Shanahan (2006) report that the view of those involved in the National Literacy Panel was that the findings of the National Reading Panel were also valid for ESL students, although such students were not included in the studies reviewed by the NRP. However, it is important to keep in mind that Garan (2001) concludes that "the panel's own words have established that the research base in its report on phonics is so flawed that the results do not even matter" (p. 502).

L2 Reading Instruction: The Two-Factor Instructional Matrix

Once students' L1 background and L2 proficiency have been assessed, judgments about instruction can be made. The Two-Factor Instructional Matrix (see Figure 4.1) recommends L1 instruction for 0-level and very limited-English-proficient students. Since this is seldom possible, except in large schools with many students of the same linguistic background, bilingual programs will not be discussed here. There are three categories of students who should not be included in L2 reading instruction. They are 1) those with no L1 literacy and 0-level English proficiency, 2) those with one to two years of L1 literacy and 0-level English ability, and 3) those with no L1 literacy and very limited English proficiency. These students must not be put into L2 reading programs; to do so is to do them a disservice. Findings of the NLP suggest strongly that first-language literacy is related to success in L2 literacy. Some have suggested that these students be placed in phonemic awareness and phonics programs. To put it bluntly, this is simply a bad idea. These students do not know what reading is and their first languages often differ greatly in the phonemes they can perceive and produce. They are almost always doomed to failure if they are included in English phonemic training and/or phonics instruction. This author agrees with Pressley's (2006) notion that many of the features of whole-language instruction are beneficial to beginning readers, in this case to beginning ESL (ELL) readers.

The very most they should be involved in is hearing the teacher read aloud and being immersed in representations of the English language. This view can probably be described as a "readiness" view since it is based on the idea that students have to have some abilities in oral English before they begin to learn to read English. It is important to remember that one of the most robust findings of the National Literacy Panel was that there is a strong relationship existing between oral English ability and success in learning to read English.

Some students can give the impression that they know no English whatsoever (see Gunderson, 2007). On the other hand, they may be able to perform on some

	0-level	Very limited	Limited	Limited fluency
L1 history None	Oral lang. dev.[a]	Oral lang. dev.[a]	Oral lang. dev. a) Printed voc. b) Word banks c) Sentence strps.	Oral lang. dev. a) Printed voc. b) Word banks c) Sentence strps. d) Pers. dicts. e) Active listen. f) Cloze[b] g) LEA h) Immersion[c]
1–2 years	Oral lang. dev.[a]	Oral lang. dev.[a] a) Printed voc. b) Word banks	Oral lang. dev. a) Printed voc. b) Word banks c) Sentence strps. d) Active listen	Oral lang. dev. a) Printed voc. b) Word banks c) Sentence strps. d) Pers. dicts. e) Active listen. f) Cloze[b] g) LEA h) Immersion[c] i) Basal DRA (L2)
3+ years	Oral lang. dev.[a] a) Printed voc. b) Word banks	Oral lang. dev. a) Printed voc. b) Word banks c) Sentence strps.	Oral lang. dev. a) Printed voc. b) Word banks c) Sentence strps. d) Cloze[b] e) Active listen. f) LEA g) Immersion[c]	Oral lang. dev. a) Printed voc. b) Word banks c) Sentence strps. d) Pers. dicts. e) Active listen. f) Cloze[b] g) LEA h) Immersion[c] i) Basal DRA (L2)

[a]L1 instruction recommended
[b]Cloze instruction beginning with sentences and progressing to passages
[c]DRTA, L1 and L2 USSR, hearing L1 and L2 reading, etc.

Figure 4.1 The Two-Factor Elementary Instructional Matrix

of the measures on the "readiness" test described in the last chapter. Scores on this test can suggest that they be involved in very basic English reading recognition tasks. Since the test consists of items believed to represent readiness skills, they can be used to teach students directly. Reference scores are presented in the Appendix. Some whole-language advocates disagree with the point of view that some students should not be involved in reading instruction. Their approach will be discussed later in this chapter.

The overall goal of all instruction suggested in this book is to provide comprehensible input for students who differ significantly in their English skills and literacy learning backgrounds. No other question is more important than "is this lesson comprehensible for Maria or Tiong, or Rupinder?"

Primary Students

Students' scores on the primary assessment shown in the Appendix can be used to begin to determine whether they should be included in direct reading instruction or not. Students who meet the criteria for inclusion in instruction can be placed as very limited speakers with one to two years' L1 experience. Of course, if an individual student has trouble with the reading content, then explicit reading vocabulary instruction should be ceased. The criteria are somewhat fuzzy, but generally for those who are administered the whole battery of subtests, a score of 0-19 indicates that the student is essentially 0-level English, 30-64 suggests a very limited or extremely low level of English ability, and 65-94 indicates that a student is ready to begin English reading vocabulary instruction.

A number of teachers have had success using scores from only a few of the subtests. More detailed information will be given in the Appendix, including subtest criteria.

Introducing Print

Discovering an elementary student's L1 literacy background is usually fairly simple. Parents, brothers, sisters, or relatives are usually good sources for this information. In some situations, however, as was mentioned earlier, L1 literacy background cannot be determined. In these rare cases the best approach is to assume the student has no L1 literacy background and place him or her in the "None" category of L1 history. The shaded area represents the instructional sequencing for students with no L1 background or unknown L1 backgrounds. Therefore, they receive oral-language development until they become limited English proficient and are then introduced to print. It is vital that they not be forced into formal reading activities until they acquire basic oral English. Any formal reading instruction in English will not be comprehensible.

This is especially important for very young students, who face the task of learning English and also learning to read English. Again, they *should not be included* in phonemic awareness programs or in phonics programs. The basic principle is that 0-level students and students of very limited English proficiency should not be included in activities that require them to have some metacognitive notion of English.

Two categories of students are "ready" to be introduced to printed words: the 0-level English-proficient student with three or more years of L1 literacy, and the student of very limited English proficiency with one to two years of L1 literacy instruction. Two procedures are extremely effective with them: print immersion and word banks. Indeed, both methods appear to help them learn oral English.

Print Immersion

Teachers who immerse students in print fill their classrooms with labels. Every desk has a name printed on it. Windows, pencil sharpeners, water fountains, walls, doors, the chalkboard—everything has a label. The teacher constantly refers to the labels and to the items.

Teacher: Class, we are ready to go outside. What is this, Amelia? (Points to the door.) Yes, you are right, this is the door. (Points to the label.)

Every opportunity is taken to draw students' attention to the print around the room. In the beginning of this process, the teacher points to the word and says, for instance, "'Door,' this says 'door.' What does this say? Yes, this says 'door.'" In this manner the teacher provides a model and reinforces correct responses. Students in such situations actually use the labels to remember the new words they learn. As students progress, the teacher allows them to provide the answer but immediately provides positive feedback, as in the example of Amelia shown above.

Word Banks

As students begin to learn that print represents language, they begin to want to know how to read specific words. In this case, each student is provided with a word bank, including such items as large milk cartons, cigar boxes (although these are now rare), large manila folders, and one-pound coffee cans. The teacher visits each student and begins the session with a review of the words already in the word bank and adds more.

Teacher: Good morning, Juan. Tell me what your words are. Here, what are these words? (Points to words.)
Juan: *Transformer, dinosaur, lunch, kickball, Christmas.* (The teacher echoes each time Juan is correct to provide positive feedback.)
Teacher: Excellent, you read all of your words correctly. What new words would you like to read?
Juan: *Elephant, Santa Claus.* (The teacher carefully prints Juan's new words and rehearses them with him.)
Teacher: This is *elephant,* good, *elephant.* What is this word? Yes, it's *elephant.* This new word is *Santa Claus.* What is this word? Yes, it's *Santa Claus.*

The teacher takes every opportunity to reinforce orally students' correct responses. These two methods are extremely effective in introducing students to print. The printed word often helps them learn oral English. In fact, such students look around the room for the word they want in particular situations. Word walls are also ways to immerse students in vocabulary and will be described later in this chapter.

Sentence Strips

Students of very limited English proficiency with three or more years of L1 instruction and the students of limited English proficiency with no L1 history should also be involved in the activities noted above. In addition, they profit from a limited form of the Language Experience Approach (LEA), the sentence strip.

Many teachers use 24-inch oak-tag strips, standard teaching material found in many elementary schools, to write students' sentences. The process is very similar to the one mentioned above.

Teacher: Good morning, Carlo. How are you? Today we are going to make some sentences. Do you have any you would like to know how to read?

Carlo: "The robots are fighting." (The teacher writes the sentence.)

Teacher: This says, "The robots are fighting." (The teacher passes her finger under the words as she reads them.) What does this say?

Carlo: "The robots are fighting."

Teacher: Yes. "The robots are fighting." Good.

The student can also be asked to form sentences out of the words found in her or his word bank; the oral reinforcement is vital. Producing sentences with words from the word bank allows students to manipulate words and sentences. Both the word bank and the sentence strips are valuable language development records. Holes punched in the ends of the sentence strips allow them to be stored on pegs or hooks in the wall. They represent a rich record of each student's language development. The sentence strips are practiced on a regular basis in a similar manner to the words in the word bank. Indeed, they can be used as evidence in student portfolios.

The activities presented so far are fairly top-down in nature. The thoroughly skills-based individual usually wishes to begin teaching students phonics skills. However, the students we have discussed so far are generally unable to cope with learning phonics and related skills, because it appears to require too much metacognitive knowledge about language. Such skills instruction may only be appropriate for older students, those who have the ability to monitor their own language learning in a way that makes phonics instruction meaningful. Teachers who are convinced their students should learn such skills must be patient and not initiate instruction until students have limited fluency in English and have been in L2 programs for at least three years. It is particularly difficult for students with these backgrounds to be asked to segment words phonemically or to sound out words.

The Alphabet

Forty years ago or so the conventional wisdom was that students who started school at 5 or 6 years of age who knew the names of the letters of the alphabet were more successful in learning to read than those who did not. The success of *Sesame Street* on television has been that many more students come to school with this skill than previously. Many immigrant students arrive with the knowledge of the alphabet in their first languages, or a substantial repertoire of sight characters, and, astoundingly, a substantial proportion appear to know the names of the letters of the Roman alphabet, at least partially, in English (Gunderson, 2007). The 0-level English-proficient student with three or more years of L1 literacy and the student of very limited English proficiency with one to two years of L1 literacy instruction should be included in instruction that teaches them the names of the letters of the alphabet, but *not* their corresponding symbol-sound relationships. Immersion in print should include models of the alphabet. There are good cultural reasons to involve these students in activities designed to teach them the names of the alphabet. The activity does represent a kind of rote memorization approach that is highly valued by the members of some cultures. Very young students also love to learn and to sing the alphabet song and memorize poems about the alphabet.

There are probably hundreds of alphabet books that are helpful for students. A sample listing of alphabet books is available at http://www.literatureforliterature. ecsd.net/alphabet_books.htm (accessed on February 11, 2007). There are a number of other websites that contain listings of alphabet books and related activities. However, be aware that many of them are commercial in nature.

Active Listening

The classrooms described so far are filled with print. Printed words and sentences are used to name and describe items surrounding the students and their own interests; and interests can be learned from the results of an interest inventory of the kind described in Chapter 2. The student who has limited English proficiency and one to two years of L1 literacy instruction knows what print represents and can produce basic, even though limited, English syntactic structures. He is able to begin to monitor, and benefit from the monitoring in an active sense, English in print. Indeed, he is able to make predictions about English. "Active listening" is designed to encourage and involve students in using their new knowledge of the structure of English. Depending upon their oral-language program, this activity should not be entirely new. The following activities are based on findings of a study by Walters and Gunderson (1985). Even though this is an old study, its findings are significant.

Walters and Gunderson (1985) studied the effects of listening to stories read aloud in L1 and L2 on L2 reading achievement. Parent volunteers were trained to be good readers of stories in Chinese or English. Randomly selected Cantonese-speaking fourth-grade ESL students 1) heard stories read aloud in Chinese for two periods of 40 minutes each week, 2) heard stories read aloud in English for two periods of 40 minutes each week, or 3) were involved in homework sessions for two periods of forty minutes each week. At the end of the 16-week study the students who heard Chinese stories scored as well on an English reading achievement test as did those who heard English stories. Having a parent volunteer and the right materials to be read aloud in L1 to students is an excellent approach to help teach students that print represents language. It also has the added benefit of exposing students to their first cultures. Active listening is not a quiet activity; therefore, one must be prepared for a great deal of oral interaction.

Active listening proceeds as follows:

1. The teacher selects material that is interesting to the students. Wordless picture books are wonderful for these activities, as are "big books."
2. Active listening is an activity that works well with individual students or with small groups.
3. The story is read aloud in sections. If possible, read so that the students can watch the print. Indeed, if possible, print should be tracked with a finger or a pointer.

4. At strategic points—for example, when something is about to happen—the reading is stopped and students are asked, "What do you think is going to happen next?" followed by "What makes you think so?"

A school librarian can help to find good books for active listening activities. Parents can be taught to conduct active reading exercises in those schools with L1 collections. The amount of oral language generated is incredible. Active listening encourages students to make predictions during reading, one of the cornerstones of the psycholinguistic model. The heuristic identifies those students who are equipped to participate. Active listening is an excellent activity to foster prediction and comprehension. However, there are times when the teacher should read aloud and not interrupt the reading to ask questions.

The Teacher Reading Aloud

ESL students need to have access to models of the English language in order to learn it. In many classrooms, access is limited to their teacher (see "ESL versus EFL Instruction" at the beginning of this chapter). Reading aloud in an uninterrupted fashion is a superb way for a teacher to model oral English, good oral reading, and enthusiasm for books and for reading. Hearing the teacher read aloud provides students with good models of pronunciation, intonation, and expression. Indeed, some have argued that it can help to develop phonemic awareness in English (see Yopp, 1995). Some teachers have a natural ability at expressive reading aloud, while others do not, but can develop it.

Trelease (2006) has published a sixth edition of his highly acclaimed *The read-aloud handbook*, which guides teachers and parents to become good oral readers for their students/children. He also has a website that is a good resource to explore at http://www.trelease-on-reading.com/rah.html (accessed on January 15, 2007). The International Reading Association (IRA) has published since 1974 booklists called *Children's choices*. The booklists are based on recommendations by teachers, librarians, and parents; however, the lists comprise the books checked out of libraries by students. The lists from 1998 to the present are available at http://www. reading.org/resources/tools/choices_childrens.html (accessed on January 15, 2007). The IRA also publishes *Teachers' choices* (accessed on January 21, 2007 at http://www.reading.org/resources/tools/choices_teachers.html) and *Young adults' choices* (accessed on January 21, 2007 at http://www.reading.org/resources/tools/ choices_young_adults.html). Sullivan (2004) published *The children's literature lover's book of lists* for students from preschool through sixth grade. It includes online resources to explore children's literature.

Technology has made it possible to involve students in hearing text read aloud. The computer can display reading material and the students can listen to it read aloud. This is a kind of active listening because the words are highlighted as they are read. It is not as interactive as actively listening with a teacher (see, for instance, www.bookbox.com, accessed on January 25, 2007) but is a positive way for students, normally one at a time in a listening center, to hear good oral reading and not rehearse oral errors. There are a number of different computer-based programs that turn printed text into oral text. However, the teacher must make certain not to use one that turns text into monotonous, computer-sounding oral language (see, for instance, www.readplease.com, accessed on January 25, 2007). The free trial versions of read-aloud programs appear to sound more robot-like than the commercial versions.

There are also a number of available commercial software programs that turn spoken language into print. Dragon NaturallySpeaking, for instance, produces software that allows PC users to input voice data into their computers and have their utterances changed into print (see http://www.nuance.com/naturallyspeaking/home/, accessed on February 11, 2007). This program requires that the user practice text so that his or her speech can be recognized and turned into print. Reeder *et al.* (2007) have studied the use of a program developed at Carnegie-Mellon University called the Reading Tutor with ESL (ELL) students. It involves students in activities in English (to be described in detail later in this chapter). One of the digital recorders this author uses for research purposes allows one to make digital recordings, input them into a computer, and then have them transcribed into text in eight different languages. Uses for these kinds of resources are discussed later in this book.

Cloze Activities

The cloze procedure can be used as an instructional activity to help students learn to read. One must be cautious, however, since cloze work can become extremely tedious and boring for students. Indeed, adult native English speakers have difficulty, especially with material like the "Missionaries" passage presented in Chapter 2. Both L1 and L2 language students find that too much cloze work is tedious.

CLOZE SENTENCES

All of the students remaining in the heuristic are equipped to deal with cloze activities. A good approach is to begin with sentences and proceed to paragraphs, being careful not to present students with cloze passages that are too taxing. Since this use of cloze is instructional, it is not necessary to stick to the deletion of every fifth word. Thus, the deletion pattern can vary in many ways. A typical cloze sentence is

Reg came to school today with his sister and his ———.

In this case, the teacher knew Reg. She was attempting to get him to be able to recognize—that is, "read"—the word *brother*. "Maze-like" alternatives may also be used.

We went to the zoo and saw giraffes, bears, and ———.

figs
was
elephants

The cloze sentence can be written on a sentence strip, with individual students asked to use their word banks to find words that will fit into the deleted slot. For students who have difficulty with cloze, visual hints can be provided by either changing the size of the deletions to match the size of the word or drawing in the word shape.

The little ⌐⟋ ran through the woods after the deer.

> after
> boy
> running

Sets of cloze sentences can be written to include particular classes of words so that students get practice with them. According to student needs, such cloze exercises as "article-deleted," "helper-verb-deleted," "pronoun-deleted," or "content-word-deleted" sentences can be used to focus on particular skills.

When cloze passages are introduced to students, they should not be any more than about half a page in length; nor should students be involved in too many cloze exercises. Very short stories with clear-cut beginnings and endings make the best passages. One very clever approach is to take a Language Experience (see "Language Experience Approach," p. 132) generated story and turn it into a cloze activity. This is done by writing the LEA story on chart paper and having target words covered up by flaps of paper with masking-tape hinges. Students read the text, make their prediction, and lift the flap to see if they are correct. The more advanced students can work in small groups. They should be encouraged to discuss their predictions.

Cloze exercises should not be used too often, nor should they be too long. A study conducted with ESL adults found that students became fatigued very quickly with cloze exercises. Indeed, the typical cloze activity was too difficult unless material was short (no more than a page) and *at least* two years below students' reading levels (Gunderson, 1989, 1995). Many skill-building workbooks use cloze or cloze-like activities to teach or develop comprehension skills. They too become tedious and boring after a time. Such workbooks are used across the grade levels and also with adults. However, they turn out to be quite deadly if overused.

Small-group work involving students' own sentence strips and word banks can be an exciting activity. In this case students use word bank words to substitute for blanks on the sentence strips. They should discuss their choices. These activities are good in small doses with material that is at least two years below students' reading levels.

Personal Dictionaries

The limited-fluency individual is quite adept at using English. Indeed, in many cases he knows what he needs to learn. He will ask how to spell a word or what a particular English word means. This student is ready for a personal dictionary. The personal dictionary can be made of heavy construction paper for covers and newsprint for pages. Elaborately bound books with blank pages purchased at the local bookstore are also quite popular. Tabs on the ends of pages show the alphabetic divisions. The procedures are fairly straightforward.

Donna: How do I spell "important"? (Has her personal dictionary.)
Teacher: Can you tell me what letter the word might begin with? Yes, it starts with *i*, so find the right page. It's *i-m-p-o-r-t-a-n-t*. (Donna writes the word in her dictionary.) What other words do you have on your *i* page?
Donna: *igloo, in, into.*
Teacher: Excellent, you remembered all your words on the *i* page.

It is amazing how useful the personal dictionary can be. Often, a student will ask how to spell a particular word and the teacher knows her students so well that she simply responds, "It's in your personal dictionary." And it is! Personal dictionaries are well used; laminated covers last longer. The best type of personal dictionary is capable of having pages added as the old ones are filled.

It is also possible for individual students to develop independently their own personal dictionaries by accessing online versions to seek out words on their own. A student's online dictionary can be found at http://wordcentral.com/aol/index. html (accessed on February 11, 2007). This is a simple site that provides definitions, word etymology, and a number of other activities. There will be a more extensive discussion of dictionary resources later in this book (see Chapter 5). Personal dictionaries can be created and maintained in word processing programs on computers. Popular resources for older ESL students are personal electronic bilingual dictionaries. Many include a pronunciation guide, a definition, and an audio reproduction of words.

The Language Experience Approach (LEA)

No other method is recommended as often for ESL (ELL) students as is the Language Experience Approach. The LEA is appropriate for students who have three or more years of L1 literacy instruction and who are limited-English or limited-fluency speakers with one or more years of L1 literacy instruction. The LEA is briefly discussed in Chapter 1. It is a fairly natural extension of work with word banks and sentence strips. The basic approach is the same:

1. Individual students or groups are asked to relate stories to the teacher. The stories may be about their experiences in or out of class. The teacher often provides experiences for students through field trips on which they acquire a great deal of background information to help them comprehend L2 stories (see the "DRTA" subsection a little later in this chapter).
2. Students' stories are recorded verbatim without changes or corrections. Correcting students tends to make LEA a negative experience and should be avoided. The teacher acts as a recorder and nothing more.
3. The student reads the story aloud. The teacher also reads the story aloud. In this manner the student begins to recognize words that are new to him.

4. A few days after it has been dictated, the story should be reread and discussed. If the student dictated new and difficult words, they should be written on flashcards and made part of his ever-expanding word bank. They should also be practiced.
5. Individual students' dictations are stapled into book form—a valuable record of their development. Students have very positive feelings about producing their own texts.
6. Students rehearse their stories and read them to the teacher, to their friends, to small groups of students, or to the whole class.

LEA is rather time-intensive for teachers, but the computer makes dictation somewhat easier. Indeed, when students become able to use the computer themselves, they can begin to use word processing programs that free them from the sometimes painful task of manual writing. There are a number of programs, however, that allow the teacher to dictate stories into the computer to be translated into print that save a great deal of time. Dragon NaturallySpeaking, for instance, changes a spoken text into written text at normal spoken-language speed (Nuance Communication, Inc., 2007). The program in essence learns to recognize a speaker's voice and is able to turn it into written text that is compatible with standard word processing programs. This approach makes the teacher's task considerably more efficient.

Class Language Experience Activities

There are many variations possible in LEA. One may wish to produce a class LEA or have small groups of students make dictations. Fields trips, school assemblies, visits by sports stars or police officers, the first snowfall of winter, the school fair, a storm, school holidays, significant news events, and so on are all experiences shared by students. The teacher leads the discussion, attempts to clarify ideas, and makes notes on a chart or on the chalkboard. After the subject has been discussed, students begin to dictate the story. At this point, suggestions and comments about such matters as form can be made. The story is read aloud by the teacher, by individual students, and by the class as a whole. LEA stories can be organized so that they share a theme—for example, all the animal stories. These are used over and over again as they are read by students. Digital video recorders can be used to record such activities. However, one must be concerned about issues related to privacy and confidentiality since digital images can find their way to the Internet and can be changed. Online wiki space is available at no cost to teachers, but discretion is essential when student-developed material is concerned.

Vocabulary Practice and LEA

LEA stories generate many vocabulary words that are new to students. It is the teacher's task to make sure they learn to recognize them. Group stories can be copied onto individual sentence strips and individual vocabulary cards and can be used as flashcards with small groups or single students. The practice should always be positive and should reinforce students' correct productions. Students can match individual words on cards with the text on the wall chart or they can match and read individual sentences. Some teachers tape vocabulary cards all over their classrooms, turning them into veritable dictionaries. This activity has been called "The Word Wall" (Green, 2003). Everyday words are added and old ones are practiced via the teacher pointing to them and asking someone what they are, repeating the correct words, and having the whole class recite them. Students actively vie for the chance of adding a new word. Green indicates that a good activity is for the teacher to say something like "I am thinking of a word that means extremely happy." The student's task is to find and read the correct word.

Immersion

Students with limited English who have three or more years of L1 literacy and all limited-fluency students benefit from many reading activities, such as Directed Reading-Thinking (DRTA), Uninterrupted Sustained Silent Reading (USSR), and hearing L1 and L2 stories read aloud. The reader is reminded that the National Reading Panel concluded that *instruction in vocabulary resulted in increases in comprehension* and that *teaching a combination of techniques is the most effective way to improve comprehension.*

Directed Reading-Thinking (DRTA)

Stauffer (1971) proposed that the typical reading lesson did not encourage students to use their natural abilities to make and confirm predictions as they read, so he developed DRTA to encourage such activities. There are several versions of DRTA. The following has been developed and used with ESL students ranging from kindergarten to adult level (Gunderson, 1995).

Active, enthusiastic prediction is the most salient feature of DRTA. Student each receive a copy of the material to be read. They should not have seen the material before. They also receive an opaque cover that each student uses to cover the first page, uncovering only the sections indicated. If students cannot do this procedure, then the story can be displayed by an overhead or digital projector and the teacher uncovers parts for the group. This system works especially well when there are students who are unable to resist the temptation to peek ahead at the story. During the DRTA the teacher asks only three questions:

What do you think this story is about?
What do you think will happen next?
What makes you think so?

Surprisingly, many teachers find it difficult to ask only these three questions, but it is better not to yield to temptation and ask other questions. They should be saved to ask after DRTA if the students appeared to have missed something essential.

The DRTA begins with the teacher asking students to uncover the title.

Meeting in the Night

What do you think this story is about?
What makes you think so?

A typical response is that the story is about spies or crooks, because such people would meet at night. All predictions are accepted.

The author's name is then uncovered:

by
Isaac Asimov

The moment the name of the author is seen, readers usually change their prediction to something having to do with science or, more likely, with science fiction. An individual's background knowledge is a powerful force in reading comprehension. Obviously, predictions would change if the author's name were Harold Robbins, Danielle Steele, Agatha Christie, or Monica Hughes.

Then some text is uncovered:

Meeting in the Night

by
Jane Doe

I have waited for nineteen years. Sometimes the clock ticking on the wall just outside my door echoes in my brain. I wait and wait, patiently watching the door, watching for him to return. As the sun sets, darkness and all the fears it brings return. The ancient building cools with the night and brings new sounds as wood and cement contract and strain against each other. Their sounds are intermittent. They both frighten me and give me hope. Is that him at the door, or is it just this damnable building?

What is this story about?
What makes you think so?
What do you think will happen next?
What makes you think so?

Typically, such responses as "It's about an insane asylum" or "It's about a political prisoner" are reported. Individuals also report that the woman will continue to wait, or she will be broken out, etc. The responses reveal readers' deep levels of comprehension, interest, and motivation. Teachers are often amazed at the depth of understanding students express during DRTA.

DRTA works well using wordless picture books. ESL students also benefit from the use of predictable books. Students sometimes spontaneously read sections aloud to confirm their predictions, often going back to the text from previous pages. This author wants to remind you that the sample story above was written for you, the reader, not for ESL students. The first task is to find good stories. The reader can be guided by the work of others such as Saccardi (1996a, b).

The following are some questions that teachers may ask concerning DRTA and some answers this author has found helpful (Gunderson, 1989, 1995):

Question: Is DRTA a reading program?

Answer: DRTA is a valuable addition to a reading program, but it is not a complete reading program.

Question: How often should I use DRTA?

Answer: It depends, of course, on your class. Once a week is quite effective.

Question: Is DRTA effective?

Answer: DRTA is very effective in developing higher-level comprehension skills. The first time one attempts DRTA, it often doesn't work well, because both the teacher and the class are uncertain of the procedures. It takes some time for the students to realize they can make incorrect predictions and not be wrong.

Question: Do I do DRTA with a whole class?

Answer: It is possible. However, DRTA appears to work best with groups of about ten. As students become more willing to volunteer predictions, it gets more difficult to manage them in a large group. There is always a marvelous metacognitive feature of reading during DRTA, evidenced by students saying such things as "You were right . . ." or "See, I told you so . . ."

Question: How can I use DRTA with very poor readers?

Answer: ESL students who are able to produce basic English syntactic structures but are unable to read well can listen as the teacher reads the passages aloud. It is amazing how well they are able to make predictions. This is a very fine method for motivating conversation.

Question: How do I find passages?

Answer: Old reading texts are good sources. Old reading kits also contain many short appropriate passages. Predictable books are excellent for ESL students (see below).

Question: What do I do about the reading problems I might observe during the DRTA exercise? Do I stop and teach the skills I see are missing?

Answer: No! This form of DRTA is dedicated to comprehension and critical reading. Nothing should interfere with students making predictions and supporting them. If it is apparent that students are having trouble with particular skills, teach them later. The only exception would be a word that *no one* in the group can read which makes a significant difference in the comprehension of the story.

Both teachers and students become addicted to this exciting prediction activity. It works well in many different situations. Indeed, some teachers use it in conjunction with television and soap operas. Adult students love to make predictions about the stories they watch. Other teachers use movies as the basis of the DRTA. In this case, different skills can be focused on, such as looking for actions and predicting what will happen next.

DRTA: A CAUTION

The foundation of DRTA as an instructional strategy in reading is that it fosters critical thinking and prediction. However, there are members of different cultural groups who find the production of critical readers inappropriate. These groups are not necessarily immigrants; see the discussion in Chapter 1 of *Mozert v. Hawkins County Public Schools*. The reader who intends to teach students in countries outside of North America should also become aware of local views of teaching and learning and of the role of reading. However, the teacher should also be aware of local views in North America as well.

Uninterrupted Sustained Silent Reading

Uninterrupted Sustained Silent Reading (USSR) or Sustained Silent Reading (SSR) makes use of a regularly scheduled block of time during which students and teachers read silently books they have selected. The teacher must provide a good model for students and therefore must be seen as actively enjoying the session. This means the teacher doesn't watch students or correct math papers. Often, whole schools set aside the same time block for USSR and everyone participates, including the principal, the secretary, and the custodian. The adults provide positive reading models. What they do after USSR is also vitally important. The teacher should share with students his or her love of reading and in particular how he or she is enjoying a particular book. Reading aloud a favorite part of a book and encouraging students to do likewise is essential to the positive modeling of reading.

Often, primary teachers have difficulty with students when USSR is first introduced, because some students cannot read silently; instead they "mumble"-read (Cunningham, 1978). They should not be forced to be quiet. After being involved in USSR for a time, they will learn to read silently. Some USSR programs fail because teachers and clerical staff are not really reading but are watching students; or there are not enough reading materials available (McCracken & McCracken, 1978). Teachers must have enough interesting materials for students to select. If students are literate in their first languages, they should be encouraged to read L1 material during USSR.

Some teachers believe that L1 activities interfere with the learning of English. There is no real evidence to suggest this is true. Indeed, as was noted earlier, Walters and Gunderson (1985) found that L1 activities did not interfere with achievement in English. After the publication of this study, the local school libraries began to stock L1 books. They report that both interest and circulation rose after doing so. Using a school district's L1 collection allows students to read about and share their own cultures with other students. It is a very motivating activity. An alternative to

USSR is for the teacher to choose to read aloud for a designated period each day (see above).

Although the National Reading Panel did not find strong evidence to support USSR, they did conclude:

> The available data do suggest that independent silent reading is not an effective practice when used as the only type of reading instruction to develop fluency and other reading skills, particularly with students who have not yet developed critical alphabetic and word reading skills.
>
> (NICHD, p. 13)

Basal Reading Instruction

The activities described so far have been mostly top-down in nature. This section describes skills-based activities that are appropriate for students of limited fluency who have L1 or L2 literacy backgrounds. There are many authorities who would recommend that basal readers never be used. (The most intense form of criticism has been referred to by McCallum, 1988, as "basal bashing.") But there are situations in which one may be required by a school district or school principal to use them, or there is no other available material. As a result of the implementation of the Reading First Act in the United States, many teachers have found themselves compelled to use basal readers, often scripted reading programs. Unfortunately, many students will have L2 literacy backgrounds involving basal readers, and in most cases, sadly, the experience has been a negative one.

As was noted previously, good children's literature became especially popular with teachers in the 1980s and into the 1990s until the Reading Wars kicked in and many critics argued that direct phonics instruction was the preferred way to teach students to read. The 2000s brought calls for instruction to be systematic and scripted. Some argued that reading instruction should be balanced. Basal readers still exist and large publishers have attempted to keep their programs salable.

As was noted in Chapter 1, a basal series is designed within a skills-based model of reading. Basal readers provide "for developmental sequences of phonics skills, word-recognition skills, comprehension skills, and so on" (Aukerman, 1981, p. 11). Basal vocabulary, as was noted before, is controlled so that only words occurring at a high frequency in the general lexicon are used; only a few words are introduced at a time; words are repeated often to ensure they are learned; and words are not encountered in text until they have been introduced.

Basal reading series usually prescribe the Directed Reading Activity or Approach (DRA) to teach individual lessons. DRA in this situation involves 1) a discussion of story background, 2) the introduction of new vocabulary, 3) guided reading, 4) story follow-up activities, and 5) related skills development. The lesson plan described here is the DRA-L2 developed by Gunderson (1985). Scripted programs have recently been adopted by many school districts in the United States. They will be described later in this chapter.

The Directed Reading Activity (DRA-L2)

STEP 1: STORY BACKGROUND AND VOCABULARY

Reading comprehension depends, in part, on the reader's background knowledge and experience (Bransford & Johnson, 1978; Anderson *et al.*, 1977; Mandler & Johnson, 1977). In the DRTA example previously demonstrated, we discussed how changing the author's name would have a profound effect on comprehension and students' predictions of story outcome. Betts (1946) noted that "the pupils should be prepared for the reading of a given selection" (p. 430). Background knowledge is vital for ESL students' comprehension (Carrell, 1981; Hudson, 1982), and DRA provides for background knowledge by developing students' familiarity with the subject of a story. ESL students also face the added burden of not knowing a great number of vocabulary words. This is particularly true when they are expected to read about something that is not found within their own culture—say Thanksgiving, for example. Indeed, they lack a knowledge of customs, idiomatic terms, and genre-specific vocabulary. Unfortunately, the DRA usually involves vocabulary instruction in isolation, or "providing pupils with the new words in each lesson in chalkboard work just prior to reading in their pupil book" (Aukerman, 1981a, p. 11). The DRA-L2 attempts to integrate background and vocabulary introduction.

The first step is to assess four areas of vocabulary in reference to the story students will read. The following items are noted: 1) new vocabulary, 2) context-dependent vocabulary (for example, "pilot" in a story about ships means something different than in a story about airplanes), 3) genre-specific vocabulary, and 4) idiomatic vocabulary within the structure of the story. The following example was taken from a third-grade classroom in which students were being introduced to a basal story about a "school fair." (See R.B. Ruddell, C. Adams, & B. Taylor, *Surprises and Prizes*, Boston: Allyn & Bacon, 1978, pp. 1-16.)

Before the lesson, the story was mapped and an outline containing the main narrative elements in chronological order was produced. The resulting structural units resemble typical story grammar elements (see Mandler & Johnson, 1977; Rumelhart, 1975; Stein & Glenn, 1979; Thorndyke, 1977). Vocabulary is ordered according to occurrence in the story, providing a set of expectations to guide passage comprehension. Illustrations are used as cues to meaning. The story structure looks like this:

1. Introduction: Family on its way to a fair.
2. Family arrives at fair: Introduction of fair features.
3. Family buys tickets to the fair: Buying features.
4. Family sees a high-wire show: High-wire features.
5. High-wire incident: Incident features.
6. Conclusion: Family jumps on net.

The teacher's guide lists 34 new vocabulary words to be introduced: *no, this, want, dad, Dave, miss, mom, fair, hurry, library, people, books, but, here, need, now, dime, win, Bell, Day, prize, ticket, jump, jumped, looked, Mrs., show, so, that, bike, fell, Ling, net,* and *Rose.* The words *fair, no, Dave, miss, mom, dad, this, hurry,* and *want* are found in the introductory section of the story, and so they should be taught first. The lesson begins in a typical DRA fashion, except that the new words and background information are integrated.

Teacher: Today we are going to read a story about a fair. (Holds up the word *fair* printed on an oak-tag strip, repeats it once, and places it into a pocket chart.) Does anyone know what a *fair* is? (Points to the word.) These are fairs. (Reveals several pictures of fairs and leads discussion of fairs.) Tiong, what is this word? (Points to the word *fair.*) Can you use it in a sentence?
Tiong: Fair. We had a school *fair.*
Teacher: Excellent, Tiong. The word is *fair.* Everyone, what is this word?

This first phase of the DRA-L2 focuses on word meanings integrated into a story or passage structure. The "fair" introduction, for instance, began with a discussion of the word *fair* and continued with the development of the first story segment, a family hurrying to a fair.

Teacher: The story today is about a fair. Dave (shows flashcard) and his mom (shows flashcard) are going to a fair (points to the word). Can someone tell me what *mom* means?
Julia: It's your mother.
Teacher: Excellent, Julia. Yes, *mom* is another word for *mother.*

Students are made aware of the words as visual units. The subtle introduction of words as visual units often helps them to remember word meanings. That is, the printed form helps the reader remember what the words are so they can concentrate on what they mean. Obviously, one should not introduce 34 words to students all at once. The teacher must judge how many words they are capable of learning and remembering. Since the words are related to particular story elements, one could limit one day's activities to one story segment.

The second phase of step 1 represents a shift in emphasis from the teaching of word meanings to the teaching of word recognition. Again, the procedure involves retention of the structure of the story, beginning with the first words that were already encountered and progressing sequentially through story elements.

Teacher: Can anyone remember this word? (Shows *fair.*)
Ricardo: That's *fair.*
Teacher: Yes, this is *fair.* (Moves finger from left to right under the word.) We know this word means a place with rides, shows, tents, and prizes. What is this word? (Students repeat the word *fair* individually and in unison.)

The word-recognition exercise can be best summed up as **Flash, Recite, Reinforce; Flash, Recite, Reinforce, and Practice.**

The teacher's task in step 1 is threefold: 1) to help students acquire word meanings, 2) to help them place the words into their speaking vocabulary while associating them with the printed forms, and 3) to provide the background or concepts to be developed through the repeated sequential introduction of vocabulary and story structure. In each case the activity uses information from other sources to help students learn a particular skill. So, for instance, story background and concepts are retained by the order in which word meanings are introduced; learning word meanings is assisted by the presence of the printed form of words; and so on.

STEP 2: GUIDED READING

Guided reading is an important factor in comprehension since it provides goals for reading. Reading can be guided globally or in increments. Guiding reading globally is more appropriate for L1 readers than for L2 readers.

Guided reading should emphasize story elements. The first element in the "fair" story describes a family hurrying to a fair. A typical guiding question would be "Read the first two pages of this story to find out why Dave is in a hurry to get to the fair." Answering the question does not require students to use any new material. During the introduction of background and vocabulary, and the sight-word practice, the students focused on this story element, the background of the element, the meaning of the vocabulary in the element, and the recognition of the vocabulary related to this element. The guided reading allows them to integrate all of these sources of information in a meaningful way. As students become more proficient, they can read increasingly greater portions of a story.

When a teacher guides reading, he or she is determining the kind of comprehension that is to take place. One should be concerned about comprehension at different levels, since comprehension at the literal level involves attention to the surface structure of a text and not to the writer's meaning. It is better to ask a question such as "Read to find out if you would be in as much of a hurry to get to the fair as Dave," followed by "Why do you think so?"

STEP 3: FOLLOW-UP

The DRA-L2, like the DRA, is designed to assure that students comprehend a text. Indeed, that is its primary goal. Follow-up comprehension activities are especially important, therefore. The standard approach is to ask students questions, either orally or on worksheets. Worksheet questions should involve all levels of comprehension. The following discussion will be about activities that differ from the typical question-and-answer worksheet format. First, a typical primary story is presented, and then examples of different comprehension activities are provided. It would be more interesting for students to read this story in DRTA fashion, by the way.

Jose and Maria Visit the Zoo

One Wednesday morning at breakfast at the D'Silva house, Mother was reading the newspaper.

"Oh, look," she said, "The zoo has a new panda bear. I think we should visit the zoo and see it."

"When can we go?" screamed Jose and Maria.

"How about this Saturday?" asked Mother. The two children nodded their heads yes. Both Thursday and Friday seemed very far away to the children. Jose complained that his fourth-grade class was boring. Maria said she couldn't sleep because she was so excited about visiting the famous panda bear of Parkville Zoo. Saturday finally arrived. The children woke up early and ran down to the kitchen.

"When are we going?" asked Maria.

Mother looked at the two excited children. "After we've had breakfast and have finished washing the dishes!" she exclaimed. The two anxious children were hardly able to finish their breakfast even though the rice and beans were wonderful. Their mother had to ask both of them to slow down and not eat too fast. Finally, they hopped into the car and left for the zoo.

"Oh no!" shouted Jose. "Look at all the people in line to get into the zoo." People were lined up to get into the zoo. Thousands of parents and children were trying to get tickets to enter.

"We'll never get in, Mama!" cried Jose.

"We'll have to wait for hours," said Maria. "Let's do something else today instead of going to the zoo."

Jose agreed and said, "Why don't we go to a movie?" Two and a half hours later, Maria and Jose were sitting in the back seat of their car as Mother was driving them home.

"Donald Duck sure was funny, wasn't he?" asked Maria.

"Do you think we will ever see the panda bear?" asked Jose. "Perhaps, someday," said Mother as they drove by the zoo, where there was still a long line of people waiting to get in.

This is not a particularly exciting story, agreed, but it is, unfortunately, like many basal stories. If the DRA-L2 were followed, the story would be divided into story segments, the new vocabulary would be isolated into each segment, and a decision would be made about how much material to teach at a time; the guided reading would involve questions at different levels. The following exercises are based on the assumption that students have read the whole story. They are designed, therefore, to assess comprehension. Students are asked to draw a map of the story showing the settings and the sequence. This kind of map requires students to go beyond the literal level and to make inferences about settings and actions. The mapping exercise can be made extremely easy. The teacher can provide some details, have students add others, or have students do the entire map—individually, or as a group. After they have finished, students should discuss their maps and give reasons why they drew them as they did. The maps shown were produced by a group of grade 5 ESL students who thought the story was dumb! The first map they produced is shown in Figure 4.2. It was based on the contents of the story and their knowledge of their home town. They put Jose and Maria's house in the corner, reasoning that since the family had to drive to the zoo, it must have been far away from their home—good logic.

However, one student finally pointed out that the family drove by the zoo again as they went home, so they settled on the map in Figure 4.3. They made the inference that the family did go to the movies. In addition, because the family had a car, the students thought they must have had money, and therefore lived in a good part of town. They also thought the family was Spanish-speaking because of the names.

The students' discussion of their map revealed that they had understood—comprehended—the passage at more than just the literal level. They inferred that the family was probably Mexican because of the breakfast they ate. They also inferred, from the comment about Donald Duck, that the family had gone to a

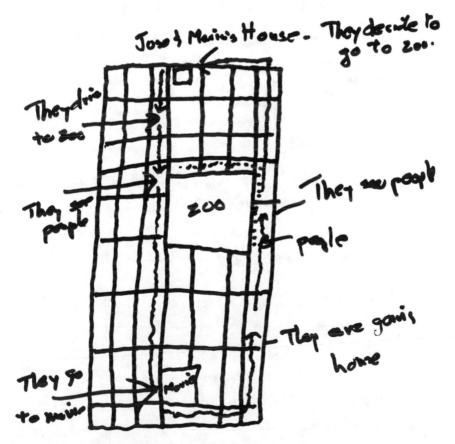

Figure 4.2 Pre-reading Map

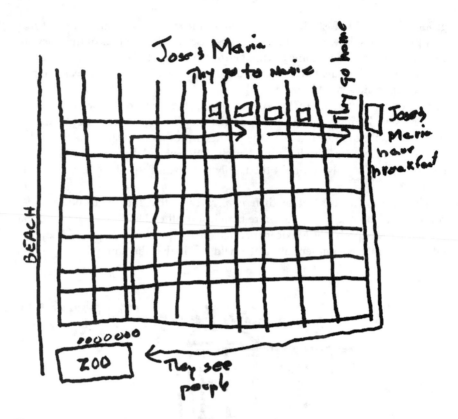

Figure 4.3 Post-reading Map

movie. Indeed, they inferred relative location of different story elements. The following is a different kind of comprehension exercise.

Estimate Maria and Jose's level of happiness.

1. When they heard they were going to see the panda bear, Jose and Maria were:

Very Happy   Very Sad

|_____|_____|_____|_____|

because_____

2. When they saw the large line at the zoo, Maria and Jose were:

Very Happy   Very Sad

|_____|_____|_____|_____|

because_____

3. When they were returning home and they saw all the people in line at the zoo, Jose and Maria were:

Very Happy   Very Sad

|_____|_____|_____|_____|

because_____

The teacher could have selected many different personality characteristics to have students analyze. The activity requires them to interpret relationships and personality traits. Discussion is important in discovering students' reasons for their answers. One could also have asked questions about the mother or the panda bear, for example.

The following activity focuses on the mother. Although the story does not explicitly describe her, one could ask probing questions such as "Was Maria and Jose's mother kind? How do you know?" or "Was Jose and Maria's mother a neat housekeeper? How do you know?" Students' comprehension could also be measured by giving them a simple exercise such as:

Maria and Jose's Mother

Maria and Jose's mother was _____

_____.

My reasons for knowing this are _____

_____

It may be that it is necessary to provide students with more help because the teacher has decided there are certain important elements she wants them to understand. The following exercise is more directive.

kind   organized   happy   anxious   disappointed   calm   bored

excited   sad   famous   responsible   patient

Make a web containing all of the words above and the following: mother, panda bear, Maria, Jose, and the people waiting in line at the zoo.

This is a fairly sophisticated task. One could provide a list of vocabulary from the text and ask students to attach individual words to particular characters or incidents. Each of the relationships should be explored orally. If the students are good readers and writers, they can write out the relationships.

The following exercise involves students inferring items involving main story items.

Jose

Jose acts in a childish fashion. Judge how childish his actions are:

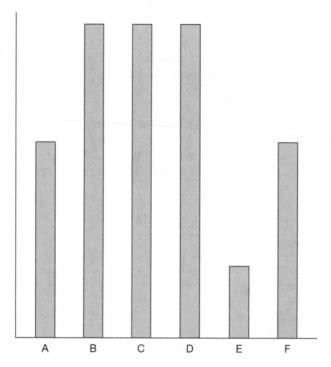

A: Mother reads the newspaper   B: Mother suggests they go to see the panda bear   C: They eat breakfast   D: They see all the people in line   E: Jose suggests a movie   F: They return home and see many people still in line at the zoo.

The student who produced this graph was fairly sophisticated. He provided reasons for each of his estimations. Students can also be asked to provide their reasons in a written or an oral fashion.

When Jose's mother is reading the paper we don't know if he is acting childish so I put the bar in the middle. When his mother said they go to the zoo, Jose act childish because he scream and act like a little baby. He was very childish when he was eating breakfast because he was eating so fast to get it over with. He was the same when he saw the people at the zoo because he said we'll never get in. He wasn't so childish when he said they want to go to a movie. If he was childish he would have cry or said something different. I can't tell if he is childish or not at the end because he only says will we ever see it mama?

This student's answers show he comprehended the passage. He was able to make inferences at many different levels. The term "childish" was selected because earlier students had made the observation. Different teachers select different concepts, but if the group is advanced, they can pick their own concepts.

These activities should be selected and adapted to match students' abilities and needs. Good evidence suggests that students will develop literal-level comprehension even if the focus is on higher-level questions. So, if a teacher asks mostly inferential questions, students will *still* develop literal-level comprehension. The following are a few general suggestions for comprehension exercises that can be adapted to meet students' needs:

1. Students change the form of the reading so that a poem becomes a story, a story becomes a play, etc.
2. Students become newspaper reporters and dictate their version of the story into a tape recorder. The teacher should check their versions to assess whether they have comprehended the story and can tell relevant from irrelevant facts.
3. Students design and build a game based on a story. The stages of the game should be based on events in the story they have read.
4. Students are given a story without the ending and are asked to write an ending. They compare their endings with the one written by the author. They should decide which is more plausible and why.
5. Students produce drawings that represent the story.
6. Students produce a play based on the contents and characters of a story. The play can be presented to the rest of the class.
7. Students model characters from a story. There should be a TV announcer who interviews them for a TV show.
8. Set up a "What's My Line" show, in which classmates must ask individual students about a role they assume. So, for instance, someone who has read a story about space travelers must assume the role and answer questions based on the material in the story.

This section has contained some activities to help develop comprehension. They should be adapted to match students' backgrounds and interests.

STEP 4: SKILLS-RELATED ACTIVITIES

Usually, the next step in DRA involves skills-related instruction. The typical skills workbook activities often do not reinforce the skills being taught in the story. For example, a series using the word *right* ("The balloon went right up into the air") used the word *right* in the context of "left versus right" in the workbook. The skills being reinforced should be the same as the ones introduced. Normally, it seems, teachers end a lesson with oral reading activities. However, unrehearsed oral reading should never be used with ESL students.

Oral Reading

It seems that most teachers are still convinced even in the new millennium that they must have students involved in oral reading activities. Students in elementary, secondary, university, and adult-level classes are almost always involved in oral reading. In nearly every case the oral reading is bad, with many teacher interruptions, with students hearing and rehearsing day after day the worst possible oral reading. Indeed, this author observed unrehearsed oral reading in an ESL classroom in April 2007. In effect, the ESL students were practicing the worst oral reading models. Students do not need to read aloud every day. If they are involved in unrehearsed oral reading, they are most likely suffering considerable damage; but oral reading is important and there are times when it should be practiced. The practice should be positive and with appropriate oral models.

As was noted earlier, the teacher should read aloud as often as possible to students. As a mature reader, the teacher provides a positive oral reading model. Students should read familiar material aloud with the teacher in a choral fashion. Indeed, they should practice the choral reading, record it, and listen to it critically as a group.

In addition to choral reading, individual oral reading should always be positive. Gunderson (1995) suggested three guiding principles for oral reading. They are:

- *never* without preparation
- *never* a great quantity
- *always* in carefully structured situations.

Oral reading should always be for an audience. If it is the teacher's goal to improve a student's oral reading, then the activities should help the student practice in a positive fashion by providing a good model to emulate. In the simplest type of practice session the teacher indicates to a student or students that they will be practicing oral reading, that they will be attempting to improve their phrasing and intonation.

Echoic Reading

The following is a typical "echoic" reading session designed to help improve students' oral reading so that they can enjoy the process. The goal of the lesson is *not* to improve comprehension, although this is a normal consequence of the activity.

Teacher: Today we are going to practice and improve our oral reading skills. Please turn to page 96. Look at the first sentence. It says, "Dave was in a hurry to get to the school fair." Will you please read that, Mario?

Mario: "Dave was in a hurry to get to the school fair."

Teacher: Well done, Mario. Did you hear how well he read that sentence? Let's read it all together the same way.

The session continues in this fashion with the teacher providing the model and reinforcing the students' correct responses. As students practice oral reading in this fashion, they will improve and they can be given larger and larger segments to read. Often a good reader in a group can provide the good model if the teacher is careful to set up conditions so that no invidious comparisons arise. Good oral reading models are extremely important for ESL students. The teacher must, absolutely *must*, provide ESL students with the opportunity to hear and emulate good oral reading models. ESL students are often hooked up to tape recorders where they listen to stories being read aloud. Often, they follow the text as the story is being read. This is a good activity. It is better, however, if the reader is real and the student is involved in active listening.

The notion of repeated reading is an old one. Students repeat reading passages aloud and the goal of the activity is to develop fluency. The National Reading Panel concluded that "*guided repeated oral reading procedures that included guidance from teachers, peers, or parents had a significant and positive impact on word recognition, fluency, and comprehension*" (p. 12). This finding appears valid for ESL students as well.

ESL students often have difficulty gaining access to good English models. Not hearing good oral reading is a problem. Without good oral models, the ESL (ELL) learner suffers. In some schools, there are few English models, and in some classrooms ESL students are placed in instructional groups where they hear over and over again the worst oral reading possible. Fluency in reading was recognized by the National Reading Panel as an important feature of instructional programs. There are a number of ways for the teacher to ensure that students hear good oral reading. The first was designed to provide students with good models of oral reading: echoic reading.

The purpose of echoic reading is to provide students with good models of oral reading and to involve them in emulating good oral reading. In some classrooms, there is only one English speaker who can provide good models of oral reading: the teacher. The echoic reading process described above works extremely well with ESL (ELL) students if the teacher, tutor, or parent volunteer puts the focus on oral reading. There are some individual students, however, who do not benefit from working in small groups. These individuals often benefit from the neurological impress method, which is a one-on-one adult–student activity.

The Neurological Impress Method

Heckelman (1969) was a speech pathologist who worked with students who were stutterers. He discovered that their stuttering ceased when he placed earphones on them that played what they were saying back to them as they spoke. He theorized that the earphones provided them with feedback. He also theorized that feedback might be a positive feature for students who had trouble reading. He developed a technique that he called the neurological impress method, which is based on an adult reader providing oral feedback for a reader as she reads.

Neurological impress involves an adult reader (you the teacher, a volunteer, or a parent) sitting next to the student, with the student sitting slightly in front so the reader's voice can be close to the child's ear. The student selects the book she wishes to read. At first the book is held by the adult, and is read aloud. The adult reads into the student's ear with fluency, careful articulation, and enthusiasm. As the adult reads, she moves her finger and tracks the text. The student reads aloud with the adult. The student is never corrected if she makes a mistake or skips a word. The adult continues to read if the student falters; often she will catch up as she hears the adult continue to read. At no point does the adult correct, teach the child, or ask questions. The focus is on the fluency of language and making the voice-to-print match. Often, sections will be read over again with enthusiasm. The session ends with the adult complimenting the student on the good oral reading.

These sessions work extremely well, and the research conducted by Heckelman showed that comprehension increased significantly, even though no comprehension activities are explicitly included in the sessions. One or two sessions a week over a semester are very dramatic in the results they produce. This author trained 11 parents in one grade 2/3 class to do neurological impress with 19 students. The results were impressive, and students enjoyed and benefited from the closeness of the activity.

ESL Reading Programs

There are published programs designed for ESL students at all levels. Often, as in the case of Michael Walker's *YES! English for children* (Menlo Park, CA: Addison-Wesley Publishing, 1983), the program is designed to teach students "Listening, Speaking, Reading, and Writing" (see pp. iv–xv of Walker's book). Such programs are highly structured and contain L2 reading skills taught in a clearly defined sequential pattern. If a series is used, it should be supplemented with activities such as the ones noted above. The ESL series are based, primarily, on a skills-based model of reading. Robinett, Bell, and Rojas (1971) (in *Miami linguistic reading* (Boston, MA: D.C. Heath, 1971), for instance, elect to use spelling patterns to introduce reading. Again, their activities should be supplemented. There are many basals available in the new millennium in the United States that are designed for ESL students, but most often they are Spanish basals. Greenwood has produced a commercial online program that introduces basic reading skills to beginning ESL students that includes both written and aural responses (see http://www.green wood.ca/index_withKeyWords.html).

Becoming a Phonics Teacher

It seems that most people in the general public and, indeed, most teachers, both mainstream and ESL, believe that students should learn phonics skills. Time after time, ESL teachers, most often those who teach older students, state that phonics skills should be taught and learned. Interestingly, it seems that teachers of adults are also constantly saying that they need to teach grammar. The belief that ESL students should learn to "crack the code" is quite pervasive among the public and in the teaching profession. Coady (1979, p. 8) stated that "ESL students typically begin by attending to more concrete process-strategies such as phoneme–grapheme correspondences." Beginners—older students, it would seem—focus on the regular relationships between letters and sounds they can isolate. They focus, therefore, on phonic relationships. Unfortunately, in English these relationships are not very reliable. It is the long-time experience of this author that phonics instruction simply does not work well until a learner has acquired a fairly substantial English vocabulary and is at the very limited level with a substantial L1 literacy background. In addition, what is ironic is that most adults are not able to remember and state any phonics rules. The exception is actually a spelling rule, "i before e, except after c."

Clymer (1963) studied 45 phonics generalizations to discover whether they were consistent in the words students encountered in initial reading texts. He found there was a high degree of variability in their reliability. Piper (1983a) selected 19 of the 45 generalizations involving vowels for further study. She concluded that since ESL students want to learn phonics, and the phonics rules available are fairly unreliable, she would examine the generalizations to see which work and which should be "reformulated to improve their utility." Piper tested the following 19 generalizations:

1. When there are two vowels side by side, the long sound of the first is heard, and the second vowel is usually silent.
2. When a vowel is in the middle of a one-syllable word, the vowel is short.
3. If the only vowel is at the end of a word, the letter usually stands for a long vowel.
4. When there are two vowels, one of which is final e, the first vowel is long and the e is silent.
5. The r gives the preceding vowel a sound that is neither long nor short.
6. The first vowel is usually long and the second short in the digraphs ai, ea, oa, and ui.
7. In the phonogram ie, the i is silent and the e has a long sound.
8. Words having double e usually have the long e sound.
9. When words end with silent e, the preceding a or i is long.
10. In ay, the y is silent and gives the a the long sound.
11. When the letter i is followed by the letters gh, the i usually stands for its long sound and the gh is silent.
12. When a follows w in a word, it usually has the sound a as in was.
13. When e is followed by w, the vowel sound is the same as represented by oo.
14. The two letters ow make the long o sound.
15. W is sometimes a vowel and follows the vowel digraph rule.
16. When y is the final letter in a word, it usually has a vowel sound.
17. When y is used as a vowel in words, it sometimes has the sound of long i.
18. The letter a has the same sound as (o) when followed by l, w, and u.
19. When a is followed by r and final e, it makes the vowel sound we hear in care.

Phonics teachers refer to the above statements as generalizations rather than rules since there are many exceptions. Piper (1983b) adjusted the 19 vowel generalizations to take into account morphology and word order. She concludes with six implications for ESL teachers:

1. Teach the rules as applying only to root words before suffixation or compounding.
2. Teach students to recognize compound words and to ignore vowel digraphs formed as a result of compounding.
3. Teach the pronunciation of unstressed vowels. Since suffixes are rarely stressed, most vowels in suffixes are pronounced as /ə / (as in attention or waited).
4. Remind students that it is the pronunciation of the *y* in the stem which determines the pronunciation of *i* in such words as *dried* and *happiest*.
5. Teach the pronunciation of *r*-colored vowels separately. An *r* following a vowel affects our perception of that vowel's quality. The problem is even greater for foreign learners who have difficulty with the English /r/ anyway.
6. Finally, do not be afraid to teach phonics. Many ESL students, convinced that English is totally unsystematic, will welcome the order suggested by these rules. Just a few rules that work most of the time will eliminate some of the guesswork involved in learning to read in English.

The following section presents some basic phonics knowledge and provides suggestions on how systematically to teach the most reliable phonics relationships. Phonics instruction is not for all ESL students. Indeed, only those with limited fluency in English and with a history of literacy training are able to cope with training in phonics. These activities require students to operate on language in a different manner from the activities discussed so far.

Phonics Primer

- *Phonic generalizations:* Spelling in English is sometimes quite irregular. The phonics teacher does not teach rules, but instead teaches generalizations because there are many exceptions.
- *Vowels and consonants:* In English, vowels are represented by the graphemes (visual symbols) *a, e, i, o, u*, and sometimes *y*. Consonant graphemes represent consonant sounds. The 26 graphemes represent, in various ways, the 44 or so English phonemes (speech sounds). They are put together in many different ways to produce syllables and words. Consonants are voiced or unvoiced; the words *pat* and *bat* differ in that the first consonant in *pat* is unvoiced while the first consonant in *bat* is voiced.
- *Word patterns:* Phonics teachers describe words by using the letters V for vowel and C for consonant.
  a. A nuclear word is a basic unit made up of the CVC pattern. Words such as *fat, met, pit, pot*, and *rut* are CVC words. This unit forms the basis for CCVC (*stop*), CCCVC (*strip*), CVCC (*wick*), CVCCC (*witch*), CCVCC (*stock*), etc. words.
  b. The CVCe pattern is called the long-vowel pattern, as in the word *bite*.
  c. Word families or phonograms are the terms phonics teachers use to describe patterns such as *at, it, uy, in*, and *eight*.
  d. Root word: This is a basic word unit. Linguists call them free morphemes.

The word *man* is a root word. A compound word is a combination of two or more root words. We can add parts to root words.

1. Affixes: Graphemes representing bound morphemes such as *un-*, *dis-*, *-ly*, and *-ness*.
2. Prefixes: Graphemes representing bound morphemes attached to the beginning of a root word, e.g., un-happy.
3. Suffixes: Graphemes representing bound morphemes normally attached to the end of root words, e.g., friend-ly.

- *Syllables:* A part of a word that contains at least one vowel sound.
  a. Closed syllable: This syllable has the pattern CVC as seen in the word *wonder* (*won-* is a closed syllable).
  b. Open syllable: Has the CV or VC pattern as in the word *empty*, which has one VCC and one CV syllable (*emp- ty*).
  c. Accented syllable: The syllable in a word that is given the most stress in pronunciation. For example, in the word *wonder*, the stress is on the *won-* syllable.
  d. Unaccented syllable: The first syllable of the word *about* is unaccented. This is a widely distributed unaccented syllable in English and is called a *schwa*. Other unaccented syllables exist at the end of such words as *little* and *garden*.

- *Consonant blends:* A blend consists of two or more consonants (i.e., CC, CCC) that are pronounced together with the sound from each being heard separately.
  a. Initial consonant blends: *bl, cl, fl, gl, pl, sl, br, cr, dr, fr, gr, pr, tr, sc, sk, sm, sn, sp, st, sw, dw, sw, tw, spl, scr, spr*, and *str*.
  b. Final consonant blends occur at the end of words: *st, sk, mp, ld*, and *nd*.

- *Consonant digraphs:* A digraph consists of two or more consonants that represent one sound.
  a. Initial digraphs: *ch, ph, sh, th*, and *wh*. The *th* digraph can be voiced (*the*) or unvoiced (*thank*).
  b. Final digraphs: *ch, gh, ph, th, tch, ck*, and *lk*.

- *Vowels:* Vowels are represented in English in many different ways. Indeed, one vowel sound is often represented by 10 or 15 graphemes or grapheme combinations, e.g., *I, kite, iron, tried, fly, high, height, buy, guide, eye, rye, style, aisle*, and *aye*.
  a. Short vowels: Phonics teachers call the following vowels short vowels: *bat, bet, bit, rot*, and *rut*.
  b. Long vowels: "The long vowel says its own name" is the standard elementary teacher's definition. The following are "long-vowel" words: *made, hide*, and *hope*.
  c. Vowel digraphs: Vowel digraphs are two-vowel graphemes that represent one phoneme as in the words *read, beast, pain, boat*, etc.
  d. Diphthongs: Some phonics teachers refer to these vowels as glided vowels. Diphthongs contain two vowel sounds, e.g., *boil, mail, pie, saw, soon*, and *cow*.

e. R-controlled vowels: When a vowel is followed by *r* or *l*, the sound is affected by the anticipatory mechanism of speech. The *r* is produced by rounding the lips, arching the tongue, and constricting the pharynx. Vowels preceding *r* are changed because the speech mechanism is changed during production of the vowel in anticipation of the *r*. The following are *r*-controlled vowels: *far, her, fir,* and *fur.*

The following lessons are based on selecting the relationships that are most reliable. Piper (1983a), for instance, found that the first pattern, CVC, had 84 percent reliability in the reading series she surveyed. The generalizations are rank-ordered and get less reliable as the discussion progresses.

There is a phonic generalization that says CVC words have a short vowel sound. If a fairly reliable initial consonant grapheme and a reliable phonogram are selected, students can be introduced to patterns that will teach them to recognize thousands of words.

Some reliable consonants: b, d, f, g, h, j, k, l, m, n, p, r, s, and t.

Some reliable phonograms: -ab -ad -ag -am -an -ap -at -ed -eg -en -et -ib id -ig -im -in -it -ob -od -og -op -ub -ud -um -un -ut

An -*an* Exercise

Make as many words as you can with the -*an* phonogram

_____an _____an _____an _____an _____an _____an _____an _____an _____an

The possibilities are nearly endless. Often a student doing such an activity suddenly realizes, often for the first time, that there are regularities in English spelling. Games can be made that involve students in such activities. The phonogram is put on the chalkboard and students are asked for a letter that will form a word. Each word and its meaning are discussed. Students can also substitute different initial consonants, read the word, and discuss its meaning. A teacher can use his or her imagination and make board games, or group games. The next step is to begin to build on the basic CVC pattern by adding initial and final consonant blends and digraphs.

Initial consonant blends

bl-, br-, cl-, cr-, dr-, dw-, fl-, fr-, gl-, gr-, pl-, pr-, scr-, sl-, spl- sp-, spr-, squ-, st-, str-, sw-, tr-, tw-, thr

Final consonant blends

-ct, -dk, -dt, -ft, -ld, -lk, -lf, -lt, -lp, -mp, -nd, -pt, -rd, -rk, -rm, -rn, -rp, -rt, -sk, -st, -sp

Consonant digraphs

ch, ck, gh, kn, ng, ph, qu, sh, wh, th (voiced and voiceless)

The possible combinations are nearly endless. The phonograms -an and -and can be added and the same exercise can be conducted, only this time students are given cards containing initial blends and digraphs. The teacher writes -and on the chalkboard. The task is to write as many real words as possible with the initial blends and digraphs given to them in combination with the phonogram on the chalkboard. (Some CVCC patterns do not follow the generalization, however. The -ind phonogram cannot be used, because it combines with initial consonants and produces "long-vowel" words such as *find*, *blind*, and *kind*.) With a little imagination, one can produce lessons and games that show students how regular English orthography is.

After students have begun to recognize the basic CVC short-vowel pattern, their knowledge can be used to help them understand and be able to recognize what phonics teachers call the "long-vowel" pattern. The CVCe pattern usually has the long sound of the vowel, as in the words *hide, kite, ride*, etc. The usual approach is to present the CVC patterns and have students supply the "silent e," making the word a long-vowel word.

Change the following short-vowel words to long-vowel words.

bit_____ cap_____ fin_____ hid_____ kit_____ mat_____ rat_____ rob_____ tap_____

Again, the combinations are nearly limitless. Board games can be made that reinforce the CVC-CVCe relationship. The phonic relationships discussed so far are fairly regular. However, there are exceptions, especially in the very high-frequency words. The CVC, with all its combinations, and the CVCe pattern have been discussed. This knowledge of the CVC pattern can be extended by introducing the "when two vowels go walking, the first does the talking" pattern, i.e., CVVC.

CVC words are selected that produce CVVC words with the long-vowel sound. The following are examples:

bed	bead	wed	weed	best	beast	bet	beat
led	lead	met	meat	men	mean	set	seat
step	steep	net	neat	red	read	bled	bleed

In each of these cases the second vowel is added after the first vowel and the first vowel now says its own name. It is possible to select CVC words with the same vowel. The quick student will look at the red-read pair and note that they "can sound the same."

bet	beet	red	reed
fed	feed	red	read
met	meet	bled	bleed
wed	weed		

Piper (1983a) found that *ee* produced the "long *e*" sound about 94 percent of the time. Again, the combinations are numerous. The purpose is to show students that there is a regularity in English orthography. The teacher should experiment a bit. The great number of logical operations that can be found is surprising, e.g., *bat–boat, flat–float, cat–coat, cot–coat, got–goat, ram–roam, bat–bait, man–main, mad–maid, lad–laid, ran–rain*, etc.

The teacher who has taught her or his students these relationships will have armed them with considerable phonics knowledge. They can produce CVC words with the short-vowel sound and all its variants (i.e., CVC, CCCVC, CVCC, CVCCC, CCVCC, CCCVCC, and CCVCCC). In addition, they know the CVCe pattern and the CVVC pattern. Each of these generalizations has a high degree of regularity—not perfect, but highly regular. Cautious teachers will probably stop at this point. Those who choose to go on, however, should realize that the orthography becomes considerably less reliable.

Some Phonograms

Adding consonants to produce or build words is a tradition in reading classrooms. Phonics teachers select phonograms such as *-eigh, -igh, -fight, -ing, -five, -ong, -ould, -udge, -ump,* and *-unny* and have students add initial consonants, consonant blends, or consonant digraphs. This is, of course, not an exhaustive list. Those who wish to become accomplished phonics teachers, transcending the bounds of the present discussion to extend their students' learning, will need a source of word families, root words, and such. An extremely valuable resource is *The Reading Teacher's Book of Lists* by E.B. Fry and J.E. Kress (San Francisco: Jossey-Bass, 2006) because it contains lists of such things as phonics skills, spelling families, affixes, and word lists.

Word Recognition

Skills-based teachers are convinced that students should learn to recognize important words on sight. Indeed, they believe students should be directly taught the important sight words. The Dolch (1936) list of 220 service-words mentioned earlier is one of the most widely used vocabulary lists in North America.

In 1936, Dolch produced "A Basic Sight Vocabulary of 220 Words, Comprising All Words, except Nouns, Common to the Word List of the International Kindergarten Union, the Gates List, and the Wheeler-Howell List." The International Kindergarten List produced by the Child Study Committee of the International Kindergarten Union contains 2,596 words obtained from the 893,256 running words spoken by a group of kindergarten students in Washington, DC. The Gates List contained 500 words of the 1,000-word list obtained from primary-level reading texts published in the early 1920s. The Wheeler-Howell (Wheeler & Howell, 1950) had the 453 most frequent words in ten primers and ten first-grade readers published between 1922 and 1929.

Dolch added some words that were not common to all three lists, because "many of these words obviously belong with others on the basic list. *Which* belongs with *who* and *that*, *done* and *goes* belong with *did* and *go*, start belongs with *stop*, and *write* with *read.* "It turns out that the Dolch list is quite powerful; in 1960, Dolch found that his words accounted for 70 percent of the words in primary reading texts and 52 percent of the words in grade 6 history texts. It is often used as a source of "readiness" skills. That is, students who are able to read all of the words on sight are thought to be ready to begin formal reading instruction. It is also used as a criterion test; so, for instance, students at the end of grade 3 are thought by some teachers to be ready for grade 4 if they can read all 220 words on sight.

Reading researchers have suggested many different alternatives to the Dolch. Indeed, the following represent just a few: 1) the Durr (1973); 2) the Gunderson (1985); the Hillerich (1974) list; 3) the Johns list(s) (1974, 1976a, b); or 4) the Johnson (1971), to name a few. As it turns out, each of these lists accounts for a great deal of the vocabulary found in initial reading texts.

A study of the vocabulary of students in grades 2, 5, 8, and 11 was conducted by this author, in which they were asked to write different kinds of written discourse. When a rank-order list using the words they produced was compiled, it accounted for as much of the vocabulary in primary texts as did the Dolch (1936), the Johns Revised Dolch List (1976a, b), the Hillerich (1974), and the Durr (1973). It was concluded that teachers could use any list as a vocabulary list since they all seemed to account for the same amount of vocabulary in beginning reading texts (Gunderson, 1984b). Actually, the Gunderson list, called the "Inner-City List," accounted for slightly more words than the other lists because it contains nouns, about 70 percent of the vocabulary.

The list has the advantage of having been developed from students' writing. Many, indeed about 33 percent, were ESL students. The list contains basic words, often function words (sometimes called structure words) such as *of, over,* and *by,* words that are often not easy to teach because their meanings are relational. One can only teach the meaning of *by,* for instance, in relation to other words. The question of how one should go about teaching these words as sight words to ESL/EFL students is an important one. The ability to use prepositions is highly predictive of reading comprehension (Gunderson, 2007).

The next section contains some suggested activities that have been successful with ESL students. Again, these activities are for students who are limited fluency in English or, in some special cases, secondary or adult-level students of lower English proficiency.

Rank Order List of Inner-City Words

the*	then*	other	talk	say*	again*
to*	get*	has	their*	wanted	an*
and*	what*	into	around*	way	all*
you*	there*	nice	ever	back	end
he*	about*	too*	everything	can't	happy
is*	all*	play*	inside	doesn't	helps

continued

I*	good*	hope*	looked	family	knew
a*	this*	much*	most	keep*	little*
me*	see*	some*	over*	kind*	next
it*	bad*	take*	since	lot	pick*
in*	out*	father	try*	name	problem
my*	will*	something	walking	only*	same
she*	boy	us*	come*	them	seen
was*	just*	got*	didn't	together	still
for*	saw*	could*	found*	did*	sure
of*	up*	how*	house	doing	walk*
that*	they*	even	well*	eat*	won't
your*	or*	help*	work*	goes*	year
his*	had*	no*	after*	last	big*
so*	want*	now*	each	need	class
with*	go*	life	give*	our*	close
have*	please*	might	problems	she's	coming
when*	think*	care	said*	should	door
very*	always*	he's	told	two	down*
but*	school	it's	also	use*	funny*
can*	who*	more	birthday	walked	gets
her*	from*	by*	first*	which*	gives
we*	love	fun	look*	another	left
like*	fine	home	sick	before*	let*
on*	tell*	make*	teacher	brother	living
because*	would*	sometimes	that's	food	made*
not*	day*	came*	years	its*	makes
do*	at*	does*	am*	looks	might
if*	why*	were*	any*	lots	somebody
don't*	man	I'm*	anything	many*	wish
him*	as*	been*	away*	may*	write
are*	things	money	long*	off*	wrong
know*	went*	open	looking	sister	
be*	took	put*	mom	than	
mother	going*	really	never*	thing	
one*	opened	right*	old*	yourself	

Note: The rank order is obtained by reading down the columns, not across the rows. An asterisk indicates that the word is included on the Dolch list.

So, if a reader has a total of 10,000 vocabulary items in it, all of these lists will account for about 7,000 of the words.

Source. L. Gunderson, One last word list. *Alberta Journal of Educational Research, 30* (1984), 259-269.

Becoming a "Flasher"

The standard approach for teaching word recognition, flashing, has been fairly well described previously in this chapter. It should be remembered that teachers flash in order to help students learn words. Effective flashing is not as straightforward as it may seem. Often, the assumption is made that simply showing a student a flashcard means he or she has learned to recognize it. The principle of **Flash, Recite, Reinforce; Flash, Recite, Reinforce, and Practice** discussed earlier in this chapter is the best method for ensuring that students will learn and remember sight words. The experienced ESL teacher usually has a big bag of tricks to help students learn new words.

A great deal of debate occurs concerning whether one should teach word recognition in context or in isolation. There is no clear-cut answer. Instead, one must judge which students benefit from context and learn words quicker when they are embedded in sentences and which learn them better when the words are isolated.

The basic problem with word lists is that they contain high-frequency words, items that are inconsistent in their grapheme–phoneme correspondence. The following discussion focuses on words from the Inner-City List that are, in fact, consistent. The following words follow the basic CVC generalization:

am	fast	must	that
an	get	not	them
and	got	on	then
ask	had	pick	think
at	him	put	up
best	hot	ran	when
big	if	red	wish
black	in	run	with
bring	it	sing	yes
but	its	sit	
can	jump	six	
cut	just	stop	
did	let	ten	

There are many methods to teach these words. One could, for instance, select all of the verbs and teach them together. The one-two-three strip works quite well (Durrell & Murphy, 1972). Three words to teach are selected—for instance, *jump, run,* and *sit*—and then written on a sentence strip in the following manner:

One-Two-Three Card

jump	run	sit
1	2	3

Students are shown the sentence strip and are asked to give the number of the word that means, for instance, ". . . ." (A good definition of the word is given, or a sentence that contains a blank space.) Students are to provide the number of the word that fits the definition or correctly fills the cloze deletion. The best procedure is to write the definitions on the back of the sentence strip, usually in the middle of the card. Definitions should not be written behind each word because this tempts the teacher to look at the particular definition and give a visual hint about which word he or she is defining.

To make this a silent activity, students raise one, two, or three fingers, or small cards with the numbers written on them. Each student raises the number of the correct answer. Unfortunately, in some classes this becomes a somewhat messy proposition. All of the short-vowel Inner-City words can be practiced in this manner with the teacher explaining that all the words follow the short-vowel generalization. The list just given represents the largest group of "regular" Inner-City words. The following represent the next largest group, words that follow the open-syllable rule. They are:

a	fly	no	try	me
be	go	she	he	we
by	my	so	I	why

There are, again, a number of possibilities. One could select the pronouns and teach them as a unit or use the simple approach referred to as the "yes–no" procedure. In this case a card with a word printed on it is held up and students are asked questions about the word. They respond "yes" or "no" or hold up a yes or no card. Questions such as "Does this word mean the opposite of *go*?" are asked. One alternative students love is "Concentration." Duplicate word cards, each of the 15 words, for instance, are placed into a deck of 30 cards and are shuffled and turned upside down on the floor or a table. The first student turns over two cards and says each word. If they match, the student collects the cards; if not, the cards are turned back over. The next player turns over two cards. The idea is to match cards and collect as many pairs as possible. The winner has the most cards at the end.

The next largest group of "regular words" on the list involves the "silent *e*" generalization. They are:

ate	five	like	make	take	write
came	gave	made	ride	white	

There are many ways to teach the CVCe generalization, as discussed earlier in this chapter. In fact, they may not have to be taught if students already know and can apply the generalization. It is amazing to observe the wide variety of teacher-developed games invented to teach students phonics generalizations.

Word recognition has been discussed in two sections of this chapter. The techniques one chooses should match one's beliefs about reading. The following is a section on word recognition having to do with word analysis. The reader should be advised, however, that this author has never seen a student actually apply the information discussed. However, many teachers believe students should be taught these skills. More importantly, many adult ESL students are convinced they want to learn such phonics skills.

Word Analysis

If students know the meanings of prefixes, root words, and suffixes, it is thought, then they will be able to read and comprehend more words. Root words are the usual items taught first. These are either Greek or Latin:

-avi-	bird	(aviator)
-caput-	head	(capital)
-ced-, -cess-	move	(precede)
-clar-	clear	(clarity)
-cord-	heart	(cordial)
-cred-	believe	(incredible)
-geo-	earth	(geography)
-homo-	same	(homogeneous)
-hydr-	water	(hydrolic)
-legis-	law	(legislate)
-lith-	stone	(monolith)
-log-, -logy-	study	(psychology)
-magn-	great	(magnificent)
-man-	hand	(manual)
-metr-	measure	(speedometer)
-micro-	small	(microscopic)
-nov-, -novus-	new	(novice)
-pac-	peace	(pacify)
-path-	feeling	(empathy)
-phon-	sound	(phonics)
-photo-	light	(photograph)
-plex-	bend	(Plexiglass)
-pod-	foot	(gastropod)
-polis-	city	(metropolis)
-psych-	mind	(psychology)
-scop-	see	(telescope)
-sign-	writing	(signature)
-tang-	hold	(tangible)
-ten-	hold	(tenable)
-vert-	turn	(convert)
-vid-, -vis-	see	(vision)
-voc-	call	(vocal)
-zo-	animal	(zoology)

To make these roots into words, one needs prefixes and suffixes. Again, there are many possibilities. Students are taught meanings of roots, prefixes, and suffixes. This knowledge helps them, it is said, to come to recognize and understand new words. It is interesting to consider the following word without reference to the lists of roots, prefixes, and suffixes, and to attempt to define the word *geometrid*. The definition is at the end of the chapter. Only one secondary student in this writer's experience has given the correct definition; never has a university student provided the correct definition without consulting the lists shown.

Many teachers are convinced that lessons focusing on suffixes, prefixes, and root words are valuable because they show students how constructive the English language is. Such lessons are appropriate for students who are fairly sophisticated in the use of English. University-level students benefit from and enjoy an activity such as "Invent a Word," which asks them to combine roots, prefixes, and suffixes to produce new words. They must be able to define the word for the class. The contest takes place after they have been introduced to the information in the lists and have been shown how Invent a Word works. The serious teacher of this information can be best described as an "annovusite" in word invention. It is this writer's hope that the activity has not left the reader "hyperpathic."

Many teachers believe students learn skills naturally, rather than being directly taught. Indeed, they object to lessons that focus on skills. Many also suggest that learning to read should be part of a "whole-language" program.

ESL teachers often speak of Latin and Greek roots with affection and many believe they represent, in many respects, CALP. But such knowledge is not as powerful as most think it is. This author has never found, for instance, any individual who is able to divide the word *helicopter* into its parts (see the end of the chapter for the answer).

Phonics and No Child Left Behind

The phonics presented in this book do not meet the breadth and depth teachers have come to expect as a result of the Reading First initiative. Indeed, the book is not exhaustive in its coverage. It is this author's experience that the study of phonics is extremely difficult for ESL (ELL) students, especially those who have little or no background in L1 literacy and very limited or no English ability. Many teachers, especially teachers of very young students, are horrified by the notion that phonics rules should be taught. The teacher should delay explicit phonics instruction until the ESL learner has developed some oral proficiency and has acquired a fairly substantial ability to recognize words in print, even though doing so is difficult professionally and politically. One of this author's biggest regrets is teaching a very bright ESL student some basic phonics rules she learned too well. The so-called rules made her reading and spelling life very difficult because of all the exceptions she encountered in print. She over-generalized and her reading/spelling life was filled with problems.

Whole-language Instruction and ESL Students

As was noted in Chapter 1, whole-language instruction is a relatively new approach to literacy instruction; it is only 30 or so years old. Its proponents are extremely positive about its benefits. Whole-language teachers involve their ESL students in the same activities as they involve their native English speakers. There are different

Prefixes		Suffixes	
Meaning	*Prefix*	*Meaning*	*Suffix*
not	a	an agent	er
	an		or
before	ante	something, an action	tion
against	anti		sion
around	circum		cion
overly	hyper	a condition	ty
highest, above	super	pertain to	al
across	trans	possible	ble
in, into not	in		able
	en		ible
	im	action or result	ment
	em	of action	
again	re	organism	id
to, toward	a	human	man
	ad	full, like	ous
	ap		ious
	at		
from, away from, apart	de		
out of, out from	ex		
together	con		
together with	com		
	col		
against, away from	op		
	ob		
before, for	pre		
	pro		
pertaining to, like	al		
	ar		
belong to	an		

versions of whole language. Generally, however, there is agreement that students begin language activities, including reading and writing, the first day—yes, even non-English-speaking students. The two major variants in whole-language classrooms are: 1) the teacher provides a written model for the students, or 2) the teacher does not provide a written model for the students, but rather lets writing develop naturally and independently.

Chow (1986) studied students enrolled in whole-language classes. The teachers in her school gave students "log books" and asked them to write in them on the first day of school, in addition to other literacy activities. Individuals who could not or would not write were encouraged to do so, but not shown how. Chow found their writing revealed five stages: 1) the prephonetic; 2) the semiphonetic; 3) the phonetic; 4) the transitional; and 5) the conventional or mature. Gunderson, Shapiro, & Froese (1988) found similar stages, but they have renamed them to make them represent students' developing sense of phonics.

The Picture Stage

Many students begin their writing development by drawing pictures. The pictures represent language and they can "read" them. The picture stage does not last more than a few weeks in whole-language classrooms.

The Prephonic (Prephonetic) Stage

Writers in the prephonetic stage produce letters or letter-like shapes. They do not understand, however, that letters correspond to sounds or words. They read their texts, but the reading varies over time. They use a small number of capital letters and numbers to write. Figure 4.4 is an example of prephonic writing.

The Semiphonic (Semiphonetic) Writer

Semiphonic writers use letters to represent words or parts of words. They have begun to understand that there is a relationship between letters and sounds. Their

Figure 4.4 Prephonic Writing Sample: "The mother is in the house."

writing is semiphonic because words are often represented by single letters (see Figure 4.5).

The letters they use to represent words are usually the letter corresponding to the first sound of the word, for example, *D* for *Daddy*. Chow refers to this phenomenon as making "phonetic hits," meaning that students have begun to associate particular phonemes of English with particular letters; they have begun to learn phonic relationships (see "Phonics Primer", p. 152).

The Phonic (Phonetic) Writer

Phonic writers know that letters represent sounds and know many correspondences. They have begun to separate letters into word units. Phonic writers rely on their knowledge of the relationship between letters and sounds to spell words and invent spellings (see Figure 4.6).

The Transitional Writer

Transitional writers begin to process words as visual units. Their writing contains many invented spellings; however, it also contains many conventional non-regular spelling patterns; for example, words such as *was*, *come*, *is*, that are not spelled the way they should be (see Figure 4.7).

Figure 4.5 Semiphonic Writing: "Andy goes in the house."

Figure 4.6 Phonic Writing: "A mommy is in the park."

Figure 4.7 The Transitional Writer: "I am playing outside with my friend."

The Mature Writer

Mature writers know many writing conventions, including "correct" spellings. They do not expend as much energy on the mechanics of writing, and their stories are longer and more complex. Note that all of the samples shown here are examples of ESL students' writing.

The examples shown above came from classrooms in which the teachers actively encouraged writing. However, they never "imposed" a writing model on students. That is, they never wrote comments on papers, because they thought such a procedure would have a negative influence on students' independent writing development. There is another school of thought about modeling, however. Some whole-language advocates believe students should be given a model of writing. These teachers begin the school year by asking students to write. If a student indicates that she cannot write, the teacher asks what she would like to write and provides the written version in the student's book. This is a kind of language experience activity. Figure 4.8 shows an example.

Teacher: "My dad is taking a walk."
Student: "My dad is taking a walk."

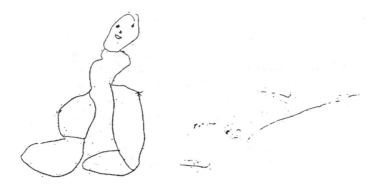

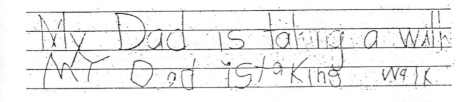

Figure 4.8 Teacher Models Writing with Student Reduction

A teacher's model is very powerful. Gunderson and Shapiro (1988) found that students enrolled in programs in which teachers provided models did not exhibit the stages mentioned above. Indeed, within a month or so, all of the students had become transitional writers. It would seem that the teacher's writing model accelerated students' writing development.

Often, as was noted above, students' writing does not resemble the mature model. It is important for the teacher to take notes or "transcriptions" of what students write. Teachers in the first group discussed above took notes at the back of students' log books or in separate teachers' logs. These notes were transcriptions of students' writing. The second group of teachers actually wrote in students' log books. They always made a positive written comment, including the essence of what students had written and, subsequently, read.

Beginning Whole Language: The Teacher as Model

All of the writing samples shown in this chapter were produced by primary-level ESL students. They are, in fact, able to produce text. The reader should decide which model best fits his or her theoretical notion of language acquisition and model of teaching. The first group of teachers believed that providing a model was imposing the adult version of language on the students. They chose, rather, to let their students develop writing in a natural independent fashion. In the second case the teachers believed they should provide a model for students to emulate. They were careful never to force students to produce "correct" forms. They always provided a model that contained the essence of what the students had written (see Figure 4.9). Indeed, there are findings that show that the writing development of the first group of ESL students does emulate that of preschool individuals, while the writing of those taught via the second model described above does not. Indeed, students who are given writing models seem to skip the first two or three stages. A teacher can do a bit of experimenting and find out which works best.

Student: "I am asking a lady for a balloon."
Teacher: "If you ask the lady for a balloon I hope she gives you one."

Whole-language teachers believe students should be engaged in meaningful language activities. Basal readers do not contain "real language" and therefore are not meaningful. Good children's literature is read aloud by the teacher, by the students individually, and in groups. Indeed, whole-language teachers establish classroom collections of good children's literature for their students. A major activity is called "chiming in," in which students read along in unison with the teacher as she reads aloud. Large-format "big books" are the material most often used for chiming in. Published big books contain material students love, and they actively chime in as the passages are read. Indeed, students often get to the point where they have memorized and enjoy reciting the poems and stories found in the big books. Chiming in provides students with a good oral reading model and helps teach them intonation and stress. They also learn to relate oral words to their printed form.

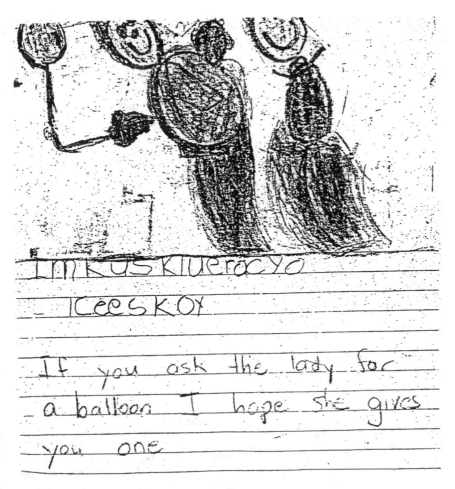

Figure 4.9 Teacher Emulates Student's Message

Drama is an important element in whole-language classrooms, because teachers believe that oral language development is extremely vital. Students often read and memorize plays or stories they have found in their books and present the stories in the form of skits. Drama is a wonderful activity that allows ESL students to hear native English speakers and encourages their participation in oral language activities. Since oral language is encouraged in whole-language classrooms they are excellent environments for ESL students.

Themes are important in whole-language classrooms and are used in interesting ways. Learning should be integrated rather than compartmentalized; therefore, the whole-language classroom does not have clearly discernible periods such as "spelling time." The teacher introduces themes around which activities are designed. In a local elementary school, for instance, all teachers focused on "Thanksgiving" as a theme at the beginning of the school year. Good children's books related to the theme were collected and placed in all classrooms; art activities focused on the theme; drama involved the theme; and students were asked to consider the theme in different ways in their writing. Through the theme, students learned about science, math, social studies, writing, spelling, vocabulary, history, and reading skills. Schools where this has been done are a wonder to behold.

The whole-language teacher's most difficult task is to keep track of students' progress. This is not an easy task. The most efficient procedure appears to be the "Reading and Writing Conference."

Conferences

Teachers who provide implicit models by writing responses to students by the very nature of the task keep records of what students are attempting to write, of their language development. Teachers who believe they should not impose an adult model must keep records, notes made in a somewhat formal period called the "conference," in this case a "writing conference." Students bring their writing to teachers, who ask questions, respond, and provide positive support. They also keep records to let them know how their students are progressing. In many situations, teachers write their comments in cursive (adult handwriting) in the back of the students' log books. These are unobtrusive comments, observations, and, in many cases, transcriptions of what students say they have written.

The transcriptions are necessary because there is not necessarily a one-to-one relationship between the student's written product and what it is the student thinks he or she has written. Other teachers write their comments in a separate book, which students do not see. These comments are used as vital signposts of student development. Both writing and reading conferences will be dealt with in detail in Chapter 5.

The teacher's role is vital and time-consuming. Often, teacher aides or parent volunteers can be trained to help provide the individual attention demanded by this learning approach. There are some valuable hints to keep in mind, as noted by Gunderson and Shapiro (1987):

1. Parents, principals, librarians, teacher aides, and other teachers in the school must understand fully the rationale behind the approach. Otherwise, they tend to react negatively to papers they see with invented spellings and no apparent "teacher corrections."
2. One must be willing to devote a great deal of time to a program. Whole-language instruction involves many of the features of individualized instruction, which demands a great deal of one-to-one student–teacher interaction.
3. Dating written products is important since it will provide an accurate record of growth in many areas. Teachers find that library daters work exceptionally well in this case.

There is a marvelous amount of specialized vocabulary used by whole-language teachers, a vocabulary that has developed over the past 30 years or so. A wonderful collection of whole-language terms has been compiled and published by Scholastic-Tab (Gunderson, 1989).

The whole-language classroom is a marvelous place to be for students. Students are not simply left to write all day. Indeed, their lives are filled with literacy activities. They read library books; they listen to the teacher read and chime in with him or her. They read their writing to their fellow students. They write to real audiences, including their teachers, their parents, and their fellow students. They publish newspapers and books. Many of the activities discussed at the beginning of this chapter are seen in whole-language classrooms. Indeed, prediction strategies, such as DRTA, are used in oral situations as well as in reading activities. Whole-language classrooms contain good children's books, ones students love to read. Drama is also an integral part of the activities in the whole-language classroom. Such activities are excellent in helping ESL students develop oral language and self-confidence. The teacher's goal is to provide an environment in which students want to talk, listen, read, and write. The learning in such environments is impressive to see.

However, there are few classrooms across North America that have teachers who strongly identify themselves as whole-language teachers, for political reasons. In both the United States and Canada, whole-language teachers appear to have become advocates of literature-based programs. In Canada, for instance, a recent study observed no basal readers in use. There were phonics activities apparent, but the observed instruction was purely literature-based with different approaches being used. These will be described in Chapter 5. A final model to be discussed is the "balanced reading" approach.

Balanced Reading Instruction

The term "balanced reading" was developed in the mid-1990s by individuals who believed there were features of both systematic phonics and whole-language instruction that were beneficial to students. Pressley (2006) wrote a book titled *Reading instruction that works: The case for balanced teaching* in which he reviewed the research literature and concluded that systematic and direct phonics instruction was a valid instructional approach for older children but not younger children. He argues strongly that whole-language instruction works better for very young students than phonics instruction, but that older students benefit more from systematic phonics instruction. Proponents of the balanced model suggest that phonics instruction should be delayed until students are out of the primary grades. The proponents of the skills-based or phonics models argue that students should be "ready" before they are included in direct phonics instruction. In many cases it appears that school-based proponents of balanced instruction interpret the model to mean teaching a little bit of everything to every student, but this is an incorrect interpretation of the term "balanced reading instruction" as formulated by Pressley and others.

The prevailing view appears to be that a balanced reading program should contain a little from each of the instructional models. This author has found that the basic problem is that no one proposes what the collection of bits should include.

Conclusion

This chapter has detailed reading programs for beginning ESL students. It provided a decision heuristic for determining 1) whether students should be involved in L2 reading activities, and 2) what programs are matched to their abilities. It was suggested that students with little or no L2 ability and no literacy background should be included in oral language programs, but not in reading programs. Reading programs for students with higher L2 abilities and more literacy backgrounds were described. They included vocabulary instruction, cloze, LEA, active participation, USSR, DRTA, and other activities. The DRA-L2 was described. It is a basic lesson plan for teaching students to read in L2 using basal readers. Basal instruction is appropriate, but not recommended, for students with a good ability in oral English and literacy instruction in L1 or L2. The pedagogical options delineated in this chapter should not be thought of as absolute. Each teacher's reading program will result from a careful consideration of her or his students' needs and abilities within the limitations of the classroom. The teacher decides who is ready to learn to read and how best to teach them. The guidelines presented in this chapter are good ones, tested by many teachers over time; but they should not determine programs. The individual teacher should.

The chapter concluded with a description of two types of whole-language instruction. Whole language is based on the idea that the traditional concept of readiness does not apply and that students should be involved in all of the literacy activities in an integrated fashion, beginning on the first day of school. When students do begin to write from the first day, their writing development appears to reveal several stages: 1) picture writing, in which text is represented by pictures; 2) prephonic writing, in which letters, numbers, and letterlike forms are used to represent text but with no relationship between letters and sounds; 3) semiphonic writing, in which there are some sound-symbol relationships, usually the first letters of words (e.g., D for *daddy*); 4) transitional writing, in which there are elements of semiphonic writing and some mature spelling conventions; and 5) mature writing, in which the standard adult conventions of spelling and sentence structure are followed. In those classrooms where teachers model writing, students' development is more rapid than in those classrooms where teachers encourage completely independent writing development. The whole-language classroom encourages speaking, listening, reading, and writing activities in a comfortable environment. The chapter concluded with a brief discussion of the notion of balanced reading instruction.

The chapter contains many ideas that can be adapted and used with ESL students, regardless of one's notion of language acquisition. The next chapter contains programs designed for older students. However, many of the ideas in this chapter can be used with them as well. Oh, by the way, "geometrid" is an inchworm. And the root words for "helicopter" are *helico* (helix-shaped) and *pter* (wing).

Explorations

Work with a partner, if possible.

1. The notion developed in this chapter is that some students are not ready to be included in direct reading instruction. How might such a student be accommodated in your classroom when you have 32 other students? What kinds of acitivities do you design for such a student? How can you assure that such a student is involved in activities that will help her develop oral language skills?
2. What is your view of balanced reading instruction? What do you think it means for ESL students?
3. Immigrant students arrive at inconvenient times during the school year, sometimes as late as June. How do you go about including them in instruction? What should you do to help them to begin to learn the importance of learning to read? What can you do to help them over the summer?
4. The basic goal in this chapter is to design programs that are appropriate for the skills, abilities, and needs of individual students. How will you plan for 32 different students?
5. Older elementary and high school students are often not included in reading instruction because their teachers believe that the academic content they teach is more important. How would you go about convincing a high school biology teacher, for instance, that she ought to focus on reading instruction in addition to academic content?

5

Teaching Older ESL/ELL/EFL
Students to Read

Introduction

This chapter contains discussions that focus on programs and techniques designed to teach older ESL students to read. The teaching of students in grades 4 through 8, intermediate students, is discussed first. Programs for secondary and adult students follow. The recommended practices and approaches are based on the notion that the instruction of ESL (ELL) students should involve comprehensible input selected relative to their English proficiency and their L1 literacy background. It also recommends activities that involve students in active participation in activities based on knowledge of their backgrounds.

Sheltered Instruction

Many of these views are also integrated in California in Specially Designed Academic Instruction in English (SDAIE), which seems to have been first mentioned in a Senate Bill in California in 1996 (California State Senate Bill 2138, 1995-1996). SDAIE programs are sometimes called "sheltered English." Their purpose is to teach academic content but in ways that support the learning of limited English proficient (LEP) students. The terms "Structured English Immersion" (SEI) and "Sheltered Content Instruction" (SCI) have also been used (see, for instance, Echevarria & Graves, 2007). The basic notion is that students need to be involved in learning content such as math and science and English, not just English. The difficulty is that some older students, those who have no English skills, either should be taught academic content in their first languages or should be involved in programs to teach them the English skills to equip them to be enrolled in programs that integrate the teaching and learning of content and English.

The concept of sheltered instruction is one that involves teachers designing academic lessons so that ESL students find them comprehensible and, in addition, so that they support students' English development. Faltis (1993) notes that sheltered instruction includes the addition of visual aids, texts that have been modified, and modifications to assignments that account for the English abilities and needs of ESL students. The term "sheltered instruction" has come to mean special content-area classes designed for ESL (ELL) students. Math, science, and social studies are the classes most often, it appears, to be sheltered.

Mohan's Knowledge Framework

In the mid-1980s, Mohan developed an early version of sheltered content instruction to help ESL students learn about the underlying theoretical aspects of content materials as well as how to deal with the specialized content skills. The typical teaching of content is "presented in verbal exposition, in textbooks, and in lectures" (1986, p. 74). Further, "the theoretical aspect of an activity contains the three knowledge structures of classification, principles, and evaluation" (1986, p. 74). A student is better prepared to deal independently with content material if he or she is given "a sense of the pattern or structure into which these details fit" (p. 75). Mohan's approach is to use tables and graphs to teach students how to use classification, principles, and evaluation to read content material. Mohan provides a general framework of knowledge structures to be used to design activities to help students learn from content (see Figure 5.1).

Students read text and put information into the correct structure frame. The activity classifies content material and helps students sort out relationships. This author is convinced that teachers who design their instruction following Mohan's framework are, in fact, providing sheltered instruction. It appears that the approach helps teachers design and implement comprehensible lessons.

The Sheltered Instruction Observation Protocol

In the mid-1990s, Echevarria, Vogt, & Short (2004) developed the Sheltered Instruction Observation Protocol (SIOP), which is widely used across the United States to guide teachers in designing their instructional programs. The overall purpose of SIOP is to guide teachers in the design of lessons that are comprehensible to ESL students. The observation protocol involves observations of eight components: "preparation, building background, comprehensible input, strategies, interaction, practice/application, lesson delivery, and review/assessment" (Echevarria & Graves, 2007, p. 57). The protocol includes 30 statements about instruction that

	Specific, practical	General, theoretical
Description		
Sequence		
Choice		

Figure 5.1 Mohan's Knowledge Framework

observers rate on a scale from 0 to 6 (from "not applicable" to "highly evident" (ibid., pp. 58-59)). Teachers learn to design their instruction following the observation protocol. Echevarria, Short, & Powers (2006) conducted a study to test the use of SIOP against a comparison group that did not involve its use. SIOP teachers were trained. Indeed, the authors note, "Project teachers spent 1 or 2 years (some teachers joined the study in 1997 and others in 1998) learning and practicing the SIOP model through an extensive professional development process; we measured implementation with the SIOP" (p. 203). In addition, the authors convened three-day summer sessions and "several reunion meetings during each school year" (p. 203). The SIOP teachers were trained to use the protocol to design studies and to implement their lessons in their classrooms. Teachers in grades 6 to 8 were included in the study. Overall, these authors noted that "Findings revealed that students whose teachers implemented the SIOP model performed slightly better than did a comparison group on an expository writing task, which closely approximated academic assignments that ELLs must perform in standards-based classrooms" (p. 195).

Sheltered instruction is based generally on the notion that the teacher's task is to make lessons comprehensible for students. To make lessons comprehensible, teachers include many visual or graphic aids, introduce key vocabulary in ways that help students to learn it, and self-monitor their own English production to assure that their language is at a level that is comprehensible to students. In some cases, teachers who work within the SIOP framework provide first-language instruction.

The purpose of the Two-Factor Elementary Instructional Matrix presented in Chapter 4 (pp. 123–124) is to design learning activities that are comprehensible to students of different English abilities and first-language literacy backgrounds. It is also designed to support literacy learning when no first-language resources are available. The matrices are also designed to help teachers match English literacy instruction for students who have no English abilities and no first-language literacy background. These are the students addressed first in this chapter.

Teaching Intermediate ESL Students to Read

It is important to differentiate terms. Elementary students, those in kindergarten through eighth grade, are differentiated by teachers as being primary (K–3) and intermediate (4–8). In the following discussion the term "intermediate" refers to a student who is enrolled in a class from fourth through eighth grade, not to that student's English proficiency. There are other grade configurations. Some school districts have middle schools and the grade configurations vary, e.g., 6–8, 7–9; others have junior high schools and senior high schools (e.g., 8–12, 9–12).

There are two categories of ESL intermediate students, those who need to learn to read English and those who have already begun to learn to read English. Teaching them to read is often more difficult than teaching primary-level students. One of the difficulties is selecting material that does not offend them because it looks "childish." The decision heuristic presented in Chapter 4 is appropriate for intermediate students who do not know how to read L2 (see pp. 45–47).

Intermediate students should not simply be placed in the lowest reading group because they are ESL students. Indeed, the slow reading group is exactly the wrong place to put ESL students. In addition, students without L1 literacy backgrounds are simply not included in reading instruction except in whole-language classrooms (see p. 179). They should not be included in formal reading instruction, because it will do more harm than good. One of the primary goals of an intermediate teacher is to teach students content material ranging from science to social studies. Since ESL students must read and learn from text, their L2 reading ability must be at the "instructional level," meaning at least 75 percent comprehension. A teacher is responsible, therefore, to help increase their L2 reading ability *before* they are required to read and learn from academic texts, or to tailor instruction so that academic content is presented at their English reading levels—that is, to provide sheltered content instruction.

Introducing Vocabulary

Zero-level English students who have not begun to learn to read in their first languages are not as rare in the intermediate classrooms as the reader might suspect. Many students from refugee families often have no or little first-language schooling and speak no English. Their potential to succeed in societies in which English is the language of schooling, learning, technology, and industry is, unfortunately, very low.

There is evidence to suggest that an early focus on vocabulary development is beneficial to them. The difficulty is finding approaches to help them learn vocabulary that is not childish. Picture dictionaries are a good resource and are described in some detail later in this chapter. There are monolingual and bilingual picture dictionaries. The use of labels for identifying common objects in the classroom described in the previous chapter is an appropriate vocabulary teaching and learning approach for these students.

Basal Reading Instruction

It is difficult to place older intermediate students into beginning basal reading programs because the texts look so "childish." The Language Experience Approach, as an alternative, does work well with these students. Some teachers, however, are somewhat uneasy about using LEA exclusively to teach older students to read, opting for a published basal program as a supplement. An alternative to a basal program is a "low-vocabulary, high-interest" series. These students must be "phased into" a basal program, following the guidelines developed in the previous chapter. Prebasal activities of the kind described in Chapter 4 are essential in teaching the students that reading is a meaningful activity.

Students are not included in basal activities unless they have L1 literacy background and they are, at least, limited-fluency L2 speakers. It is unfortunately all too common to see non-English-speaking children in reading groups or in whole-class reading activities where they are completely lost about what is taking place. Many teachers are convinced they should include older students in reading instruction because "even if they don't know what's going on, they may learn something from being in a reading group." Intermediate students must learn to read quickly. Basal readers, unfortunately, are usually not the place for them to begin. In essence, basal readers do not provide them comprehensible input. It is also just as disheartening, or perhaps scandalous, to see ESL students who speak little or no English involved in instructional programs teaching academic content in English. As was noted in Chapter 1, there is a significant difference between learning to read and learning from reading. It is at about grade 4 that students typically begin to be taught content systematically and are expected to read to learn. Students who speak no English and have no schooling backgrounds are in serious trouble. These students should likely be in pull-out programs that teach them English. The best kinds of pull-out programs teach English and academic content in an integrated fashion similar to the sheltered programs mentioned above.

Basal readers designed for native English speakers are inappropriate for intermediate students for several reasons. Basal authors write their initial texts so that they contain many high-frequency words. They assume the students have these words in their vocabulary. Indeed, they also make assumptions about students' oral-language development. Initial texts contain many irregular past-tense verbs; they use words in a strange out-of-context fashion (e.g., the word "you" in many texts can refer to someone in the text or to the reader); they contain "unnatural" sentences; and they contain unfamiliar L2 cultural content. Each of these items represents a formidable block to beginning ESL students. The beginning ESL student's vocabulary does not contain many irregular past-tense verbs. Even native English-speaking students have difficulty with the use of such pronouns as "you" in beginning texts. One could opt for basal readers designed for ESL students because they are likely more appropriate.

The authors of ESL basals take into consideration that there should be a better match between students' L2 language ability and the language in their reading texts. Rebane (1985) analyzed a typical ESL basal series and found that it contained many words having the lexical morpheme *ing*. This is one of the first lexical morphemes learned by children. The authors of the ESL series, therefore, assume that the first lexical morpheme learned by ESL students is also *ing*, so they fill their texts with it. Unfortunately, the typical ESL series uses decontextualized language, bizarre sentence patterns, strangely repetitious language, and stories that do not contain familiar cultural content. Generally, basal readers are inappropriate for beginning ESL students. If ESL students are "ready" for a basal series, each lesson must be carefully guided. The DRA-L2 described in the previous chapter is an appropriate lesson plan. Several items are especially important to successful basal instruction.

Background information is vital to comprehension and must be developed carefully and completely. Indeed, vocabulary knowledge may not be as important to comprehension as background knowledge. The DRA-L2 teaches background knowledge and vocabulary within the structure of the story. Basal reading series are not intrinsically bad. Indeed, McCallum (1988) believes that "basals serve an important function", that "basal programs are source books for reading instruction" (p. 207) and should be used as sources of materials and approaches. DRTA activities encourage students to use their background knowledge. The added advantage of DRTA is that it helps students come to know that they do not need to read every single word in a passage in order to comprehend it.

Many teachers, and indeed many ESL students, feel that phonics and word-recognition activities are vital to learning to read. It was suggested that younger ESL students may not benefit from phonics instruction because it requires a kind of metacognitive activity they may not developmentally be able to do. Older students are more likely to be able to function in this metacognitve fashion. If a teacher is convinced that his or her intermediate students need to learn phonics, the teacher must be sure that they have the necessary literacy background, adequate level of L2 proficiency, and ability in metacognitive functioning that learning letter–sound relationships requires. For these students, the phonics activities presented in Chapter 4 are appropriate. There is some evidence to suggest that beginning ESL (ELL) students benefit from instruction in scripted programs, but only initially. There are basal reading series written in Spanish that are used in some bilingual programs. The difficulty is that other than Spanish, L1 basal readers are not readily available. Intermediate students can benefit from whole-language instruction. It is clear to this author that whole-language programs work well when implemented and managed by committed advocates.

Whole Language

The principal advocates of whole-language instruction are typically primary teachers. However, there are whole-language programs in both intermediate and secondary ESL classrooms. In many respects, introducing, initiating, and maintaining such a program with older students is more difficult than it is with younger students because of the attitudes they have usually developed concerning the act of writing. Typically, they associate writing with "school work." They have learned that writing they turn in will be scrutinized, annotated with red marks, and, yes, given a grade. Most intermediate ESL students will probably not have been enrolled in whole-language classrooms, and will have the usual expectations about what is required of them in writing. It is especially difficult for them to write in English. A secondary immigrant student had an interesting comment about the English reading instruction she received. When asked if knowing how to read in her first language had helped her to read English, she reported, "No cuz I had to learn the whole-language. It was like I was a baby and I had to speak again" (female, 15 years old, Spanish-speaking) (Gunderson, 2007, p. 273).

It is best for the teacher to explain very carefully that the teaching approach most likely will be different from what they have experienced before. Students should be given a log book. The teacher explains that he or she will read and react in the log book but will not make any of the usual teacher marks and notations, nor will they be "graded." The teacher will also be writing in a log. Indeed, on certain days, after writing what he or she thinks is an especially interesting, beautiful, or meaningful passage in the log, the teacher will read it to the class. The teacher explains to the class that he or she hopes students will do the same. Students should be made to be comfortable with reading their own material aloud and allowing others to read their material.

In addition, students will be reading many different books, mostly those that are of interest to them, not an assigned reading textbook. Students soon learn that they will be working individually. One of the interesting things that happens with whole-language students is that they come to love to write and do so with a vengeance. Indeed, it is not unusual to observe an ESL student gleefully writing 35-page essays (Gunderson and Shapiro, 1988). The intermediate whole-language teacher quickly adopts and adapts individualized instructional approaches.

Individualized Reading

There are three basic objectives in individualization: 1) to allow students to select their own reading material from a wide selection of appropriate material; 2) to provide students with reading material that is appropriate for their abilities, skills, needs, interests, and motivations; and 3) to provide teachers with the opportunity to monitor, assess, and measure students' reading progress in order to plan and maintain appropriate individual instructional programs.

Teachers in whole-language programs are guides rather than teachers. The basic goal in whole-language classrooms is to make the learning environment comfortable, natural, and holistic. Teachers may guide students in choosing reading material, but must never interfere with their choices. One must, therefore, have a large collection of books, magazines, and other reading materials in the classroom. The following discussion will focus on materials that are of interest to students generally and to different subgroups of students specifically.

Selecting and Maintaining a Classroom Reading Collection

Whole-language teachers as quickly as possible discover their students' interests. The quickest method is to ask. The most efficient approach is to work with small groups and conduct an oral interest inventory. The alternative is to develop a group-administered interest inventory as discussed in Chapter 2. Some students have fairly negative attitudes toward reading. A reading interest inventory can help the teacher to identify them (see Chapter 2). The interest survey is used to begin the selection of materials and to match students and materials. The oral survey is more flexible than the written form, since the teacher can pursue sub-interests.

The teacher-librarian, if there is one, and the local public librarian are invaluable resources for a reading program. They can be asked about high-interest low-vocabulary texts, designed primarily for boys, which contain highly motivating stories with limited vocabulary requirements. The Series Canada (Don Mills, Ontario: Collier-Macmillan, 2000) texts, for instance, have such titles as *Dope Deal*, *Runaway*, *Burn Out*, and *Hot Cars*. There are thousands of books that are written in this fashion, and the Internet is an exciting resource for finding them. Indeed, the local public library is a good source of such books, and some libraries have web pages (see, for instance, the Watertown, Massachusetts, library list of High Interest Low Vocabulary Fiction books at http://www.watertownlib.org/high_interest_low_

vocabulary_fic.htm, accessed on January 23, 2007). Often, school districts have multiple copies of these kinds of books, which can be used to form instructional groups around interests or themes. School storerooms often have discarded but useful materials such as old basal readers and reading kits. Old materials, such as individualized reading kits, are valuable because they contain graded material that can be used as DRTA passages or interest stories. Recently, publishers have also produced informational text at lower readability levels, such as the "Start to Finish Library" at http://www.donjohnston.com/products/start_to_finish/library/index. html (accessed on January 23, 2007). They help teachers provide comprehensible input. In essence, these kinds of programs help the teacher provide sheltered instruction by controlling the difficulty of the academic texts.

Reading and Writing Conferences

A whole-language program demands that the teacher keep in close contact with individual students to monitor their reading and writing progress. Since students are reading and writing independently, their work is unique. Teachers respond to, question, and monitor each student's progress. This is no easy task because it requires the maintenance of careful records. It is best to keep a conference log book to record who has been seen, when they were seen, and the essence of the meeting.

WRITING CONFERENCES

Many teachers maintain two kinds of writing conference. The first involves communicating with a student through writing, usually in the form of comments in their log books. The second kind of conference is the direct one-to-one meeting in which students' progress, their interests, and so forth are discussed. During these conferences, suggestions about the direction of students' writing can be made.

READING CONFERENCES

The primary goal of a reading conference is to monitor, encourage, and guide an individual student's progress. During the reading conference the teacher should take careful notes about what the student is reading and any suggestions for further reading. Occasionally the teacher may ask the student to read aloud in order to evaluate her or his performance. This will suggest whether or not the reading material is appropriate and help to guide the student's progress.

Conferences are important to both the writing and reading programs. Every student must be seen on a regular basis. Two different systems work effectively: 1) the regularly scheduled conference, and 2) the teacher-initiated conference based on student progress. In the first case, the teacher publishes a regular conference schedule. So, Terry always meets with her teacher at 9:30 on Thursday mornings. This system is limited by its inflexibility. Often schedules are interrupted by such school activities as fire drills and school rallies. There are a number of online resources teachers can use to initiate and maintain conference schedules, and a number of commercially available scheduling systems that allow students to view the teacher's schedule and to sign up for sessions independently. In addition there are free calendars available for use (e.g., http://www.google.com/googlecalendar/event_publisher_guide.html, accessed on September 29, 2007).

The second approach is for the teacher to monitor his or her conference log and call on students when needed. There is no regular schedule. The basic limitation of this approach is that some students may be missed if the conference log is not regularly monitored and maintained. The major complaint about this individualized approach is that teachers find there is not enough time in a week to conduct good conferences with everyone. Accurate and careful note taking by the teacher is the most important aspect of conferencing. In order to maximize conference sessions, one may opt to use a standard information form containing basic questions and observational categories. A typical form is as follows:

Conference Log

Name _____   Date _____

Story/Chapter/Book   _____

Comprehension   _____

_____

Suggestions for further study   _____

_____

_____

Oral reading analysis   _____

_____

Writing (Dated)   _____

Subject   _____

Invented spellings   _____

Suggestions   _____

Skills needs   _____

Group conferences are a possibility. One can use the information gained from the interest session to form natural conference groups. So, for instance, a conference could be scheduled with the science fiction group. Group conferences are rather limited regarding the amount of assessment and information one can gain.

Assessment and Skills Instruction

Some teachers feel somewhat uneasy about having students select and read their own books. These teachers feel they want to know more about students' needs, skills, and abilities. Indeed, many teachers are convinced that they themselves should teach the skills students need to learn. In this respect, conferences are important. In addition, the most important assessment involves the students' writing.

Students' Writing

It was noted earlier that students' writing was not graded in the traditional fashion. However, writing should be viewed as a source of vital skills information. Whole-language teachers scrutinize their students' independent writing carefully. They note students' invented spellings. In those cases in which they see consistent patterns, they use the information to form instructional groups. So, for instance, one teacher noted that a great many of her students were having trouble spelling words ending with "le," as in *tumble* and *trouble*. She called together the group of six ESL students who were having the difficulty and taught them the skill.

Managing a Whole-Language Program

Classroom management is fairly easy if one teaches students in three ability groups; even easier if there is only one group. The whole-language classroom is considerably more difficult. Good, accurate notes about students' individual progress must be maintained, with all entries dated. If students are not able to date their writing, the teacher should. A teacher's conference log is essential. This author observed a teacher using an online calendar that all her grade 7 students could monitor to make conference appointments and keep track of students' progress.

Management issues are so crucial to the success of a whole-language classroom that this author has recommended a step-by-step approach (Gunderson, 1995). This author noted that the whole-language programs that appeared to work the best at the intermediate level were those the teachers had taken several years to achieve a step at a time. Uninterrupted Sustained Silent Reading (USSR) or Sustained Silent Reading (SSR) involves students reading silently books of their own choice at a regularly scheduled time during the school day. The most impor-tant feature of USSR is that during the silent reading process the adult reading models in the school and classrooms must be seen to be reading and to be enjoying it. No one—including the principal, the secretaries, or the custodians—is excluded from the silent reading session. Often signs are posted in schools alerting visitors about SSR. Students see adults as avid interested readers. The teacher often ends the SSR sessions with short conversations with students about how good the book he is reading is, how wonderful the author is, and how much he looks forward to reading the next book. This is the time that non-readers can peruse picture dictionaries.

Students are also asked to make daily journal entries. Whole-language teachers ask their students regardless of their backgrounds to maintain such journals. Often, intermediate-age ESL students begin making entries into their journals that are pictorial only. This author has also seen students writing in their own languages in their journals. An exciting development in some students' writing is that there occurs a stage when both English and the first language are written. This author has seen Chinese-English mixed entries in the journals of intermediate-grade students. This is an exciting development because it provides evidence that the student is learning to read and write English. Whole-language teachers meet often with individual students and usually refer to these sessions as conferences.

Conference records should be as complete as possible. In addition to careful individual notes about students' progress, a log of all conferences should be maintained. A wall chart containing a list of students on one side and calendar dates on the other makes a good visual record for everyone to see. An alternative is the online calendar referred to earlier. The teacher should develop a shorthand code to let everyone know when they have had a conference, what kind, and what outcomes are expected. Again, the ultimate record keeper is the computer. The local user-friendly computing teacher is a good source of information about management programs. Management is the most difficult aspect of whole-language instruction. The usual individual conference requires about 15 or 20 minutes of one-to-one meeting time. It is difficult to see every student every week, and interest conferencing is a way of making conferences somewhat more efficient. If a group of students has been involved in reading the same book, for instance, they can be met as a group. Individualized reading programs are difficult for teachers because of the great deal of one-to-one contact time they require. Some teachers rely more on a published program to teach ESL students to read.

Teaching Secondary Students to Read

This author visited a secondary school in Florida that had ESL classes of various kinds and schedules. Several of the classes were scheduled over two class periods to provide the teachers with 80 minutes of time to devote to language arts. The reading portion consisted of 1) the teacher directing students' attention to the story to be read; 2) students taking turns reading (poorly) aloud; and 3) students writing the answers to the questions at the end of the story. These activities took up about 40 minutes of class time. The class was a waste of student and teacher time. The lesson was a failure because students were not properly prepared for the reading, they rehearsed oral errors, and follow-up activities were not designed to help them learn. Secondary students do not have time to waste. Whatever program or methods are chosen, the teacher must be sure that students are actively engaged in learning. Unfortunately, ESL (ELL) students in secondary schools often disappear from academic courses and many drop out of school altogether (Gunderson, 2007). Oakes and Guiton (1995) investigated instructional practices in a large urban high school and found that many Latino students were placed in the vocational track, where they languished academically.

There are a few whole-language instruction classes designed for secondary ESL students, and many secondary ESL teachers have opted to implement some features of whole-language instruction in their classrooms. The important consideration is that secondary ESL students need to learn to read as quickly as possible because their success depends on their ability to comprehend and learn from text. Most teachers believe that direct, intensive instruction in reading is essential. It is somewhat unusual to find a secondary student who has had no L1 literacy instruction; however, it does happen. The secondary matrix is shown in Figure 5.2.

There are two types of students who need reading instruction: those who do not know how to read, and those who have been unsuccessful in learning or have not progressed far enough to contend with the content texts they are expected to read. The following examines the first group.

Students who have not learned to read in their first languages are not as unusual as the reader might think. Often they come from refugee camps. In 2005, for instance, a single 18-year-old refugee from Kenya arrived in this author's city. She was originally from Somalia and she had never learned to read or write in her first language and she had 0-level English. Designing an instructional program for her was extremely difficult and time was not on her side. A basic problem is that the context of her experiences did not include many of the items and experiences that teachers can normally assume students have. She had no experience with books, nor did she know what such common items as electricity and television were.

Even though many authorities would disagree, this author recommends that students who do not know how to read in their L1s should be introduced to print immediately upon being enrolled in the ESL class. They should be involved in activities such as those introduced at the beginning of Chapter 4, vocabulary and LEA activities. The goal should be to make sure that they acquire basic reading

L1 literacy	0-level Very limited	Limited	Limited fluency
None	Survival	Survival	Survival Special
2–6 years	Survival Special	Survival Special	Survival Special General Content*
7+ years	Survival Special	Survival Special Content* Technical	Survival Special General Content*

Figure 5.2 Two-Factor Secondary Instructional Matrix

Note. An asterisk beside a category indicates an issue that will be addressed in Chapter 6.

skills. It may sound pessimistic, but these students will not usually succeed in academic courses. They must learn survival reading skills. The program for adults discussed below focuses on vocabulary vital to survival generally. Secondary students need to learn, and quickly, school survival vocabulary. The following is a list of some important school vocabulary:

GIRLS	BOYS	PRINCIPAL	OFFICE
NURSE	VICE-PRINCIPAL	HALL PASS	CAFETERIA
GYM	COUNSELOR	CUSTODIAN	LIBRARY
AUDITORIUM	ATTENDANCE	EXIT	FIRE
ALARM	UP	DOWN	OUT
IN			

The list is not exhaustive; different words will be important to survival in different schools. These words should be taught directly. They should be written on large word cards. The students should be taken around the school and be shown the vocabulary within the school. If possible, the trip should be photographed with a digital camera so that pictures can be used to illustrate the LEA story that can be written, afterwards, with the words being taught. Photographs and a story montage can also be stored and retrieved by members of the class if the teacher has access to the Internet. Free space is available for teachers on Wikispaces for Educators at http://www.wikispaces.com/site/for/teachers100K (accessed on November 6, 2007). Wikis will be discussed in Chapter 6.

After students have been taught school survival words, they should be taught general survival words. The section dealing with adult survival reading later in the chapter will identify other words to teach. These students are not ready for further reading programs until they have acquired at least a limited proficiency in English. They cannot be taught using a general reading series. They are ready for special reading programs only after they have acquired survival vocabulary and knowledge of basic syntactic structures. They cannot learn from academic texts. To put them into academic classes where texts are in English and the instruction is in English is to do a great disservice to them and to their teachers. These students are prime candidates for first-language classes, but that may not be an option in many districts. If they are older, they are more at risk of dropping out (Gunderson, 2007). They are also prime candidates for being assigned "bilingual buddies." Bilingual buddies are individuals who share the same first languages and are able to provide support in students' first language in cases where bilingual classes are not available. Bilingual buddies are also useful in academic classrooms. The computer lab in a large urban high school, for instance, has designated bilingual buddies to help scaffold students' needs to understand vocabulary and processes in English through their first language. Bilingual buddies define English vocabulary and explain content for students.

The basic notion behind the instructional matrices is to provide comprehensible input for learners based on their language and literacy backgrounds. This author's experience is that teachers who are outstanding in their interactions with ESL (ELL) students make certain that input is comprehensible by including the following features in their instruction:

- realia (real objects and materials)
- manipulatives (drawings, posters, brainstorming-clusters, graphs, tables, maps, props, multimedia presentations, storyboards, storymaps)
- visuals (study prints, textbook illustrations, overhead-projected prints, reproductions of paintings, and documents)
- graphic organizers
- planned opportunities for interactions between all the students in a classroom (cooperative learning, collaborative learning, and student-generated stories based on personal experiences).

Limited and Limited-Fluency ESL Students—No L1 Literacy

Normally there are very few limited or limited-fluency students with no L1 literacy. There are some, however, and they too are at risk as far as success in academic courses is concerned. There are also a great number of students who have an L1 literacy background, but in reality they are not particularly literate in their first languages. This author met a grade 6 Spanish-speaking student from Mexico who was fairly fluent in English, but his reading and writing in Spanish were not very sophisticated. His writing was filled with invented Spanish spellings that demonstrated he was applying his primary-level Spanish knowledge to his L1.

These students should be introduced to survival vocabulary and the important function words. Indeed, they should be explicitly taught to recognize and read the words from a list such as the Inner-City. The sight word approach discussed in Chapter 4 works fairly well for these students. They know basic English and they understand and can produce basic syntactic structures. Their reading tasks will be eased if they are equipped to recognize on sight high-frequency words, especially the function words. The skills-based teacher teaches them directly. Those who believe in the psycholinguistic notion teach them in context. The whole-language teacher objects to the suggestion that the words should be directly taught and assumes that having students read and write daily will teach them the basic words as a consequence of the activity. It appears that vocabulary is learned best when activities focus on word groups or categories.

COMPREHENSIBLE VOCABULARY: PICTURE DICTIONARIES

The following is an example that focuses on the category "dog." The class is shown a picture of a dog, and students help to create a web.

Illustrations are essential for these students. The best illustration to use is one that shows a fairly "standard" dog, so that it represents the category. Generally, students have good world knowledge that they can apply, in this case knowledge

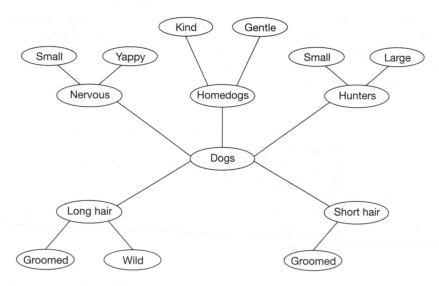

Figure 5.3 A Dog Web

about dogs. English is their problem. The first step is to identify several different kinds of dog (e.g., poodle, German shepherd, greyhound, beagle). Pictures are used to generate discussion about likenesses and differences. One of the best resources, by the way, is a good picture dictionary. Picture dictionaries are organized around categories and show illustrations of items with English attached. A good, affordable paperback called the *Oxford-Duden Pictorial English Dictionary*, published by Oxford University Press, presents items in both inclusive and exclusive categories. An extraordinary source of comprehensible input is the *Stoddart Colour Visual Dictionary* (1993), which uses computer-generated images that have different parts labeled in English. This author has seen intermediate-grade students, especially boys, leafing through this particular dictionary for extended periods of time. The *Oxford-Duden* is good because it provides pictures in categories, so learners can see members of categories and their names. The Internet also contains comprehensible input that is bilingual. Richman, for instance, provides color photographs with English-Spanish vocabulary (http://www.my-spanish-dictionary.com/dict 065.htm, accessed on November 6, 2007). Figure 5.4 shows a sample from Richman's online bilingual dictionary.

An especially exciting online resource is the "All Free Dictionaries Project," which provides multiple visual images in English and 66 other languages. This is really the ultimate resource in providing comprehensible input with L1 support for those students with literacy backgrounds (http://www.dicts.info/index.php?tab=picture, accessed on November 9, 2007).

Words should also be printed on cards so that students can practice recognizing them in isolation and matching the illustrations with them. Discussion can also be directed towards similar and/or dissimilar features (e.g., size, short vs. long hair).

Figure 5.4 Online English-Spanish Dictionary

Source. Image from www.my-spanish-dictionary.com. Copyright by Jacob Richman. Permission to reprint granted by Jacob Richman.

Feature Analysis	
Dog	
big	small

These activities help students to begin to understand and associate words in English both with objects and with printed words. Generally, if students are familiar with the content of a particular category (e.g., they know about the different animals that belong to the "dog" category), working with related items helps them associate English words with their printed forms. The wise teacher selects categories that are important to students, say foods or cars. Often, as a consequence of discussion of a category, students use function words such as *the, of,* and *to.* These should be noted and flashcard practice should be included.

There are incredible online resources to help the teacher locate and utilize comprehensible input. Students themselves at some point can also learn to access comprehensible input independently, although many learn to use technology before they can read print. Pictures can help to provide comprehensible input. Comprehensible input related to vocabulary can be found, for instance, at Dicts.info at http://www.dicts.info (accessed on October 1, 2007). This web page provides illustrations to show the meanings of words. The illustrations are labeled in English and five other languages simultaneously. In addition, other languages ranging from Afrikaans to Welsh are also available. A very brief definition in English is also provided.

The Internet Picture Dictionary at http://www.pdictionary.com/ (accessed on October 1, 2007) is a free online resource that presents illustrations for words either alphabetically or categorized into groups such as "animals," "schools," and "transportation." The illustrations are colorful and appear to be computer generated.

The resources at Picture Dictionary at http://www.pidic.com (accessed on October 1, 2007) are slightly more complex than the Internet Picture Dictionary. This free dictionary shows an illustration of the word if it is concrete, usually a noun, accompanied by definitions. Other words include just definitions or attempts to represent meaning by an illustration.

The Visual Dictionary, http://www.infovisual.info/ (accessed on October 1, 2007), is a free online picture dictionary that features content that is fairly technical and complex. It categorizes words and presents diagrams that have parts labeled in English. An incredible resource is called the Visual Thesaurus (http://www.visual thesaurus.com/, accessed on October 2, 2007). The Visual Thesaurus is available in a free trial version online for a very modest monthly fee or as a software package one can load onto a computer. It works best with students who have basic English reading skills. It is presented here because it is a superb source of comprehensible input for teachers. Higher-level students, to be discussed later, also find it to be an extraordinary resource since both images and related URLs can be quickly accessed.

The user enters a word such as "dog" into the Visual Thesaurus and gets a diagram like the one shown in Figure 5.5. The diagram is in color and the nodes (the circles) are in different colors to represent different categories (i.e. nouns, adjectives, verbs, and adverbs). A user can click on the word "dog" and hear a pronunciation of the word, conduct an instant search of the Web for pages that are related to the word "dog," and conduct an instant Web search for images related

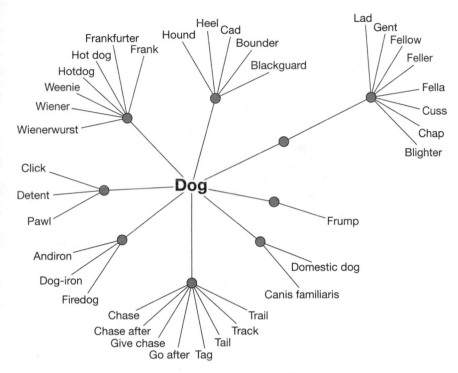

Figure 5.5 Visual Thesaurus Dog Web 1

Source. Images from the Visual Thesaurus (http://www.visualthesaurus.com). Copyright 2002–2007, Thinkmap. All rights reserved. Reprinted with permission.

to the word "dog." Clicking on the nodes will develop a diagram related to the category of the node. Clicking on the node attached to domestic dog results in the diagram shown in Figure 5.6.

This is an extraordinary resource for teachers seeking comprehensible input. It is also an excellent resource for students who may be classed as having limited-fluency English ability, have L1 literacy backgrounds, and are able to use the Internet independently. Such students will be discussed in detail later.

So far, students with no L1 literacy background have been discussed. After they have learned survival vocabulary and to recognize sight words and interest vocabulary, they are ready to be placed into special reading programs discussed later.

Limited and Limited-Fluency Students—Six Years' or Less Schooling

Most secondary students have had some literacy training in either L1 or L2. It is the unusual secondary student who has had no training; that is, the "true" secondary student. Recently, students who are actually in their early twenties have

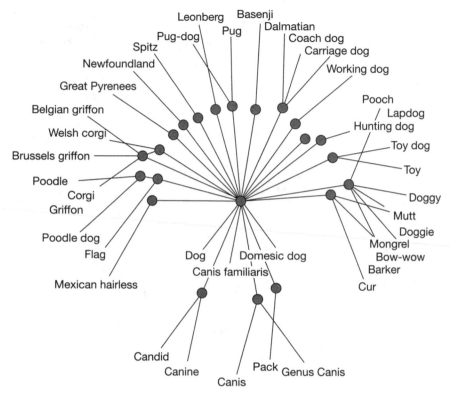

Figure 5.6 Visual Thesaurus Dog Web 2

found their way into secondary classrooms. They are there for several reasons, mostly political and economic. Many have had no literacy training. The immigration vector for one 19-year-old Pakistani refugee included Iran, Turkey, Germany, Quebec, and British Columbia—and no formal schooling.

There are secondary ESL students who have had six years or less of literacy training in L1. Their needs and abilities are often somewhat different from those of students with six years or less of L2 training. In the first case, students must be introduced to L2 reading; they are often anxious to learn to read. The second group of students are already able to read L2, with varying degrees of success. A program designed for the needs of the first group should focus on survival vocabulary and the learning of significant sight words such as those on the Inner-City list. The goal of their reading program should be to develop their skills quickly, so that they can learn from text written in English. In many schools these students attend ESL classes for a very limited time, during which they are expected to develop L2 skills to a level that will permit them to succeed in academic classes. However, they should not be enrolled in academic classes until they can perform at an instructional level. This is a very difficult task to accomplish in most secondary schools because they must be enrolled in classes of some kind. Often, unfortunately for them and for their teachers, they end up in classes such as art because administrators believe such classes do not require anything but minimal English skills. This is a great disservice to them, to the discipline, and to the teachers. Sheltered content instruction is appropriate, but in many schools the necessary resources are not available. The classroom teachers are often the last, best hope for these students to succeed in school and in life.

To discover student "content" reading level, assessments should be made. The cloze procedure, scored according to the criteria given in Chapter 2, can be used to discover students' content comprehension levels. Indeed, no ESL student should be enrolled in a content class that is not sheltered until she or he is able to read the material at an instructional level. In fact, it is also a disservice to enroll native English-speaking students in classes in which they cannot read the material at an instructional level. Reading programs for those students without L2 literacy training should be intense. All of the activities mentioned in Chapter 4 are appropriate. Students should be immersed in vocabulary activities. They should be involved in LEA. As soon as they begin to be able to read, they should be involved in special reading programs. Indeed, it may be that they should also be included in a general reading program carefully matched to their needs and abilities.

Students with six years or less of training in L2 literacy, and in many cases three or four years in L1, who have limited or limited-fluency command of English, must be carefully and closely assessed in L2 reading performance. A large number of these students will be behind their grade level in L2 reading ability—some because they have not had the right teaching programs, others because they have learning problems. The ESL teacher will have to determine which students have learning problems and which simply need more study. The determination is not always easy.

It is not unusual to encounter a student who is seven or eight years below grade level in L2 reading ability (Gunderson, 2004, 2007). The student should not be enrolled in content classes where the texts are too difficult. An important task is to discover whether the student has a learning problem. Any secondary student who has been involved in L2 literacy training for three to six years who is reading at four or more years behind grade level is a candidate for further assessment. Differentiating students with learning problems from those with reading problems is not always easy, especially when their L2 background is limited to six years or less. The following is a checklist of behavioral features that are often associated with students who have learning problems.

- persistent inability to remember sight words
- persistent bizarre spellings
- persistent reversal of letters and/or words
- inability to maintain attention to tasks
- emotional instability

- easily frustrated by reading tasks
- consistent failure to learn to read
- slow, laborious word-by-word reading
- hyperkinetic behavior in the classroom
- persistent avoidance of language-arts activities
- persistent inattention in class.

Many students with learning problems are unable to remember sight words even though they have practiced them repeatedly. However, a student who has great difficulty remembering sight words is not *necessarily* one who has a learning problem. The student who consistently spells words in a bizarre fashion may have a problem, but not necessarily. Some students reverse letters when they write them, while others read "saw" when the word is actually "was."

Emotional ability is difficult to deal with. Some students overreact emotionally to things others would disregard or shrug off. The hyperkinetic student is unable to sit in one place for very long. The student with a learning problem is often easily frustrated by reading tasks, is unable to pay attention for very long, and often avoids language-arts activities. One student in a local school district routinely gets permission to go to the bathroom at the beginning of the language-arts period and never, quite conveniently, returns to the reading lesson.

There are several important points to remember. If a secondary student demonstrates one or more of these features, it does not mean *necessarily* that he or she has a learning problem. It does mean, however, that the student should be monitored closely, and further assessment by the school or school district psychologist should be sought. One must be cautious and not overreact. Many students may display a large number of these features and not have learning problems. Indeed, the onset of many of these behaviors often occurs with the onset of puberty. Any student who consistently demonstrates a "cluster" of these features should be monitored carefully. The course of action is not to label the student as having a learning problem, but to talk to the school principal or school psychologist to try to get further assessment. The significant problem is that identifying a disability in an ESL (ELL) student is no easy task. Often, school psychologists use an IQ test to determine whether or not a student has a disability. Gunderson & Siegel (2001) argue that the use of an IQ test and a discrepancy model of a learning disability is not appropriate for ESL students because of the built-in biases of the test. They conclude that thoughtful classroom teachers who observe students' language behaviors can begin to identify ESL students who have learning disabilities. It is not easy, however. Indeed, it may be that a student can be L1 literate and L2 reading disabled (see Gunderson, 2007).

The most important task is to teach such students some usable reading skills, most likely related to survival (see the next section).

Students with Seven or More Years of Literacy Training

This author found that ESL students in secondary schools were, on average, in ESL support classes for about three and a half years (Gunderson, 2007). However, students' grades in their academic courses went down after they lost their ESL support. Many will have learned to read successfully and will be enrolled in content classes, where they successfully compete with their native English-speaking classmates. A large number of these students are so successful that teachers do not know that they are, in fact, ESL students. The secondary ESL teacher normally deals only with students who have had extensive L2 training when they are behind and have problems dealing with the rigors of content classes. It must be determined whether students are simply behind or whether they may have learning problems. The student who consistently demonstrates a cluster of the behaviors noted above should be recommended for further intensive assessment. "Cluster" means five to seven of the features, but even this can vary. Normally, such an assessment will include teaching prescriptions. It is important to be willing to err on the side of concern. That is, it is better to find out that one's concerns are unfounded than to fail to express them and let a problem pass unnoticed. Sometimes the consequences are lifelong and negative.

A few years ago this writer received a call from a 25-year-old university graduate who was concerned that his first language, Chinese, was still interfering with his English. In fact, he wanted help in eliminating his Chinese accent. The results of an interview were quite interesting. He had immigrated when he was 9 years old, studied in mainstream classrooms for ten years, studied at the university for four years, and received a BA degree in chemistry. Unfortunately, his speech was extremely difficult to understand. He was convinced that his use of Chinese at home had interfered with his English pronunciation. In fact, his speech had only the tiniest hint of an accent, but he had a pronounced lateral lisp. He had been in English-speaking classrooms for 14 years and all of his teachers had apparently thought his speech problem was related to his first language. After six months of regular sessions with a speech pathologist, his speech has improved considerably. Nevertheless, it is more difficult to deal with the problem at 25 than it would have been at 9.

The first step in designing or selecting a program for secondary students who have had literacy training is to assess their L2 reading ability, since classes have an extremely wide range of L2 reading abilities. Indeed, it may not be possible to use a single ESL reading series because it does not adequately account for the wide range of L2 abilities. One can opt for having multiple reading programs and individualized instruction, not an easy task, especially since class size seems to be increasing across North America. The task, though difficult and time-consuming, is quite straightforward. The following is a checklist of activities to be kept in mind when planning group and individual reading activities for students with seven or more years of literacy training:

1. Assess the students' oral English proficiency.
2. Assess students' L2 reading ability using:
   a. a word list like the San Diego Quick Assessment to obtain a "shotgun" measure of reading level.
   b. their oral reading performance on a passage selected from the material they are expected to be placed in (a running record; see Chapter 2)

    c. a cloze test based on materials at different levels, with the scoring altered to account for content words (see Chapter 2)

    d. an Informal Reading Inventory for those students believed to have particular difficulties. Use a published IRI or one made up from materials to be used in the program.

3. Measure the students' ability to recognize survival vocabulary, including words contained on a list such as the Inner-City.
4. Assess the students' content reading knowledge by administering a Group Reading Inventory based on content materials students are asked to read.
5. Design students' programs:
   a. Identify and group students who need work on basic function words.
   b. Identify and group students who need to learn content skills.
   c. Form groups for instruction so that students' reading levels are instructional for the material they are expected to read.
   d. Identify students who will be unable to comprehend and learn from content texts.
   e. Establish student folders so that a record of their abilities, needs, and progress can be kept.
6. Select appropriate reading programs and supplementary materials.
7. Initiate instruction.

A reading program for each student that teaches survival vocabulary, specific reading skills, general reading development, and content reading skills should be designed. Record keeping is very important, especially if an individualized reading program as described above is implemented. The procedures described are helpful in keeping track of students' progress, as well as assisting in putting together instructional groups.

The reading record is a powerful instrument that allows one to isolate individual student needs, abilities, and interests, and to record reading development over time. A reading record is more informative than a conference report because it is more comprehensive. A reading program may involve a published reading series that is augmented with DRA-L2, LEA, DRTA, writing activities, phonics activities (analyzing students' writing reveals which phonics skills need to be taught), vocabulary exercises, mapping, semantic webbing, echoic reading, choral reading, interest grouping, independent interest reading, USSR, special reading, and content reading (see Chapter 4).

The secondary teacher's primary goal is to provide students with the skills they need to read and learn from content texts. Indeed, their very survival in our technological society may depend on it.

Special Reading Programs

Since individual needs and interests are so powerful in determining the degree to which a student learns, special reading programs that take these features into account are an essential component of the secondary reading program. After an interest inventory (either oral or written) has been conducted, a group and/or individual reading test has been administered, students' oral proficiency has been gauged, the instructional level in content material has been surveyed, and their interests have been discussed, then the teacher can design a program that will teach students to read material in a specific subject area. Most often it will be an area they want to learn about. A Special Reading Inventory is easy to develop. Here is a section of such an inventory:

Special Reading Inventory

I am interested in reading and learning about:

1. Sports:

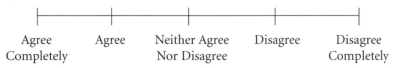

| Agree | Agree | Neither Agree | Disagree | Disagree |
| Completely | | Nor Disagree | | Completely |

2. Local Recreation Centers:

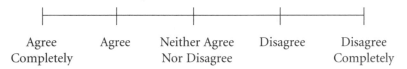

| Agree | Agree | Neither Agree | Disagree | Disagree |
| Completely | | Nor Disagree | | Completely |

3. Getting a driver's license:

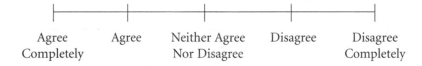

| Agree | Agree | Neither Agree | Disagree | Disagree |
| Completely | | Nor Disagree | | Completely |

4. Applying for a job:

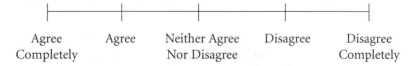

| Agree | Agree | Neither Agree | Disagree | Disagree |
| Completely | | Nor Disagree | | Completely |

The teacher decides what items should be included in an interest inventory. Special reading programs are appropriate for students of limited fluency with no L1 backgrounds and all students (with much caution) with six or more years of literacy training. The following is based on the driver's license manual of British Columbia, Canada. It was developed for a group of eight secondary ESL students who had indicated on their interest inventories that they wanted to read and learn about the subject.

The Insurance Corporation of British Columbia publishes *Road Sense for Drivers* to teach potential drivers basic rules and regulations related to driving and

Reading Record

Name _____   Grade _____

Enrollment Date   _____

Initial Assessments:

_____   _____

Test   Results

_____   _____

Test   Results

Outcome:

_____   _____

Placement   Program

Content Reading Skills:

_____

Grade Level   Skills needs   Program

Strengths and Weaknesses: _____

_____

PROGRAM COMPLETION NOTES:

_____   _____   _____

Placement Completed   Program Components   Success Completed

_____   _____   _____

Needs   Recommendations   Other

_____   _____   _____

Content level   Content Needs   Content
                                                                    Recommendation

_____

Overall comments, recommendations, and observations.

_____

getting a driver's license. The manual is 154 pages long and contains text and many illustrations. It is available online and in print (http://icbc.com/licensing/lic_utility_resman_drivers.asp, accessed on November 25, 2007). The online version divides the text into ten chapters. If you peruse the chapters online you can see how complex the organization of the text is. Look at some individual pages and notice the complex manner in which the texts are presented. Some issues related to the Internet and readers will be presented in Chapter 6.

The readability of the manual was explored. Using Fry (see p. 70), based on three 100-word samples, revealed a mean of 149 syllables and 6.9 sentences for a grade 8 level. Raygor resulted in a mean of 27 words of 6 or more letters in the same three passages selected for the Fry for a readability level of grade 7. All of the students had extensive literacy backgrounds. A 250-word passage that had been turned into a cloze test showed that three of the students were at instructional level, while the others were at the frustration level. The text was too difficult for most of the students in the group. However, they were highly motivated to read and learn from this text; and none, on the basis of several reading tests administered to them, were more than two years behind the level of the text. The text is surprising in that on the surface it looks quite simple; however, when one looks carefully at the text it is quite complex, with many illustrations and accompanying text (see Figure 5.7).

Next, it is a good idea to find out what students know about the subject. The easiest procedure is simply to ask them and keep notes as students brainstorm what they know about the subject. In this case their knowledge was limited. Essentially, they knew they needed to know about signs, driving rules, and "laws of the road." Two of the students, new to the country, had very little experience with cars, but they were eager to learn as much as possible.

A content analysis revealed that the manual contains sections such as Be a Thinking Driver; Control Panel; Safety Restraints for Children; Starting, Signs, Signals and Road Markings; Using Lanes Correctly; and Speed Control. Readers are expected to memorize sign shapes, learn new vocabulary, learn about handling an automobile, learn about dealing with other drivers while on the road, and learn basic motor vehicle laws. As a teacher, one could use the blood, sweat, and tears approach to this reading—the ultimate form of sheltered content instruction. That is, one could take a page at a time and read individual paragraphs, painstakingly explaining new vocabulary and concepts sentence by sentence or word by word as the group encounters trouble. In effect, one becomes an instant talking dictionary, syntactic and semantic analyzer, and background developer. Indeed, the teacher shelters instruction and tries to make the input as comprehensible as possible. The blood, sweat, and tears approach works but should only be used in those cases where students must learn new material as a matter of survival. The following is a typical special reading program lesson; this one concerns a section of the manual entitled See, Think, Do.

The following are important features of this section of text:

1. Going faster than the posted speed is against the law.
2. The greater your speed, the harder it is to control your car.

Chapter 3 – Signs, Signals and Road Markings

School, playground and crosswalk signs

These signs tell you the rules to follow in areas where you need to be extra cautious.

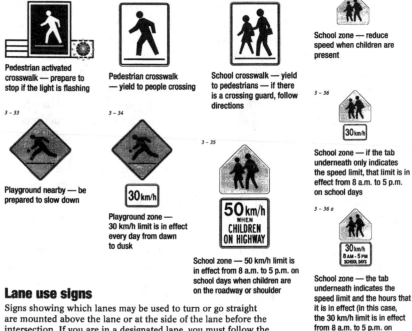

3 – 29 Pedestrian activated crosswalk — prepare to stop if the light is flashing

3 – 30 Pedestrian crosswalk — yield to people crossing

3 – 31 School crosswalk — yield to pedestrians — if there is a crossing guard, follow directions

3 – 32 School zone — reduce speed when children are present

3 – 33 Playground nearby — be prepared to slow down

3 – 34 Playground zone — 30 km/h limit is in effect every day from dawn to dusk

3 – 35 School zone — 50 km/h limit is in effect from 8 a.m. to 5 p.m. on school days when children are on the roadway or shoulder

3 – 36 School zone — if the tab underneath only indicates the speed limit, that limit is in effect from 8 a.m. to 5 p.m. on school days

3 – 36 a School zone — the tab underneath indicates the speed limit and the hours that it is in effect (in this case, the 30 km/h limit is in effect from 8 a.m. to 5 p.m. on school days)

Lane use signs

Signs showing which lanes may be used to turn or go straight are mounted above the lane or at the side of the lane before the intersection. If you are in a designated lane, you must follow the direction indicated by the arrows. You may not move into or out of a designated lane while you are in an intersection.

3 – 37 Turn left only

3 – 38 Continue straight only

3 – 39 Go through or turn left

3 – 40 Go through or turn right

3 – 41 Vehicles from both directions must turn left, no through traffic allowed

3 – 42 Vehicles in both these lanes must turn left

29

Figure 5.7 Page from the British Columbia Driver's Manual

Source. RoadSense for Drivers: BC's Save Driving Guide (North Vancouver, BC: Insurance Corporation of British Columbia, 2007). Copyright 2007 by the Insurance Corporation of British Columbia. Reprinted by permission of the Insurance Corporation of British Columbia.

3. Speed limit signs are always in kilometers per hour.
4. The basic speed limit in British Columbia is 80 kilometers (48 miles) an hour *unless otherwise posted.*
5. The basic speed limit in cities and towns is 50 kilometers (30 miles) an hour unless *otherwise posted.*
6. You can be a hazard by driving too slowly.
7. The speed limit near schools is 30 kilometers (18 miles) an hour.
8. The speed limit near playgrounds is 30 kilometers (18 miles) an hour.
9. The speed at which you have control of your car is the basic speed limit.

The text is simple and contains many illustrations. Vocabulary is a bit tricky. The following words must receive special attention: *posted, limit, speeding, handle, frustrated, impeding, traffic flow, conditions, tempted, press, zones, dawn, dusk, hazard.*

There are two objectives in special reading programs: 1) to teach students reading skills; and 2) to teach students information that is, for some reason, of interest and value to them. The vocabulary words are written on flash cards and are introduced to students before they read the text, in the order in which they occur. Everything possible is done to teach the context-based meanings of the words.

Teacher: Today we are going to read a section of the driver's manual that deals with speed and distance. The first difficult vocabulary word you are going to see is *posted.* Juanito, do you know what this word means?

Juanito: Let me see, my dictionary don't have it, but it has *post* to mean "a stake set upright in the ground to serve as a marker or support."

Teacher: The definition is related. Let me draw a post on the chalkboard. This is a post. If I put a sign on the post then we say that the information on the sign has been posted. Wai Chi, if I draw a sign on this post and write this on the sign, tell me what is posted here.

Wai Chi: Thirty kilometers [18 miles] per hour is posted.

Teacher: Right. So in this case, the posted speed limit is 30 kilometers [18 miles] an hour. So *posted* means shown somewhere along the road on a post so we can see it. Sometimes posted can also mean that the sign is put on a wall of a building. What kinds of information is posted on page 29?

Each of the vocabulary items is developed in this fashion. It is quite incredible to consider page 29 (Figure 5.7) because it contains so much information. The sign with the two children (upper right), for instance, states that one should reduce speed when children are present, while the sign just below it contains the note that the same sign with "30 km/h" posted below it is in effect from 8:00 a.m. to 5:00 p.m. There are, however, a total of five signs that include children on this page. Each one, although they appear similar, means something different. Although the overall readability level is grade 7 or 8, the manual is much more difficult to read and to learn from than material of grade 7 or 8.

It is wonderful to watch ESL teachers in action. They spare no amount of energy or personal dignity to teach students vocabulary. The following is a portion of a modified study guide (see Chapter 6 for a discussion of study guides) to help students read and comprehend new material. It focuses on the identified concepts and target vocabulary. Before reading new material, students should have practiced recognizing the vocabulary words and practiced using their meanings. Before reading, the study guide is read aloud by the teacher and discussion is directed at guiding students to read and answer the questions.

Speed and Distance

Read Paragraph 1: Traveling faster than the _____ speed limit is against the _____. Why do you think this is true?

_____

It says that traveling faster than the posted limit is the greatest _____ of accidents. Why do you think this is so?

_____

Read Paragraph 2: The greater your speed, the harder it is to

_____

How do you think posted speeds are chosen?

_____

Read Paragraph 3: This paragraph says that the posted speed is the fastest you can _____ drive under ideal conditions. What does this mean?

_____

_____

The guide contains the identified vocabulary and directs students' attention to the important concepts and facts being described. Follow-up exercises should focus on important content items discussed in the passage. Students are normally interested in reading a driver's manual so they can get a driver's license. If this is the case, then follow-up activities should include not only discussions of the material read, but also practice tests involving real-life activities. That is, they should be given a real multiple-choice test, one similar to the actual test. The British Columbia Insurance Corporation provides samples of tests online at the address noted earlier. A webbing activity, since it shows the overall form and content of the chapter, is also a good follow-up exercise.

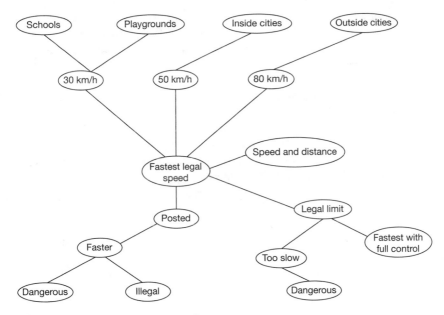

Figure 5.8 Speed and Distance Web

Students involved in this lesson learned how to recognize and understand new vocabulary in English and learned information they needed to know. The teacher-developed special reading program is an essential component of the secondary ESL program.

Published special reading programs are available and are discussed further in Chapter 6. Special reading programs are useful in teaching vocabulary and reading skills. The best ones are developed around interests and needs and are designed and developed by teachers. One of the standard teacher-developed special reading programs involves the use of the daily newspaper. It is only after students have developed a fairly good grasp of English that they should be introduced to general reading programs.

General Reading Programs

Teacher-developed programs are excellent; however, it is also possible to augment them with a published reading series. Published programs are general in scope, often more difficult than their "level" designation would indicate. Published programs are generally appropriate for students with literacy backgrounds and *at least* limited proficiency in English. Generally, students who do not have a literacy background should not be included in a published reading program until they have attained limited fluency in English. Such students will succeed, given much teacher help. One should not rely solely on an ESL reading series. Students should be placed in material that is at their instructional level through one of the procedures discussed in Chapter 2. There are hundreds of ESL materials. These will not be listed here, however, because information is readily available on the Internet and any list published here would be out of date in a fairly short time.

If one opts for a general published reading program, the following items are important to remember:

1. General reading programs are often more difficult than their "level" indicates. Therefore, one should:
   a. Measure readability using a readability formula to make an initial judgment of the program's suitability for a class.
   b. Measure how well students read the text by administering a series of cloze tests based on the reading program materials.
   c. Assess the background knowledge required to read different selections in the program.
2. Familiarize students with both the concepts and the new vocabulary to be introduced in particular selections of the program before their independent reading.
3. Never allow students to read a story "cold." They must be carefully introduced to new vocabulary, especially when vocabulary is context-specific in meaning (e.g., pilot of a ship).
4. Always ensure that the activities at the end of a selection focus on meaning rather than on surface structure details.
5. Never include students in a general reading program if they cannot comprehend it at an instructional level.

The major goal of a secondary teacher is to provide students with the skills they need to read and learn from content texts. Teachers who have ESL students must be prepared to use many different approaches and programs. They must be willing to spend a great deal of time planning and designing programs that meet the individual needs and abilities of their students. A student's future is often in the hands of the reading teacher. They must be equipped to meet the challenges of learning from text. These issues are addressed more closely in Chapter 6.

Teaching Adults to Read

Adult ESL students have various reasons for learning to read English. Figure 5.9, the Two-Factor Adult Educational Matrix, divides L1 literacy background into three broad areas: 1) no L1 literacy background, 2) two to six years' L1 literacy background, and 3) seven-plus years' L1 literacy background. Adults vary in significant ways related to their backgrounds and their motivations. The following discussion focuses on adults who might be best characterized as adult basic English students. These are individuals who wish to develop basic reading skills to cope with the day-to-day English literacy requirements needed to live in an English-speaking environment. These individuals do not want to learn enough to read an academic text to learn, or to gain enough English literacy skills to pursue higher-level degrees, or to qualify for professional certification. The issues related to such students will be presented in the next chapter.

	0-level Very limited	Limited	Limited fluency
L1 literacy None	Survival	Survival Special Experiential	Survival Special Experiential General
2–6 years	Survival Special Experiential	Survival Special Experiential	Survival Special Experiential General Content* Technical*
7+ years	Survival Special Experiential	Survival Special Experiential Content* Technical*	Survival Special Experiential General Content* Technical

Figure 5.9 Two-Factor Adult Educational Matrix

Note. An asterisk beside a category indicates an issue that will be addressed in Chapter 6.

0-Level/Very Limited English and No L1 Literacy Background

Adults with no L1 literacy background and little, if any, proficiency in English are often the most difficult individuals to teach. They do not associate print with language. They have never had to rely on writing and reading in any way to survive. Indeed, one occasionally encounters an individual from a non-literate culture in the classroom. Often, such adults find themselves in a large urban area enrolled in programs designed to teach them to speak, read, and write English. It is difficult to gauge who is more frustrated, teachers or students. There is not enough time to develop English proficiency to the level where these students can be placed into reading programs. They must be introduced to survival reading to equip them to recognize and read important vocabulary. The following is a list they should learn very quickly:

WOMEN	MEN	LADIES	GENTLEMEN
TOILET	BATHROOMS	STOP	GO
WALK	DON'T WALK	ENTER	POLICE
BUS	CAUTION	FOOD	OPEN
CLOSED	EXIT	DO NOT ENTER	IN

continued

OUT	DANGER	HOT	COLD
WARM	LOW	HIGH	ON
OFF	POWER	POISON	GROCERY
RICE	TEA	COFFEE	WATER
EMERGENCY	HOSPITAL	DOCTOR	CLINIC
AMBULANCE	ENTRANCE	SMOKING	SCHOOL
WORK			

Direct observation and instruction are superior activities. In other words, the teacher must take students out of the classroom and bring them into "the field." This author remembers all too well a most embarrassing moment that occurred when he was showing a group of adult male Cambodians how to use the facilities in the bathroom of the secondary school they had just enrolled in. As an ESL teacher, this writer had carefully written words on flashcards so they could be used to teach the students to recognize important words. It soon became apparent, however, that simply showing them the word "urinal" and having them practice recognizing the word, which they did successfully, was not enough to get the concept across. But, although I will avoid recounting the details, the reader is assured that these students did learn the essentials and could recognize related survival words.

The list gives survival words for students in an urban setting. Other words for different settings will probably need to be selected. They are not randomly ordered. *Go, stop*, and *walk* are definitely related, but so is *don't walk*. The 0-level or very limited adults with no L1 backgrounds do not seem to benefit from other reading activities, so the focus should be on improving their English and increasing their sight vocabulary of survival words.

Students with L1 Literacy Backgrounds

The following activities are designed for students who have L1 literacy backgrounds or who are limited English or limited-fluency English proficient.

EXPERIENTIAL PROGRAMS

Experiential reading programs involve students in "real" activities rather than the decontextualized classroom lessons often used to teach them. They are referred to here as experiential even though they are language experience activities, because they involve the teacher giving students experiences in areas that may be new to them. LEA and the vocabulary exercises described in Chapter 4 are also appropriate and helpful for students at these levels. The decision heuristic labels these activities as experiential reading programs. The focus must be on meaningful material organized into themes. The following, for example, is organized around the theme of "riding the bus."

Students are introduced to the theme and the vocabulary associated with the theme. So, for instance, the teacher introduces vocabulary cards on large cardboard sheets along with pictures to illustrate meaning.

Teacher: This is *bus*, everybody. (Students repeat the word *bus*.) The bus carries people. (Shows a picture of a bus.) We are going to take the bus. The driver drives the bus. (Shows the word *driver*, and students repeat the word.)

The teacher practices recognizing words with students. At one point he or she separates the words and the pictures and has students match words with pictures. The next step is to go catch a bus. The teacher brings along the flashcards and associates their new vocabulary with items encountered during their trip. A digital camera makes a good record of the trip, especially since the pictures can be downloaded onto a computer and easily integrated into experience stories. One could also use a video recorder to add the element of sound. A trip can involve a stop at a library, police station, hospital, restaurant, or some other place associated with vocabulary previously introduced. The Internet (see Chapter 6) provides exciting new possibilities for including students' activities in various forms such as oral, visual or both. See, for example, the Multi-Literacies Project at http://multi literacies.ca/index.php/folio/viewGallerySlideShow/220/334, accessed on October 24, 2007. After a visit, the follow-up activity reinforces the vocabulary introduced. This time students identify objects for the teacher, using the flashcards as needed. Free wiki space is also an important resource in developing, storing, retrieving, and using such materials (see Chapter 6).

The Experience story is very important at this point. If the trip is photographed or videotaped, it is a visual record to help students generate a story. The teacher, since these students have so little English, may have to take the lead in writing the story—making sure to involve students in the photographs and in the stories (e.g., "Mrs. Trang is waiting for the bus"). Even though these activities are essentially reading activities, they help develop oral English skills. The following is a portion of a story written by a group of adult ESL students.

A Bus Trip

The class is walking to the bus stop. (Photograph) Mr. Baht is waiting for the bus. Mr. Vu is waiting for the bus. (Photograph) The class is waiting for the bus. (Photograph) The bus comes down the street. (Photograph) The bus stops at the bus stop. (Photograph) Mrs. Lao gets into the bus. (Photograph) Mrs. Lao pays the bus fare. (Photograph) Mrs. Lao sits down. (Photograph)

There are no pronouns since at this point, students would have difficulty understanding them. The sentences are all in present or present progressive tense. The words students were introduced to before the trip are reinforced and practiced. However, other words have entered into the reading activity, words such as *into*, *the*, *is*, and *at*. One suffers great anguish when trying to introduce such words to students. At this level the task is to get across the meaning of the sentence without focusing on the function words. Learning these will come with time. In this fashion, students learn survival words and are introduced to meaningful print. They begin to learn that print represents language and they learn survival vocabulary. If one follows this procedure and visits the school's homemaking department (if it has one) or kitchen, a local restaurant (menus are wonderful teaching materials), a grocery store, a hospital, a recreation center, a police station (caution, however, because some students are afraid of officials in uniforms), a fire station, and a department store, students will have been introduced to and learned hundreds of vocabulary words, and, most importantly, vital survival words. Each experience will provide material to last for at least a week of study. Field trips can be organized in such a way that they do not involve money. A class can walk to the local market. (The owner should be consulted first!) It is surprising how many trips can be arranged for little or no money. These students need meaningful activities that cannot be adequately provided in classroom environments.

Adults at all levels of oral proficiency will benefit from programs such as the one described on p. 174 as an initial program. However, those with no L1 literacy background and 0-level or very limited proficiency will progress in L2 reading very slowly. The words representing the most difficulty for them in oral English are function words. These, as discussed earlier, represent significant portions of written text. They can come to be able to read survival words and the simple texts generated for them. In the real world, however, they are generally frozen at the survival level.

One should not give up, however, because there are occasional, marvelous exceptions. Interestingly, adult students, especially older ones, find it easier to learn in adult environments than in other kinds of classrooms. That is, adult ESL students learning English in a "senior citizens' center," for example, are more likely to participate and learn than those in a secondary or elementary school or some other center where there are younger people. It seems they feel freer to talk, to discuss, and to learn in such an environment. This feature makes an enormous difference in the older adults' learning of English. Special reading programs are the next step for these students. They should be designed around students' interests. The special program described earlier is a typical series of lessons focused around a theme based on interests.

Obviously, there are many kinds of adult ESL students who have reasons for wanting to learn to read English or to improve their reading ability in English. The survival reading program can also be termed a special program, since the activities are focused in a particular area. The special program is designed to match students' interests and needs. A published general reading program is acceptable only if 1) it is related to a student's needs and interests, 2) it is at the student's instructional level, and 3) it is supplemented by the teacher with materials generated by the student.

The adult decision heuristic divides literate adults into two groups, those with one to six years of literacy training and those with seven or more. Six years is, of course, a rough predictor of reading knowledge. It appears that six years represents a kind of average for many adult students, especially those from Third World nations. The seven-plus group usually includes students who have finished university studies and have, in many cases, studied English.

In San Francisco, for instance, there is a former school principal from Argentina, a medical doctor from Vietnam, a biochemist from Taiwan, and a dentist from Indonesia who are enrolled in an evening English language program to improve their reading abilities. Each of these students had studied English prior to immigrating to the United States. Unfortunately, their programs had focused on reading technical material, not on developing fluency in speech or reading. The teacher's primary goal was to improve their reading comprehension and their oral English.

DIRECTED READING-THINKING ACTIVITY (DRTA)

Readers of English use their knowledge of syntax and semantics, their personal experiential background, and their knowledge of the world to make predictions in reading. ESL readers also apply their syntactic and semantic knowledge as they read, but their ability to apply this knowledge may be limited by their English proficiency. In addition, their personal and world knowledge is directly related to their first-cultural backgrounds. ESL readers object to the notion that they do not have to read every word in order to understand a text. Indeed, their basic approach is most often to use their dictionary to understand every word in an English text, a procedure that both slows their reading rate and lowers their comprehension. DRTA and DRTA-like activities promote prediction in the reading of ESL adults (Gunderson, 1995).

A study was conducted by this author to investigate adult ESL students and DRTA. It was thought that DRTA was a superior method for developing students' abilities to make predictions and to comprehend text. Six English instructors at an English-language institute participated in the study. Three of them were trained to teach reading by using the DRA and three were trained to use DRTA. Permission to use stories from *Unusual stories from many lands*, written by Arlo T. Janssen (Englewood Cliffs, NJ: Prentice Hall, 1985) was granted by the publisher. Teachers in the study used the Janssen stories as part of their reading programs. The first exploratory study involved some 150 students at different levels of English proficiency. Students were given reading lessons using the same stories. However, the kind of instruction they received varied: 1) students were taught using cloze activities based on the stories, 2) students were taught using the DRA L2 as a basic lesson plan, 3) students were taught using DRTA, and 4) a group of students were used as a control (they were not taught using any of the other approaches). The study lasted four months, beginning in September.

The cloze students were given the stories with every fifth word deleted. They were asked to work in small groups and decide on what words should be supplied. Other students, using the same stories, were taught using DRA-L2 with a special emphasis on developing background knowledge. The DRTA groups were given the stories and asked to make predictions. The results are as follows:

The DRA-L2 and DRTA groups thought the stories were quite interesting. Indeed, they were very enthusiastic about them. The cloze group, involved with the same stories, thought they were boring and uninteresting. The DRA-L2 and DRTA groups scored higher on measures of L2 comprehension at the end of the study than did the cloze group. Indeed, the cloze group and the cloze instructors hated the approach. Many different versions of the cloze instruction were tried in order to make it more interesting, including deletion of every fifteenth word, maze-like deletions, and oral deletion work. However, the attempts failed. The results show that cloze as an instructional activity quickly becomes boring and repetitive. It focuses the students' attention on low-level syntactic constraints and must be used with caution.

DRA-L2 and DRTA did not appear to result in different levels of achievement, but DRTA students reported in their logs much more enthusiasm than the DRA-L2 students. Indeed, one group of Japanese students were unable to read only part of a story at a time. They were too anxious to see the end of the story and would immediately uncover the conclusion. It was necessary to cut the stories into sections, giving them only a part of the story at a time. This procedure worked quite well, but the room often became rather messy, with parts of stories floating around. The DRTA group was superior in achievement to the DRA-L2 group in one respect: they were much better at comprehending inferential questions than were the DRA-L2 group.

In a second study, about 125 students were divided into six different classes; three used DRA-L2 and three used DRTA. Students were adult English teachers whose L1 was French. They varied tremendously in their English ability. At the end of the study, those in the DRTA group were superior to those in the DRA-L2 group in L2 comprehension. DRTA is a valuable approach that can be used in many different situations. It can be used with such items as newspaper articles, movies, film strips, oral stories, and content texts. It is amazing how adaptable DRTA is. One can have students write predictions. DRTA is a valuable addition to oral, reading, and writing programs. Indeed, it adapts extremely well to many different situations.

The highly motivated ESL student can be placed in a general reading program if his or her L2 skills are at the instructional level. These students benefit greatly from such programs if the teacher is careful to teach each lesson so that new vocabulary and background knowledge are meticulously developed. Published special reading programs may also be appropriate since they appeal to students' interests.

Conclusion

This chapter contained discussions of reading approaches and programs designed to teach intermediate, secondary, and adult-level ESL students to read. It began with a discussion of intermediate students in which it was suggested that teaching older students to read can be more difficult than teaching younger students because reading materials matched to their older students' needs and abilities are often too childish. It was suggested that ESL students should not be included in reading instruction if they have no L1 literacy history and 0-level English ability. Including these students in formal reading instruction is fruitless, often causing the development of negative attitudes toward reading.

Whole-language instruction requiring the teacher to implement and maintain careful records on an individual basis was discussed. So, too, were individualized programs, a basic component of whole language. An example of an interest inventory was given to show how students' background motivations can be matched with texts. Classroom library collections allow the teacher to provide material in a classroom to match students' interests.

Textbooks containing low-vocabulary requirements designed to be of high interest were described. It was pointed out that reading and writing conferences allow teachers to keep track of students' progress. Skills instruction, for those teachers who believe in it, was also discussed. It was suggested that students' individual writing represented a valuable assessment instrument for the teacher.

Basal reading instruction with ESL students is successful only with students of limited to limited-fluency ability who have had L2 literacy instruction. ESL basals contain different kinds of vocabulary from those designed for native English speakers.

Secondary students need to learn to read as quickly as possible. Programs must be designed to match their backgrounds, needs, and abilities in L2. A secondary decision heuristic was provided that measures these two features. Programs to teach secondary students were divided into 1) programs for 0-level and very limited English, *and* six years or less of L2 training; 2) limited English and limited-fluency English, *and* six years or less of L2 training; and 3) students with more than six years of L2 training. ESL students with many years of L2 training who are behind their grade level in L2 reading ability may have learning problems. The chapter offered procedures for discriminating between those with learning problems and those simply behind in reading.

Special reading programs are designed to include students' interests. A special reading inventory is a kind of interest assessment that discovers what students would like to read and learn about. From the results of such an inventory the teacher is able to design and implement a reading program in a particular interest area, such as "the driver's license program." General reading programs are published by firms to teach students to read. Often they are more difficult than their level designation indicates and caution must be used before including students in a general reading program. General reading programs were described and a list of precautions given.

Programs to teach adult ESL students to read were also discussed. Adult students are often among the most difficult to teach, especially those who have little English and no L1 literacy training. Survival reading programs that teach essential "emergency" vocabulary are therefore important. The experiential approach for teaching adults to read uses local trips as a basis for generating stories and vocabulary to learn. Once adults begin to be able to read, they should be included in special reading programs designed to meet their interests.

Highly motivated and educated adult ESL students may learn to read L2 very quickly. They should be included in survival reading programs followed by special and general reading programs. DRTA, which focuses on active prediction during reading, is an excellent method for helping these students develop orally, in reading, and in writing.

This chapter has presented methods and approaches for teaching older ESL students how to read in L2. The methods set out in both Chapters 4 and 5 should be adapted to meet the needs, abilities, and interests of students. Since each student is an individual, no one program or approach works for all. Once again, the ESL teacher must take extraordinary measures to provide the right program for each student. This chapter and Chapter 4 have presented many approaches and methods to teach literacy. They can, and should, be combined in hundreds of different ways to help students learn to read. The following chapter focuses on students who need to learn from reading rather than students who need to learn to read.

Explorations

Work with a partner, if possible.

1. Some immigrant students arrive when they are in their late teens and begin high school with no English skills, but a need to learn to read. Unfortunately, they do not have five to seven years to wait until they learn the CALP they need to learn in their academic classes. What kinds of instructional programs do you design for these students? What kinds of sheltering do you provide?
2. The Internet represents an incredible resource that has, unfortunately, negative features. How do you explore the Internet with ESL (ELL) students in a way that teaches them about the incredible resources but also the negative features?
3. Comprehensible input is one of the most important features of good ESL instruction. How do you as the teacher go about locating, evaluating, and using comprehensible input for your ESL students? How can you train them to find comprehensible input independently?
4. Adults are often the most at-risk students. How would you go about making certain that your adult students explored their English-speaking environments independently? This is often the most difficult task for ESL students. Indeed, many adult students, usually women, end up becoming isolated. As their children grow and become more socialized into English and the community, they become even more isolated and lonely. How would you go about supporting their integration into their new communities?

6

Teaching Academic Reading

Introduction

Learners are often asked to read, comprehend, and learn material from textbooks, computers, the Internet and a variety of other media. Students in general have difficulty reading and learning from text of various kinds. They have to learn, for instance, to read and comprehend Internet-based text that is presented in extremely complex and interconnected ways. This chapter contains discussions of content-area reading instruction. The discussions in this chapter will develop strategies to help students read and learn from informational texts primarily. However, there will be a short discussion of critical literacies and multiliteracies (see Chapter 1) as they relate to ESL (ELL) students. There are various terms that have been used to refer to reading relative to students and their particular literacy needs; these terms will be addressed first.

Content Reading, English for Special Purposes, and English for Occupational Purposes

There is a long tradition in North American reading pedagogy to refer to instruction that equips learners with strategies to read and comprehend text as "content reading." Many books have been written for teachers in the area (see, for instance, Martha Rapp Ruddell (2001), *Teaching content reading and writing*, New York: Wiley). Authors have primarily covered issues related to teaching English-speaking high school and university-level students strategies to read and comprehend their academic texts. Second-language educators have additionally used a variety of terms to designate underlying differences in students.

There are a number of different terms that occur in the ESL literature: English for Special Purposes (ESP), English for Academic Purposes (EAP), English for Business Purposes (EBP), English for Occupational Purposes (EOP), and English for Vocational Purposes (EVP). Actually, many of these categories have also been divided into subcategories (see, for instance, Dudley-Evans & St. John, 1998). For purposes of this book, the overall category "content literacy" is used to denote reading and writing related to the act of learning content. The term "content" is used because it was the term first used in the area of reading pedagogy. Content literacy is divided into English for Special Purposes and Adult Basic English. The abbreviation ABE is normally used to refer to Adult Basic Education. However, in the context of this book it is used to refer broadly to the kinds of literacy skills an adult learns to survive in an English-speaking environment. The adult reading programs described in the previous chapter are characteristic of this category of learning. The key feature of these students is the need to learn the basic literacy skills necessary to get along in society and to gain employment, although the work is usually at a lower level.

English for Special Purposes is divided into two categories: English for Academic Purposes and English for Occupational Purposes (see Figure 6.1). The focus of Academic English is on adult-level students who are most often college and university-level students who are attempting to gain entrance to a college or university in an English-speaking post-secondary setting or who are already enrolled in such a setting and need to learn the literacy skills they need to survive in university-level classes. The sad fact is that many university students who have gained entrance to a program on the basis of their scores on a test such as the TOEFL are woefully unprepared for the difficulties of reading and learning from academic texts. The two largest groups of students who need occupational English appear to be those who wish to enroll in an institution to study to get certified to gain employment in an occupation such as electrician or airplane mechanic and who wish to get recertified in a profession such as nurse, social worker, or medical doctor. In the first case the learner has to learn both the trade and the vocabulary. In the second case the individual must learn the English to allow her or him to apply the knowledge gained in a program in another language to an English environment. These students often have the most difficulty adjusting to a new country where their deep expertise in fields such as medicine or social work is masked by their limited English abilities. This author has known surgeons and engineers who have had to work as dishwashers because of their limited English skills. The bottom line is that the United States has much to offer if one's English is good enough.

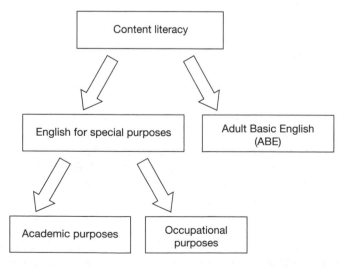

Figure 6.1 Content Literacy

Content Reading and L2 Reading Ability

There are several options available concerning adults and content material: 1) make sure that the material they are asked to read is at their "instructional level," 2) provide support to help them read texts (sheltered content instruction), 3) enroll them in courses that teach academic content without texts, 4) explicitly teach students content reading skills, 5) teach academic courses in the students' first languages, 6) systematically simplify all texts they are asked to read, or 7) assume they will never learn from text and give up. Some secondary teachers, it would seem, have opted to ignore ESL students' special needs, pretend they are not in their academic classes, and go on with business as usual (Gunderson, 1986b, 2004, 2007). Students, even native English-speaking students, must learn how to learn from reading. College- and university-level students need urgently to learn content reading skills. High school students who have limited English fluency and more than seven years of schooling also need to learn content reading skills.

Content Reading Materials

Content reading instruction involves teaching the special reading skills needed to read, comprehend, and learn from textbooks used in classes such as social studies, mathematics, biology, physics, and economics. Textbook authors have, probably under the guidelines imposed by publishers or by the constraints and requirements imposed by particular subjects, developed particular content writing styles.

It is important to demonstrate why it is so difficult for both English-speaking and ESL (ELL) students to read and comprehend their content texts. You, as the ESL teacher, will also have to face the realization that some content material is too difficult even for you because of your background and the depth of knowledge of content vocabulary and technical issues required by some academic texts. A casual perusal of a modern secondary-level academic text demonstrates dramatically that knowledge has also changed in profound and significant ways.

The science that secondary students study today is incredibly complex and advanced compared to the science of 20 or 30 years ago. This author has observed grade 12 biology classes in which DNA was the focus. The instruction included a great deal of information that was not known in the mid-1990s. Books have also evolved in the way they present text. Textbook authors and publishers produce books filled with graphics, text boxes, glosses, flow charts, and many other features they believe will help students learn academic content. The problem is that students are seldom taught to read complex texts, and, as a result, the texts are more difficult for them to read and comprehend.

Content texts are different in *many* respects from elementary reading texts. Content reading material:

- contains more complex sentence structure than reading texts
- contains more abstract vocabulary than reading texts
- contains more specialized vocabulary than reading texts
- is generally more abstract than material in reading texts

- contains different kinds of visual aids (such as graphs, maps, charts, and time-lines) than do reading texts
- is generally more difficult than reading material designated for the same grade level
- requires students to read, comprehend, and learn new material from text
- is more "information packed" than reading texts
- is more "concentrated" than reading text
- is usually written in a style different from reading texts
- contains more difficult vocabulary, often with non-standard meanings (e.g., *conductor* in a science class is different from *conductor* in a music class).

Chamot & O'Malley (1987), partly on the basis of Cummins' work, developed the Cognitive Academic Language Learning Approach (CALLA) to help ESL (ELL) students learn academic content. Their model has three components: "(1) a standards-based curriculum correlated with grade-appropriate content subjects, (2) academic language development focusing on literacy, and (3) instruction in the use of learning strategies" (Chamot, 2006, p. 21). These authors argue that the teacher's first task is to choose important topics and teach learning strategies to assist students to learn both the content and the English associated with the content. The approach also focuses on the explicit teaching of learning strategies. Students learn how to use strategies to learn from written material. Chamot (2006, pp. 34–35) lists questions to guide teachers' planning that include such items as:

- How will I find out what my students already know about the content topic and what related experiences they have had?
- How will I find out what language skills and learning strategies they can already bring to this type of task?
- What vocabulary needs to be taught?
- What is the best way to present this content so that students understand the concepts?
- What language skills will they use?
- What learning strategies do I need to model, explain, or remind them to use?
- What kinds of activities will help my students apply the new information?
- What language skills will they be practicing?
- How will they apply learning strategies during practice activities?
- What is the best way for my students to assess their own learning of language, content, and learning strategies?
- How can I connect the topic of this lesson to students' own lives, culture, and language?
- How does this topic connect to other content areas?

In the 1991 edition of this book, this author recommended very similar approaches and procedures for teachers who wished to design academic reading programs for ESL students. The first step in designing an academic reading program is to discover whether students are able to cope with the special features of a content text and the general requirements of the content course, an endeavor requiring two assessments: a content reading inventory and a cloze procedure. The teacher is advised to consider the local curriculum guides to identify "required" content or "standards" to be included. At the university level this includes reviewing students' course syllabuses.

The content reading inventory reveals the students' needs and abilities in dealing with content features, whereas the cloze procedure reveals whether students will be able to comprehend and learn from the written discourse. Both types of assessment were described in Chapter 1. If a student is not able to comprehend the text at an instructional level, the text is too difficult. It is fruitless to ask the student to read the text independently. Instead, she must be given intense reading instruction until her reading ability increases to the level at which she can understand the text. Those who cannot deal with the special content features of a text will not be able to read and comprehend it adequately and must be enrolled in a program designed to teach students how to "read" such features. Indeed, some may be at the instructional level in cloze, but below in content-reading ability.

Quick Content Assessment Measure

A content-reading assessment measure was described in Chapter 2. Results of such a measure provide a great deal of information for a teacher to begin to design programs to teach students the skills they need to read and understand academic material. This author has used a quick-and-dirty assessment procedure that provides some fairly reliable information concerning students' comprehension of a particular text. The Quick Content Comprehension Measure is quite easy to administer. Select a passage of 100 or more words from the academic text students are assigned. A selection of approximately 250 words appears best. Photocopy the selection, including any graphics, and give it to students. Ask students to read the text and to highlight any words they do not know or have trouble understanding. The time limit for this assessment is three minutes per hundred words. The following is a rough or fuzzy indicator of students' content comprehension:

- 0–10 highlighted words per 100 words—Independent
- 11–20 highlighted words per 100 words—Instructional
- 20 or more highlighted words per 100 words—Frustration.

These readers should not have trouble with function words such as *have*, *of*, and *were*, so these should not be highlighted. If they are, this is a signal that the students must focus on basic English. The assessment provides an overall assessment of students' content comprehension of particular reading material. However, it often provides teachers with convincing evidence that they must focus their instructional programs on academic vocabulary and content structures.

As was noted in Chapter 1, there are many skills students need to learn in order to comprehend text. The following list contains a number of these skills. The activities that follow are either general, in that they teach students many of the skills, or specific, in that they teach one or two of the skills:

1. recognize the significance of the content
2. recognize important details
3. recognize unrelated details
4. find the main idea of a paragraph
5. find the main idea of large sections of discourse
6. differentiate fact and opinion
7. locate topic sentences
8. locate answers to specific questions
9. make inferences about content
10. critically evaluate content
11. realize an author's purpose
12. determine the accuracy of information
13. use a table of contents
14. use an index
15. use a library card catalog
16. use appendices
17. read and interpret tables
18. read and interpret graphs
19. read and interpret charts
20. read and interpret maps
21. read and interpret cartoons
22. read and interpret diagrams
23. read and interpret pictures
24. read and interpret formulae
25. read and understand written problems
26. read and understand expository material
27. read and understand argument
28. read and understand descriptive material
29. read and understand categories
30. adjust reading rate relative to purpose of reading
31. adjust reading rate relative to difficulty of material
32. scan for specific information
33. skim for important ideas
34. learn new material from text.

The number of skills a content reader must acquire is surprising. Most people, it would seem, acquire them independently by struggling with content material. Unfortunately, students are seldom explicitly taught the skills needed to read, comprehend, and learn from content texts. The discussions in this chapter will describe content reading skills, those that students need to learn from academic texts. Intermediate, secondary, and university students need to be able to read content texts.

In addition, the chapter will delineate some programs to help students comprehend "technical" material. The distinction is essential. Technical reading programs are designed to help students read from and understand "special" texts, often containing especially complex material. ESL authors often refer to this as English for Specific Purposes. There are highly L1 literate students who are attempting to study technical material, often at the graduate university level. "Technical" reading programs equip students to read and comprehend the difficult material found in such treatises as "Humanist Epistemology," "Selenium Sensitivity in Heat Transient Environments," and "Human Neuroanatomy."

The following discusses the standard features of content material, those that often cause students difficulty. These features are associated with "content structure." Indeed, they are a kind of "background knowledge" that students need in order to understand both academic and technical texts. Being able to use these features as "signposts" of content structure will allow students to comprehend and learn this material more easily and quickly. Generally speaking, content and technical reading are appropriate only for students who have attained at least limited-English fluency or who have substantial L1 literacy backgrounds (see the adult heuristic in Chapter 5).

Textbook authors are constrained by their media. Textbooks contain information to be learned, and authors attempt to present information in coherent, organized ways. The following exercises can teach students that content material contains some fairly standard structures. By using SQ3R, an activity that focuses on surface features of text that correspond to the content structure, students are equipped to comprehend, independently, content material. The discussion begins with purpose and reading rate.

Purpose of Reading and Reading Rate

Mature readers change their reading rates depending upon their purposes for reading and, of course, the "difficulty level" of the material being read. Reading entertaining narrative while sitting in front of a warm fireplace is considerably different from reading a treatise on realist epistemology in preparation for a final exam. Readers "slow up" when their reading material is difficult. But since reading rate is also related to purpose, readers often speed up their reading when they are "skimming" or when they are "scanning."

SKIMMING

The first step in SQ3R, an important content activity, is to skim the material, looking for general ideas. Skimming is a form of reading that is faster than general reading. Its purpose is to discover general information from a text. Skimming is a valuable skill to learn, one to be used as a strategy for assessing information sources, discovering main ideas and themes, and assessing whether material should be read more thoroughly.

How does one determine, before it is purchased, whether a particular book meets one's needs? How does one determine whether a book contains the information needed for a particular project or class? How does a reader locate sections of a text he or she needs to read more closely? How do students discover information that helps them write questions about text they are going to read?

Skimming is the answer. The following features are signposts to look for while skimming:

- the title
- any descriptive information provided by the publisher
- any foreword, preface or introduction
- the table of contents (especially the chapter titles)
- information highlighted in some way (e.g., text that is presented in boxes).

When teaching students how to skim, provide them with a text they have not seen or read before and ask them to read the text for a purpose (e.g., read to find out what a passage is about), but time them. For example, allow them to read for only 15 seconds. After a few practice sessions with different passages, students learn what it means to skim. In truth, most university-level ESL students are uncomfortable with the concept of skimming, because they are convinced their task is to read and comprehend every word in the text. It is an unfortunate feature of university-level students' reading of content that they often read in a laborious word-by-word fashion and highlight every item of vocabulary they do not know. This author has seen texts that have had more unknown words highlighted than known words.

Since it is an important skill in SQ3R, skimming should be carefully taught before SQ3R is taught. After students have skimmed a passage, they are asked to write down as many items as they can. If the purpose is to discover the "main" ideas, let them work in groups at the end of the reading and compile lists of main ideas from their reading. Such activities should begin with short passages, perhaps sections of chapters, and progress to whole books. Students should be challenged to skim and discover the major contents of a book within two minutes. It is amazing how much information they can discover if they have been taught which features of a text are the signposts of important information. Skimming is also a necessary skill in the "technical prediction" activity described later.

SCANNING

If one wants to find out what the most important grain crop in Kansas is, it is not necessary to read an entire chapter word for word. One can scan the material and look specifically for the desired information. The cheapest materials for teaching scanning are newspapers, since, very often, the local newspaper will provide old, but free, copies on a regular basis. In many large cities, for instance, the daily morning newspaper will deliver free copies of its Tuesday edition on Wednesdays to educational institutions.

To begin scanning instruction, overheads of some articles should be prepared. Before students see an overhead, they are given an instruction such as "Read this paragraph to find out who the new president of Russia is." There are two alternatives to the process. Students may raise their hands as soon as they know the answer, or they may independently write down their answers after having seen the article for 20 seconds. With practice, students will come to understand scanning. Both skimming and scanning provide a foundation for the teaching of other content reading strategies like SQ3R.

Study Guides

The goal of the following activities is to help students become independent in applying systematic study skills to reading material. Study guides are transitional aids to help students become independent content readers. They help students begin to focus on text in an organized fashion, before they read and as they read. A general study guide identifies what the teacher thinks is important in a particular passage or chapter of text. It calls students' attention to certain text features and asks them questions about the features. A typical study guide might be:

1. Look at the title of the chapter on page 45. What kind of subjects do you think will be covered in this chapter?
2. Look at the subtitle on page 45. It says "Genetic Engineering." What is genetic engineering?
3. There is a diagram on page 46 entitled "Cloning." What is cloning?
4. The word *antibodies* is used on page 48 in paragraph three. What does *antibodies* mean?
5. What is the main idea of paragraph five on page 49?
6. What is the sequence of events depicted in the chart on page 50?
7. Write a short paragraph describing the moral considerations scientists must have in genetic engineering. Do you agree with the author's position in paragraph three on page 53?

Many teachers rely on study guides to help their ESL students comprehend texts. However, these should be viewed as transitional aids. If they are used too often, students begin to consider them simply as more worksheets. Indeed, after a while students will not consider information that is *not* on the study guide, scanning the text only for the information the teacher has identified as important. A study guide can be used to help students learn to develop their own content background information, through the SQ3R.

SQ3R

SQ3R was developed to increase students' retention of content material (Robinson, 1961). It stands for "Survey, Question, Read, Recite, and Review." It is an effective procedure for reading and comprehending text, and it helps students develop their own study guides independently. The following is a list of the steps used in SQ3R:

1. *SURVEY*—Survey the material to be read, beginning with the title. If there is a chapter outline, survey it to discover the main topics or ideas. If there isn't a chapter outline, use the table of contents for the same purpose. Read the titles and subtitles found in the chapter. Read captions and titles associated with all of the graphic aids. Read any summaries the author has included. Often an

author will pose important questions in the text—look for them. Also look for any special vocabulary words. Often these are highlighted with bold type or italics and the definitions are given in a glossary at the back of the book. Otherwise, a trip to the dictionary is essential.

2. *QUESTION*—Use a sheet of paper on which to write the questions which will serve as a study guide. Formulate questions involving all titles, subtitles, summaries, and graphic aids. "What is the significance of the chart on page 3?" and "Why does the author condemn some kinds of genetic research?" are the kinds of questions that can be formulated.

3. *READ*—Read the chapter carefully to answer the questions and take notes as the reading progresses. In many cases a question formulated earlier will be slightly off-base. After reading each portion of the text, reformulate questions when necessary and answer them. It is often best to read in sections and to recite at the end of each section.

4. *RECITE*—Chapters are usually written in major sections and set off by headings or titles. At the end of each section, stop to recite the answer to the questions developed for the section. Answer questions, either orally or in writing, without looking back at the section.

5. *REVIEW*—After finishing the chapter, review it completely, looking at questions and answers. Again, it is often better to review a section at a time.

SEQUENCING THE LEARNING OF SQ3R

SQ3R is an effective study strategy if introduced and taught correctly, but it is time-consuming and students will not apply it successfully without much guidance. The first step is to introduce the activity as a class effort.

The students who are to learn SQ3R should be brought together as a group. They should be told that they will be learning something called SQ3R, a method for helping them improve their reading in such subjects as social studies and history. Each step of SQ3R is described. A typical passage from a content text, one containing as many features as possible discussed so far, should be used to illustrate the process.

The digital projector works well for this group activity. Students' attention is focused first on the title and then on some text. They are asked to generate questions, which the teacher then writes on the board. In effect, students scan the text to identify important items. Since they have previously been introduced to this skill, this is not an entirely new strategy. This procedure is followed until questions have been developed for the whole passage. Then the passage is read to answer each question, a form of scanning. The students answer each question aloud and their responses are recorded on the chalkboard or overhead. Students practice reciting the answers without looking at the text and conclude the activity by reviewing the text to make certain the answers are correct. In this manner, SQ3R has been demonstrated to students step by step. To make certain that they master SQ3R, however, and are able to apply it independently, one can use a "special study guide," which is described later.

Often, the most difficult part of SQ3R for ESL students is the construction of questions. If during SQ3R, a reader finds that his or her question is wrong, it can be rewritten when the passage is read. This is a valuable feature of SQ3R. Students can be provided with worksheets with different titles, subtitles, or visual aids that will generate different kinds of questions. They can be asked to turn subtitles such as "Postmodern Architecture" into questions such as "What is postmodern architecture?" or "What does the term *postmodern architecture* mean?" and "What does the author think about postmodern architecture?"

MARGIN GUIDES

After SQ3R has been introduced and taught, and the steps have been rehearsed by the group, students are ready to apply them independently. As a transitional tool it may be useful to provide students with a "margin guide" that visually marks items students should take into account. The guide is usually about 1 inch wide with its length being the same as the page size of the material being read, so it can be aligned with the text.

The students line up the margin guide to match the edge of the appropriate page, and it points out the features that should be made into questions. A guide for a large chapter would consist of as many thin margin notes as the number of pages in the text. Punching holes in the tops of the guides and connecting them with a shower ring works quite well; margin guides do not get lost or out of order. Laminating such guides assures they last for more than one usage. As was mentioned, the margin guide is the transitional stage from a teacher-produced study guide to students' independent application of SQ3R. Students often complain of the time and energy the SQ3R activities require. However, it should be pointed out how well comprehension and learning improve. Done consistently, SQ3R improves comprehension, retention, and learning from text.

SQ3R teaches students to focus on text features that authors use to signal important or significant material. SQ3R improves reading comprehension because it establishes a kind of "content background knowledge." For ESL students the major block is often creating questions. Consequently, they may need guided practice in writing them. The goal is to help students to construct sentences that are beyond the literal level. As was noted previously, literal questions involve surface structure features and do not require much more than memory capacity. Caution should be exercised, however, since many content books stress details, and the task of students in these courses is to learn and remember details. Who would want, for instance, a medical doctor who could not remember the major nerves, a task involving remembering details?

Variants of SQ3R: PQRST and SQRQCQ

SQ3R is a valuable strategy for readers of content and technical texts, as we have seen. Thus, variations of SQ3R have been developed for such areas as science and mathematics. Spache (1963) devised PQRST (Preview, Question, Read, Summarize, Test) for science materials. The following outlines the system:

- *Preview:* Skim all the material.
- *Question:* Formulate questions to guide reading.
- *Read:* Read the material to answer questions.
- *Summarize:* Summarize information learned.
- *Test:* Compare summary with material in text.

Fay (1965) developed SQRQCQ for mathematics, especially for written mathematics problems:

- *Survey:* Skim the problem to determine what kind it is.
- *Question:* Figure out what is being asked in the problem.
- *Read:* Read for details and ascertain relationships in the problem.
- *Question:* Ask what processes should be used.
- *Compute:* Do the problem.
- *Question:* Decide whether the answer is correct by analyzing the facts involved.

Both approaches ask students to be more logical about their reading and to formulate independently guides to help them understand text.

SQ3R and its variations allow students to develop independently a kind of study guide that increases their comprehension of portions of text, usually chapters, large passages, or overall math problems. Students should also be equipped to deal with the many different kinds of content features found in typical texts.

Content Assessment

So far, the lessons have been directed toward developing independent study strategies through skimming and scanning, study-guide directed reading, SQ3R, PQRST, and SQRQCQ. In Chapter 2 a content assessment was discussed. Such an assessment measures what content skills students need to know in order to read and comprehend a particular text. In the portion of a class record that follows, students were tested on these content features found in a social studies text:

1. table of contents
2. glossary
3. find main idea
4. read maps
5. follow directions
6. follow a sequence of cause and effect statements
7. read and interpret pie charts and bar graphs
8. read and understand "flow" maps.

The following is a portion of the class record (Figure 6.2). The numbers at the top refer to the skills in the list just given. The class record shows that the students in this class have different needs and abilities. It allows the teacher to isolate individuals needing skills development and it also identifies instructional groups. In this case, only Duk Sue has trouble with glossaries and the table of contents. He

Class record								
	1	2	3	4	5	6	7	8
Jose	X	X		X			X	X
Mohammed	X	X		X		X	X	
Suki	X	X		X	X	X	X	
Jakob	X	X	X	X	X	X	X	X
Sylvana	X	X	X	X	X	X	X	X
Duk Sue				X	X	X		X

Figure 6.2 Content Reading Class Record

can be taught individually to use these content features. Direct instruction in these skills will help him deal with the requirements of the text. Jose, Mohammed, Suki, and Duk Sue all need to learn how to find the "main idea" in the text. They can be assembled as a group for instruction.

Texts for courses such as geography, history, social studies, economics, sociology, and psychology often contain writing that is expository in nature. They are usually also filled with graphs, charts, timelines, and maps that students must gain information from. Vocabulary may be specialized, and readers are often asked in such texts to consider and arrive at "main ideas."

Mathematics texts contain many symbols and mathematical formulae, in addition to text. It is important that students be able to translate symbols into English and English into symbols, as in "word problems." Word problems can present a major obstacle to comprehending mathematics texts. A reader must be able to decide what is essential to a problem, what is insignificant, and what operations should be done in what order. A mathematics reader must be able to follow directions. Diagrams are especially important in mathematics texts. In addition to difficult vocabulary, mathematics texts may be filled with intense analytical discourse.

Science texts also contain specialized, difficult vocabulary and complex, analytical expository prose, in addition to charts, graphs, diagrams, and mathematical equations. Science texts often require students to analyze data and hypothesize about outcomes of particular events or experiments.

Courses in the humanities require the reading of different kinds of texts altogether. English literature courses require that students read texts containing narrative. Students are asked to consider texts, to analyze characters' motivations, to judge events, to draw inferences, and to decide what is "good" writing. Often students are asked to interpret "styles" of writing. Other texts in the humanities ask students to interpret moods and feelings and consider the importance of events or trends in fashion, art, or music.

Many university-level ESL students are enrolled in business and economics courses. They attend English courses anxious to learn how to read better, so that they can read their texts. They are often frustrated because teachers do not teach them the content skills they need to be able to read their difficult, technical texts. The reading teacher's task sounds almost impossible. What makes the task even more difficult is the reading teacher's knowledge that many of these students depend on him or her to teach them to read material that will help them in their careers.

Depending upon the subject area, some skills are more vital than others. Determining the difference between fact and opinion, for instance, is more important in reading newspapers and political science texts than it is in reading a mathematics or a physics text. Other important features of some academic textbooks are graphic features and editorial features. Content and technical texts, depending on the academic field, have different graphic and editorial features. This is also true of the Internet, as we shall see later in the chapter.

Teaching the Reading of Graphic Aids

The first step in teaching students to gain information from graphic aids is to direct attention to them in the first place. Readers often ignore them, not realizing they contain important information. It may be that the first step is to provide students with some data, some information, and have them produce a graphic aid that represents it. For instance, they can be asked to depict the number of L1s in their class in some graphic way. The concept of graphic aids should be introduced and discussed, including actual examples of aids ranging from graphs and maps to technical illustrations. It is important for students to learn the different kinds of information available so they can come to comprehend and learn the presented material. Graphic aids may contain the following kinds of information:

1. Raw data—pie charts, bar graphs, maps, statistical tables, and other such aids provide raw data. These aids allow a reader to answer such questions as "How many tons of apples are grown in Washington State in October?" and "What is the average rainfall in Chicago?"
2. Comparative data—pie charts, bar graphs, interaction diagrams, and other such aids provide comparative data. They allow the reader to answer such questions as "What state produces the most apples?" and "Which drug is more effective for teenage girls than for teenage boys?"
3. Descriptive data—illustrations, photographs, diagrams, and other such aids provide information about objects. These aids allow the reader to answer such questions as "What is the configuration of a B1 bomber?", "What are the parts of a neuron?", and "What are the parts of the eye?"
4. Process data—photographs, illustrations, technical illustrations, and similar aids provide answers to such questions as "How does osmosis work?", "How does the internal combustion engine work?", and "What are the macroeconomic forces that affect supply-side inflation, and how do they work?"

5. Logic; theoretical propositions—such aids as tables of arithmetic proofs, visual models, and logical statements reveal mathematical relations, logical proofs, and theoretical relationships. They can answer such questions as "What is the proof of the Pythagorean theorem?", "How do you compute total resistance in the following circuit?", "How does one determine truth from belief?", and "What are the hypothesized relationships in the 'psycholinguistic' model of L2 reading?"

Students must determine what kind of information is available in a graphic aid. Are raw data, comparative data, process data, or theoretical propositions presented? The answer determines the kind of processing to be used. A single graphic aid can, in fact, present information of all five categories, depending on the author's intent. A collection of graphic aids that students may encounter should be used as teaching material. As was noted above, the first step is to introduce the concept of graphic aids and have the class construct different kinds. This is an entertaining and powerful learning situation, especially for ESL adults, who bring a marvelous world knowledge to the task. The following is a discussion of some actual graphic aids taken from content and technical sources. The first is from a study of ESL reading-achievement testing (Table 6.1). The table shows years in English school, Comprehensive Test of Basic Skills (CTBS) scores (a reading-achievement test), and L1 and L2 students. There are many questions that could be formulated from such a statistical table. Here are a few:

TABLE 6.1 Years in English School and CTBS Mean Percentile Scores for L1 and L2 Students

Years		Vocabulary		Comprehension		Total Reading	
		L1	L2	L1	L2	L1	L2
1	X		14.30		21.38		15.79
	sd		12.34		18.13		12.07
2	X		35.26		40.74		37.37
	sd		20.35		23.58		23.09
3	X	40.00	52.57	36.91	49.83	37.68	51.74
	sd	26.92	23.50	25.80	22.45	27.76	21.95
4	X	39.65	52.36	43.25	45.67	40.80	49.07
	sd	28.84	28.80	24.92	26.81	25.90	27.84
5	X	38.81	58.60	38.83	52.46	38.76	56.86
	sd	24.44	13.97	27.04	22.73	26.21	18.23

Source. L. Gunderson, Reading achievement assessment of L1 and L2 students in regular classrooms. *TEAL Occasional Papers*, 8 (1984), 31–41.

1. What is the relationship between L1 and L2, years in school in English, and mean percentile scores on the CTBS? (This question was formulated from the title, an excellent strategy.)
2. Which group scored highest?
3. Did the L2 group benefit from English instruction?
4. In what reading area (i.e., vocabulary, comprehension, total reading) did L2 students change the most?
5. What is the effect of English school on the reading achievement of L2 students?

There are, of course, many other questions that could be formulated. The text of the article might discuss all of these questions; on the other hand, it might not. The careful reader poses such questions and answers them from the graphic. The careful or critical reader may even learn information the original author did not. Different readers may have different conclusions about the results and may have to read the original article to discover the actual findings. These are good questions for SQ3R, too!

Sometimes a graphic reveals relationships in a dramatic way. Figure 6.3 shows the outcome of a study of adults reading idiomatic and literal text. The graphic is quite informative. The following are questions a reader could ask:

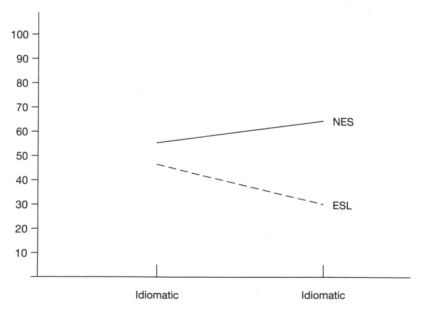

Mean percentage scores of native English speakers (NES) and ESL students reading a literal passage and an idiomatic passage

Figure 6.3 A Statistical Interaction

Source. L. Gunderson, K. Slade, and D. Rosenke, The cloze response patterns of L1 and L2 students to literal and idiomatic text. *TESL Canada Journal,* 6, 1 (1988), 60–66.

1. What are L1 and L2 students' mean scores on literal and idiomatic passages?
2. Which group scores highest (lowest) on literal-level passages?
3. Which group scores highest (lowest) on idiomatic text?
4. What is the relationship between literal/idiomatic text, L1/L2, and comprehension? (The simple answer is that idiomatic text improves English speakers' comprehension, while it lowers ESL adults' comprehension.)
5. What is a hypothesis that would, or could, have predicted the findings presented in this graphic?

ESL teachers have a primary role in revealing how to gain meaning from graphic aids. In many cases, students will have to be explicitly guided through several exercises before they are able to formulate questions above the literal level.

Editorial Features

Once a reader has understood a text, she or he must make judgments about the author's message. Is the content true or is it opinion? Is it propaganda? Are the author's arguments logical and supported? Is the material valuable? Secondary ESL students must be taught to make judgments about text. Adults, on the other hand, generally through experience, have come to understand that print does not necessarily mean truth. There are some exceptions, however. An editorial from the local newspaper provides the opportunity for students to identify statements of truth and of opinion. It is amazing how critical ESL students become after they are taught some of the vocabulary that often distinguishes fact from opinion:

> should
> may be
> perhaps
> would
> possibly
> if
> might

These words clearly signal statements of opinion. On the other hand, what makes a sentence such as "Bigbie's watermelons are the best in the world" a statement of opinion rather than fact? Asking students to signify which sentences are fact and which are opinion is easy. Indeed, they simply put an "F" by sentences that are factual and an "O" by those that are opinion. Teaching them to distinguish fact from fiction is more difficult; but once they begin to evaluate statements such as the following, they become very critical readers:

1. About 50,000 people are killed in automobile accidents every year in the United States.
2. Cigarettes are possibly the most dangerous health hazard in the world.
3. Acme Car Sales Company sells the best cars in California.
4. Happiness is the most important element in life.

Print and editorial features must be part of the secondary and adult ESL students' reading program, especially the secondary program. To read content texts requires skills and strategies in many areas. The following discussion will briefly focus on the university-level technical reader.

Technical Reading: Co-sheltered Instruction

Technical reading involves complex material requiring specific background knowledge. Technical reading is content reading, but more complex, difficult, and informational. It often involves material that ESL teachers do not know or understand. The reading instruction must involve co-sheltering.

The concepts in technical reading are complex and often extremely difficult to understand, and the content-specific vocabulary is specialized, perhaps best called jargon. There are published programs to teach technical English and reading. For instance, the Regents Publishing Company has a wide range of materials for teaching ESL students, with such titles as *Electrical and Electronic Engineering in English, Atomic Energy in English, Civil Engineering in English*, and *Restaurants and Catering in English* (New York: Regents Publishing Company, various dates). However, the ESL teacher is often the only resource available.

Students at the university level often confront extremely complex and information-packed courses. The following is a portion of an article that is a serious consideration of what can be learned from text. The essential question is: Can a reader come to know, in the hard sense of the term, from reading? How can a reader actually come to know, for instance, that London is in England if he reads it—or can he? This is a vital question for teachers because, as noted above, they should be dedicated to producing critical readers of text. The following is a fairly dense piece of writing that requires a critical reader to understand it:

> Scheffler concludes that the final test of adequacy of evidence is "roughly equivalent to that of **good reasons**, or a **good case**" (Scheffler, 1965, p. 59). Terry's statements are subject to several interpretations. First, we cannot conclude that Terry believes that evil spirits cause disease (hence X believes that Q), unless we ask her explicitly, "Do you believe that evil spirits cause disease?" As teachers we often err in assuming that students know something because they correctly answer questions within a particular set of parameters: that is, they respond correctly relative to something they have read. Many scholars have correctly provided the answer, "the square on the hypotenuse is equal to the sum of the squares on the other two sides" simply because they have read and remembered it. That one reports the statement cannot be construed to mean either X knows that Q or X believes that Q. In fact, there may be the case in which we ask Terry what causes disease and her answer is, "evil spirits" because she has read it. She may disagree. Readers may have no compelling belief in "knowledge" acquired through reading. Obviously, the opposite is also true, the case in which a reader believes because she has read it. Belief based solely on reading lacks the weight of good reason or good case, especially for more mature readers. Knowledge cannot be attributed by

virtue of X reads that Q. Several conditions may result from X reads that Q: 1) X reads that Q, X believes that Q; 2) X reads that Q, X does not believe that Q; 3) X reads that Q, X believes that Q, and knows that Q; and 4) X reads that Q, X does not believe that Q, but knows that it is written that Q. Knowledge can only be attributed from reading when the reader is able to give good reason.

(Gunderson, 1986a, p. 252)

The vocabulary and the concepts in this text are not particularly difficult, but the text is packed with propositions that may or may not add to comprehension. It is likely that the ESL (ELL) teacher will have little difficulty helping students in the following activity. The process for understanding is fairly simple. Students:

1. Skim the text to find any unknown vocabulary and list the vocabulary on a sheet of paper. (On inspection, only the use of such phrases as "X believes that Q," "X knows that Q," and "X reads that Q" seem like something out of the ordinary.)
2. Identify, if possible, an introductory sentence or paragraph that communicates the main idea(s) to be developed or a final paragraph or sentence that summarizes the main ideas. (The first sentence may represent the main idea, but the last one surely does: "Knowledge can only be attributed from reading when the reader is able to give good reason.")
3. Make a list of ideas they expect to encounter in the text.
4. Identify what new information they expect to learn from the text.

This information is organized into a form that will help reveal relationships, sometimes called a graphic organizer (Herber, 1978). Barron (1979) views the best kind of graphic organizer as one a student helps to build. University-level students become quite adept, after careful guidance, in developing their own. Figure 6.4 is a graphic organizer based on the reading text shown above. It was developed by a graduate language education student whose L1 was Mandarin. The students found that the organizer helped them read and comprehend the passage better than if they

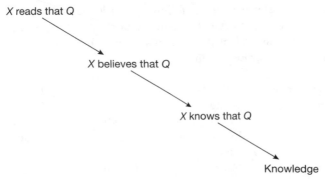

Figure 6.4 Pre-reading Graphic for Scheffler

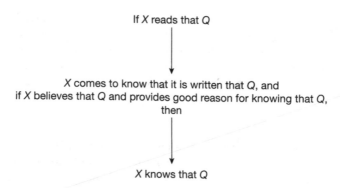

If X reads that Q

X comes to know that it is written that Q, and
if X believes that Q and provides good reason for knowing that Q,
then

X knows that Q

Figure 6.5 Post-reading Graphic for Scheffler

had read it "cold." They also found that the initial graphic did not represent the text accurately, but a post-reading graphic, a kind of visual outline, helped them understand the text. Some have referred to this kind of visual outline as mapping or webbing. The post-reading graphic is an outstanding way to represent relationships that exist in text (see Figure 6.5).

It is often embarrassing to be helping university graduates when one does not have the background to understand the texts they are asked to read. The procedures discussed so far do provide skills that allow students to understand technical texts. The following exercises are designed to help students master extremely complex material—indeed, material that is often beyond the level of the ESL teacher. The following activities represent a kind of synergy between the teacher and the students. This author calls it co-sheltered instruction since the teacher helps students with the reading, while students help the teacher to understand academic-based vocabulary and content.

Content Prediction Activities

Many texts are difficult to comprehend because of the significant vocabulary load. Teachers can identify vocabulary in advance of students reading the text and present it to them. A reading assignment on crustaceans in a secondary science class began with the ESL teacher providing the following words she had taken from the text in the belief they were important to the understanding of the passage. The teacher did not, in fact, know all of the particular words, but could identify them as important because they looked important.

Abdomen	Animals	Antenna	Barnacles
Branchiopods	Carapace	Chela	Cirripedes
Copepods	Crabs	Crayfish	Crustaceans
Cuticle	Exoskeleton	Fishlice	Head
Insects	Larva	Life Cycle	Lobsters
Malocostracons	Nauplius	Oceans	Ostracods
Parasitic	Plankton	Pleopods	Prawns

Regeneration	Shrimp	Slaters	Thorax
Trunk	Wood Lice		

The basic rule here is that students should not be completely unaware of the material. They should have some background knowledge. They are asked to organize the words into a web before they read the passage. Figure 6.6 shows a pre-reading web completed by a group of grade 12 ESL students.

The students explained that the web was created because they knew that crustaceans were animals and were the topic of the passage to be read. The list is a long one, so they were written on individual cards and were organized on the top of a table to help make sense of them. The manipulation helped them come up with categories: kinds, individual characteristics, environment, and an unknown category. They further decided that there were common and scientific names for crustaceans, so they divided them into these two groups. The scientific names were selected on the basis that they looked like and sounded like scientific names, although no one really knew them. After the web had been finished, students were able to generate some questions to be asked to guide their reading of the passage, e.g., Are crustaceans animals? Are the terms "branchiopods," "copepods," "branchiopods," "cirripedes," "malacostracons," and "pleopods" the scientific names of crustaceans?

Students read the passage to find out whether or not their pre-reading web reflected the content of the passage. They were asked to discuss the passage and to rearrange their webs on the basis of the passage's content. Figure 6.7 shows the grade 12 ESL students' post-reading web.

They were asked to explain their reasons for changing their web, and their discussion convinced the teacher that they had read and understood the text. The teacher also learned a great deal about crustaceans from the students' conversations.

Students can also explore their knowledge through the use of the Internet or through the use of the Visual Thesaurus described in the previous chapter. The Visual Thesaurus is particularly helpful because it generates webs to show relationships between and among vocabulary words within an overall category such as "crustacean."

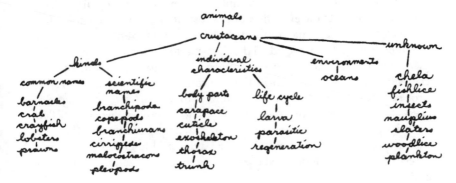

Figure 6.6 Crustacean Pre-reading Web

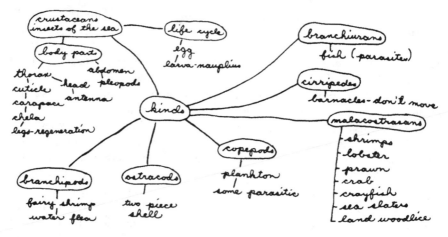

Figure 6.7 Crustacean Post-reading Web

Ogle (1986) developed an approach called K-W-L (Know, Want to Know, Learned) that was expanded by Carr & Ogle (1987) to include mapping (similar to a web). Students begin by making a list of items they know about a subject such as "crustaceans." These words are written on a worksheet under the category "know." The next step is the generation of questions they want to know and what they expect to find out in the reading. These questions are placed under the "want to know" column. The passage is read and students focus on what they learned from the reading. K-W-L works well for students, but they require more English ability than in the activity described above.

In the cases noted so far, the teacher is able to identify potential vocabulary difficulties. But this doesn't always work. In some cases the text is so specialized and difficult that the teacher may not understand it, as can be observed in the following piece of technical writing, but the university-level content-expert ESL students have the technical backgrounds to help them understand the text.

A computer model has been formulated using existing empirical relationships to predict the evolution of microstructure during the hot rolling of steel strip. Isothermal restoration and recrystallization results were obtained from tests conducted on the Cam-plastometer and the Gleeble. The principle of additivity has been employed so as to apply isothermal recrystallization kinetics to non-isothermal conditions such as the hot rolling process. IRSID's model has been utilized to characterize the static recrystallization that occurs after the deformation process, whereas Sellars' model was employed to describe the metadynamic recrystallization. The microstructure obtained from CANMET pilot mill tests showed excellent agreement with the model-predicted degree of recrystallization and resulting grain size.

(Devadas, 1989, p. 1)

This paragraph is part of a larger text, one filled with what may be for the teacher complex concepts and difficult vocabulary. The prediction process begins with students listing the technical vocabulary they believe will be encountered in the text. They explain their choices to the teacher. In essence they are sheltering vocabulary instruction to the teacher, particularly when he asks for explanations or expansions of information given to him by the students.

PREDICTED VOCABULARY   VOCABULARY NOT PREDICTED

MAIN IDEAS OR PROPOSITIONS

Since these students are experts, and since they know background and related vocabulary, predicting vocabulary is not difficult. The prediction process works best in small groups but is also an independent activity, one that serves the student well as a study strategy. After the prediction process, students skim the text to identify vocabulary predicted and not predicted and to identify sentences that seem to express main ideas or propositions. In some cases, items predicted are not found; to the expert in an area, this can be important information. The main ideas are also turned into questions. Finally, the questions are listed and the related vocabulary attached:

How can one predict the evolution of the microstructure during the hot rolling of steel strips?
 Cam-plastometer, Gleeble, isothermal recrystallization kinetics, IRSID's model, Sellars' model, CANMET pilot mill tests

How is the principle of additivity used?
 isothermal, recrystallization, kinetics, non-isothermal conditions, hot rolling process

By identifying main ideas or propositions and vocabulary, students produce a study guide. They then read carefully to answer the questions. The teacher can guide students through most texts and help them produce questions, even though he may not actually understand the content. Indeed, the teacher's ignorance may be beneficial to the process, since he asks questions to clarify concepts and vocabulary.

Expert readers also benefit from an activity in which they do not note vocabulary items before they read, but simply make predictions about what will be in the text. Before reading the passage, students brainstorm and list everything they know about the subject. The following, printed on top of a page, will function as a brainstorming worksheet. In this case, the passage to be read is about "culture shock."

Culture Shock

Things known and predicted   *Things not predicted*

After lists have been produced, they are read aloud. As they are, the teacher writes them on the chalkboard and asks about items he doesn't understand. Students quickly become avid teachers themselves and like to explain terms and concepts to their English teachers.

The passage is read and items correctly predicted are checked, while items not predicted are noted in short statement form. The teacher directs attention to the chalkboard, and items correctly predicted are checked off as the teacher asks students to clarify them. Any item that was predicted and not found in the text is noted and discussed, and possibly researched. This prediction activity works with students at all levels. They become actively engaged in text and do comprehend materials well.

Some technical reading involves making decisions about editorial features of text. This basic prediction activity can be used in a slightly different way to help students become critical readers. In this case a statement is generated, probably by the teacher, or by students reading the title or subtitle of a section of text. The following is an example:

Free trade is good for the United States, Canada, and Mexico.

Before reading

AGREE   DISAGREE

After reading

AGREE   DISAGREE

Before reading the text, students discuss the issues and produce statements that support or oppose them. Usually, teams produce both kinds of statements, especially if the issue is contentious. They should explain their statements and provide support. Depending upon the group, it may be desirable to write the statements on the chalkboard and discuss each item. The passage or chapter is read, and students again meet to discuss whether they agree or disagree with the statement, producing observations, or "proof," from the text that are recorded. The teacher who believes students benefit from reading text critically and expects them to learn new viewpoints should expect, therefore, the AGREE/DISAGREE statements to change after reading. The procedure is a powerful one and produces very critical readers.

The strategies discussed produce good content and technical readers. They do require time. It has been suggested that these strategies draw readers' attention to features of text that, in many cases, may represent a kind of content structure. In essence, these examples represent co-sheltering or co-scaffolding as students who are content experts help guide their teachers' instruction in the reading of related content material in English.

Critical Literacy

The term "critical literacy" has traditionally meant in the reading research community that a reader comprehends a passage and has the ability and knowledge to judge whether the content has validity or is substantiated in some way. This was the kind of critical approach taken above. Many of these critical reading skills can be used to help develop critical literacy. Critical literacy has come to mean that a reader or writer can explore and analyze the underlying power relationships that may marginalize him or her or members of other groups in some way, either implicitly or explicitly. Critical literacy is subsumed within the general concept "critical pedagogy."

In some societies the written word developed as a way to keep track of inventories for traders. The Phoenicians, for instance, were traders and travelers who kept careful written records of the items they traded (Dirringer, 1968). On the other hand, the historical precedent for many societies was that writing was sacred in nature. Ancient Egyptian, for instance, was written and read exclusively by priests (Dirringer, 1968). Bibles were illuminated in the Middle Ages so that the average human being, one who could not read the words, could understand their content. Readers did not question texts, because they contained the "truths" that readers sought to understand. The basic notion was that print represented truth, and, further, that what was in print was objective and without bias. Many people in this new millennium are still convinced this notion is true (see Chapter 3), and this belief has been extended to material presented on the Internet.

Many human beings around the world have grown up without questioning what is written in texts. We have had an explicit faith that everything written is true, that our governments, our newspapers, our textbooks present objective and unbiased truth. We also believed without question what our teachers taught us. As teachers, we have not questioned the implicit and explicit cultural content of the material we teach. Many of us have lived our lives without questioning our learned cultural beliefs. We assume that our views are correct and the views of others are not. We have come to believe, for instance, that all of the great thinkers of the past were members of the Western world. We never questioned our textbooks that represented other human beings in stereotypic ways. Critical literacy helps us to do so. In critical literacy, readers attempt to understand the power relationships between their ideas and the ideas presented by the author of the text.

Freire published a book called *Pedagogy of the oppressed* (1975) in which he criticized what he called the "banking concept of education." He argued that teachers treated students like empty vessels that they filled up with knowledge. In this view the teacher is the one who chooses the content and the students' job is to make certain they learn it. It seems that a fair number of human beings also have this view of teaching and learning, as we saw in Chapter 3. Freire argued that in this view teaching was oppressive. He also argued that the purpose of teaching should be to raise learners' critical consciousness about social conditions, both their own and that of others.

There are different kinds of critical literacy, but it seems that all of them involve an active, challenging approach to reading and textual practices. Critical literacy is the analysis and critique of the relationships among texts, language, power, social groups and social practices. It consists of ways of looking at written, visual, spoken, multimedia, and performance discourse to question and challenge the attitudes, values and beliefs that lie beneath the surface.

Teachers who take a critical literacy approach help students to learn how to examine explicit and implicit meanings in texts; how to evaluate the purpose of the text and the author's implicit and explicit intentions; to judge how and when texts are not neutral, represent particular views, silence other points of view and influence people's ideas; how to question and challenge how discourse has been constructed; to appreciate and understand multiple meanings associated in texts; and to help students get involved in addressing social injustice. This author's experience is that engaging students in dialogue about such issues is the best way to get them involved in understanding critical literacy.

An essential question to ask is, "Is this text fair?" There will, of course, be different points of view and different answers, usually related to individuals' backgrounds and cultures. Reviewing the differing responses is a good way to explore which positions or "voices" are represented by the discourse and how the different readers are positioned relative to it. How does the text portray age, gender, cultural groups, sexual preference, political stance? Whose views appear to be highlighted or privileged and whose views are marginalized or excluded? What worldview is presented and what kinds of social relationships are presented?

Students can be guided to question the author. What kind of person is the author? Whose views does she value? Whose views does she marginalize or exclude? What views does she assume that the reader shares with her? The difficulty is that there is no actual single critical literacy curriculum that teachers can adopt and use. There is no critical literacy method that can work across contexts. Indeed, what works in one educational setting likely will not work in another. In essence, you, the teacher, must develop your own program to develop critical literacy. However, there are some general activities that appear to be useful.

The use of drama can help students to take points of view and to critically evaluate issues. Verriour (1994) suggests an activity he calls "Vignette." The teacher selects a photograph that has characters in it such as a historical picture of a family. Students study the picture and act out what they view as the features that represent the roles in the picture. The teacher and other classmates ask questions of the "actors" and ask them to explain items such as regional clothing that might be in the photograph. This author has used this technique with adult ESL students and it appears to work fairly well, although some individuals from different cultures have trouble participating at first. Pictures of individuals from different cultures help students to analyze and ask questions about roles, family structures, and power relationships.

Drama is a powerful tool to help students understand and address serious issues such as racism and bullying (see, for instance, Belliveau, 2005, 2006). Caution must be exercised by the teacher in using drama with ESL students because they may view the task as demeaning, uncomfortable, or inappropriate in a school setting. Drama does work to help students begin to identify differences in how human beings view different issues. Goldstein (2004) wrote a script for a play based on the findings of her ethnographic study of a school that had an influx of immigrants from Hong Kong. The script was designed to be read or performed for audiences. Goldstein's student teachers were asked to rewrite parts to represent different viewpoints of different characters. They were also asked to write or act out different conclusions. These activities helped students to analyze critically the power relationships between those who spoke English as a first language and those who were L2 speakers, between teachers and students, etc. This kind of activity helps students to begin to be able to critically analyze written texts. Indeed, it also begins to help them become critical in a world filled with many different kinds of texts or discourses or representations.

Multiliteracies

This author teaches undergraduate and graduate university students. The undergraduate students are all in their early twenties and are training to be teachers, and the graduates are mostly teachers who are in their late thirties and forties. The surface differences related to age are readily apparent. However, there are under-lying differences in their knowledge and experience that are strikingly apparent. The undergraduate students know about technology in a way that graduates do not. The undergraduates are deeply involved in instant text messaging, word processing, searching the World Wide Web, listservs (although they believe this is a very dated technology), bulletin boards, blogs, wireless access and Facebook (http://www.facebook.com/), and other personal presences on the Web. The undergraduates use social networking technologies extensively while the graduates are generally unaware they exist. In a class of 38, with 22-year-old students study-ing to become teachers, it is rare to encounter someone who does not know of these technologies. Those who do not are almost always older students who have returned to university after careers in some other field. It is clear that the definition of what constitutes text or discourse and what constitutes literacy is changing rapidly. It has been referred to by some as "multiliteracies."

As was noted in Chapter 1, ten language researchers met in 1994 in New London, New Hampshire, to talk about the state of the art of the teaching and learning of literacy. They concluded:

> We decided that the outcomes of our discussions could be encapsulated in one word – multiliteracies – a word we chose to describe two important argu-ments we might have with the emerging cultural, institutional, and global order: the multiplicity of communications channels and media, and the increasing saliency of cultural and linguistic diversity.
>
> (New London Group, 1996, p. 67)

They also concluded that the term "multiliteracies" represents a broader view than what they called "mere literacy." The traditional view of literacy focuses on language. The view that reading is based on a predictable relationship between letters and sounds is one that is related to the idea that it is possible to identify a correct and stable usage. Multiliteracies, on the other hand, involves considerations of ways of representing meaning in wider ways than simply through written or oral lan-guage. Meaning can exist in architecture and in art, on the Web, and in communities developed in different areas of the world. Multiliteracies are related to different cultural ways of representing, and they change relative to local rather than imagined universal views. In many respects, advocates of multiliteracies view literacy much the way Freire did when he advocated that students should learn to read the world rather than simply the word. The difficulty with the term "multiliteracies" is that it has not been broadly accepted. Potts (2007) notes, for instance, that as of summer 2007, the term was not listed in any reference book that she consulted. In researching related topics, she has concluded that the concept of multimodality appears to be gaining more acceptance within the literacy community.

To address adequately the concept of multiliteracies is beyond the scope of this book. However, it is clear that multiliteracies are a fact of life in ESL students' lives, especially older students. Many are familiar with hand-held bilingual dictionaries that provide definitions in print or as synthesized speech. Some also provide visual images to accompany definitions. Two typical approaches can be seen at Franklin Electronic Publisher's Website at http://www.franklin.com/estore/dictionary/BES-1890/ and Vistawide at http://www.vistawide.com/languages/gifts_electronic_translators.htm. The reader is reminded that these are examples of commercial sites that feature electronic bilingual dictionaries, and the fact of their mention should not be considered recommendations for the products. Hand-held bilingual dictionaries are based on hypertext linking. They are multimodal and they are examples of the use of multiliteracies.

Print-based documents are normally read in a linear fashion. Nelson (1965) defined hypertext as "a body of written or pictorial material interconnected in such a complex way that it could not be conveniently represented on paper." The Visual Thesaurus discussed in Chapter 5 is an outstanding example of the use of hypertext. The World Wide Web is based on technology that links texts of vastly different kinds. The "http" in the typical Web address stands for "hypertext transfer protocol." The Visual Thesaurus presents print in the form of semantic webs, but it also makes links between one's computer and Internet-based visual images and Internet-based websites.

Dobson & Willinsky (in press) refer to digital literacy and write from an interesting historical perspective. They conclude, "Digital literacy does appear to be leading to greater literate participation in a wide range of activities, brought on by the ease of writing, greater linking of ideas and text, and at least the promise of universal access to knowledge" (p. 21). Digital literacy is not necessarily Internet based. One view of multiliteracies, however, appears to be that the Internet is an integral feature. Leu & Leu (2000) have produced a volume that guides the teacher in using the Internet to teach. It is vital that students learn about such a valuable source of information that exists in such incredibly complex multimodal and hypertextual forms. The reader is urged to explore books such as that by Leu & Leu to discover how to teach students to become Internet literate since this book cannot adequately do so.

It is possible, however, to provide examples of how powerful the technology is and how Internet literacy is different from that which occurs with standard print forms. Some have argued that Internet literacy is significantly different from, and a transformation of, literacy (see Leu, 2000), while others conclude, "Yet what we see of this literacy is remarkably continuous with the literacy of print culture right down to the very serifs that grace many of the fonts of digital literacy" (Dobson and Willinsky, in press, p. 1). To be fair, Leu focuses on the Internet, while Dobson & Willinsky refer to digital literacy, not necessarily to the Internet.

The power of the Internet relative to reading can be seen in the work of John McEneaney (2000). Access the following Internet address (it's an online paper titled "Learning on the Web: A content literacy perspective" and published by *Reading Online*, an electronic journal published by the International Reading Association): http://readingonline.org/articles/art_index.asp?HREF=mceneaney/index.html (accessed on October 27, 2007). McEneaney (2000) notes in the abstract that

> The objective of this article is to describe (and, in one version, to illustrate by example) how new web technologies can be applied to assist readers both in integrating content and in maintaining a process focus as they navigate complex expository text. The central concept behind the approach described is that of the learner's "path."

Click on the "traditional hypertext" and begin navigating the article. Notice that McEneaney provides a graphic overview to help you comprehend the text. The text is complex and its structure is determined to a great extent by you, the reader, who end up navigating the text in the way that makes sense to you. Your students will need to learn about navigating and about reading hypertexts and you will have to teach them, probably explicitly in at least some of the cases. The Leu & Leu text cited above is likely a good place for you to start, although it is focused on activities for younger students. An online resource that is helpful for older ESL students is the *The Internet TESL Journal* (http://iteslj.org/, accessed on October 27, 2007).

One of the amazing features of the Internet is that projects from around the world can be accessed and explored. To provide suggestions for the use of multi-literacies or multimodal teaching and learning is not possible here, but there are projects that are accessible that will demonstrate the power and possibilities with ESL students. There are hundreds of thousands of projects worldwide that involve students in multiliteracies and multimodal teaching and learning. One large-scale coordinated project was developed in Canada. It can be seen at The Multiliteracies Project at http://multiliteracies.ca. The coordinators note:

> The Multiliteracy Project is a national Canadian study exploring pedagogies or teaching practices that prepare children for the literacy challenges of our globalized, networked, culturally diverse world. Increasingly, we encounter knowledge in multiple forms – in print, in images, in video, in combinations of forms in digital contexts – and are asked to represent our knowledge in an equally complex manner. Further, there is international recognition that Canada's linguistic and cultural diversity are a source of its strength, and a key contributor of Canada's social and economic well-being. The challenge is to assist our schools in helping students to achieve a more diverse folio of literacies.

> (http://multiliteracies.ca, accessed on October 26, 2007)

The project includes schools in five districts across Canada and one non-affiliated school at grades that vary from kindergarten to high school. A typical elementary school project can be seen at http://multiliteracies.ca/index.php/folio/viewSchool Projects/16 (accessed on October 26, 2007). This particular page contains the folio of Admiral Seymour Elementary School multiliteracies activities. Click on the "Blue Sea Creatures" link (http://multiliteracies.ca/index.php/folio/viewProject/237, accessed on October 26, 2007). On this page you will find a folio of projects. Click on one, say "Henry's Water Book," and flip through the pages of the material—mostly written—produced by Henry (http://multiliteracies.ca/index.php/folio/view GalleryBook/237/407/0, accessed on October 26, 2007).

The secondary-school projects are more complex and more multimodal. Access http://multiliteracies.ca/index.php/folio/viewDocument/222/9431 (accessed on October 26, 2007) to view a grade 8 (high school in this district varies from grade 8 to 12). This project, by Hughes (2006), shows the kind of multimodal representations that high school students can be involved in (click on the screen to see the student-animated and narrated production related to Shakespeare's sonnet "Shall I Compare Thee to a Summer's Day?").

Students are also able to contribute via their first languages, as can be heard at http://multiliteracies.ca/index.php/folio/viewDocument/238/11358 (accessed on October 26, 2007). Click on the icon of the cassette and listen to students speaking their first languages (in this case Cantonese). Early (in press) and Early, Potts, & Cohen (2005) explore the issues related to developing such programs. Potts (2007) makes the following points about multiliteracies:

- that the theoretical frames for multi- and new literacies largely ignore the students' multilingual resources and their potential for furthering academic achievement
- that the particular affordances of moving across and between modes rarely explore the contributions such activities may offer EAL students (see Early, in press)
- that such theories will continue to experience difficulty gaining traction if there is no public means of communicating their contributions to students' continuing academic development
- that such pedagogies are plausible, practical and well within the range of students of all ages, socioeconomic backgrounds, and ethnicities/countries of origin.

College- and university-level academic students will find that the Internet is filled with comprehensible input that will help them to learn the technical and academic English they need to succeed in the academic classes. It seems as though many of them have some understanding of the Internet and its possibilities. However, it is this author's experience that many have a view limited to what they have accessed for personal reasons. The teacher must demonstrate how students can access comprehensible input. This author continues to be shocked at how surprised international students are when they are shown such resources as online bilingual visual dictionaries. This seems like an important first step for a post-secondary instructor.

Wikis

Wiki software makes it possible to create, edit, and link Web pages and to make them password protected so that only their creators (and students) have access. These pages can contain a variety of student- and teacher-generated materials. The best-known wiki is Wikipedia (http://en.wikipedia.org/wiki/Main_Page, accessed on November 6, 2007), which allows anyone to access and contribute material. The use of a wiki has become extremely straightforward and easy, requiring little if any technical expertise. The bottom-line requirement for the establishment of a wiki is space on a server. The multiliteracies projects referred to earlier are located on a server. This service normally requires financial support. However, free wiki space for teachers can be found at http://www.wikispaces.com/site/for/teachers100K (accessed on November 6, 2007). This author, with minimal technical skills, was able to set up a wiki page and upload various materials to it. Having students contribute to a wiki demonstrates in concrete ways the power of the Internet.

The Internet contains content of various kinds. As was mentioned above, however, it is essential for teachers to make certain that Internet users know and understand the importance of being critical consumers of Internet-based information. The issue of critical literacy is especially important for individuals who rely on the Internet for information for educational or professional purposes. Technical advances have made the Internet increasingly democratic in that accelerating numbers of people have both access to and the ability to create material for the Internet. This democratic feature requires users to be critical since the accuracy, validity, reliability, purpose, and veracity of the material must be questioned. Indeed, there are extremely talented human beings who enjoy creating movies of phenomena such as flying saucers that are artificial but appear real to the viewer. The critical literacy skills described above are also important for Internet users to consider.

The first question focuses on the generic top-level domain found in the URL. The address extensions .com, .edu, .gov, and .org, for instance, generally refer to, repectively, business or commercial sites, post-secondary (generally American) sites, American governmental sites, and sites normally associated with professional organizations. Does the site appear legitimate? The generic top-level domains .edu, .gov, and .org provide a tiny bit of assurance concerning the legitimacy of the site, but one can be easily fooled. Is there a recognized authority associated with the site? As was noted earlier, Scheffler concluded that the final test of adequacy of evidence is "roughly equivalent to that of good reasons, or a good case" (1965, p. 59). Thoughtful Internet users question the material they find. They ask questions such as:

* Is the author of the material identified?
* If so, what are her or his credentials?
* If not, is there an organization or group associated with the material?

- If so, what kind of organization is it and what are its purposes?
- What kind of evidence supports any claims made?
- Is the evidence credible, substantiated, reliable, or valid?

Questioning the content of the Internet is roughly the same as the activities noted in the "Editorial Features" section (pp. 229–230). However, there are additional considerations. In some cases it may not be enough to believe your eyes or your ears. The digital nature of information makes it possible to produce "text" that may appear real but is not. The ESL teacher is put in the role of both language teacher and technology teacher.

Conclusion

ESL students must learn to read and learn from texts if they are to succeed in school. Indeed, they must also learn to become literate in a multimodal sense and be able to process and understand digital material. At the intermediate, secondary, and university levels, reading from content texts is a survival skill. It was suggested that the teacher has several options with ESL students: 1) make sure that the material they are asked to read is at their "instructional level," 2) provide support to help them read texts (sheltered content instruction), 3) enroll them in courses that teach academic content without texts, 4) explicitly teach students content reading skills, 5) teach academic courses in the students' first languages, 6) systematically simplify all texts they are asked to read, or 7) assume they will never learn from text and give up. It was suggested that content skills should be explicitly taught when students needed to learn them.

Content materials were described and discussed. Differences between reading books and content books are that content books contain more complex sentence structures; more difficult non-concrete items of vocabulary; more specialized, and therefore difficult, vocabulary; generally more abstract material; different kinds of visual aids such as graphs, maps, charts, and timelines; more difficult reading material; more new material; material that is more "information packed" and "concentrated", material usually written in a different style; and more vocabulary with non-standard meanings (e.g., "conductor" in a science class is different from "conductor" in a music class). Information on the Internet is often even more complex because it can contain sound, images, movies, and complex links that students must learn to comprehend and use.

The first step is to assess what content skills students know and do not know. The content reading assessment provides such information. The chapter listed many content skills that could be included in an assessment. In addition, a content skills record was described that allows the teacher to identify content instructional groups.

The discussion of instructional strategies begins with purpose of reading and reading rate and describes how students can be taught to change their reading rates relative to their tasks. Activities were presented to develop the important techniques of skimming and scanning. A general study guide was presented to focus ESL students' attention on text features that allow them to comprehend and learn from text. A margin guide, one that helps focus attention on text features to be turned into comprehension questions, was developed. SQ3R was introduced and the sequence in which it is best taught was described. Two variations—one for reading science, PQRST, and one for mathematics, SQRQCQ—were discussed.

Graphic aids are an important content feature to be read and understood. Graphic aids provide different kinds of information: raw data, comparative data, descriptive data, process data, and logic or theoretical propositions. Strategies were provided that help ESL students learn to read and comprehend graphic aids. Editorial features represent yet another content area to be developed in ESL students. This content area requires students to become critical readers, to judge what is fact and what is opinion, to recognize propaganda, to judge the content of what they read. Some suggestions for instruction were made.

Technical reading, sometimes referred to as English for Specific Purposes, requires students to read complex texts in which the vocabulary and content are often extremely difficult. ESL students in graduate university courses and adults wishing to become recertified as doctors or other professionals want to be taught how to become better readers of technical texts. Several approaches are described that allow teachers, naïve in technical terms, to help students develop their reading skills.

This chapter has not contained any simple answers to the problems ESL students face when they attempt to read content or technical texts. The teacher's role is to guide students in the development of the study strategies that will help them learn from text. Often, the survival of these students is based on their ability to read and understand text written in English. Indeed, the ESL instructor makes an important contribution to, for example, a trained doctor who can do nothing but wash dishes because he or she can't read and understand enough English to pass a medical test. Many such students fail because of reading skills, while others pass because their teachers understood the importance of both reading and study skills. This chapter has provided a basis on which to design programs that will equip students to learn from content texts. To be successful, ESL teachers must take the ideas, extend them, and change and adapt them to the needs of their particular students.

Explorations

Work with a partner, if possible.

1. College and university students are often in difficult dilemmas. They learn that their English reading ability is not advanced enough for them to read and comprehend their academic texts. How do you go about providing support for them so that they understand that they are not simply academic failures, but are having trouble because their English abilities are not advanced enough for them to read and understand their complex texts, even though they may have easily passed the TOEFL and that they should be involved in reading instruction?
2. Some of your students may be asked to read and comprehend material that is too difficult for you, the teacher, because you do not have the prerequisite

academic background. How do you go about helping these students read and comprehend their very difficult academic texts?

3. The Internet has made it very easy to find material and to download it and use it. Plagiarism has, unfortunately, become a fairly regular feature of university life. Some students from some cultures believe that reproducing great portions of a text—usually without citations—from identified experts is a sign of respect for them. How do you go about changing these attitudes in a positive way?

7

The Past, Present, and Future of ESL Reading Instruction

The Past

The first edition of this book was published in 1991 and many dramatic developments have taken place since then. One readily apparent change is that in 1991 not a single Web-based citation was made, while in this book many have been. There have been other changes.

In the United States, many educators have opted to change the abbreviation ESL to ELL (English Language Learner) to better represent students who are studying English as a third or fourth, and so on, language. In 1991 the Internet was used almost exclusively by university researchers and govenment personnel, but today its use is widespread in ways never predicted in 1991. Different search engines have made the Internet a valuable information resource available in millions of homes. The term "multiliteracies" was not used or applied to instruction in 1991 as it is in this new millennium, and critical literacy was usually associated with reading comprehension. One feature seems to have stayed the same, however. There are hundreds of millions of human beings around the world who study English. If anything, there appears to be a rapid acceleration in the numbers of individuals who wish to study English.

The Present

In 1991 this author reported that Cheng (1988) had noted that 50 million Chinese adults were studying English, and most of them were involved in activities designed to teach them to read. It is reported today, however, that about 175 million in the school system in China are studying English (see *Newsweek* at http://www. msnbc.msn.com/id/20216718/site/newsweek/, accessed on October 13, 2007). In the same *Newsweek* article it was also reported that the British Council predicted that 2 billion human beings will be studying English by 2010. The 2008 Olympic Games has resulted in a renewed interest and effort in China to study English. English is viewed as the international language of science, technology, and, perhaps most importantly, commerce. It also appears that the predominant language of the Internet, for the moment at least, is English. Millions of immigrants to English-speaking countries face the task of learning to speak, read, and write English. Teaching students to read is a primary function of the teacher. Unfortunately, the "state of the union" of ESL/EFL reading instruction was not good in 1991 and it continues not to be good in the new millennium (Gunderson, 2007).

ESL Reading Research

In 1991 this author noted that both reading and ESL researchers had explored many issues involved in students learning to read in their second, third, or fourth languages and that there appeared to be a growing interest in ESL/EFL reading issues and research. He also stated that although a healthy interest in ESL/EFL reading issues existed, there were many issues that had not been adequately addressed. They included such items as:

- L1–L2 interactions
- cultural differences
- social features
- motivation
- learning styles
- purpose for reading
- reading styles
- differential effects of genre
- discourse differences
- specific background
- world knowledge
- sex differences
- vocabulary knowledge
- relationship between L1 and L2 proficiency
- teacher variables
- classroom variables (e.g., EFL versus ESL)
- L2 proficiency variables.

In many respects, these issues have not been well explored and continue to need further research. In 2000 this author noted, "The definition of reading will broaden, and literacy researchers will become embroiled in more complex questions about its definition" (Gunderson, 2000b, p. 69) in response to the question, "How will literacy be defined in the 21st century?" The New London Group's influence appears to have increased and solidified after the publication of Cope & Kalantzis's edited volume (2000). It is clear that researchers and educators have become involved in more complex discussions of the nature of literacy. Indeed, there is a current focus on critical literacy within a multiliteracies or multimodal context.

This author noted in 1991 that

It is hoped that the development of ESL/EFL reading models and notions will be a primary goal for ESL reading researchers. At this time there is no adequate model to account for the nonliterate, non-English-speaking 5-year-old from Laos enrolled in a mainstream kindergarten, the 30-year-old dentist from Vietnam attempting to learn to read well enough to pass a certification examination, and the 70-year-old illiterate from Cambodia who must learn to read survival signs and basic oral English. No current model can account for the phenomenon of older adult ESL students appearing to learn better in "senior citizens' centers" than they do in institutions that also enroll younger students.

(Gunderson, 1991, p. 172)

In 1991 there was no credible model of ESL literacy, although Bernhardt published a review of the literature and proposed a model (Bernhardt, 1991). There were and have been multiple attempts to model L2 literacy after first-language English models. Bernhardt (2000) tested an L2 model that accounted for a great deal of the variance in the system. Gunderson (2007) tested an L2 literacy model. He concluded that L1 literacy background was a powerful variable, but the most powerful was L1 literacy pedagogy. The model that this book is based on is that the provision of comprehensible input depends on individual students' language and literacy skills—a view supported by the authors of a recent study, who state, "the impact of any particular instructional strategy appears to depend on children's language and literacy skills" (Connor et al., 2007, accessed at www.sciencemag. org/cgi/content/full/315/5811/464/DC1 on October 14, 2007). This basic view guided the development of the 1991 instructional matrices and the work presented in this revision.

The U.S. federal government entered into the debate about reading instruction by funding the National Reading Panel to review what works best to teach English speakers literacy skills and the National Literacy Panel to review what works best to teach ESL (ELL) students literacy skills, bilingual or English instruction. Findings were limited. However, it is important to keep in mind that Garan (2001) concluded of the National Reading Panel's findings, that "the panel's own words have established that the research base in its report on phonics is so flawed that the results do not even matter" (p. 502). The National Literacy Panel findings were also somewhat disappointing. Slavin and Cheung (2005), who were members of the panel but opted to quit and conduct their own independent review, concluded, "The most important conclusion from research comparing the relative effects of bilingual and immersion programs for English learners is that there are too few high-quality studies of this question," and (of the 17 studies that fitted their qualifications) "12 revealed bilingual education resulted in higher scores, while English immersion resulted in no superior performances." August & Shanahan (2006) report that the view of those involved in the National Literacy Panel was that the findings of the National Reading Panel were also valid for ESL students, although such students were not included in the studies reviewed by the NRP. So, almost two decades later, after significant effort, it seems there is still a great deal of research to be conducted.

There are fascinating areas to be explored. Background information determines, to a great extent, how well an individual comprehends a particular text. Teaching "background" has been shown to have good effects on comprehension, at least for mainstream secondary students. Are there superior methods for teaching students background information in ESL classrooms? In EFL classrooms? In mainstream classrooms? Adults learn English phonics skills so quickly, and overuse them. Is there a developmental relationship between L1 reading proficiency and L2 phonics knowledge? Who are the students that should be taught phonics, if any? What would an ESL interactive reading program look like? Is whole language the answer for teaching ESL students to read and write? Is there an approach that works best in EFL classrooms to teach reading? Are there certain teachers who are more successful as ESL reading teachers? If so, why? What pedagogical approach can help ESL students learn to be critical readers or to become able to understand and use the informational sources available on the Internet? These and hundreds of other questions should be addressed, and they will be.

Gunderson, Eddy, & Carrigan (submitted for publication b) explored how the number of ESL students in elementary classrooms affects reading achievement, both theirs and their English-speaking classmates'. It seems that issues related to EFL are taking on more importance as classrooms across North America become less like ESL (ELL) and more like EFL environments. What needs to be done to equip teachers to become knowledgeable about EFL methodologies? Mainstream teachers appear woefully unprepared to teach ESL students the literacy skills they need. How will they be prepared to meet the needs of their students when they are actually immersed in EFL environments in North America?

New technologies will be developed to allow mainstream teachers to incorporate more English models into their classroom instruction—technology, for instance, that will allow language students to be immersed in English regardless of their geographic location and the lack of availability of such models in their communities. In essence, English learners will be able to access virtual interactive English communities. The Internet represents the promise of such integration. The online version of the TOEFL, for instance, involves students in activities that represent the language occurring in academic classrooms, but without real interactivity.

Professionalism

It is lamentable that there is such a wide gap between those who are experts in ESL (ELL) and those who are experts in literacy research. Mainstream literacy researchers, it seems, become ESL experts by simply including such students in their studies. On the other hand, ESL researchers appear to become literacy experts simply by including literacy measures in their studies. There is a need for deep ESL literacy expertise. There is the need for researchers and educators who are ESL (ELL)-literacy experts. At present, these individuals are divided by history, organizational affiliations, and allegiances that do not serve them, students, or their "disciplines" well.

The Future

For the moment English is a predominant language in science, in technology, and on the Internet. Some individuals have referred to this dominance as hegemony (see, for instance, Macfadyen *et al.*, 2004). English is viewed negatively by many as being responsible for marginalizing other languages and cultures. Interestingly enough, this may not always be the case. Students of this author argue that English is the vehicle for discovering and maintaining first cultures in ways not previously possible. For instance, the YouTube website at http://www.youtube.com/watch?v= N2RIAS_zFZg (accessed on November 3, 2007) shows clips from the first movie ever made in Konkani, a regional language of the penisular west coast of India. It was found by searching the Web in English. Members of various diasporas search the Internet in English to access material representing their heritage, such as poetry written in Russian (http://www.litera.ru/stixiya/poets.html, accessed on November 3, 2007), Korean movies (http://www.youtube.com/watch?v=nwcmaXojf2Q, accessed on November 3, 2007), and Mexican movies (http://www.youtube.com/ watch?v=g9gZe-SDuDk, accessed on November 3, 2007). First-cultural materials are accessible in English on the Internet. English is helpful to individuals who wish to research their own cultural heritages. English may be hegemonic, but it is also powerfully liberatory.

This book was written with the countless students who struggle to learn to read English around the world in mind. It has discussed programs for students of all ages, educational backgrounds, language proficiencies, and motivations. They are extraordinary individuals. They vary in age, color, cultural background, worldview, language ability, motivation, interest, sex, socioeconomic status, educational background, and belief in the value of education. These are important variables to consider in the design of ESL programs.

There is one variable, however, in which ESL—not necessarily EFL—students seem to vary less widely. That is determination. Wai Chi is a Chinese immigrant from Hong Kong who works part-time in her uncle's laundry and is a secondary student struggling with courses in English, chemistry, hygiene, social studies, French, and trigonometry. She spends five to seven hours a day doing homework. Steven Arellano is an immigrant from Italy, a secondary student in academic courses, a soccer player, and a part-time worker in his father's flower shop. He spends three to five hours a day doing homework. Erik Vuong, an immigrant from Vietnam, works eight hours a day as a busboy in a Chinese restaurant, studies English two nights a week in an English program run by a California school district, attends a vocational school to study jet mechanics, and does two to three hours of homework every day. Paul Zbesinski, an immigrant from Poland, an engineering major at a large university, and a pizza delivery man, studies English twice a week in night school, has English tutoring six hours a week, does homework for five to seven hours a day, and has a very high grade-point average in his engineering courses. Jesse Abarco is an immigrant from the Philippines who is a trained biochemist, has a family of four to support, works in a Greek restaurant as a busboy, studies technical English at a local university extension program, and waits for the day he can pass his certification examination to become a practicing laboratory technician.

All these students struggle to learn English. Except for a change in names, these are real people, determined to learn English because it is the key to their success. They sleep short hours and work long ones. They are determined, and their determination is shared by many ESL students, a feature that endears them to teachers. To such students, teachers should be dedicated. They do not "bring down the level" in classes, as many seem to think. They are not mentally slow, as many teachers assume, because of their English.

Both teachers and researchers should be as dedicated to the task of finding better methods and approaches to teaching literacy in English as these students are to learning.

Explorations

Work with a partner, if possible.

1. Some have speculated that the Internet has made differences related to socio-economic status and access even more pronounced than it was before the development of the technology. What is your view? Are students in poor countries or communities disadvantaged even more by the lack of access? If so, how could the situation be improved? If not, why not?
2. What is your view of the potential for technology to create virtual teaching and learning communities where ESL/EFL students could learn by interacting online rather than with other human beings? What would be the negative aspects of such a teaching and learning approach, if any?
3. What do you predict will be the changes in ESL/ELL/EFL pedagogy in five years, ten years, or twenty years? What do you think should be the focus of research in the area over the next decade?

Appendix: Informal Primary-Level Language and Literacy Test

The purpose of the following assessment is to measure primary students' language and literacy skills to determine whether they might benefit from literacy instruction in English. The following items are easily constructed. Indeed, you can assemble this assessment package in a fairly short time. Suggestions for management of your assessment package will be given at the end of this Appendix. The test should be administered at a small table if possible since the table itself will form part of the test.

Assessment 1: Responding to Questions

This is an oral assessment administered in a one-on-one session. This assessment should take place in a fairly quiet place with as few interruptions as possible. Ask the following questions and record the student's answers, if any. You should record responses on a student record form (see below).

1. What's your name?
2. How old are you?
3. Where do you live?
4. Who lives with you here?
5. What food do you like to eat?
6. What game do you like to play?

Answers are usually one or two words in length. If answers are more complex, make note of them, but one point is given for each correct response regardless of the length of the utterance, for a total of six points for this subtest.

Assessment 2: Following Directions

This test involves the student being able to follow directions. It requires knowledge that is somewhat more complex. You will need the following items to be placed on the table where you are administering the test: an eraser, a book, a ruler, and a piece of paper.

1. Please give me the eraser.
2. Put the ruler under the book.
3. Open the book.

4. Pick up the paper.
5. Put the paper in the book.
6. Close the book and put it on the table.

Score one point for each correct response, for a total possible score of six.

Assessment 3: Reciting the Names of the Letters of the Alphabet

Ask the student to recite the names of the letters of the alphabet in order. Score one point for each correct letter produced in order up to 10 (up to the letter J). Ten is the total possible score even if the student is able to produce all letters accurately.

Assessment 4: Copying a Sentence

Print the following in large, primary manuscript writing. Ask the child to copy the sentence.

The boys and girls are going to school.

Score the copying: 0—unable to copy; 1—able to copy two or three letters; 2—able to copy about on third of the letters; 3—able to copy about half of the letters; 4—able to copy about two-thirds of the letters; 5—able to copy nearly all of the letters; 6—able to copy all of the letters, including both capital and small letters accurately. Judgment is an important scoring variable in this case. If the letters are terribly primitive but recognizable, they should be scored as correct. If the sentence is copied, but as a line of letters with no spaces, subtract one point from the total score.

Assessment 5: Writing Numbers 1–20

Ask the student to write in English the numbers from 1 to 20. The following scoring rubric is used.

- No numbers written: 0 points
- 1–5 numbers: 1 point
- 6–10 numbers: 2 points
- 11–15 numbers: 3 points
- 16–20 numbers: 4 points.

Order is important, so numbers score only when they are in the correct positions. It is often difficult to count items as correct because the writing may be so completely illegible.

Assessment 6: Printing the Alphabet

Ask the student to print the letters of the alphabet in order.

- No letters produced: 0 points
- 1–5 letters: 1 point
- 5–10 letters: 2 points
- 11–15 letters: 3 points
- 16–20 letters: 4 points
- 21–26 letters: 5 points.

Order is important, so letters are scored correct only when they are in the correct order. It is often difficult to count items as correct because the writing may be so completely illegible.

Assessment 7: Upper- and Lower-Case Letter Recognition

Print the following in large, primary-size script. Ask the student to read the letters aloud to you.

A	G	N	B	T	S	Q	I
p	c	e	i	f	b	u	y

Score one point for each correct response for upper-case and lower-case letters. So, the upper-case total possible is 8 and the lower-case total possible is also 8.

Assessment 8: Single- and Multiple-Digit Number Recognition

Print the following numbers on a card. Ask the student to read the numbers aloud to you.

2	4	5	8	3	9	7	6
13	28	87	51	60	106	1,000	

Score one point for each correct response. The total possible for single-digit numbers is 8 and the total possible for multiple-digit numbers is 7.

Assessment 9: Color Recognition and Naming

This test involves naming six colors: red, yellow, blue, black, green, and white. Many versions are possible; one standard letter-size page with six colored squares or six separate 3 × 5 cards each with a different color. The easiest alternative, however, is to purchase a box of crayons that contains all of the colors. The child identifies the colors of one crayon at a time. This author has noted that a small box of eight crayons usually does not have a "white" crayon, but the box of 12 does. Some teachers have opted to use paint samples they found at paint stores. Score one point for each correctly identified color for a total possible correct score of 6.

Assessment 10: Body Parts Recognition and Naming

This test measures students' ability to recognize and name parts of the body. The following should be printed on a separate page. These are sketches; some teachers have opted to use clip art from the Net.

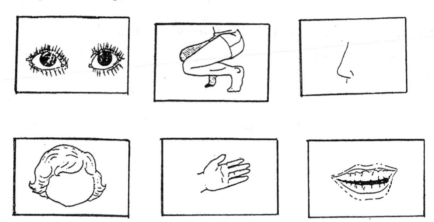

Figure A.1 Sketches of Six Body Parts

Score one point for each correctly identified body part, for a total possible correct score of 6. Record any correct responses since this will help identify possible items for instruction.

Assessment 11: Recognition and Naming of Common School Items

This test measures students' ability to recognize and name common school items: pencil, paper, chair, table, and crayons. The items to be named in this test are common school items that should be collected and kept in the Assessment Kit. (It is interesting to note that crayons are a common school item in North America, but not necessarily in other parts of the world.) Score one point for each correctly identified school item for a total possible correct score of 5. Keep a record of the items not identified.

Assessment 12: Connecting Words and Pictures

The following assessment asks students to draw a line from a printed word to a picture that represents the word.

Score one point for each correctly connected word and picture, for a total possible score of 9 for this assessment.

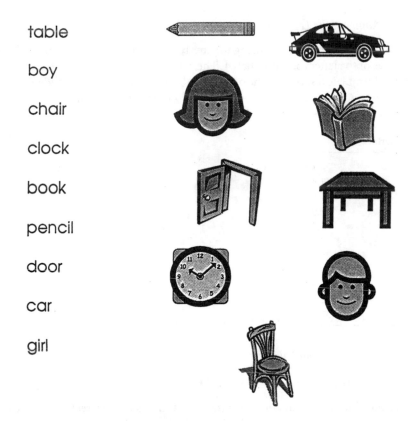

table

boy

chair

clock

book

pencil

door

car

girl

Figure A.2 Word–Picture Connection Task

Assessment Criteria and Instructions

Oral Language (Questions and Directions)

The following table shows the overall percentage of primary students who correctly responded to the questions and the directions tests. Overall, 25.60 percent of the students responded accurately for all questions and 21.20 percent for following directions.

Student no.	Questions	Directions
1	60.9%	35.3%
2	48.8%	23.3%
3	33.4%	37.5%
4	34.5%	34.4%
5	34.8%	33.6%
6	32.6%	33.7%
Total	25.6%	21.2%

Reciting Names of the Letters of the Alphabet

The following represents the scoring for the 1,300 primary-level students reciting the names of the letters of the alphabet. The response A, B, C, D seems to represent a kind of formulaic response to the question. About one-fourth of the students were able to respond in this fashion, while roughly 40 percent could not recite any of the names of the letters of the alphabet.

No. of letters

10	20.1%
9	1.4%
8	1.0%
7	0.9%
6	1.2%
5	2.0%
4	25.5%
3	6.0%
2	1.2%
1	2.0%
0	38.6%

Recognition: Letters and Numbers

UPPER-CASE LETTERS

The second column displays the percentage of students who correctly named each of the capital letters, while the third column shows overall percentages of students related to number of items correct. So, in this case 51.7 percent could not identify any of the letters.

Letter	Correct	Items Correct
A	46.2%	0 (51.7%)
G	39.5%	1 (1.2%)
N	39.0%	2 (2.3%)
B	40.6%	3 (2.8%)
T	40.4%	4 (2.4%)
S	40.4%	5 (1.8%)
Q	40.5%	6 (1.7%)
I	37.5%	7 (2.4%)
Total correct	33.7%	8 (33.7%)

LOWER-CASE LETTERS

The following table shows data concerning the percentage of students who accurately named each of the lower-case letters and the overall percentage of students who had 0 to 8 items correct. Overall, students were less likely to recognize and name lower-case letters than they were upper-case letters.

Letter	Correct	Items Correct
p	37.8%	0 (55.6%)
c	41.5%	1 (2.2%)
e	36.2%	2 (0.9%)
i	38.0%	3 (3.0%)
f	37.9%	4 (2.4%)
b	35.5%	5 (1.6%)
u	35.5%	6 (1.7%)
y	36.2%	7 (2.3%)
Total	30.2%	8 (30.2%)

NUMBER RECOGNITION

About half of the students could not recognize and name any of the single-digit numbers and about 80 percent could recognize none of the multiple-digit numbers.

Correct	Single-Digit	Multiple-Digit
0	49.3%	77.7%
1	0.5%	2.6%
2	1.2%	3.0%
3	2.7%	2.7%
4	3.7%	1.2%
5	1.7%	3.2%
6	1.3%	4.4%
7	1.6%	5.2%
8	38.0%	

Writing

Students were asked to copy a sentence, to write the letters of the alphabet, and to write numbers. The following table represents their scores.

Score	Sentence (6)	Alphabet (5)	Numbers (4)
0	44.0%	52.0%	46.0%
1	30.7%	30.1%	30.6%
2	16.5%	1.0%	10.3%
3	2.2%	2.6%	4.8%
4	0.9%	7.8%	8.3%
5	2.2%	6.2%	
6	3.6%		

Typical responses to these items are shown in the following three figures.

Figure A.3 Copying a Sentence

This student copied the letters so that they are legible; however, she did so without spaces between letters. Her score for this was 4 (5, but 1 subtracted because of the lack of spaces).

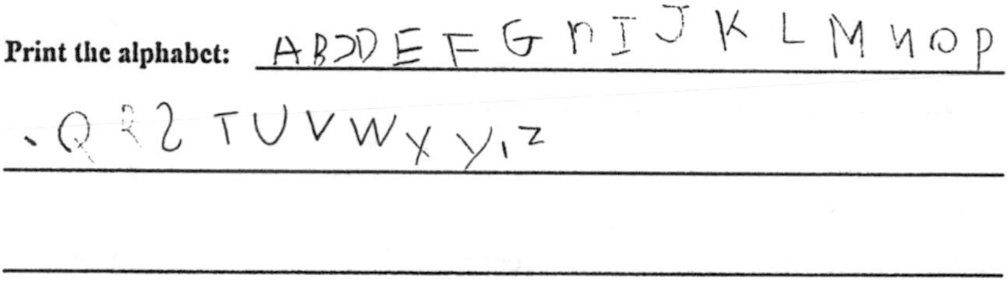

Figure A.4 Writing the Alphabet

The student scored 5 points for this subtest. All of the letters are in order, but some were reversed. Reversals are very typical for beginners.

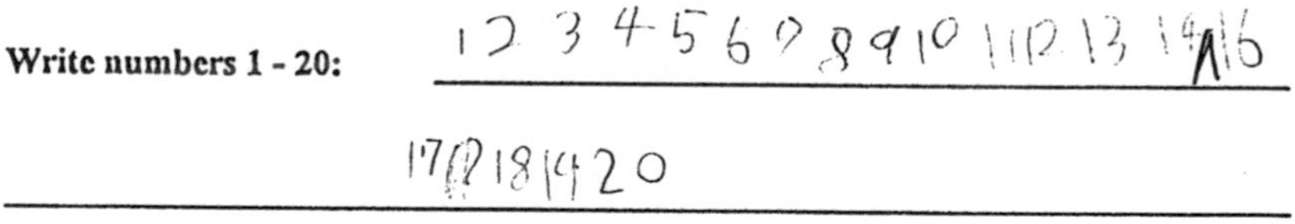

Figure A.5 Writing Numbers

The student missed only one number (15), so her score was 4.

Recognition: Colors

Scores for the recognition of six colors are shown in the following table.

Color	Correct	Total Correct
Red	50.4%	0 (47.1%)
Yellow	49.3%	1 (2.1%)
Blue	48.9%	2 (1.7%)
Black	45.4%	3 (1.6%)
Green	47.4%	4 (3.0%)
White	44.9%	5 (3.0%)
Total	41.5%	6 (41.5%)

Recognition: Body Parts

Scores for the recognition of six body parts are shown in the following table.

Body Part	Correct	Total Correct
Nose	50.3%	0 (47.8%)
Hand	45.6%	1 (2.0%)
Mouth	46.0%	2 (2.2%)
Leg	33.1%	3 (2.4%)
Eyes	48.7%	4 (5.9%)
Head	42.9%	5 (8.3%)
Total	31.3%	6 (31.3%)

Recognition: School Items

Scores for the recognition of common school items are shown in the following table.

School Item	Correct	Total Correct
Pencil	47.5%	0 (49.7%)
Table	40.9%	1 (4.2%)
Paper	40.1%	2 (3.5%)
Chair	43.4%	3 (4.2%)
Crayons	33.9%	4 (9.2%)
Total	28.9%	5 (28.9%)

Connecting Word and Pictures

Students were asked to connect, with lines, printed words with the correct pictures. The following table shows their scores.

Word–Picture	Correct	Total Correct
table	26.0%	0 (48.0%)
boy	39.0%	1 (12.0%)
chair	26.0%	2 (8.6%)
clock	37.0%	3 (3.2%)
book	26.0%	4 (2.3%)
pencil	35.0%	5 (2.5%)
door	22.6%	6 (3.2%)
car	33.6%	7 (1.6%)
girl	33.0%	8 (2.5%)
Total	16.0%	9 (16.0%)

Interpretation

Scores are broadly interpreted into three criterion: zero-level English, extremely low English, and readiness English. It is important to remember that these overall categories are bounded by fuzziness. Variations in scores can represent the experiential history of an individual rather than an overall level of knowledge. The ability to recite the letters of the alphabet, for instance, was more widespread in this primary population than this author expected. It may be that *Sesame Street* has had an influence around the world. The following are the criteria for all of the subtests:

Assessment	Total Score	Zero-level	Extremely Low	Ready
1. Questions	6	0–2	3–4	5–6
2. Directions	6	0–2	3–4	5–6
3. Recite Alphabet	10	0–4	5–7	8–10
4. Copying Sentence	6	0–3	4–5	6
5. Write Alphabet	5	0–2	3–4	5
6. Write Numbers	4	0–1	2–3	4
7. Upper Case	8	0–2	3–5	6–8
8. Lower Case	8	0–2	3–5	6–8
9. Single Numbers	8	0–2	3–5	6–8
10. Multi-digits	7	0–2	3–4	5–7
11. Colors	6	0–2	3–4	5–6
12. Body Parts	6	0–2	3–4	5–6
13. School Items	5	0–1	2–3	4–5
14. Words and Pictures	9	0–2	3–7	8–9
Total	94	0–29	30–64	65–94

The complete battery of tests takes a fairly long time to administer, so teachers often opt to use only some of the tests, but using the scoring rubric above for the subtests. Some administer the recognition portions only, while others administer only the oral portions. Some have opted to use the first three subtests—questions, directions, reciting alphabet—as the subtests they find most useful in their classrooms to determine readiness for English instruction, while others have opted for an English recognition score using upper-case, lower-case, colors, body parts, school items, and connecting words and pictures to determine readiness for instruction.

Individuals who use this test opt to create a separate scoring sheet and a student response sheet. In addition, they also create a "kit" to contain the realia for the test.

References

Alemán, A.M.M. (2006). Latino demographics, democratic individuality, and educational account-ability: A pragmatist's view. *Educational Researcher, 35*, 25–31.

Anderson, R.C., Reynolds, RE., Schallert, D.L., & Goetz, E.T. (1977). Frameworks for comprehending discourse. *American Educational Research Journal, 14*, 367–381.

Andrew, C.M., Lapkin, S., & Swain, M. (1978). *Report on the 1978 evaluation of the Ottawa and Carleton French immersion programs, grades 5–7.* Toronto, ON: Ontario Institute for Studies in Education.

Ashton-Warner, S. (1963). *Teacher.* New York: Bantam Books.

Ashworth, M.N. (1979). *The forces which shaped them: A history of the education of minority group children in British Columbia.* Vancouver, BC: New Star Books.

Auerbach, E.R. (1993). Reexamining English only in the ESL Classroom. *TESOL Quarterly, 27*, 9–29.

August, D., & Shanahan, T. (Eds.) (2006). *Developing literacy in second language learners: Report of the national literacy panel on language-minority children and youth.* Mahwah, NJ: Lawrence Erlbaum Associates.

Aukerman, M. (2007). A culpable CALP: Rethinking the conversational/academic language proficiency distinction in early literacy instruction. *The Reading Teacher, 60*, 626–635.

Aukerman, R.C. (1981). *The basal reader approach to reading.* New York: John Wiley.

Baldwin, R.S., & Kaufman, R.K. (1979). A concurrent validity study of the Raygor Readability Estimate. *Journal of Reading, 23*, 148–153.

Banks, J.A. (1991). *Teaching strategies for ethnic studies* (4th ed.). Needham Heights, MA: Allyn & Bacon.

Barik, C., & Swain, M. (1975). Three-year evaluation of a large scale early grade French immersion program: The Ottawa study. *Language Learning, 25*, 1–30.

Barron, R.F. (1979). Research for the classroom teacher: Recent developments on the structured overview as an advance organizer. In H.L. Herber & J.D. Riley (Eds.), *Research in reading in the content areas: The fourth report.* Syracuse, NY: Syracuse University, Reading and Language Arts Center.

Bartoli, J.S. (1995). *Unequal opportunity: Learning to read in the U.S.A.* New York: Teachers College Press.

Bates, E. (1976). *Language and context: The acquisition of pragmatics.* New York: Academic Press.

Bates, E., Benigni, L., Bretherton, I., Camaioni, L., & Volterra, V. (1977). From gesture to the first word: On cognitive and social prerequisites. In L. Rosenblum (Ed.), *Conversation, interaction, and the development of language.* New York: John Wiley.

Baumann, J.F., & Heubach, K.M. (1996). Do basal readers deskill teachers? A national survey of educators' use and opinions of basals. *Elementary School Journal, 96*, 5, 511–526.

Belliveau, G. (2005). An arts-based approach to teach social justice: Drama as a way to address bullying in schools. *International Journal of Arts Education, 3*, 136–165.

Belliveau, G. (2006). Using drama to achieve social justice: Anti-bullying project in elementary schools. *Universal Mosaic of Drama and Theatre—IDEA Publications, 5*, 325–336.

Bernhardt, E.B. (1991). *Reading development in a second language.* Norwood, NJ: Ablex Publishing Corporation.

Bernhardt, E.B. (2000). Second-language reading as a case study of reading in the 20th century. In M.L. Kamil, P.B. Mosenthal, P.D. Pearson, & R. Barr (Eds.), *Handbook of reading research* (3rd ed.) Mahwah, NJ: Lawrence Erlbaum Associates.

Betts, E.A. (1946). *Foundations of reading instruction.* New York: American Book Company.

Bond, G., & Dykstra, K. (1967). *Coordinating center for first grade reading instruction programs.* Final report, United States Department of Health, Education, and Welfare. Minneapolis: University of Minnesota Press.

Bormuth, J. (1967). Comparable cloze and multiple choice comprehension test scores. *Journal of Reading, 10,* 291–299.

Bourne, K.R. (1972). *The Bourne method.* Baltimore County, MD: Essex Community College Press.

Bowen, J.D. (1969). A tentative measure of the relative control of English and Amharic by eleventh-grade Ethiopian students. *Workpapers in TESL, 2,* 68–98. Los Angeles: University of California at Los Angeles.

Braithwaite, L. (1974). Problems of race and colour in the Caribbean. *Caribbean Issues, 1,* 1–14.

Bransford, J.D., & Johnson, M.K. (1978). Considerations of some problems in comprehension. In W.G. Chase (Ed.), *Visual information processing.* New York: Academic Press.

Brown, R. (1973). *A first language: The early stages.* London: George Allen & Unwin.

Brown, Y. (2001). Personal communication at the University of British Columbia, September.

Burns, P., & Roe, B.D. (2002). *Informal reading inventory: Preprimer to twelfth grade* (6th ed.). Boston: Houghton Mifflin.

California State Senate Bill 2138, Regular Session 1995–1996. Retrieved March 30, 2007, from http://info.sen.ca.gov/pub/95-96/bill/sen/sb_2101-2150/sb_2138_cfa_960418_111701_sen_comm.html.

Carr, F., & Ogle, D. (1987). K-W-L plus: A strategy for comprehension and summarization. *Journal of Reading, 30,* 626–631.

Carrell, P.L. (1981). Culture-specific schemata in L2 comprehension. In R.A. Orem & J.F. Haskell (Eds.), *Selected papers, 9th Illinois TESOL/BEAnnual convention and the first Midwest TESOL conference.* Chicago: TESOL/BE.

Carrigan, T. (1998). Personal communication, Richmond, British Columbia, Canada.

Carroll, J., Carton, A., & Wilds, C. (1959). *An investigation of "cloze" items in the measurement of achievement in foreign languages.* Cambridge, MA: Harvard University Laboratory for Research in Instruction [ED 021513].

Carter, T. (1970). *Mexican Americans in the Schools: A History of Educational Neglect.* New York: College Entrance Examination Board.

Cazabon, M.T., Nicoladis, E., & Lambert, W.E. (1998). *Becoming bilingual in the Amigo two-way immersion program.* Santa Cruz, CA: University of California at Santa Cruz. Also available at http://repositories.cdlib.org/crede/rsrchrpts/rr03.

Center for Research on Education, Diversity and Excellence. (2002). *A national study of school effectiveness for language minority students' long-term academic achievement final report.* Retrieved June 22, 2004, from http://www.crede.ucsc.edu/research/llaa/1.1_final.html.

Chall, J.S. (1958). *Readability: An appraisal of research and application.* Athens, OH: Bureau of Educational Research, Ohio University.

Chall, J.S. (1967). *Learning to read: The great debate.* New York: McGraw-Hill.

Chamot, A.U. (2006). *The cognitive academic language learning approach: An update.* In R.T. Jiménez & V.O. Pang (Eds.), Race, ethnicity, and education: Language and literacy in schools. New York: Praeger.

Chamot, A.U. & O'Malley, J.M. (1987). The cognitive academic language learning approach: A bridge to the mainstream. *TESOL Quarterly, 21,* 227–249.

Chang, J. (2001). Chinese speakers. In M. Swan & B. Smith (Eds.), *Learner English: A teacher's guide to interference and other problems.* Cambridge: Cambridge University Press.

Cheng, G.H. (1988). Teaching English as a Foreign Language in China. *TESL Canada Journal, 5,* 88–93.

Ching, D.C. (1976). *Reading and the bilingual child.* Newark, DE: The International Reading Association.

Chomsky, N. (1975). *Reflections of language.* New York: Pantheon Books.

Chow, M. (1986). Measuring the growth of writing in the kindergarten and grade one years: How are the ESL children doing? *TESL Canada Journal, 4,* 35–47.

Clark, H.H., & Clark, E.V. (1977). *Psychology and language: An introduction to psycholinguistics.* New York: Harcourt Brace Jovanovich.

Clay, M.M. (1979). *Reading: The patterning of complex behavior* (2nd ed.). Auckland, New Zealand: Heinemann.

Clay, M.M. (1985). *The early detection of reading difficulties: A diagnostic survey with recovery procedures.* Portsmouth, NH: Heinemann.

Clay, M.M. (1988). Exploring with a pencil. *Reading Today, 6,* 5.

Clay, M.M. (1991). *Becoming literate: The construction of inner control.* Portsmouth, NH: Heinemann.

Clay, M.M. (2001). *Change over time in children's literacy development.* Portsmouth, NH: Heinemann.

Clymer, T.F. (1963). The utility of phonics generalizations in the primary grades. *The Reading Teacher, 16,* 252–58.

Coady, J. (1979). A psycholinguistic model of the ESL reader. In R. Mackay, B. Barkman, & R.R. Jordan (Eds.), *Reading in a second language: Hypotheses, organization and practice.* Rowley, MA: Newbury House Publishers.

Condon, J.C., Jr. (1973). When people talk with people. In C. David Mortenson (Ed.), *Basic readings in communication theory.* New York: Harper & Row.

Connor, C.M., Morrison, F.J., Fishman, B.J., Schatschneider, C., & Underwood, P. (2007) Algorithm-guided individualized reading instruction. *Science, 315,* 5811, 464–465.

Cope, B., & Kalantzis, M. (Eds.) (2000). *Multiliteracies: Literacy learning and the design of social futures.* New York: Routledge.

Crawford, J. (1989). *Bilingual education: History, politics, theory, and practice.* Trenton, NJ: Crane Publishers.

Crawford, J. (1997). *Best evidence: Research foundation of the bilingual Education Act.* Washington, DC: National Clearing House for Bilingual Education.

Crawford, J. (1999). Life in a politicized climate: What role for educational researchers? Paper presented at the Linguistic Minority Research Institute Conference on the Schooling of English Language Learners in the Post 227 Era, Sacramento, CA, May 1999. Available at http://ourworld.compu serve.com/homepages/JWCRAWFORD/LMRI.htm.

Cummins, J. (1981). The role of primary language development in promoting educational success for language minority students. In California State Department of Education (Ed.), *Schooling and language minority students: A theoretical framework.* Los Angeles: California State Department of Education.

Cummins, J. (1984). Wanted: A theoretical framework for relating language proficiency to academic achievement among bilingual students. In C. Rivera (Ed.), *Language proficiency and academic achievement.* Clevedon, UK: Multilingual Matters.

Cummins, J. ([1985] 1991). Interdependence of first- and second-language proficiency in bilingual children. In E. Bialystok (Ed.), *Language processing in bilingual children.* New York: Cambridge University Press.

Cummins, J. (1998). Beyond adversarial discourse: Searching for common ground in the education of bilingual students. Presentation to the California State Board of Education. Retrieved January 8, 2004, from http://ourworld.compuserve.com/homepages/JWCRAWFORD/cummins. htm.

Cummins, J. (2000). Putting language proficiency in its place: Responding to critiques of the conversational/academic language distinction. In J. Cenoz & U. Jessner (Eds.), *English in Europe: The acquisition of a third language.* Clevedon, UK: Multilingual Matters.

Cummins, J., & Swain, M. (1983). Analysis-by-rhetoric: Reading the text or the reader's own projections? A reply to Edelsky et al. *Applied Linguistics, 4,* 23–41.

Cunningham, P.M. (1978). Mumble reading for beginning readers. *The Reading Teacher, 31,* 409–411.

Cziko, G.A. (1983). Another response to Shanahan, Kamil & Tobin: Further reason to keep the cloze case open. *Reading Research Quarterly, 18,* 3, 361–365.

Darnell, D. (1968). *The development of an English language proficiency test of foreign students using a Clozentropy procedure.* Boulder: University of Colorado.

Dauzat, S.V., Dauzat, W., Otto, W., & Burton, K. (1978). *Steck-Vaughn adult reading.* New York: Steck-Vaughn Publishing.

DeFord, D.E. (1980). Young children and their writing. *Theory into Practice, 19,* 157–162.

DelFattore, J. (1992). *What Johnny shouldn't read: Textbook censorship in America.* New Haven, CT: Yale University Press.

Devadas, C. (1989). The prediction of the evolution of microstructure during the hot rolling of steel strip. Unpublished doctoral dissertation, University of British Columbia, Vancouver, British Columbia, Canada.

Dirringer, D. (1968). *The alphabet* (Vols. 1 and 2). New York: Funk & Wagnalls.

Dobson, T. & Willinsky, J. (in press). Digital literacy. In D. Olson & N. Torrence (Eds.), *The Cambridge handbook of literacy.* Pre-print version retrieved October 16, 2007, from http://lerc.educ.ubc.ca/fac/dobson/courses/lled565d/pdfs/digitalliteracy.pdf.

Dolch, E.W. (1936). A basic sight vocabulary. *Elementary School Journal, 36,* 6, 456–460.

Dolch, E.W. (1960). *Teaching primary reading.* Champaign, IL: Garrard Press.

Downing, J. (1962). *To bee or not to be: The new augmented Roman alphabet explained and illustrated.* New York: Cassell.

Dudley-Evans, T., & St. John, M.J. (1998). *Development in English for specific purposes: A multidisciplinary approach.* Cambridge: Cambridge University Press.

Duff, P.A., & Uchida, Y. (1997). The negotiation of teachers' sociocultural identities and practices in postsecondary EFL classes. *TESOL Quarterly, 31,* 451–86.

Durr, W.K. (1973). A computer study of high-frequency words in popular trade juveniles. *The Reading Teacher, 27,* 37–42.

Durrell, D.D., & Murphy, H.A. (1972). *Speech-to-print phonics.* New York: Harcourt, Brace & World.

Dyson, A.H. (1981). Oral language: The rooting system for learning to write. *Language Arts, 19,* 776–784.

Early, M. (in press). Adolescent ESL students' interpretation and appreciation of literary texts: A case study of multimodality. *Canadian Modern Language Review.*

Early, M., & Gunderson, L. (1993). Linking home, school, and community language learning. *TESL Canada Journal, 1,* 99–111.

Early, M., Potts, D., & Cohen, S. (2005). *From literacy to multiple-literacy; Designing learning environments for knowledge generation.* Symposia at AILA 2005: The World Congress of Applied Linguistics, Madison, WI.

Echevarria, J., & Graves, A. (2007). *Sheltered content instruction: Teaching English language learners with diverse abilities* (3rd ed.). Boston: Allyn & Bacon.

Echevarria, J., Short, D., & Powers, K. (2006). School reform and standards-based education: A model for English-language learners. *Journal of Educational Research, 99,* 195–210.

Echevarria, J., Vogt, M.E., & Short, D. (2004). *Making content comprehensible for English learners: The SIOP model* (2nd ed.). Needham Heights, MA: Allyn & Bacon.

Edelsky, C. (1990). *With literacy and justice for all: Rethinking the social in language and education.* London: Falmer Press.

Edelsky, C., Hudelson, S., Flores, B., Barkin, F. Altwerger, J., & Jilbert, K. (1983). Semilingualism and language deficit. *Applied Linguistics, 4,* 1–22.

Ellis, R. (1986). *Understanding second language acquisition.* Oxford: Oxford University Press.

Ellis, R. (1994). *The study of second language acquisition.* Oxford: Oxford University Press.

Faltis, C. (1993). Critical issues in the use of sheltered content instruction in high school bilingual programs. *Peabody Journal of Education, 69,* 136–151.

Fay, L. (1965). Reading study skills: Math and science. In A.J. Figurel (Ed.), *Reading and inquiry.* Newark, DE: International Reading Association.

Ferreiro, E. (1986). The interplay between information and assimilation in beginning literacy. In W.H. Teale & E. Sulzby (Eds.), *Emergent literacy: Writing and reading.* Norwood, NJ: Ablex.

Fitzgerald, J. (1995). English-as-a-second-language learners' cognitive reading processes: A review of research in the United States. *Review of Educational Research, 65,* 2, 145–190.

Flaitz, J. (2006). *Understanding your refugee and immigrant students: An educational, cultural and linguistic guide.* Ann Arbor: University of Michigan Press.

Flesch, R. (1955). *Why Johnny can't read.* New York: Harper.

Freire, P. (1975). *Pedagogy of the oppressed.* New York: Herder & Herder.

Gallaudet, E.M. (1888). *Life of Thomas Hopkins Gallaudet.* New York: Holt.

Gamez, G.L. (1979). Reading in a second language: "Native language approach" vs "direct method." *The Reading Teacher, 32,* no. 6, 665–670.

Garan, E. (2001). Beyond the smoke and mirrors: A critique of the National Reading Panel report on phonics. *Phi Delta Kappan*, *82*, 7, 500–506.

Gates, A.L. (1926). *A reading vocabulary for the primary grades*. New York: Teachers College, Columbia University.

Gates, A.L. (1940). The place of the basal books in a reading program. *Teachers' Service Bulletin in Reading*, *1*, no. 6. New York: Macmillan.

Gee, J.P. (1992). *The social mind: Language, ideology, and social practice*. New York: Bergin & Garvey.

Gersten, R., Woodward, J., & Schneider, S. (1992). Bilingual immersion: A longitudinal evaluation of the El Paso program. *READ*, ERIC Document Reproductions, p. 1–42.

Goldenberg, C. (2006). Improving achievement for English-learners: What the research tells us. *Education Week*, *25*, 34–36.

Goldstein, T. (2004). Performed ethnography for critical language teacher education. In B. Norton & K. Toohey (Eds.), *Critical pedagogies and language learning*. Cambridge: Cambridge University Press.

Goodman, K.S. (1965). A linguistic study of cues and miscues in reading. *Elementary English*, *42*, 639–643.

Goodman, K.S. (1976). Reading: A psycholinguistic guessing game. In H. Singer & R.B. Ruddell (Eds.), *Theoretical models and processes of reading*. Newark, DE: International Reading Association.

Goodman, K.S. (1992). Why whole language is today's agenda in education. *Language Arts*, *69*, 354–363.

Gray, W.S., & Leary, B.E. (1935). *What makes a book readable?* Chicago: University of Chicago Press.

Green, J. (2003). *The word wall: Teaching vocabulary through immersion* (2nd ed.). Toronto: Pippin Publishing.

Greene, J.P. (1998). A meta-analysis of the effectiveness of bilingual education. Austin, TX: University of Texas. Retrieved November 24, 2007 at http://ourworld.compuserve.com/homepages/jwcrawford/greene.htm.

Gunderson, L. (1983a). ESL students: Don't throw them to the sharks. *Highway One*, *6*, 33–44.

Gunderson, L. (1983b). A readiness word list. *Prime Areas*, *25*, 34–36.

Gunderson, L. (1984a). Reading achievement assessment of L1 and L2 students in regular classrooms. *TEAL Occasional Papers*, *8*, 31–40.

Gunderson, L. (1984b). One last word list. *The Alberta Journal of Educational Research*, *30*, 259–269.

Gunderson, L. (1985). L2 reading instruction in ESL and mainstream classrooms. In J. Niles & R. Lalik (Eds.), *Issues in literacy: A research perspective*. Rochester, NY: The National Reading Conference.

Gunderson, L. (1986a). An epistemological analysis of word recognition. *Reading-Canada-Lecture*, *4*, 247–254.

Gunderson, L. (1986b). ESL students and content reading. *TESL Canada Journal*, *4*, 49–53.

Gunderson, L. (1989). *A whole language primer*. Richmond Hill, Toronto: Scholastic-Tab.

Gunderson, L. (1991). *ESL literacy instruction: A guidebook to theory and practice*. Englewood Cliffs, NJ: Prentice Hall Regents.

Gunderson, L. (1995). *The Monday morning guide to comprehension*. Toronto: Pippin Publishing.

Gunderson, L. (1997). Whole-language approaches to reading and writing. In S. Stahl & D. Hayes (Eds.), *Instructional models in reading*. Englewood Cliffs, NJ: Lawrence Erlbaum Associates.

Gunderson, L. (2000a). Voices of the teenage diasporas. *Journal of Adolescent and Adult Literacy*, *43*, 692–706.

Gunderson, L. (2000b). How will literacy be defined in the 21st century? *Reading Research Quarterly*, *35*, 68–69.

Gunderson, L. (2004). The language, literacy, achievement, and social consequences of English-only programs for immigrant students. In J. Hoffman & D. Schallert (Eds.), *The NRC Yearbook*. Milwaukee: National Reading Conference.

Gunderson, L. (2006). But she speaks English! In R.T. Jiménez & V.O. Pang (Eds.), *Race, ethnicity, and education: Language and literacy in schools*. New York: Praeger.

Gunderson, L. (2007). *English-only instruction and immigrant students in secondary schools: A critical examination*. Mahwah, NJ: Lawrence Erlbaum Associates.

Gunderson, L. (2008). Bilingual education. In S. Mathison & D.W. Ross (Eds.), *Battleground schools*. New York: Praeger.

Gunderson, L., & Anderson, J. (1999). An exploration of internet access for literacy teachers and learners. *Computers in the Schools, 15*, 5–11.

Gunderson, L., & Anderson, J. (2003). Multicultural views of literacy learning and teaching. In A.I. Willis, G.E. Garcia, R. Barrera & V.J. Harris (Eds.), *Multicultural issue in literacy research and practice*. Mahwah, NJ: Lawrence Erlbaum Associates.

Gunderson, L., & Shapiro, J. (1987). Some findings on whole language instruction. *Reading-Canada-Lecture, 5*, 22–26.

Gunderson, L., & Shapiro, J. (1988). Whole language instruction writing in 1st grade. *The Reading Teacher, 41*, 430–437.

Gunderson, L., & Siegel, L. (2001). The evils of the use of IQ tests to define learning disabilities in first- and second-language learners. *The Reading Teacher, 55*, 48–55.

Gunderson, L., Shapiro, J., & Froese, V. (1988). The effects of models on the writing development of students in grades one and two. Paper presented at the Annual Convention of the National Reading Conference, Tucson, AZ: December.

Gunderson, L., Slade, K., & Rosenke, D. (1988). The cloze response patterns of L1 and L2 students to literal and idiomatic text. *TESL Canada Journal, 6*, 60–67.

Gunderson, L., Eddy, C., and Carrigan, T. (submitted for publication a). An examination of ESL ratio in reading achievement in mainstream classrooms.

Gunderson, L., Eddy, C., & Carrigan, T. (submitted for publication b) An exploration of critical ESL mass in mainstream classrooms.

Guthrie, J.T., Seifert, M., Burnham, N, & Caplan, R. (1974). The maze technique to monitor reading comprehension. *The Reading Teacher, 28*, 2, 161–68.

Gutierrez, A.L. (1975). Bilingual education: Reading through two languages. In D.E. Critchlow (Ed.), *Reading and the Spanish Speaking Child*. Laredo, TX: Texas State Council of the International Reading Association.

Harman, S., & Edelsky, E. (1989). The risks of whole language literacy: Alienation and connection. *Language Arts, 66*, 392–406.

Harris, B. (c. 1690). *The New England Primer*. Boston: Benjamin Harris Printer.

Harris, D.P., & Palmer, L. (1986). *CELT examiner's instructions and technical manual*. New York: McGraw-Hill.

Heckelman, R.G. (1969). A neurological impress method of remedial-reading instruction. *Academic Therapy, 4*, 277–282.

Helfand, D. (2000). Decades later, frustrated father is phonics guru. *Los Angeles Times*, Orange County Edition, January 10, A1 and A16.

Henk, W.A. (1982). Commentary: A Response to Shanahan, Kamil, and Tobin: The case is not yet clozed. *Reading Research Quarterly, 17*, 4, 591–595.

Herber, H.L. (1978). *Teaching reading in content areas*. Englewood Cliffs, NJ: Prentice Hall.

Hillerich, R.L. (1970). ERMAS: A beginning reading project for Mexican American children. *The National Elementary Principal, 1*, 80–84.

Hillerich, R.L. (1974). Word lists: Getting it all together. *The Reading Teacher, 27*, 353–360.

Hipple, M.L. (1985). Journal writing in kindergarten. *Language Arts, 5*, 22–26.

Hoffman, J.V., McCarthey, S., Elliott, B., Bayles, D.L., Price, D.P., Ferree, A., *et al.* (1998). The literature-based basals in first grade classrooms: Savior, Satan, or same-old, same-old? *Reading Research Quarterly, 33*, 168–197.

Hoole, C. ([1660] 1912). *A new discovery of the old art of teaching school*. Syracuse, NY: SUNY Press.

Howard, E.R., & Sugarman, J. (2001). *Two-way immersion programs in the U.S.* Washington, DC: Center for Applied Linguistics. Retrieved October 30, 2007, from http://www.ncbe.gwu.edu/ncbepubs/reports/bestevidence/index.htm.

Hudson, T. (1982). The effects of induced schemata on the "short circuit" in L2 reading: Non-decoding factors in L2 reading performance. *Language Learning, 32*, 1–31.

Huey, E.B. (1908). *The psychology and pedagogy of reading*. Cambridge, MA: MIT Press.

Hughes, A. (2006). *The Shakespearean sonnet through multimodal analysis.* Retrieved October 22, 2007, from http://multiliteracies.ca/index.php/folio/viewProject/222.

International Kindergarten Union (1928). *A study of the vocabulary of children before entering first grade.* Baltimore: International Kindergarten Union.

Ishiyama, F. (1995). Culturally dislocated clients: self-validation and cultural conflict issues and counseling. *Canadian Journal of Counseling, 29,* 262–275.

Jastak, J.F., Jastak, K., & Wilkinson, G. (1984). *Wide range achievement test.* Wilmington, DE: Jastak Associates.

Jastak, S., Wilkinson, G., & Jastak, J. (1984). *Wide range achievement test revised* (6th ed.). Wilmington, DE: Jastak Associates.

Johns, J.L. (1974). Should the Dolch list be retired, replaced, or revised? *Elementary School Journal, 74,* 375–380.

Johns, J.L. (1976a). Some comparisons between the Dolch Basic Sight Vocabulary and the word list for the 1970s. *Reading World, 15,* 144–150.

Johns, J.L. (1976b). Updating the Dolch Basic Sight Vocabulary. *Reading Horizons, 16,* 104–111.

Johnson, D. (1971). A basic vocabulary for beginning reading. *Elementary School Journal, 72,* 29–34.

Jones, M.B., & Pikulski, E.C. (1974). Cloze for the classroom. *Journal of Reading, 17,* 432–438.

Kaufman, M. (1968). Will instruction in reading Spanish affect ability in reading English? *Journal of Reading, 11,* 521–527.

Keagy, J.M. (1824). *An essay on English education together with some observations on the present mode of teaching the English language.* Harrisburg, PA: Pennsylvania State Board of Education.

Klare, G. (1963). *The measurement of readability.* Ames, IA: Iowa State University Press.

Klare, G.R., Sinaiko, S.W., & Stolurow, L.M. (1971). The cloze procedure: A convenient readability test for training materials and translations. *Institute of Defense Analyses,* log No. 4070–11774. Arlington, VA.

Kloss, H. (1978). *The American bilingual tradition.* McHenry, IL: Center for Applied Linguistics and Delta Systems.

Krashen, S. (1982). *Principles and practice in second language acquisition.* New York: Pergamon Press.

Krashen, S. (1999). *Why Malherbe (1946) is NOT evidence against bilingual education.* Retrieved July 24, 2005, from http://ourworld.compuserve.com/homepages/JWCRAWFORD/Krashen4.htm.

Krashen, S., & Terrell, T.D. (1983). *The natural approach.* New York: Pergamon Press.

Kroeber, A., & Kluckhohn, C. (1954). *Culture: A critical review of concepts and definitions.* New York: Random House.

Lado, R. (1964). *Language testing: A scientific approach.* New York: McGraw-Hill.

Lambert, W.E., & Tucker, G.R. (1972). *Bilingual education of children.* Rowley, MA: Newbury House.

Larson, D.N., & Smalley, W.A. (1972). *Becoming bilingual: A guide to language learning.* Pasadena, CA: William Carey Library.

Larsen-Freeman, D. (1986). *Techniques and principles in language teaching.* Oxford: Oxford University Press.

Leu, D., & Leu, D.D. (2000). *Teaching with the internet: Lessons from the classroom* (3rd ed.). Norwood, MA: Christopher-Gordon Publishers.

Leu, D.J., & Zawilinski, L. (2007). The new literacies of online reading comprehension. *New England Reading Association Journal, 43,* 1–7.

Leu, D.J., Jr. (2000). Literacy and technology: Deictic consequences for literacy education in an information age. In M.L. Kamil, P. Mosenthal, P.D. Pearson, & R. Barr (Eds.), *Handbook of reading research* (Vol. 1). Mahwah, NJ: Lawrence Erlbaum Associates.

Leu, D.J., Jr., Kinzer, C.K., Coiro, J.L., & Cammack, D.W. (2004). Toward a theory of new literacies emerging from the Internet and other information and communication technologies. In R.B. Ruddell & N. J. Unrau (Eds.), *Theoretical models and processes of reading* (5th ed.). Newark, DE: International Reading Association.

Lewis, G.L. (1965). Bilingualism: Some aspects of its history. *Report on an international seminar on bilingualism in education.* London: Her Majesty's Stationery Office.

Li, G. (2006). *Culturally contested pedagogy: Battles of literacy and schooling between mainstream teachers and Asian immigrant parents.* Albany, NY: State University of New York Press.

Lopez, M., & Gunderson, L. (2006). Oaxacan parents' perceptions of literacy. In R. Jiménez & D. Ong-Pang (Eds.), *Race, Ethnicity, and Education*. Westport, CT: Routledge (Taylor & Francis).

Lucas, T., & Katz, A. (1994). Reframing the debate: The roles of native languages in English-only programs for language minority students. *TESOL Quarterly, 28,* 537–561.

Luke, A. (2004). Two takes on the critical. In B. Norton & K. Toohey (Eds.), *Critical pedagogies and language learning*. New York: Cambridge University Press.

Macfadyen, L.P., Roche, J., & Doff, S. (2004). *Communication across cultures in cyberspace: A bibliographic review of intercultural communication*. Münster, Germany: Lit Verlag, and Piscataway, NJ: Transaction Publishers.

MacGillivray, L., Ardell, A.L., Curwen, M.S., & Palma, J. (2004). Colonized teachers: Examining the implementation of a scripted reading program. *Teaching Education, 15,* 2, 131–144.

Mackey, W.F. (1972). *Bilingual education in a binational school*. Rowley, MA: Newbury House.

Mandler, J.M., & Johnson, N.S. (1977). Remembrance of things parsed: Story structure and recall. *Cognitive Psychology, 9,* 111–51.

Mann, H. (1841). *A lecture on the best method of preparing and using spelling-books*. Boston: Bavdeen.

Mann, H. (1844a). *Seventh annual report of the Board of Education together with the seventh annual report of the secretary of the Board of Education*. Boston: Massachusetts School Board.

Mann, H. (1844b). *Reply to the remarks of thirty-one schoolmasters*. Boston: Lothrop.

Manning, J. (1975). Reading instruction in elementary school. Lecture given at the University of California, Berkeley.

Mathews, M.M. (1966). *Teaching to read historically considered*. Chicago: University of Chicago Press.

Matsumura, S. (2003). Modeling the relationships among interlanguage pragmatic development, L2 proficiency, and exposure to L2. *Applied Linguistics, 24,* 465–491.

McCallum, R.D. (1988). Don't throw the basals out with the bath water. *The Reading Teacher, 42,* 3, 204–208.

McCracken, R.A., & McCracken, M.J. (1978). Modeling the key to sustained silent reading. *The Reading Teacher, 31,* 406–408.

McEneaney, J.E. (2000). Learning on the web: A content literacy perspective. *Reading online*. Retrieved October 27, 2007, from http://readingonline.org/articles/art_index.asp?HREF=mceneaney/index.html.

McEneaney, J.E. (2006). Agent-based literacy theory. *Reading Research Quarterly, 41,* 352–371.

McGuffey's Eclectic Readers. New York: American Book Company, 1836.

McKenna, M.C., Robinson, R.D., & Miller, J.W. (1993). Whole language and research: The case for caution. In D. Leu & C.K. Kinzer (Eds.), *Examining central issues in literacy research, theory, and practice*. Chicago: National Reading Conference.

McLeod, J., & McLeod, R. (1977). *GAP*. Sydney, Australia: Heinemann.

McLeod, J., & McLeod, R. (1990). *NewGAP*. Novato, CA: Academic Therapy Publications.

Mellgren, L., & Walker, M. (1977/78). *YES! English for children*. Philippines: Addison-Wesley.

Modiano, N. (1968). National or mother tongue language in beginning reading? *Research in the Teaching of English, 2,* 1, 32–43.

Mohan, B. (1986). *Language and content*. New York: Addison-Wesley.

Moll, L. (1992). Bilingual classroom studies and community analysis: Some recent trends. *Educational Researcher, 21,* 20–24.

Moore, S. (1998). Bilingual betrayal. *National Review*. Available at http://www.onenation.org/1098/101298a.html.

Morphett, M.V., & Washburne, C. (1931). When should children begin to read? *Elementary School Journal, 31,* 496–508.

Morrow, L.M., Gambrell, L.B., & Pressley, M. (Eds.) (2003). *Best practices in literacy instruction* (2nd ed.). New York: Guilford Press.

Moustafa, M., & Land, R.E. (2002). The reading achievement of economically-disadvantaged children in urban schools using *Open court* vs comparably disadvantaged children in urban schools using non-scripted reading programs. In the 2002 Yearbook of the Urban learning, teaching, and research Special Interest Group of the American Educational Research Association.

Mozert v. Hawkins County Public Schools, 827, F. 2d 1058 (6th Cir. 1987), *cert denied,* 484 U.S. 1066 (1988).

Murdock, G.P. (1945). The common denominator of cultures. In R. Linton (Ed.), *The science of man in the world crisis*. New York: Columbia University Press.

Natalicio, D. S. (1979). Reading and the bilingual child. In L.B. Resnick & P.A. Weaver (Eds.), *Theory and practice of early reading*. Hillsdale, NJ: Lawrence Erlbaum Associates.

National Center for Education Statistics (NCES) (2004). *Language minorities and their educational and labor market indicators: Recent trends*. U.S. Department of Education, Institute of Education Sciences, 2004–009.

National Center for Education Statistics (2005). *National Assessment of Adult Literacy (NAAL)*. Retrieved September 8, 2007, from http://www.nifl.gov/nifl/NAAL2003.html.

National Institute of Child Health and Human Development (NICHD) (2000). *Report of the National Reading Panel. Teaching children to read: An evidence-based assessment of the scientific research literature on reading and its implications for reading instruction*. NIH Publication No. 00–4769. Washington, DC: U.S. Government Printing Office.

National Literacy Panel (2003). Retrieved December 12, 2005, from http://www.cal.org/natl-lit-panel/index.html.

Nelson, T.H. (1965). A file structure for the complex, the changing, and the indeterminate. *Association for Computing Machinery's 20th National Conference* (84–100). New York: Association for Computing Machinery.

New London Group (1996). A pedagogy of multiliteracies: Designing social futures. *Harvard Educational Review, 66,* 60–90.

Nuance Communications Inc. (2007). Dragon NaturallySpeaking. Retrieved September 22, 2007, from http://www.nuance.com/naturallyspeaking/.

Oakes, J., & Guiton, G. (1995). Matchmaking: The dynamics of high school tracking decisions. *American Educational Research Journal, 32,* 3–33.

Ogle, D. (1986). K-W-L: A teaching model that develops active reading of expository text. *The Reading Teacher, 39,* 564–570.

Oller, J., & Conrad, C. (1971). The cloze technique and ESL proficiency. *Language Learning, 21,* 183–195.

Olson, D. (1989). Literate thought. In C.K. Leong & B.S. Randhawa (Eds.), *Understanding literacy and cognition: Theory, research, and application*. New York: Plenum Press.

Olson, D. (1992). When a learner attempts to become literate in a second language, what is he or she attempting? The forum. *TESL Canada Journal, 20,* 18–22.

Ovando, C.J. (2003). Bilingual education in the United States: Historical development and current issues. *Bilingual Research Journal, 27,* 1–24.

Palmer, T.H. (1837). On the evils of the present system of primary education. Paper delivered at the American Institute of Instruction, August.

Peirce, C. (1844). Lecture delivered to the American Institute of Instruction, August.

Piaget, J. (1973). *Memory and intelligence:* New York: Basic Books.

Piper, T. (1983a). Guidelines of phonics with ESL learners. *The Reading Teacher, 3,* 87–97.

Piper, T. (1983b). Phonics and the ESL learner. *Reading-Canada-Lecture, 2,* 56–62.

Pirbhai-Illich (2005). The educational pathways and outcomes of ethnic and linguistic minority students. Unpublished doctoral dissertation, University of British Columbia, Vancouver.

Potter, T.C. (1968). *Taxonomy of cloze research*, Part 1: *Readability and reading comprehension*. Inglewood, CA: Southwest Regional Laboratory for Educational Research and Development.

Potts, D. (2007). Personal communication, University of British Columbia, October 2007. See also http://multiliteracies.ca/ (accessed 15 October 2007).

Pressley, M. (2006). *Reading instruction that works: The case for balanced teaching* (3rd ed.). New York: Guilford Press.

Radwanski, G. (1987). *Ontario study of the relevance of education, and the issue of dropouts*. Toronto: Ontario Ministry of Education.

Ramirez, J.D. (1992). Executive summary. *Bilingual Research Journal, 16,* 1–62.

Ramirez, J.D., Yuen, S.D., & Ramey, D.R. (1991). *Executive summary of final report: Longitudinal study of structured English immersion strategy early-exit and late-exit transitional bilingual education program for language minority students*. San Mateo, CA: Aguirre International.

Rankin, E.F., & Culhane, J.W. (1969). Comparable cloze and multiple-choice comprehension scores. *Journal of Reading, 14,* 193–198.

Ransom, P. (1968). Determining reading levels of elementary school children by cloze testing. In J.A. Figurel (Ed.), *Forging ahead in reading* (pp. 259–263). Newark, DE: International Reading Association.

Raygor, A.L. (1977). The Raygor readability estimate: A quick and easy way to determine difficulty. In D. Pearson & J. Hansen (Eds.), *Reading: theory, research and practice.* Clemson, SC: National Reading Conference.

Rebane, K. (1985). A word frequency distribution study of language presented to young ESL students. Unpublished Master's thesis, University of British Columbia, Vancouver.

Reeder, K, Early, M., Kendrick, M., & Shapiro, J. (2007). Listening to diverse learners: The effectiveness and appropriateness of a computer-based reading tutor for young Canadian language learners. In F. Zhang & B Barber (Eds.), *Handbook of research on computer-enhanced language learning.* Hershey, PA: IGI.

Rice, J. M. (1893). *The public school system of the United States.* New York: Century Publishing.

Richard-Amato, P.A. (1988). *Making it happen: Interaction in the second language classroom: From theory to practice.* New York: Longman.

Rivera, C. (Ed.) (1984). *Language proficiency and academic achievement.* Clevedon, UK: Multilingual Matters.

Robertson, D.J., & Trepper, T.S. (1974). The effects of i.t.a. on the reading achievement of Mexican-American children. *Reading World, 14,* 2, 132–139.

Robinson, F.P. (1961). *Effective study.* New York: Harper & Row.

Rosen, C.L. (1970). *Assessment and relative effects of reading programs for Mexican Americans: A position paper* [ED 061000]. Arlington, VA: ERIC Document Reproduction Services.

Rossell, C.H. (1998). *Mystery on the bilingual express: A critique of the Thomas and Collier study.* Retrieved on December 8, 2005, from http://www.ceousa.org/READ/collier.html.

Rossell, C.H., & Baker, K. (1996). The educational effectiveness of bilingual education. *Research in the Teaching of English, 30,* 7–74.

Ruddell, M.R. (1980). Personal communication, University of California, Berkeley, Berkeley, CA.

Rumberger, R.W. (1995). Dropping out of middle school: A multilevel analysis of students and schools. *American Educational Research Journal, 32,* 583–625.

Rumelhart, D.E. (1975). Notes on a schema for stories. In D.G. Bobrow & A. Collins (Eds.), *Representations and understandings.* New York: Academic Press.

Saccardi, M.C. (1996a). Predictable books: Gateways to a lifetime of reading. *The Reading Teacher, 49,* 588–590.

Saccardi, M.C. (1996b). More predictable books: Gateways to a lifetime of reading. *The Reading Teacher, 49,* 668–670.

Samad, A.A. (2002). Brief review of Somali caste systems: Statement to the committee on the eliminations of racial discrimination. Retrieved October 30, 2007, from http://www.idsn.org/pdf/Africa/somalia.pdf.

Saville, M., & Troike, R.C. (1971). *A handbook of bilingual education.* Washington, DC: Teacher of English to Speakers of Other Languages.

Scheffler, I. (1965). *Conditions of knowledge.* Chicago: Scott Foresman.

Schieffelin, B.B., & Ochs, E. (Eds.) (1986a). *Language socialization across cultures.* New York: Cambridge University Press.

Schieffelin, B.B., & Ochs, E. (1986b). Language socialization. *Annual Review of Anthropology, 15,* 163–191.

Schmidt, P.R. (1998). The ABC's model: Teachers connect home and school. In T. Shanahan & F.V. Rodriguez-Brown (Eds.), *National Reading Conference yearbook* 47. Chicago: National Reading Conference.

Schmidt, P.R. (2000). Emphasizing differences to build cultural understandings. In V. Risko & K. Bromley (Eds.), *Collaboration for diverse learners: Viewpoints and practices.* Newark, DE: International Reading Association.

Schmidt, P.R. (2001). The power to empower. In P.R. Schmidt & P.B. Mosenthal (Eds.), *Reconceptualizing literacy in the new age of multiculturalism and pluralism*. Greenwich, CT: Information Age Press.

Schmidt, P.R. & Izzo, A. (2003). Home/school communication for literacy development. Paper presented at the Educational Research Conference, January, Honolulu, Hawaii.

Schmidt, P.R., & Ma, W. (2006). *50 literacy strategies for culturally responsive teaching, K–8*. Thousand Oaks, CA: Corwin Press.

Schumann, J. (1978a). The acculturation model for second-language acquisition. In R.C. Gingras (Ed.), *Second language acquisition and foreign language teaching*. Washington, DC: Center for Applied Linguistics.

Schumann, J. (1978b). Psychological factors in second language acquisition. In J. Richards (Ed.), *Understanding second and foreign language learning: Issues and approaches*. Rowley, MA: Newbury House.

Schumann, J. (1986). Research on the acculturalization model for second language acquisition. *Journal of Multilingual and Multicultural Development*, 379–392.

Shanahan, T. (1983). A response to Henk and Cziko. *Reading Research Quarterly*, 18, 3, 366–367.

Shanahan, T., Kamil, M.L., & Tobin, A. (1982). Cloze as a measure of intersentential comprehension. *Reading Research Quarterly*, 17, 229–225.

Shapiro, J., & Gunderson, L. (1988). A comparison of vocabulary generated by grade 1 students in whole language classrooms and basal reader vocabulary. *Reading Research and Instruction*, 27, 40–46.

Sharp, D. (1973). *Language in bilingual communities*. London: Edward Arnold.

Sherman, L.A. (1893). The literary sentence-length in English prose and the decrease of prediction. *Analytics of literature*. Boston: Ginn.

Slavin, R.E., & Cheung, A. (2005). A synthesis of research on language of reading instruction for English language learners. *Review of Educational Research*, 75, 247–284.

Snow, C.E., Burns, M.S., & Griffin, P. (Eds.) (1998). *Preventing reading difficulties in young children*. Washington, DC: National Academy Press.

Spache, G.D. (1963). *Toward better reading*. Champaign, IL: Garrard Press.

Staff writer (2005). U.S. Department of Education declines to publish report on literacy education of bilingual children. *Reading Today*, 23, 1.

Stahl, S.A., & Miller, P.D. (1989). Whole language and language experiences approaches for beginning reading: Quantitative synthesis. *Review of Educational Research*, 16, 175–186.

Statistics Canada (2001). Neighborhood income and demographics. http://www.statcan.ca/english/IPS/Data/13C0015.htm.

Stauffer, R. (Ed.) (1967). *The first grade studies: Findings of individual investigations*. Newark, DE: International Reading Association.

Stauffer, R. (1971). Slave, puppet or teacher? *The Reading Teacher*, 25, 24–29.

Stein, N.L., & Glenn, C. (1979). An analysis of story comprehension in elementary school children. In R.O. Freedle (Ed.), *New directions in discourse processing*. Norwood, NJ: Ablex Publishing Corporation.

Stone, M.H., Jastak, S., & Wilkinson G. (1995). *Wide range achievement test* 3. Wilmington, DE: Jastak Associates.

Sullivan, J. (2004). *The children's literature lover's book of lists*. San Francisco: Jossey-Bass.

Sulzby, E. (1986). Writing and reading: Signs of oral and written language organization in the young child. In W.H. Teale & E. Sulzby (Eds.), *Emergent literacy*. Norwood, NJ: Ablex Publishing Corporation.

Swain, M. (1981). Bilingual education for majority and minority language children. *Studia Linguistica*, 15, 15–31.

Swan, M. & Smith, B. (Eds.) (2001). *Learner English: A teacher's guide to interference and other problems* (2nd ed.). Cambridge: Cambridge University Press.

Taylor, W.L. (1953). Cloze procedure: A new tool for measuring readability. *Journalism Quarterly*, 30, 415–433.

Thomas, W.P., & Collier, V. (1997). *School effectiveness for language minority students*. National Clearinghouse for Bilingual Education. Retrieved October 16, 2007, from http://www.ncbe.gwu.edu/ncbepubs/resource/effectiveness.

Thomas, W.P., & Collier, V.P. (2002). *A national study of school effectiveness for language minority students' long-term academic achievement.* Santa Cruz, CA: Center for Research on Education, Diversity, and Excellence.

Thorndike, E.L. (1921) *The teacher's word book.* New York: Teachers College Press.

Thornyke, P.W. (1977). Cognitive structures in comprehension and memory of narrative discourse. *Cognitive Psychology, 9,* 77–110.

Trelease, J. (2006). *The read-aloud handbook* (6th ed.). New York: Penguin Books.

Tucker, G.R., Lambert, W.E., & D'Anglejan, A. (1973). Cognitive and attitudinal consequences of bilingual schooling: The St. Lambert project through grade five. *Journal of Educational Psychology, 65,* 141–149.

U.S. Census Bureau (2001). Ability to Speak English for U.S. Residents Ages 5–17, 2000. Retrieved October 30, 2007, from http://factfinder.census.gov/home/saff/main.html?_lang=en/.

U.S. Commission on Civil Rights (1975). *A better chance to learn: Bilingual–bicultural education.* Washington, DC: Clearinghouse of U.S. Commission.

Valette, R.M. (1967). *Modern language testing.* New York: Harcourt, Brace & World.

Verriour, P. (1994). *In role: Teaching and learning dramatically.* Toronto: Pippin Publishing.

Vontress, C.E. (1988). Counseling the racial and ethnic minorities. In G.S. Belkin (Ed.), *Counseling: Directions in theory and practice.* Belmont, CA: Wadsworth.

Walters, K., &. Gunderson, L. (1985). Effects of parent volunteers reading first language (L1) books to ESL students. *The Reading Teacher, 39,* 66–71.

Watkins, E. (1922). *How to teach silent reading to beginners.* Chicago: Lippincott.

Watt, D., & Roessingh, H. (2001). The dynamics of ESL drop-outs: Plus ça change . . . *Canadian Modern Language Journal, 58,* 203–222.

Wheeler, H.E., & Howell, A.E. (1950). A first-grade vocabulary study. *Elementary School Journal, 31,* 52–60.

Willig, A. (1985). A meta-analysis of selected studies on the effectiveness of bilingual education. *Review of Educational Research, 55,* 269–317.

Xu, H. (2000a). Preservice teachers integrate understandings of diversity into literacy instruction: An adaptation of the ABC's Model. *Journal of Teacher Education, 51,* 135–142.

Xu, H. (2000b). Preservice teachers in a literacy methods course consider issues of diversity. *Journal of Literacy Research, 32,* 505–531.

YEAR 2000 (1988). *The British Columbia primary program.* Victoria, BC: The Queen's Printers.

Yoes, D. Jr. (1967). Reading programs for Mexican-American children of Texas. *The Reading Teacher, 20,* 313–318, 323.

Yopp, H.K. (1995). Read-aloud books for developing phonemic awareness. *The Reading Teacher, 48,* 538–542.

Zehr, M.A. (2001). California's English fluency rate helps fuel debate. *Education Week, 21,* 23.

Zehr, M.A. (2003). Reports spotlight Latino dropout rates, college attendance. *Education Week, 22,* 12.

Zintz, M.V. (1975). *The reading process: The teacher and the learner* (2nd ed.). Dubuque, IA: William C. Brown.

Author Index

Subject Index